AMERICAN EDUCATION

Its Men,

Ideas,

and

Institutions

Advisory Editor

Lawrence A. Cremin
Frederick A. P. Barnard Professor of Education
Teachers College, Columbia University

AMERICAN EDUCATION: *Its Men, Ideas, and Institutions*
presents selected works of thought and scholarship that have
long been out of print or otherwise unavailable. Inevitably, such
works will include particular ideas and doctrines that have been
outmoded or superseded by more recent research. Nevertheless,
all retain their place in the literature, having influenced educational thought and practice in their own time and having provided
the basis for subsequent scholarship.

CREATIVE EXPRESSION

*The Development of Children
in Art, Music, Literature
and Dramatics*

Edited for

THE PROGRESSIVE EDUCATION
ASSOCIATION

by

GERTRUDE HARTMAN
and
ANN SHUMAKER

ARNO PRESS & THE NEW YORK TIMES
*New York * 1971*

Reprint Edition 1971 by Arno Press Inc.

Reprinted from a copy in
  The University of Illinois Library

American Education:
  Its Men, Ideas, and Institutions - Series II
ISBN for complete set: 0-405-03600-0
See last pages of this volume for titles

Manufactured in the United States of America

Library of Congress Cataloging in Publication Data

American Education Fellowship.
    Creative expression.
    (American education: its men, ideas, and
institutions. Series II)
    Originally published as four special numbers of
Progressive education, 1926, 1927, 1928 and 1931.
    Includes bibliographies.
    1. Education--Experimental methods.
2. Creation (Literary, artistic, etc.)
I. Hartman, Gertrude, 1876-   ed.
II. Shumaker, Ann, 1899-1935, ed. III. Title.
IV. Series.
LB1026.A5 1971   371.3   79-165717
ISBN 0-405-03706-6

CREATIVE EXPRESSION

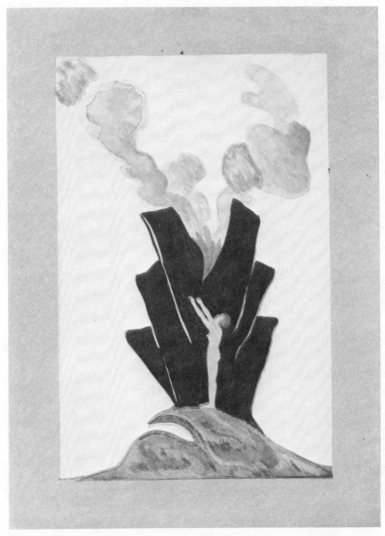

FLAMES

Painted by a thirteen-year-old student, at the Walden School, New York

CREATIVE EXPRESSION

*The Development of Children
in Art, Music, Literature
and Dramatics*

Edited for

THE PROGRESSIVE EDUCATION
ASSOCIATION

by

GERTRUDE HARTMAN
and
ANN SHUMAKER

THE JOHN DAY COMPANY

New York

MANUFACTURED IN THE UNITED STATES OF AMERICA

FOR THE JOHN DAY COMPANY, INC., NEW YORK

BY THE QUINN & BODEN COMPANY, INC., RAHWAY, N. J.

FOREWORD

THIS volume meets a need of which we have been conscious for a long time. So numerous have been the calls for additional copies of the special numbers of *Progressive Education* devoted to Creative Expression through Art, Literature, Music and Dramatics, that the files have long since become exhausted.

The first of these special numbers, the one on Art issued in 1926, was received by teachers and parents with enthusiasm and even amazement. It marked a definite turning point in art instruction in American schools, for teachers recognized in those delightful color reproductions of the paintings of children the true art quality of naïve and childlike products which they had heretofore been overlooking in their own classes. The number on Art, edited by Miss Hartman, was so successful that, in the following year, she produced the number on Music, and in 1928, the number on Literature. To complete the series, the Dramatics number was issued in 1931.

Because of the unique emphasis on the child's own modes of self-expression through all of the creative arts, as opposed to more adult standards of finish and perfection, these numbers became a valuable reference source in schools, libraries and teacher training institutions. Second- and even third-hand copies of the separate numbers have long been at a premium.

We are under a debt of gratitude to The John Day Company for now bringing all of this material under one cover, preserving it in permanent book form, and making it available to the many readers whose earnest requests we have until now been unable to fulfill.

ANN SHUMAKER.

CONTENTS

CONTENTS

Creative Expression Through Music
Edited by GERTRUDE HARTMAN

Creative Expression Through Literature
Edited by GERTRUDE HARTMAN

CONTENTS

Creative Expression Through Dramatics
Edited by ANN SHUMAKER

CREATIVE EXPRESSION
THROUGH ART

THE CREATIVE SPIRIT AND ITS SIGNIFICANCE FOR EDUCATION

Hughes Mearns

THAT is the title suggested by the editor. My own preference was "All God's Chillun Got Wings" until I remembered that all God's chillun are not permitted to use them. I visit many schools which, in spite of a modern cheerfulness and a seeming acquiescence of pupils, are to me places where the wings of God's children are gradually and painlessly removed. High marks are given to them who know least about flying; future advancement is open only to those who keep their feet always on the ground. When the creative spirit strives here and there to flutter, it becomes an activity that must be practiced in stealth, rarely with full approval of the authorities.

In *Creative Expression* one sees the creative spirit in action, sometimes in full flight; and these are but representatives of myriad activities; hundreds of illustrations had to be left out for lack of space and only the pictorial could be shown, for the creative spirit is something more than a product in clay and canvas: it is dancing, rhythmic living, a laugh, a flash of the mind, strength of control, swiftness of action, an unwritten poem, a song without words; it is life adding its invisible living cells to more and abundant life. But these pictures will serve; for the object is to tempt the unbeliever to loiter a moment at the shrine of the true gods. Our argument may not move him, but the grace of our service may win him into the faith.

To the unbeliever, then, I address myself when I would tell of the creative spirit and its varied manifestations; and also, of course, to those who believe but would have their faith strengthened. The creative impulse is more easily observed in young children but the housewife who bakes unerringly without book or recipe knows it; the carpenter fashioning a cupboard to his own notion of shape and line, the office man given free sway in the phrasing of a sales advertisement, the lawyer playing upon the mood of judge and jury, these practice it without knowing it; my true love's letter is the perfect product of instinctive artistry; all our adult ways of interacting one with another, in short, call on the creative spirit, and our life is artistic or dull in proportion to our creative gifts. But adults are in the main wingless; convention, tribal taboos, mechanistic living, long years of schooling, something has stilled the spirit within or walled it securely. It is to children we must go to see the creative spirit at its best; and only to those children who are in some measure uncoerced.

Outwardly it is harmony; a unity of eye, hand, bodily muscles, mind; a concentration upon the object of desire that sets the world aside. It is frequently balked by the need of special information or of special skill; these are the obstructions that it must surely overcome or the heart's desire is not achieved and the spirit dies; these, too, are the strategic places where the wise teacher is at hand with just the right assistance. But of that later; the outward picture concerns us now. Not only is there harmony of mind and body but there is the closest connection between the thing conceived as worthy to be done and the media necessary— brush, paint, wood, metal, clay, blocks, script, tool, machine.

It flourishes, of course, in what we call play, but mindful of our religious inheritances, in which play has been conceived as touched with evil, I hasten to note concrete illustrations of play that has taken on all the characteristics of work: a butterfly collection occupying five steady years which brought technical knowledge of family and species, of habitat, environment, breeding, and culture, of correspondence with other collectors and with foreign sales agents, and an ability to present orally to an assembly of several hundred children and adults the serious business of preparing such a collection and to lead the discussion that followed with the skill of experience; a study of biological specimen that led an elementary-school boy first to museums and then to summer school (Wood's Hole) until all unwittingly the avocation put him so far outside the rôle of pupil that an ornithologist and later a marine biologist claimed that they must talk to the lad as a colleague and defer to him in his special scientific field; an elementary-school boy who constructed photostatic apparatus and motion-picture cameras from lard cans found on the village refuse pile and from odds and ends picked up at rummage sales; a young artist who built herself a five thousand dollar studio through a persistently applied scheme of savings, earning, and commercial borrowings.

Illustration of such activity is at hand in every classroom including the college classroom if one has the skill to look for it. The common ingredient in each case, that which makes it different from formal instruction, is that the "urge to do" is self-engendered; it seeks its own way to fulfillment; it is not stopped by time, space, apparatus, or by teachers or school administrators, although because of the last two it may often conceal every outward trace of interest in the thing that occupies the main tracts of the mind, in this regard behaving like a conquered people in the presence of the ruling race. It may even at these

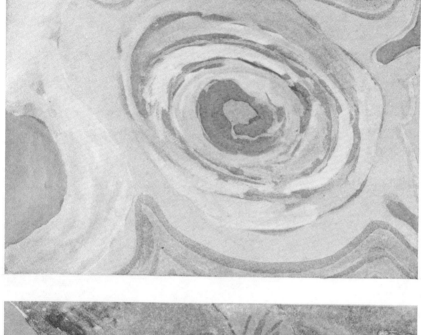

Keith School, Rockford, Ill.

WHEN YOU ARE DIZZY

(Age 12 years)

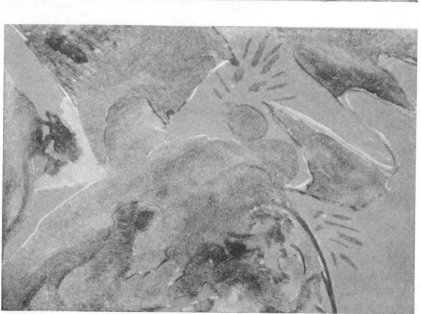

Keith School, Rockford, Ill.

THE SOUND OF A BRASS BAND

(Age 11 years)

(*Age 16 years*)　　　　　*Keith School, Rockford, Ill.*

RADIATION

(*Age 15 years*)　　　　　*Keith School, Rockford, Ill.*

times assume a cautious stupidity; for neither to the unsympathetic nor to the arrogant and unfeeling will it confess an interest in the inner dream. Under unfriendly questioning it may even deny, and thus through clumsiness and inexpertness get into the coil of adult morality.

II

When the creative spirit is at work, not only are body and mind co-operating with instinctive harmony to secure the desired result, but the language art is functioning at a high degree of excellence. A child may speak haltingly in classroom recitation, or in a school "composition" write with despairing inadequacy, who in the midst of a bit of self-initiated artistry, the making of a toy motor boat, a radio set, a cartoon, or a poem, will talk with the effectiveness of an inspired expert. In his own language and idiom, of course, and provided you do not bring with you the flavor of the impossible linguistic standards of adult perfection. You may ask questions then, if you are not of the forbidding sort; and if you have an ear for right rhythmic speech you may have cause to marvel at the language sense that these youngsters really have; and you may wonder why we as teachers do not take advantage of the gifts that children have in this line instead of damming—both spellings apply here—their utterance through our insistence on the use of an alien tongue.

The claim for "lessons" and "home assignments" is that they teach persistence, but who can equal the persistence of children when engaged in creative work? Ask the mothers and fathers who have tried to keep up with the demands of their offspring for continuous attention to a loved story or game! And the work which they set for themselves is not stopped by the ending of the day; it carries over, day after day, until the accomplished end is reached. The astonishing paintings that decorate Miss Keelor's room (second grade) were not done at a sitting. Day by day they grew. She has just told me the history of one remarkable water color of an autumn orchard, how the house and the trees and the far-off hills came slowly to their present places in the picture and then one morning a shy voice confided, "I was thinking about it last night in bed, so I put some apples on the tree as well as on the ground, for, of course, they all wouldn't have fallen off, would they? And the red apples are so pretty I wanted more of them." A teacher has just dropped in to tell me of a remarkable speech delivered from a most unexpected source at a recent Lincoln Day assembly. "It was done with such ease and masterfulness," he said, "with the modesty of a trained speaker, and yet it was the boy's first serious public appearance. We found out that he had been at work for weeks in various libraries. He had concentrated on a bibliography that no teacher would have had the heart to give any one as an assignment, even in the old days; and no one knew he was at it! He saturated himself with material like an expert research student, and then calmly talked out of full knowledge. The school is so thrilled by it that they are thinking of naming him for the most responsible position in the vote of the pupils, chairman of the Student Council, a most coveted office, I tell you, and never held but by the all-around best man in the place!"

"And no one knew he was at it!" That is a quality that must not be missed, in which regard these young artists are one with the older artist. The same artist-shyness is here, the same fear of spoiling the picture through the wrong word from outside; even suggestions, the artist knows, are dangerous until the work is finished. And flattery can knock one out of the humor—shatter the inspiration—as well as dispraise, or stupid misunderstanding, or nagging (parents and teachers, elder sisters, and governesses, please take notice!), or that unfeeling looking-over-the-shoulder which has dished many a promising canvas. Artists and children hide from onlookers until enough of the work is done to insure a possible completion (that's why they should have their own rooms, studios, workshops). But they work cheerfully enough among their own kind; so in some schools the artistic work is done out of hours and teachers never hear of it; but in the schools that are represented in *Creative Expression* one senses that the artist has been protected from the cold eye of the outsider. "I'm painting that red barn," I heard a Woodstock celebrity once say to a group of gushing ignorants, "but if you ask me what I am painting, I shall have to go fishing for a week." He was bitter with a sense of outrage at their unfeeling impertinence in hovering over him, but all they said was, "Isn't he just *screamingly* funny! And don't you *love* it! It *is* the barn you're painting, isn't it? I'm just *crazy* about it!" And as he folded up his work he remarked hopelessly, "I'm off! Fishing it is!"

But at the right moment they want praise like any other artist. Or, rather, they want what the artist-student calls a "crit." "Oh," cried one of Miss Keelor's little boys, "you didn't hang mine up!" It was a moment of real torture. Miss Keelor brought the painting out slowly (while, no doubt, she thought hard) and looked at it again. "I didn't think it had enough in it," she explained, but not with an air of really knowing. "So much space here," she mused, and then looked at the pictures of the others. He looked too and understood. "I could do some more!" He caught the idea eagerly, explaining spiritedly new thoughts that began to come to him with a rush. And away he went, satisfied with the judgment.

And at other times, just like real artists, they are dismayed at praise. You hang their pictures; they are grieved. "It is not good enough,"

THE RESCUE

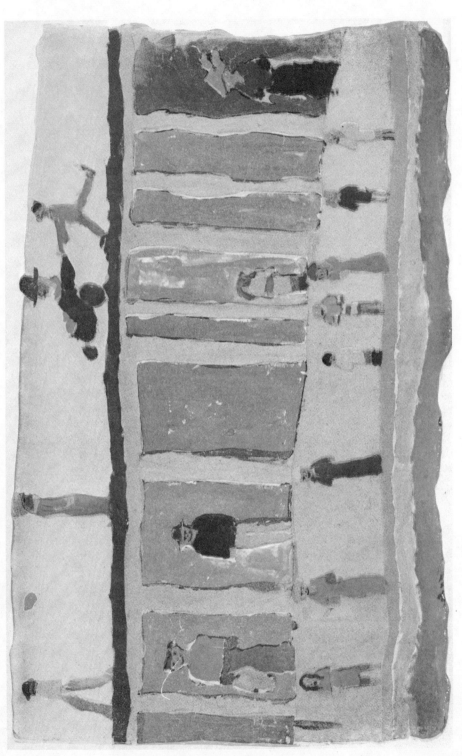

ATLANTIC CITY

Washington Montessori School

(*Age 5 years*)

they say in real distress and go sturdily to work to make a better one to take its place. Every one who has been intimate with gifted poets and painters knows how difficult it is to get them to pack their work off to magazines or to exhibitions. To go through the agony of such necessary business is one of the last things learned by the professional; and more often than not it is his prudent and practical wife who supplies the needed motivation.

III

This then is the torrential force that comes unbidden out of the mysterious recesses of personality and fashions things out of wood, color, fabric, clay, and words; the thing that dances, sings, leads a dozen dramatic reincarnations; the thing that drives a small child into profound research or sets him digging into a difficulty with the energy of a dog at a woodchuck hole; whose ways are sure, whose outcome is beauty. Not that I would say that the conscious end is beauty. Children seem to be driven by an inner necessity of putting forth something; that it shall turn out to be beautiful is not their concern; their impulse at its best is to place something in the outside world that is already (or almost ready) in their inside world of perceiving, thinking, feeling; they measure their success or failure by the final resemblance of the thing done to the thing imagined. And in their best moments they seem to know exactly what to do: the muscles ripple in perfect harmony to the right touch, line, blow; in painting the brush is swung fearlessly and surely, in pottery the punches and patches are thumbed without hesitation. In this regard they are in tune again with the professional artist. Experience has loosened his fears; he trusts his instinct for level, balance, the swift adjustings of his medium and his materials to satisfy those flashing demands from within.

One needs to emphasize here that the modern discovery of the child as artist—a very ancient bit of knowledge, of course—is coincident with the realization of the beauty of primitive art generally. The child is a genuine primitive. He needs little or no instruction, but he must have materials and his surroundings must be such as to call his effort worthy; he is susceptible to condemnation and will give up all his precious art and lose one of the most gracious of nature's gifts—for, alas, it may be easily lost—if his overlords command. The art of the uncivilized tribes, ancient and modern, is just that untutored art of our own children. And now that we are treasuring every trace of the craft of the primitive peoples, the native art in Africa, Mexico, Egypt, the South Seas, it is fitting that our educational leaders should be rediscovering with joy and understanding the work of our own young "natives."

The undeniable result, however, is beauty; and fortunately we do not in these days need to justify it. Here and there, to be sure, its utility is questioned; but the sense of its importance in American life is growing at such bounds that we no longer worry over the eventual result. Some further argument is necessary, however, to meet the demands of those ascetics, often in power in education, who still have faith in information, in assigned tasks, in "the discipline of difficulty" and other fading theories of the way of life.

Those of us who have watched young life grow from dependent insecurity to independent power through the opportunities for the cultivation of the spirit which the newer schools afford, are assured that something ever so much more important than a beautiful product is the result of the new freedom in education. Personality develops with the springing certainty of a dry seed dropped into moist earth. Character emerges; and with it knowledge, a kind of wisdom, so sure in its judgments as to make us listen and attend rather than command and instruct. Taste is never, as with us, a hypocrisy. Confidence comes into the spirit and thrives there, for fear and bewilderment—the acknowledged tools of the older education—never yet begot faith in oneself. New hungers arise, new desires, new satisfactions, and these are the very food of education. The cultivation of the creative spirit makes for great artists, giant scholars and thinkers; it is the recipe for distinction.

The story of the leaders of the race is the story of those who cultivated the creative spirit in spite of the schools. Why is it, I wonder, that we have never taken that lesson to heart? The masters of men have ever refused formal education, or they have revolted, or they have evaded instruction, or have cleverly turned it to their own uses. But these are the strong of will who have fought their way to the right to be free. The mass has not been strong of will; a little fluttering of the wings, and then an acceptance—that is their story. The newer education is learning the uses of the mysterious forces of the spirit through which one may literally educate oneself for all the important needs of living. It is like the heart beat; no one has found the source of its power but no one doubts that the source is within us. The creative spirit is another heart; it will keep us alive if we give it a chance to beat for us; it may be stilled, but there is then no more life.

IV

Education is at last learning to use the natural creative impulses. At present it is experimenting, and the results are good; it has no assured technique as yet, but the beginnings are in sight. There is a general agreement that the school life should be free from arrogant authorities; that the teachers should be guides rather than instructors, and that these should be learning about children rather than certain about children; that the school environment should be rich in suggesting material for

Lincoln School, New York

Rosemary Junior School, Greenwich, Conn.

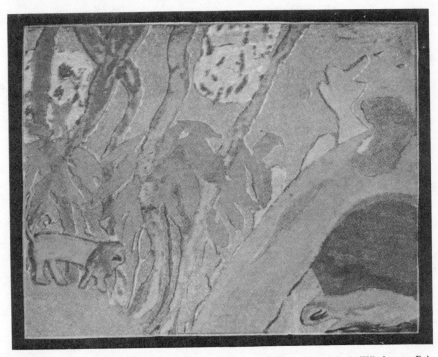

(Age 9 years) *Tower Hill School, Wilmington, Del.*

(Age 8 years)
Rosemary Junior School, Greenwich, Conn.

VIKING SHIPS

(Grade VI) *Winnetka Public School, Winnetka, Ill.*
THE FJORDS OF NORWAY

the creative impulses, and that the unfolding of the best personality should be watched and noted as important rather than "marks" in
assigned home tasks called "lessons."

When those of us who have dealt with children on this side of their
nature meet, we talk a different jargon from the professional pedagogue
because our classrooms are set to another rhythm than that of our more
military brothers; nor do we speak so despairingly of the work of school
children, rather we ply one another with this and that astonishing product of their effort. Information we do not prize so much—"the world is
so full of a number of things!"—nor the "skills" that one will sup-
posedly need at maturity (mostly very bad guesses, as any textbook
thirty years old will abundantly testify); nor are we much attracted
by the prevailing drill psychology ("Force them to do it a certain number of times and they will continue to do it joyfully for life") which we
are apt to classify flippantly with the claim of the New England cate-
chism as a formula for insuring the pious life. In this connection I
am reminded of the illiterate Kentucky mountaineers in the army whom
we insisted upon teaching to shoot from the shoulder; with the gun
at the hip these lads could pick the whiskers off a bouncing rabbit!

We dispute in the most friendly and heated manner when we meet,
for we are very much concerned that no mistakes shall be made in a
matter so vital to human kind. One group of "progressives," for instance, believes so much in "growth theory" that it will hardly permit
any instruction at all. It banks all upon Nature. With these "naturalists"
some of us have delightful disputes. Nature is wonderful, as all the
poets tell us, but we, some of us, don't trust her altogether. She is a
powerful Djinn to summon, and also a lusty, sly wench. We must make
Nature work for us, that is our contention; but, of course, we should
know what help and what interference we may expect of her. Because
of having written a book on the poetry of youth I am in constant receipt
of sheaves of bad poetry from all parts of the country. "See what my
children have done without any instruction whatever!" is the tenor of
the accompanying letters. My pity goes out to the children; so obviously
have they needed some one to be by to point out the way. Not to tell
them what to say! Heaven and Poesy forbid! But they never should
have been allowed, I say as I read, to continue to write in the style of
yesteryear, and even in the style of the year before yesteryear; and their
copyings, their hackneyed phrasing, and their silly platitudes should
have been gently made known to them—an art of teaching required here
that is nothing but the highest. If growth under pleasantly free surroundings were all of the new education, then my occupation is gone;
for I conceive of my professional skill as something imperatively needed
to keep that growth nourished.

Notably is this true of drawing, painting, and color work generally. Children do very good work and they do very bad work. If no one is by to suggest to them the difference they may never grow in taste, in discriminating art judgment. Nature, the jade, may or may not help them. They may even turn away from the sure voice of the instinctive creative spirit within them to copy the work of others or, worse, to copy themselves.

The teacher must know enough to entice them into the right road. And just any teacher will not do; scholarship here is a smoky flare, and the diploma, Master of Pedagogy, is not exactly enlightening. Children, for example, are often too satisfied; then they need an immediate experience with something better than they have hitherto known. Nothing so surely disgusts one with poor work as a goodish experience with something better. But it must not be too much better. (At this point the standardized teacher presents the "classics" in literature and in the fine arts, with the usual classic result.) The newer type of teacher, herself always more artist than teacher, knows the better, really knows it for what it does to one; and she knows how to place it in the child's life so that—most important!—it may be wholly acceptable.

Further, children are balked by difficulties in the handling of materials, how to make an effective linoleum block, for instance, or what to do with color that changes when brought into contact with other colors; they want to know the uses of crayon, charcoal, grease pencil, India ink, the mechanics of enlarging illustrations for the printer, and so on endlessly. It is the new business of the teacher to provoke children into wanting to know about these and other varying matters, and then to provide materials and such help as is asked for.

Growth is not enough, nor is environment enough, unless, as I believe it should be, the teacher is considered an essential part of the environment. Richer results may be expected of children than the standardized schoolmaster has hitherto considered possible; richer results may be expected from those even who are leading the way in the progressive schools; and that richness will come no faster, I suspect, than the coming in greater numbers of the gifted artist-teacher.

v

We talk of these and other matters when we meet professionally, but we consider it no particular justification of our work that the "free children" surpass the controlled children not only in an enlarged and gifted personality but in the customary school branches. Superintendent Washburne of the Winnetka Schools has the proof, if any one is interested. We note the fact, to be sure, because of its influence upon parents and upon the powers that control educational organization and administration. We may win our argument by way of the results in the standardized tests—and we do not despise winning our argument—but our main interest lies not there but in the sure knowledge we possess of the effect of our sort of education upon the mind and spirit of youth.

I BELIEVE

That life itself is the finest of all arts and that its richest realization is art's supreme excuse for being.

That human life is the progressive evolution of the spiritual nature of God and that the measure of growth in the appreciation of the beautiful in the conduct of life is also a measure of the true and the good in man's character.

That the mission of art is to teach a love of beautiful clothes, beautiful households, beautiful utensils, beautiful surroundings, and all to the end that life itself may be rich and full of beauty in its harmony, its purposes, and its ideals.

That the spirit of art lifts the artisan from the plane of the animal laboring to provide itself with creature comforts, to the plane of man working to the end that he may thereby most fully and deeply live the spiritual life of human idealism.

That the spirit of art is to lighten the labor of the artisan while at work, no less than to ennoble his leisure by the uplifting influence of its appropriate use.

That art appreciation and art values in human life grow most consistently and most toward life control by the exaltation of the element of beauty in all things—the pursuit of life's common needs and the conduct of man's daily intercourse, no less than in the abstracted idealizations of these relationships of man to man, and man to God conceived and produced by the imagination of artistic genius.

That all progress in art lies in the expression of the experiences, the hopes, the ideals, and the aspirations of our own environment, of our own times, and of our own lives. The past is studied to refine and stimulate creative effort for the expression of the life of the present, not to become a substitute for it.

That the appreciation of beauty in the thousand common things of daily life will result in the final appreciation of beauty as a dissociated ideal.

from MY ART CREED

FREDERICK GORDON BONSER.

THE DEVELOPMENT OF CREATIVE IMPULSES
IN ART CLASSES

L. Young Correthers

THE teacher who is trying to extract something in the form of original drawing or painting from the modern child, has attacked a difficult problem. He does not even know what name to give his course. The present idea of what constitutes "Art," is a hotly disputed point and he is none too sure of his own attitude toward it. The old comfortable days when one could sit back and quote Ruskin are gone. If the teacher is in sympathy with the conservatives and their nicely formulated rules of perspective, chiaroscuro, balance, and so forth, and plans to follow their guidance, the mere glancing from his window at the newer forms of office buildings or the design of modern clothing or even the picking up and handling of the latest books and magazines should cause him to alter and readjust his decision. If he is a real progressive, he will realize that following the conservative point of view will make his work deadly and dull, and that the charm of the undiscovered which is the most fascinating phase of creative life will be entirely lacking. He will decide, as have so many others, that after all, what has been done, has been done—so why do it again?

On coming in contact with his pupils he discovers that the mind of the modern child is filled to overflowing with images and pictures derived from the flood of illustrated children's books with which it has been deluged, from the moving pictures, the rotogravure section of the daily newspapers, as well as from many visits to the museums and picture galleries with their endless collections of the bric-a-brac and pictures of the ages. Place before one of these sophisticated little people a drawing board and a box of colors, ask him to do something original and he will turn out a color arrangement suggested by something from the storehouse of his memory. When analyzed it will yield up nothing new. Most likely you will find naïve or weak echoes of the assortments of valentines and Christmas cards that he has received, window displays gazed at, or a color arrangement suggested by the "Interior Decoration" atmosphere in which he lives. In short, the average child of today tends to reflect in his work, his made-to-order existence. Everything—work, play, games, and amusements—is provided by others.

He is simply a small cog in a highly organized machine and must move in the prescribed path. It is too much simply to ask him to create something that has not existed. The best that he can do is to take bits from various memories and reassemble them. There are of course exceptions. There are children who are wisely limited as to playthings, who are given raw materials with which to work, but in our present stage of educational development they are sadly in the minority.

To interest and encourage the child in original creation one must of necessity present something new. It would be the height of folly to place a child in a room hung with the works of the old masters and ask him to compete with them. If, however, we make a bold stand and reject everything that has been done, we at once enlist his sympathy and he becomes enthusiastic over this adventure into the unknown. Planting the idea is a simple matter. Explain that we are no longer interested in telling stories in pictures as that is done more successfully in books, that flowers and vegetables are more attractive in gardens than when hung on living room walls, that we can get a better and more satisfying understanding of rhythm and theme development from an orchestra than from any amount of paint, and that landscapes and views are more thrilling when framed in an automobile window than in dusty gilt, and he will understand. He will agree with you that modern photography is very skillful in obtaining likenesses of people and that living representations of the life of other times and other lands are often adequately handled by the directors of the film studios and the theaters, that it seems a useless and wasteful thing to use one art solely for the interpretation of another. The question then arises, what is there left for us to do? The logical answer is that we can arrange color patterns and combine forms in such ways that they will give to the beholder reactions that are not given by the written or spoken word, by music, dancing, or the drama.

The child, feeling that he is at liberty to do anything that he pleases, and that the result will be judged only from the point of view of his sincerity and truthfulness and not by laws formulated by experts of the old schools, will attack his work with the energy born of the joy of creation. The appearance of a class awakened to this joy is very different from that of a group working along the old arts and crafts methods, trying to produce something that will resemble a model, an illustration in a book or a past experiment dug up from the memory of the training period of the teacher. Perhaps all of this sounds hazy and up in the air, so it may be well to give an account of an actual working out of the theory.

In one school in this country where work is being carried on along these lines, the studio is a large well-lighted room at the top of the

(Kindergarten)   Tower Hill School, Wilmington, Del.

A RAINY DAY

(Age 7 years)   Lincoln School, New York

THE FARMER GATHERING APPLES

(Grade II)   *North Shore Country Day School, Winnetka, Ill.*

NEGRO FIELD WORKERS

(Age 7 years)   *Lincoln School, New York*

THE CITY AT NIGHT

Shady Hill School, Cambridge, Mass.

Lincoln School, New York

(Age 8 years)

A SET FOR AN ORIGINAL PLAY DEALING WITH HENRY HUDSON, MADE ON AN OLD SHEET

building. The simple but peculiar equipment consists of chairs, long tables, a sewing machine, laundry tubs, and vessels for dyeing, a carpenter's bench, a large scrap-box of textiles, leather and woodworking tools, modeling clay and plaster, and shelves holding tempera, oil, water-colors, and brushes. At one end of the room is a small stage with a proscenium arch and curtains, equipped with spotlights and gelatine screens for trying out light effects.

The classes are small, rarely exceeding twelve. A class, of say thirty, in the throes of creative activity would probably result in the collapse of the teacher. There is very little lecturing but a great deal of good-natured criticism by fellow workers. The favorite medium of expression seems to be the use of tempera on large sheets of bogus paper. Some, however, attack their problems in wood, leather, metal, stone, embroidery, or even in the making of doll-like figures of stuffed cloth. It is interesting to note that the children usually start expressing their ideas in two dimensions and progress to three dimensional work. As all materials have the same value—that of being merely vehicles used for visualization—it seems to make no difference to either boys or girls as to what they use or whether they are at the sewing machine or the carpenter's bench.

The first part of each period is devoted to talk—a free-for-all discussion of what can be done, what cannot be done, and possible methods of accomplishing results. The workers are not encouraged to tell too specifically of what they are about to do, as it has been discovered that many individuals experience the thrills of creation in discussion and when the working out takes place the result is found to be labored and uninspired. The teacher attacks an individual piece of work at the same time as the pupils and accepts their criticism as easily as he gives his. All the projects started do not reach completion. If at any time the material seems to run away with the idea, or the subject is beyond the worker's power of expression, the project is abandoned and a new one started. The old one may be taken up later from a fresh angle or in a different medium. Everything that is finished is left in the studio for a time so that it may be exhibited and discussed when cold. Many things are found weak or inadequate when not more than seven days old and are often destroyed by their creators. The one thing insisted upon is sincerity. The only thing demanded as to technique is that it must be straightforward, not muddled, and must show a conscious seeking after color pattern and significant living form. There are those who cannot at first evolve original forms. These are encouraged to take some natural living form and, selecting a portion of this, use it as a starting point. Sometimes when no idea comes to the worker, the actual handling or playing with the material results in a suggestion.

Most of the ideas expressed are more or less serious and seem to be based on a past emotion or experience of the creator. Here are some of the titles given by the workers to their projects: *Feelings on Entering a Large Building, Being Submerged, Disappearance, Growth, Awakening, Paganism, Sleep, How the Leaves Feel When Rain Touches Them, Coming from Sunshine into Shadow, Depth.* These are for the most part executed in paint. The older students sometimes attack very abstract subjects, such as *Envy, Kindness, Satisfaction* and *Fear.* It is interesting to note that the first attempts are usually simply mingled shades of color, no forms being discernible. At first strong colors are used, reds, blues, and crude greens. The next stage shows a refining of the color sense and the colors become weak half tones. This process is continued until the sheets of paper are covered with shadings so quiet that they finally resolve into neutral tints. From this point a fresh start is usually taken and the interest in form awakens. The younger children are addicted to the use of the circle and the arc, while the older ones make a conscious effort to avoid such simple forms as circles, triangles, and squares.

Various arrangements of color have been applied to cloth by means of painting, embroidery, and dyeing. Objects have been cut from wood, sometimes, but more rarely from stone, and have also been riveted together from copper. An interesting phase has been the creation of peculiar animal-like forms in various materials. Experiments have also been carried out using the monotype process and linoleum blocks.

Some of the work is crude, some frankly ugly, some beautiful, but there is a joyous spontaneity about it all that is delightful. The spirit of attack and enthusiasm has carried over and shows its result in other forms of study. It is too early yet to decide what has really been accomplished, but the school sponsoring the work feels assured of this, that there is a keen interest in creation through the mediums of color and form, and that a desire has been awakened to produce original things, not for the pleasure of possession but to realize the joy of creation.

PLASTIC ART

Willy Levin

ARCHIPENKO, the great sculptor, has said very cleverly, "Art begins where Nature ends." These words really express almost entirely my philosophy of art. The impressions we get in our everyday life, worked over in our minds with the help of our senses and our inner self, make the foundation of art. Nature is only a means for us to bring out what is in us.

Before I begin to speak about the creative ability of children and how I help them create, I must say that I am not a professional teacher, but primarily an artist whom life has thrown into a teacher's profession, and very interesting I find, is the study of a child's creative soul. But please overlook it if my technical terms are not professional.

During my five-years' experience with children in clay modeling, I have become convinced that every child can create, and the fewer standards we force upon them the richer will be the creative results obtained. The only standards I recognize for them in using certain materials are: technique, which grows with the child; proportion and movement, when they get to be ten years of age, and form after that age. In short, I give them some crude elements of fundamentals when they are old enough not only to understand but to experience them, and the expression of this living-through of the thing is the creation. A child does not reason, does not recognize rules; it wants to do a thing, it does it. It is the teacher's task to draw out of them just the one right thing which is the creation.

A child sees things differently, therefore it expresses itself differently from grown-ups, it is personal, it is an expressionist; it feels strongly and impulsively, and goes away from nature instinctively, that is, it exaggerates—which really is the aim of all art. To force our conceptions upon children is to suppress them, to kill their imagination, their spontaneity, to take away their creative ability: this is what happens in the old school, and what makes the greatest difference between the old and the progressive school in teaching art.

The ability of children to create differs; some are naturally more artistic than others, have natural feeling for proportion, for composition, and so on, due to certain circumstances in life, such as heredity, environment and others.

I also have been asked to tell how I work with the children to get results. This is the hardest thing to do, because it can't be formulated. You have to feel the thing the child wants to do, to think their thoughts, in short to become a child yourself, and to be able to do so, you must have the soul of a child, and unless it is so and only so, you can't get results.

I often have been asked the questions: "Do you give children models to copy?" "Do you tell them what to make?" No, the only help I give them in choosing the subject (if they don't come full of ideas themselves) is to go through their class program with them which suggests subjects to the children. Another thing I sometimes do is to let them squeeze the clay and develop the forms suggested by it. In modeling figures (by figures I mean animals as well as human figures) children always begin with the details of the figure and by and by produce the whole. They make the feet first or the head, putting in the eyes, nose, and mouth, which seem to them the most important; even in pottery they often make the cover of a dish before they make the dish. I let the small children go ahead in this way, showing them only how to work the parts together so they don't fall apart in drying. But when they are about nine years old, I ask them to make the whole figure at once, or to produce the biggest part of the figure first. I get this result through the question: "Which is the biggest part of the figure?" They usually say the body, though occasionally I have answers like the head or the feet. Here the question of proportion comes in for the first time. I ask them to compare their own heads with their own bodies, and ask which is larger. When they are about eleven years of age they begin to model figures in movement. I have them make primitive armatures. They continually try out the pose themselves, in order to experience, to feel the movement. The understanding of form-construction grows with the growth of the child's mentality. When I feel that the child can understand form, I explain the construction of the human body to them in an elementary way. I show them the big forms of the body and the joints, to make them understand that twisting or bending of the parts can only be done at the places where joints exist. But they only model movement, not form. I have noticed that children instinctively compose their designs well; they have a natural feeling for balance. They show it mostly in getting their designs into a tile. They experience it still more in modeling groups, in which I encourage them when they are older, as it takes them into composition in a wider sense.

Our materials are clay, which can be fired, and plasteline, which does not harden. In order to preserve the objects modeled in this medium, they have to be cast in plaster of paris. Besides figure work we do a great deal of pottery. We use the Indian Coil method in building by hand,

(*Age 12 years*)   *Walden School, New York*

(Age 9 years)   *City and Country School, New York*

(Grade III)   *The Lincoln School, New York*

(Grade V)   *The Lincoln School, New York*

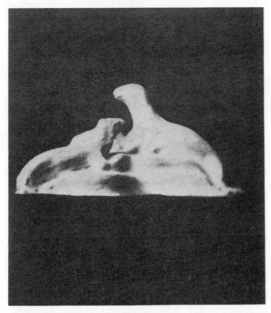

(Age 12 years)   *City and Country School, New York*

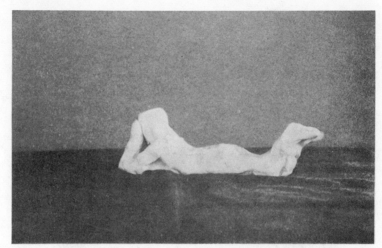

Shady Hill School, Cambridge, Mass.

(Age 11 years)   *City and Country School, New York*

Carson College, Flourtown, Pa.

Public School 45, New York

CHILDREN WORKING AT CLAY MODELING

Edgewood School, Greenwich, Conn.

Ethical Culture Branch School, New York

Shady Hill School, Cambridge, Mass.

SOAP AS A MEDIUM FOR SCULPTURE

Art has recently discovered the possibilities of soap as a plastic medium. The use of soap makes possible in schools a technique hitherto not possible. Before the recognition of its value as a means of self-expression, clay, wax, and plasticine were used as plastic mediums. But soap is used not as a modeling material but as one to be carved. It is clean and easily manipulated. In fact, the average child can cut it with a precision which he would have difficulty in doing in the moister clay or plasticine. This clean-cut quality of soap makes it possible for a child to translate his imagination directly into plastic forms resembling ivory in their beautiful texture and color. Even young children can produce results which give a satisfying tone and finish obtainable only in marble itself.

(Age 9 years)   *(Age 10 years)*   *(Age 8 years)*

Francis Parker School, Chicago, Ill.

(Age 7 years)
Chevy Chase Country Day School, Chevy Chase, Md.

(Age 12 years)   *City and Country School, New York*

but the children often find their own individual ways. Some who have patience enough learn how to use the primitive Kick Wheel. I fire their pottery and figures when they are technically well made. We put colored glazes on, and the children learn something about changes of materials going through a firing process. I let the little ones paint their clay things with water colors. They learn how to use their brushes on clay, but I seldom fire their work, nor do they glaze it.

By the time the children are eight years old they make finished products. For decoration of these, we use besides colored glazes, underglazes, colored clays, et cetera, and as they grow older, they learn many other techniques of decoration.

In my opinion, the best medium for little children to work in is clay; it hardens enough so it can be painted or varnished. It is very important to make them knead their clay before they begin to model. Besides learning the technique of preparing clay, it develops their finger muscles. For older children clay is advisable only with the purchase of a kiln. It is too disappointing to children who have worked hard at a vase or a bowl or at any other piece of pottery, not to be able to finish the article; that is: to fire it in a kiln, glaze it and fire it again to make it waterproof.

THE ARTIST AND THE CHILD

Peppino Mangravite

THE ordinary methods of attempting to foster the creative impulse have proved so unsuccessful that an entirely new approach must be made. My idea of a teacher of art is a person who is clairvoyant, who is able to penetrate the mind and soul of a child. A teacher must comprehend what the child wants to do. He must never interfere with the child's mental image by telling him how to begin. The idea—the mental picture—must be the child's. Once he is started a teacher can help him.

Getting the idea started is really the most difficult part of a teacher's work. What shall be the teacher's approach to the child's nature in order to stimulate him to express himself through the medium of art? It is most essential for the teacher to establish the right relationship between himself and the child. He must gain the child's confidence and establish within the child the desire to create, or he will not do anything. One of the most difficult situations to meet arises when children say, "I can't do this." I always answer, "Why?" Sometimes they can tell and sometimes they cannot. If they can answer, I can help them at once. If not, I must find out why they cannot. Sometimes I say to a child, "Very well, if you can't draw anything, don't try to, but suppose I should ask you now if there is anything you would love to do." The child answers perhaps, "Go swimming."

"Do you like to swim and dive?"

"Yes."

"Do you like to go alone?"

"No."

"How many should you like to have with you, and do you like children or grown-ups?"

He answers perhaps, "About three children."

"Well, do you like to go in the ocean, or a lake, or a pool?"

"In the lake."

"Are there trees around the lake? Tell me about it." You see, I am developing his mental picture. We are working it out together, but the ideas are all coming from him. When I feel that he has the picture sufficiently in mind I say, "All right, now draw it for me. Draw me a picture of the place you would like to go swimming in. I should like to see the kind of place you like."

When I am confronted for the first time with a young child or a group of children I sometimes appeal to their sense of humor by caricaturing with a few quick strokes on the blackboard some animal with which they are familiar—first the eyes, then the contour of the head, and so on. Soon the children recognize the creature. While I am drawing I talk to them and the room is filled with laughter and merriment. In this short time I have established a favorable relationship with the children; their sense of strangeness has disappeared. They look upon me as a sort of magician who, with a piece of chalk, can transform the blackboard into a living circus. By this time all the children are eager to draw— but draw what? I tell them that they may draw anything they like. They wonder what to draw and how to begin. Sometimes I suggest that they can visualize the picture more clearly on the cleaned blackboard if they think hard enough, or in their minds, if they close their eyes and think hard. Closed eyes—eyes with gaze lost in space—the approach of vision. Soon things are under way, pencils moving in every direction on large sheets of light gray paper, rolling tongues, firmly set lips—then, behold the creation!

I look about and discover that Bob and Jane have too extensive a vision for the sheets of paper they have. I notice that Bob has extended the drawing of the cow's tail on the other side of the paper, while Jane has drawn what is apparently a part of a haystack out on the drawing-board. This indicates a lack of sense of limited space. It is a quite common characteristic of young children. When it is manifest I give the children what is known as the boundary lines—the four lines, an

(*Age 7 years*)   *Potomac School, Washington, D. C.*

THE THREE KINGS

Ethical Culture Branch School, New York

HOUSE WITH CHIMNEY AND FIRE ESCAPE

inch or two from the edge of the paper, within which the picture must be drawn.

At the other end of the room Michael calls for help. He is distressed because the color combination of his picture looks queer. "What is wrong with this? Please help me get the right color." I answer, "How do I know what is wrong with it? If I were painting it, I would know. Now, if it were my picture, I would go a distance away from it, relax physically, look at it, and find out what colors go best." He walks away from his picture, looks at it, and soon returns happy. "I see now," he says. "The greens and blues are too raw for the other colors."

A sense of color harmony is one of the fundamentals of art that must be developed in working with children. I get children to work out harmony of color through using various combinations, but never by standardized methods. Out of standardized systems can come only commonplace conceptions. Emotional reaction is what counts most in working out new color combinations and new harmonies. My aim with children is to keep them always experimenting. This experimentation is to me one of the most fundamental characteristics of my work. In order to be really creative in life, we must ever look forward, creating new things—vital, strong figures—or new combinations of old things. Experimentation keeps alive the soul, out of which springs a new and beautiful growth—a new emotion. If then in the classroom today we discover one method of painting, tomorrow we shall be in quest of another.

I begin color work with four-year-old children and I also begin clay modeling with this age children. Young children see the world in one dimensional plane because of their lack of experience with things. Our sight is a complex faculty. It consists of visual sensations plus the memory of sensations of touch. Before children can comprehend things through the sense of sight they must get the idea through touch. The young child has a natural instinct to touch everything. It is his surest way of learning about the world in which he lives. As the child works with his fingers with clay, gradually he will come to understand the second and the third dimension. Later on he will be able to discern these things through the sense of sight alone.

Sometimes a child even gets a vision of the fourth dimension. A very exceptional child came to me one day and said, "I am tired of expressing nature and life; I want to paint something else."

My answer was, "Why, Buzzy, what else is there to express?"

He said, "There are other things to express; I want to draw gods."

"How would you draw a picture like that?"

"That is what I don't know."

"Well, what made you think about it?"

"One day, last summer, when we were away, I was lying out under a tree on the hilltop, when all at once I saw gods among the clouds."

"What did they look like? Tell me."

"I can't."

"Close your eyes and see if you can see them again."

He did. I said, "Now draw without opening your eyes the picture in your mind." When he had finished, the drawing looked like a strange bird among some clouds. It seemed to me that he needed a conception of space, in order to express the idea more clearly. After thinking it over for two days, I came to the conclusion that perhaps the best way was by means of a funnel. I had him look through the funnel. He finally drew a picture of circles, conical shapes, infinite space. It is really beautiful and absolutely abstract. He called it, *The Gods*.

As we work I talk to the children trying to explain to them the inner meanings of things in the simplest language. I try to recall to their minds vivid experiences they have had and impress upon them that it is nature and life they must express, but not the mere reproduction of the things they see. If a child is painting a tree, for instance, I tell him that it is not the outline that counts. He must think how the tree developed. First it was a tiny seed, then it grew and put forth sprays, leaves, buds, flowers, fruit. I lead the children to imagine things, I tell them to think of the inside of things instead of the outside, for my aim is to encourage imaginative and creative rather than reproductive art. It is not representation but creation. Representation is literal; creation is spiritual.

It is because of my belief in the true creative vision of children that I disapprove of illustrated children's books. In such books we have a triangular arrangement so far as mental imagery is concerned: first, that of the person who wrote the book; second, that of the person who illustrated the book (and of course this must necessarily be different from that of the author, because a second person cannot possibly express what another person conceives); third, that of the child who is reading the book. Such a situation cannot but be confusing to the child. If the words of a book are meant to evoke pictures, why the accompaniment of pictorial representation?

Modern children are becoming increasingly less imaginative. There was a time when children's imaginations were nurtured by nature and life. Now they are overwhelmed by illustrated books, trips to art galleries and museums, and the like. Art can be brought into the lives of our children not by sending them to museums but by bringing them closer to nature and life. Looking at pictures, if it teaches them anything, teaches them the art of imitation. Art must express the age in which it is created. How can a child express any other age when it is the age in

(Age 8 years)   Potomac School, Washington, D. C.

North Shore Country Day School, Winnetka, Ill.

THANKSGIVING

Washington Montessori School

(Age 8 years)

(Age 6 years)   *Junior Elementary School, Downers Grove, Ill.*

Park School, Baltimore, Md.

LARGE BATIK HANGING

which he is living that he feels? Children should not be allowed to go to galleries and museums until they have learned to realize the emotional beauty of the lines of a factory or a locomotive; until they understand that it is exaltation and not edification that they must seek in art; until they can comprehend that forms can be expressive and significant without resembling anything. Music is the purest of the arts because it is abstract expression; visual art should be the same. My children are not allowed to look at picture books, for it distorts their sense of reality. I want them to create freely from the experiences and images they have in their minds. The child is often more right about these things than we are. We are sophisticated; we have lost the creative vision; the child approaches art as a naïve and simple creature. If we could only add to the intelligence of the artist the unspoiled vision of the child, we should create art in naïve forms. While I am teaching the child what I know about art, he is teaching me life—the fundamental principle of art—he teaches me to look at life as naïve forms.

I believe that it is absolutely impossible for any one who is not an artist to succeed in teaching art. The made-to-order teacher of art depends upon standardized methods rather than upon his own sensibilities. No one but an artist has the delicate intuition to sense what another person is trying to express. Art education, as I conceive it, aims at nothing but sharpening sensibilities and strengthening power of expression. Ouspensky clearly describes this in his fascinating book, *Tertium Organum*. "He" (the artist) writes Ouspensky, "hears the voices of stones, understands the whisperings of ancient walls, of mountains, rivers, woods, and plains. He hears the voice of the silence, understands the psychological differences between silences. All art in essence consists of the understanding and representation of these elusive differences." This poetical understanding of the world only an artist can impart.

CREATIVE EXPRESSION THROUGH THE BLOCK PRINT

Florence E. House

NOT many years ago block printing was introduced into the schools of this country. It has become very popular. Some children who cannot express themselves in other art forms will express themselves freely in a wood or linoleum cut. For this and other reasons the block print has come to its own in the schools. The school magazine needs an attractive cover, or it may be that end sheets would add to the beauty of a book that is being made. At Christmas time children enter almost spontaneously into a block-printing experience. The library needs a bookplate or a child wishes to make one for his own little library at home. Sometimes a poster is wanted for a school program or play. The wood or preferably the linoleum cut is an easy and an inexpensive way to supply these needs.

There are various methods in use today in the making of block prints. The suggestions here are a simplified process to be used with children from nine to twelve years. The design as originally drawn may be reversed by placing it on the carbon side of impression paper. After tracing over the lines, the back of the paper will show the drawing reversed. This may be transferred to a piece of grade A linoleum which for convenience has been painted with white tempera paint. Designs which leave a maximum of linoleum in mass and provide for comparatively little to be cut away seem most appropriate for this medium. Lines may be incised with a veiner, or the cutting may be done with a penknife or razor blade having but one sharp edge. The tool should be held slanting outward to make the base slightly larger than the surface. It need not be cut deeper than one-sixteenth of an inch. The block may be inked by means of a printer's brayer rolled over a slab of glass or marble, on which a small quantity of ink has been placed. The brayer should be rolled over the block lengthwise and crosswise. The printing can best be done by placing the linoleum on the paper and putting it through a clothes wringer. This goes still better when children improvise a shelf fastened to the wringer and on a level with the lower cylinder. Quite rapid printing may be done in this way. If the block is mounted, a letterpress may be used to make the impression. If that is not available, a mallet would do. If mounted type high, it may be placed in any school

(Age 14 years)   Skokie School, Winnetka, Ill.

(Age 12 years)   Shady Hill School, Cambridge, Mass.

IF WE COULD SEE GRENDEL AS A SHIP GOES OVER HIS HEAD

(Age 11 years)   *City and Country School, New York*

(Age 11 years)   *City and Country School, New York*

THE BRONX

THE HALF MOON

LINCOLN'S BIRTHPLACE

BENJAMIN FRANKLIN

From Our Story Book, written, designed, and printed by Pupils of Public School 45, New York City

Park School, Baltimore, Md.

Park School, Baltimore, Md.

printing press. It would be interesting for the children to compare the method described above with the process used by the Orientals, that of using an ink ball, laying the paper on the inked surface and rubbing it to make the impression. Children sometimes pull off a proof in the same way.

This work not only takes children into a new and delightful craft, but goes still further by giving them the possibility of a program full of activity and so full of stimulating content material that they express themselves freely and creatively when opportunity arises. For instance, children about ten or eleven years of age at work on a medieval nativity play and saturated with the medieval setting are as quaint and naïve in their prints as were the artists of that day when they pictured the star, the Mother and Child, the angels, the shepherds and kings. In a school where this really happened some of the groups studied quite deeply into the historical setting of the Christmas tree, taking up not only the Scandinavian myths, but also all the pagan festivals of the sun and the symbols which came to be used on the tree. What could be more natural than to use some of these symbols on their blocks?

There is another way in which the block print can enrich the lives of the children. I mean a study of the beginnings of block-printing and its development to the present time. Children would enjoy following block printing through the five centuries of existence in Europe to its present revival both here and abroad, or to reach still further back into its Asiatic beginnings to the time when the first inked impressions on paper were made in China.

Imagine with what interest and delight children will follow this historical development while having the experience of making a print of their own, and with what appreciation they will examine and pore over prints of all kinds and of every time and place.

It would be quite worth their while also to make a collection of prints. They could easily get the modern ones in the current magazines, such as those of Rockwell Kent. They would enjoy owning the funny little cuts in the *New England Primer* and the "One Thousand Quaint Cuts" from *Books of Other Days*, or the whimsical blocks of the fifteenth and sixteenth centuries or of the early Renaissance. They could get acquainted with Dürer and Holbein not only as painters but as famous block printers of their time. They would value the St. Christopher dated 1423, not only because it is considered by most authorities to be the earliest known print in Europe, but for its quaint conception of the medieval mind and its combined crudity of proportion and beauty of line. Then there is the *Ars Moriendi* or *The Bible of the Poor* with its forty pictures meant to give religious teaching to the illiterate people of the Middle Ages. To come to our own time again, there are the reproductions of the old masters done so skillfully in wood by Timothy Cole and Henry Wolf. Fine Japanese color prints are also easy to obtain. They are an interesting study in themselves and would naturally lead to a study of the modern four-color process and other methods of illustration in use today.

All this material, and more too, will give children in the elementary school a rich background of history, an added appreciation of beautiful prints of all times, an interest in the modern processes of today, and a desire to express in their own blocks interests which they have, not in commonplace ways but with individuality and which, in spite of crudities, have a beauty of their own.

CREATIVE WORK AT THE MODERN SCHOOL

Elizabeth Byrne Ferm

THE educational value of the art work of the Modern School at Stelton, New Jersey, cannot be measured by its technique, color, line, or subject. Its distinction and value lie in its being a pure reflection of the inner life of the child. There are no external stimuli, suggestions, or examples; there are no art talks; no art walks; no journeys to museums. The children are free to paint all day or no day. Pencils, crayons, paints, paper, canvas are accessible—just as clay, wood, metal, reed, yarn and type are accessible.

It is safe to say that no school was more devoid of decoration than the building of the Modern School. No Venus; no Apollo; no Winged Victory. Not even photographs of beautiful things or places. Just an ordinary building with unattractive rooms. If there was any esthetic influence it was indirect, like the skyline, the fine sunsets, the distant blue range of the Watchung mountains, a brook, and a few trees. The immediate surroundings were flat.

We did not regard art in terms of sculpture, drawing, printing, literature, dancing, music or acting. We recognized art as self-expression, as a revelation of the spirit projected outwardly. We believed that man, to know himself, was necessitated to objectify his inner life in the very outermost, that that outermost might serve as a mirror to reflect his image. This belief made us zealously guard the outposts of the child's life. So many good people are always ready to do things for children.

Copying a Rembrandt or a Botticelli may be an aid in acquiring style, taste, or technique, but we did not look upon imitation or reproduction as art. Art meant more to us than any of these accomplishments. We saw in art the signature of the child's inner life.

Modern School, Stelton, N. J.

Edgewood School, Greenwich, Conn.

CANTERBURY PILGRIMS

Tower Hill School, Wilmington, Del.

Francis Parker School, Chicago, Ill.

PALM BEACH

Did the glorious sunsets provoke the children to work so freely and joyously with color, or was their free, independent use of color a reflection of an inner state or need? We did not probe the children to find out. We were satisfied that their work was spontaneous and creative. We pondered over the crude endowment or environment of the children and the esthetically beautiful conceptions that the children gave birth to in their work. Our conclusion was that a child has more opportunity for expansion in a crude than in a finished surrounding; that equipment very often clogs the space in which the child needs to exercise himself physically and spiritually. If a child is surrounded by models of perfection where can he find a place for his crude effort? By presenting models of beauty we erect standards which may react on the child by obscuring the spiritual value of his own expression.

Believing that the great reservoir of human creativeness is inexhaustible, we religiously withdrew from the child so that he might discover himself in his work and also, incidentally, that we might discover him. We were not trying an experiment; we tried to provide an environment in which the child might experiment. Our experience taught us that life is realized and enriched through creativeness; that it is unrealized and impoverished by repetition, imitation, and reproduction. We maintained that idling was better than copying and reproducing.

Art cannot be separated from life for it is life revealed. The cooing of the infant is his first music; the kicking of the infant's legs is his first rhythmic dance. The child's early drawing of the spiral and circle is his first art expression. The spiral and circle reveal the homogeneous, spiritual at-oneness of his stage of development. Every object made from an inner impulse, no matter how insignificant or useless it may appear, is a creation, and bears the hallmark of the creator upon it. We have observed that when the older children express themselves in drawing, they make pictures actually resembling themselves.

An unhampered child is always self-active and creative. He is absorbed in his own interests and is therefore reluctant to receive suggestion or direction from the outside. He needs no encouragement to do things. His own impulses and desires are so alive and urgent they keep him busy fulfilling the promptings of his own being. Outside suggestion or direction only serves to interrupt and retard the work of the self-active child.

In the early stages of a child's development he is satisfied with any form which he can create. He is possessed by the spirit of his own activity and finds his satisfaction in the doing of the thing. The concrete forms made by the child reflect back to him his own image and likeness. Through his own activity his vague purposeless feelings assume a shape which makes visible and tangible to him the indwelling force which necessitated his activity. He is able to relate the form which he has created to himself because he has not been diverted from his own center by outer suggestion or direction. He has left his impression on matter and through that impression he has learned the properties of matter. Through his creation he develops a knowledge of himself as a creator. At the same time he recognizes that every visible form exists and is manifested through and by means of the spiritual impulse indwelling in the thing itself. In the degree that he recognizes himself in his acts he in that degree is able to understand the cause of existing things surrounding him. When the child feels satisfied with the form of his creation it no longer holds for him as vital an interest, but until he senses it as complete he is urged on and on until he perfects it. In the time and order of a child's development he becomes critical and exacting toward his own work. But before that takes place the form is always subservient to the spirit and we find the child engrossed in his own creation.

When a child is directed from the outside to do this or that thing, he is not exercising his own power. He may be active, but he is not self-active. He can gain no consciousness of the force indwelling in his own nature so long as he is subject to guidance and direction. The impression that outside direction leaves on the child is a sense of unsureness. Direction implies that the natural inclination and impulse of the child are not in accord with the demand of the outside, so the child is left in doubt of himself and unsure about his outside relations. The child who has been subjected to direction is always noncreative, restless, exacting, and capricious. He has been trained to look to the outside for suggestion and direction. If the outside fails to supply him he is lost and confused. Suggestion becomes such an accepted thing in the life of such a child, that to be left to his own resources for even a few minutes is a cause of complaint. In the midst of his own unexplored nature, his own inexhaustible resources, the child is a beggar—stunted and starved, dependent upon the outside for help because that is where we adults have led him to believe that the source of supply exists.

One day I found a block of wood on one of the tables with a design carved on it. That woodcut dropped from a clear sky. It was the origin of the wood and linoleum cuts that appeared in the children's magazine. A child had played with the block and then dropped it. We adults marveled over the how and where of the creations that followed, but the children treated them as normal every-day affairs. It was but necessary to provide the raw material for them to find their expression.

Perhaps the greatest reward that came to us was that every creator had his place in the sun with the children. They seemed to realize that each creation was a contribution to the whole social body. The recognition that was accorded to a new accomplishment was very beautiful. It gave us a vision of a new society founded on creativeness instead of rivalry and competition.

Sometimes I think that because a creation must have its root in the inner life and come from an inner necessity it is spiritually recognized by other creators because they also work from within, where there are no standards, no loss, no gain. It establishes a creative fraternity. This may seem very speculative. It is, however, the only solution that I have been able to come to. The bare, bald fact was, that not one case of envy or disparagement by the children was manifested in all the years of our creative work. Even dispositions and temperaments that did not combine freely were united when they expressed themselves creatively.

Very naturally the questions must arise as to whether there is any place for past achievements in the present demand for creative expression; whether or not there is any connection, any bridging over of the past to the future; whether the past is to be ignored or included in our present educational life.

To these questions I would reply that the past is the stream from which the present flows. It is irrevocably bound up in the present. To become conscious of the relation of the past and present the individual must first realize himself in his own creations before he is capable of recognizing the creations of others. If he can trace his outer attainments to an inner prompting, urge or impulse, he is then ready to review and comprehend his relation to the past. Until he understands himself he is incapable of understanding others. In truth, he cannot even see them correctly. Art is synonymous with the inner life of humanity. The artist is moved by an inner need for self-expression. We must become conscious of this before we can respond or vibrate to our past inheritance. The past is ours, let us include it in our life with insight and understanding.

How shall we educators know when the child is ready for connection with the past? Our study of the child indicates that the adolescent stage reveals the need and time. The youth shows less confidence in taking the initiative and less satisfaction in his own accomplishment. He turns his back on his inner promptings and faces round towards the external world. He tries to understand the external by absorbing it. His necktie, shoes, clothes, hair, and manners are as true copies of the external as he can get or make. He identifies himself with the forms of the past. It is like a complete surrender to the forms of life and a repudiation of the spirit of life. The novitiate is not long however, for the youth who has been creative and who has ventured away from his own creative center, soon realizes that the formalities and externalities of society have their origin in a spiritual need similar to his own. He journeys back to his own life, enriched by his outer experience. He has enlarged his outlook and has gained consciousness of the underlying unity in the great diversity of human expression.

MAPS AS ART EXPRESSION

Lucy Sprague Mitchell

IF A map means the representation of a part of the earth's surface with reference to the relative position of certain factors, then it is fair to say that in the City and Country School, maps begin in block building. The general floor play of "boats" on "water," or "elevated" on "streets," or "trains" on "land," early develops into ferries, ocean-liners, barges in the Upper and Lower Bays or on the Hudson, the Sixth Avenue Elevated crossing the familiar streets around Twelfth Street, or the Pennsylvania Railroad. So that with five-year-olds a floor scheme will often represent true locational relationships actually observed by the children in their trips. Of course much practice in orientation of the children in their own immediate surroundings—their classroom in the building, their school in reference to their homes, and so on, precedes and determines such observation. These floor maps are incident to play. They are simply the children's recall of particular aspects of their actual experiences.

From the early floor-scheme maps where water may appear as wavy chalk lines on the linoleum floor and four or five buildings important to the children appear as block constructions placed in their relative positions and where the block-constructed boats or the bench-made autos and trucks move along their respective highways—from these early floor maps there is a logical development to the decorative map of the world, or to a symbolic map of Indian tribes and their modes of life, or to a scientific map of the life of cows in the United States in relation to the kind of lands and kind of workers needed for their progress from the grassy plain to the table. The early orientation of the children facilitates the translation of geographic observations into symbols. This early use of symbols to record their own observations leads to an understanding of scientific maps of human or earth factors, and to consequent ability to use such scientific maps independently as tools in their own study.

But it is equally true that the maps originated as play—a reliving of an actual experience. This play element persists in the development of map making in the school until it reaches a pitch of organization which ranks many of the maps as art. The children in the early stages make no distinction between science and art in their recalls of their experiences. With the older children—perhaps from ten to twelve—their keen

(Age 9 years)

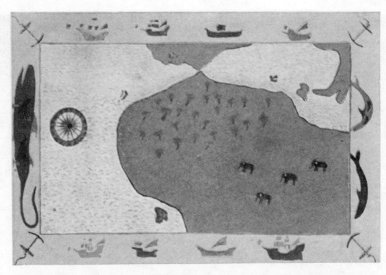

A CHART DRAWN AND USED BY A BOY TAKING PART OF SEA
CAPTAIN IN A MEDIEVAL PLAY

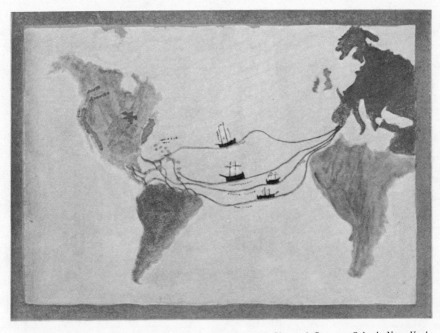

THE ROUTES OF THE EXPLORERS

THE FRENCH AND THE INDIANS
SMOKING THE PEACE PIPE

THE FRENCH FORT WHERE CHI-
CAGO NOW STANDS

EARLY CHICAGO

(Grade III)

Hawthorne School, Glencoe, Ill.

SCENES FROM A MOVING PICTURE MADE WHILE STUDYING CHICAGO HISTORY.
THE WHOLE IS ON A REEL SEVERAL YARDS LONG

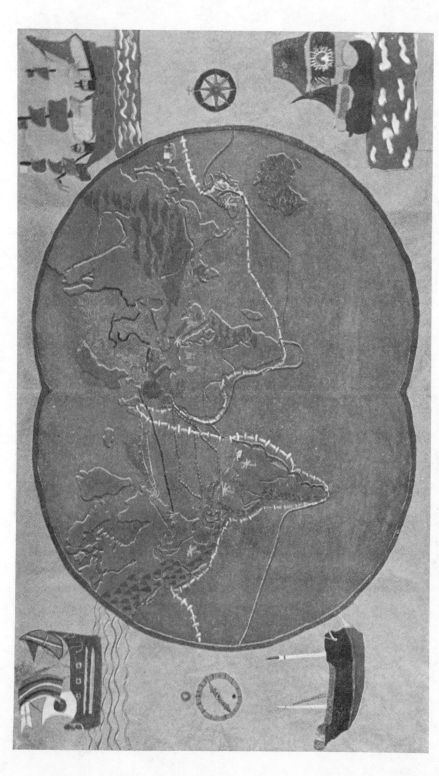

(11 year old group)

THE PERIOD OF EXPLORATION AND EXPANSION

analysis of all their own processes makes many of them distinguish between play maps and real maps. There is no absolute or genuine distinction, however. It is merely a matter of emphasis. The play map pretends to less accuracy than the real map. The real map on the other hand seldom appears in the school without some element which the child put there for the sake of form or beauty, rather than as a help to the understanding. It has, therefore, a play, an art, element. Maps as tools for study and maps as expressions of form do not conflict in the children's minds. Is it too much to hope that the children will never make the devastating divorce of these two elements which make most adults feel that a scientist cannot be an artist or an artist a scientist?

ART IN THE LIFE OF THE CHILD

Florence Cane

THE world of art is truly a cosmos. It contains within it the whole drama of life. The creative process is life itself revealing all its phases: conception and growth, play and work; its problems, conflicts, failures, overcomings, and achievements. Therefore art may hold within it possibilities for the development of the child in relation to life far more important than the possibilities for the development of the artist. Too often man has identified himself with his art in a false way: pinned his ego on his art and said, "If my art is great, I will be great." I do not believe this to be true. On the contrary, I believe that man is like a tree and art is one of the fruits of that tree. The fruit is a measure of that tree's worth. The quality of the painting inevitably develops if the child develops as an individual, and equally the child grows with his growth as a painter. Therefore the direction of my teaching has been towards the liberation and growth of the child's soul through play and work and self-discipline involved in painting.

The play spirit is the primary one. The creative impulse is born of it and without play art cannot exist. Art always starts in play, otherwise it is not art, and it must preserve this element or lose its purity. I mean play in the sense that it springs from an inner wish for satisfaction of the true self. In early youth this satisfaction seems to be completely achieved.

> Heaven lies about us in our infancy
> Shades of the prison house begin to close
> Upon the growing boy.

As the child matures, the possibility of complete achievement slips away from him, but in his effort to approximate it the element of work enters in. His search for truth and beauty drives him on to infinite labor. This labor must always be related to the play—the inner wish to express the unattainable—or it is no longer art and contains neither beauty nor truth. When outer standards enter, such as the desire to please, to be accepted, to receive praise and fame, the shrine is desecrated and art takes flight. In the play aspect lies the instinctive, irrational, and unconscious; the black as well as the white; the grotesque and crude as well as the beautiful; the wild as well as the controlled. Its outpouring is like the unfolding of life; it brings with it release and joy. Perhaps it is the recognition of both these values that makes this work vital. The young child is uncritical and easily pleased; endless fantasies stream forth; their projection through the painting makes a channel for the subjective life, builds in the child a faith in himself and forms the beginning of his own center. Man is born with the creative impulse and this impulse may become the means of revealing and developing the self. The work side being a continuation and development of the play becomes more conscious and directed; it brings in its train strength and power, the ability to conquer difficulties, and achieve a completed thing.

Though I speak of work and play as two aspects they occur in the same work of art and one must do nothing to separate them. In the play side lies the instinctive creative impulse that must be cherished above all else; in the work side lies the searching need for perfection, the development of the material thrown up by the first. The first is like the birth of life, the second is its overcoming and transforming. This must come in natural stages adapted to the individual needs of each student. Infinite care must be taken to do nothing that may stifle the creative impulse.

Creation is a process like life itself. It rises out of a state of quiet, a sacred spot where the miracle is born. Out of the dark, the unconscious, a spring wells forth, and like a stream cutting its own bed through the meadow it flows. After this process a detachment sets in and the artist views, judges, and develops according to his taste and maturity. In the young child or a great genius a state of unity may exist and the two processes occur at the same time. Because of this simple unity in the young child painting is play for him and he is better off with almost no teaching. The creative fantasy must be respected and allowed free play a long time before any laws of art can be brought to the child without harm. The expression of feeling or the representation of objects as they appear to the comprehension of the child are essential to the building of an inner honesty and a faith in his own powers. A flower may appear larger to a child than himself. He should be permitted to make it so without comment. For if he gives up belief in his own concept for that of the adult's, a conformity may begin which leads to sterility. If, however, his ideas and feelings are permitted to flow freely regardless of whether they appear clear or confused to the adult, they will satisfy him. As he makes these fantastic patterns and forms he gains empirical experience. In placing colors next to each other often enough he discovers harmony; in interlacing lines he finds rhythm; and in opposing masses he learns balance. So in this early period there is little teaching except to show the child how to take care of the material and to use his body freely as he paints.

But when he grows older a change gradually takes place in him. At about ten or eleven years he is no longer so easily pleased. He becomes critical. The thing projected in canvas does not conform to the inner image and the child becomes dissatisfied. But his desire to achieve in his painting what he imagines drives him on to a search for truth. He enters a new period, the second stage of creation. He no longer merely plays; he works. At this time teaching is needed. The teacher must give the children whatever technical help they require individually as the need appears, but more important than that she must keep them related to their own center, the source, continually leading them back to themselves for the answer whenever possible. All through the years when they are acquiring technique she must see to it that the door to their imagination is kept open. The greatest harm that teachers of art can do is to let the acquiring of technique postpone or exclude creation. Form is man's language for expressing his spirit and if the spirit slips away the form is empty and dead.

Building on these observations the general plan of art in the Walden School is somewhat as follows: The young children from two to ten are given free use of materials: crayons and large paper, water-colors, post-card colors, and clay. They draw, or paint, or model, at will—just as they play with blocks or toys. As it is a free spontaneous impulse and only followed as such, it will be impractical to have a special teacher come in regularly. So the class teacher has care of the children in art as well as in their regular work. I go in at the beginning of the year a few times and give the class teacher my point of view. The teachers, furthermore, obtain their own creative experience by learning to paint in a special class for teachers. The teachers' class is an interesting development that has grown out of our experimentation. A number of teachers wanted to paint and asked me whether they could. I consented to try the experiment. Now many of them come regularly and are doing very interesting work; and it actually does have an immediate liberating effect on the work of their children.

I begin by giving the child carefully chosen materials, materials that respond well. The crayons must be soft enough to mark easily, not to require pressure, and yet not so soft they will smudge. Paper must be good enough in quality to take the strokes well and hold them. If it is too coarse the child's efforts are often balked. Water colors must be moist in order to respond. Brushes must be large to help keep the work free. There is always a tendency to cramp and niggle. In using post-card colors for young children, if they are to help themselves and keep the work clean, a systematic plan must be made. I give each child a china palette with the divisions for the colors. The large jars of colors stand in a row on a table covered with oil cloth. In front of each large jar stands a small empty jar with a wooden mustard spoon. The

Lincoln School, New York

SPACE

Mohegan Modern School, Peekskill, N. Y.

child can help himself to a color with this spoon, place it on his palette, replace the spoon in the empty jar, ready for the next child to use. By this method the problem of waste and mixed colors is done away with. I teach the children such practical details as the need to dip the brush in water before using a new color, to change the water frequently when it gets muddy, to start work on the upper part of the paper first so as to avoid smearing, or in using crayons the need of keeping them sharp and clean. All such small details are the means towards giving the child the power to express what he wants. Often discouragement comes from simply not knowing how to keep the colors clear or the brushes clean. A class teacher who does not paint herself may be unaware of the importance of these matters. I want to cultivate in the child a love of his tools, such as good craftsmen always have. It builds something in the child. The care he gives his materials reflects in his painting and then in his life. In learning to make his strokes with care he finds he needs a supple brush; the washing of it properly is therefore closely related to good work.

Next as to the free use of his body: If the child is working in a standing position I see that he is well balanced so that he may sway easily from one foot to the other. One should be able to dramatize a gesture, as a dancer or an actor would. For the arms I try to teach large gestures with the shoulder as a working point. So often the children cramp themselves and use only the finger muscles. I tell them that all their joints, the wrist, elbow, and shoulder are pivots to work from as reliable as the center of a compass. When they draw I want them first to feel the line they are going to make and then trust the arm to do it. Here may be found the difference between fear and faith, and the line shows it. Let the child mark two points far apart on the paper and join them with a curve. There are two ways: if he tries timidly to guide the line in a cramped fashion it will be poor and uncertain because it is determined by fear; but if he swings it in freely trusting the arm, the line will assume a beautiful strong curve and express the organic use of the whole being.

Having given the child his materials, I trust him to do what he wants and let him continue to draw or paint as long as his interest lasts. To the extent he is content with his work I am assured the thing projected on paper corresponds to the image within. One little girl of five said of her painting, "It looks the way you feel inside."

At the ages of ten or eleven the plan changes. The children leave their classroom and come to me in the studio. All of their work is more differentiated now and is being carried beyond mere spontaneous impulse. Here they are given oil paints, or colored inks, or linoleum, or wood blocks, or clay. Besides the direct painting we are trying to develop some of the practical arts. The students have decorated rooms, not only mural painting, but all the workman side—the scraping, crack filling, and ordinary painting. They also decorate lockers and doors, and paint screens. They have printed a magazine and illustrated it with their own wood blocks. They have put on plays and made their own costumes and scenery. The competent, confident way in which they tackle these jobs assures us that the undirected early work is bearing its fruit.

Having sketched the general plan of art in the school I will outline my approach to the work. I believe that art is a search for the unattainable and that craft work is a search for the attainable. The difference, if clearly realized, defines the approach. Since it is the unattainable, the immortal thing we seek, naturally it is within the child's own soul the source is found. It is because I have this faith in children and build their faith that they respond as they do. It is for this reason that I do not volunteer criticism. I feel it is a violation of the creative process for one human being to interrupt or direct another. Who knows what the vision of the worker is, except the worker himself, and how can a teacher be of use except at the point of dissatisfaction when the worker has reached an impasse? Therefore I wait until I am asked for help. It is not only what is taught but when that is important. I never lessen the child's self-criticism. I must ask him what he thinks is poor and by questioning find out what he meant to do; then show him how he failed, and find a way to come nearer to his conception. It calls for all one's understanding and all one's technique, for with the right direction—not correction—the child should move on; a new door should be opened where he will perceive more directly, or feel more deeply, or think more clearly.

I never suggest a subject; it is always the children's choice. If one says occasionally she doesn't know what to paint I talk with her until I draw out of her a hidden wish for something she wanted to do but was afraid she couldn't. It is very interesting to observe how the interest will flag if they attempt to paint something they don't really care about; but if they attempt something that is really dear to them, no matter how difficult it is, the necessary energy is there. That is why it is so important for them to choose their own subject.

Here follow a few illustrations of common difficulties and the way I try to meet them. A very conscientious boy was trying to paint a landscape; he was thoroughly dissatisfied with it; the sky, hills, and lake were wooden, dark, and lifeless. I realized that he was in bondage to the object. He was so definitely searching for a literal likeness to the object that he had lost all sense of joy in it, all natural feeling of design

THE MERMAID AND THE MAGIC BOAT

(Age 14 years)

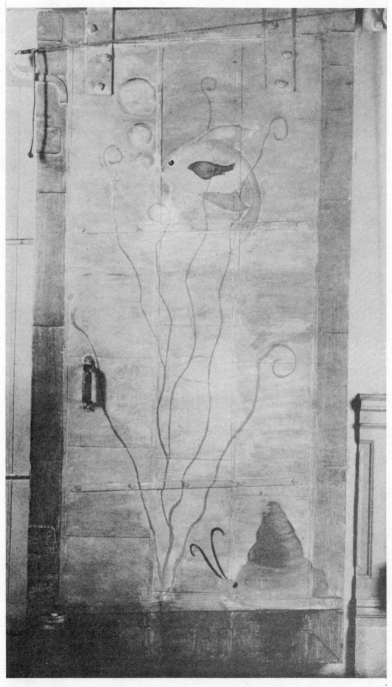

AN UNSIGHTLY FIRE DOOR IS CONVERTED INTO A THING OF BEAUTY
AND GAY COLOR AFTER A VISIT TO THE AQUARIUM

(*Age 15 years*)   *The Walden School, New York*

AN APRIL DAY

FAIRIES DANCING IN THE MOONLIGHT

(Age 15 years)

and color. It was simply three parallel strips of blue sky, green hills, and blue lake. After several suggestions on my part had helped not at all, I said to him, "Sometimes a horse must drive in harness with a definite direction to go to, and sometimes he needs to run loose in a field just for the fun of romping. How would you like to take a canvas and just play with color and shapes and romp like the pony in the field?" A most sudden change took place. He was delighted at the idea and began at once making rapid free lines all over the canvas. He drew a large tender flower in the center surrounded by forms and many colors and shapes, by far the most light and clear color he had ever used. It was as if my words had revealed his play side to him, which brought up fantasy, and in its train intuition and sensation came to his aid. He had been dealing almost entirely in thought before he was ready for it.

Another way to release a child from the bondage of the object is to turn the painting upside down, then he sees it freshly as design and can judge whether he likes it as pattern; he can see the color as harmonious or otherwise, rather than the colors literally conforming to the object. He frees himself from the slavery of representation and usually discovers what is next to be done.

The problem of relative value in color is a constant one. For instance, a model is posing; she is an Assyrian woman, dusky skin, shimmering peach-color costume against black background. One of the girl students starts to paint the face, quite a dark color. She is building it against the white canvas and the dark tone seems true; but the moment she adds the black background the face appears too dark because in relation to black it seems light, just as before against white the skin seemed dark. The same thing applies to the relative amount of red in the skin and the draperies. There seemed to be a great deal of red in the face until the drapery was added. Then the face needed more yellow in order to bring out the greater amount of red in the drapery. So I try to give children the general idea through the particular problem—that value and colors are not absolute, but only exist in relation to the others. A further development of the idea of relativity comes out in another case. A student was doing a three-quarter figure seated with hands in the lap. All was going well until she struck difficulty in the arms and hands. They remained wooden and cramped. She persisted in trying to get them right and concentrated on them alone. She forgot where the arms grew from, what they were resting on, and what they were seen against. I said, "If you would stop thinking only of the hands and see them in relation to the whole body perhaps they would come of themselves. They rest between the two thighs and their large curves contain them. Paint in the beautiful cool shadow back of them, developing the legs they rest on rather than the arms and hands themselves, and feel and paint the form of the whole body back of them; they will live in relation to it."

The same sort of thing happened with regard to the object in relation to its background. One girl came to the school whose work was always on a shallow level. She always painted a simple silhouette like a poster. She put in no background at all or only a flat tone without much meaning or relation to the object. I asked her why she didn't develop the rest of the picture, and she said, "Oh, I always spoil it if I do." I explained to her that the environment was so closely related to the object that one could not exist without the other—like the relation of herself to her environment. So I asked her to try, and said that I would help her if she got into trouble. A change took place. The next thing she did was a ship at sea, and as she made the effort to relate her ship to the world about it, her painting assumed depth and beauty such as it never had before.

The problems connected with light are many of course, as it is so important and difficult a part of painting. A child will say, "What is the matter with the sky? It seems the color blue sky looks to me, and yet this doesn't look like sky. It is solid like blue cloth." I answer, "Perhaps the reason may be you have tried to match the blue of light with the blue of paint. Now light is a transparent medium and paint an opaque one. The range in light is much greater than in paint. So we can only suggest light relatively. When we want to suggest the blue of the sky in paint, we have actually to paint it a much lighter color than it seems in order to suggest light." I also explain to them how a ray of light is pure white, and as it strikes an object is broken up into the spectrum; even a speck of dust may be sufficient to do this. And so in the sky we find red and yellow as well as blue, each keyed high with white. The use of the prism to show them the spectrum is valuable here.

There is also a problem in dealing with different types of children. Some need to be stimulated to use their imagination, and some to be disciplined in mastering form. For instance, one student is an introvert, with feeling and intuition as superior functions, the other student an extravert, with sensation and thought as superior functions. The former has her own center well established; she works best from imagination, needs very little stimulus from the outside. If she wants to know how a figure looks in a certain position it is best for her to see it only a few minutes, secure her acquired knowledge and then work from memory. If she observes an object too long it destroys her unified conception. Perhaps she will never need a model for long periods because this method of working develops the perceptive eye. Mental notes doubtless go on all the time her eyes are open and the needed information is being

CHILDREN PAINTING THE SCENERY FOR ONE OF THEIR PLAYS

The Man of the Winter Nights

The wind is loudly calling,
The snow is deeply falling,
And through it all an old man comes,
The "Man of the Winter Nights".

He is old and bent, but still he comes
To his castle of silver, the "Fair Moonlight."
And as he comes, the trees all bow
To their King, the "Man of the Winter Nights.

(Age 12 years)   Carson College, Flourtown, Pa.

ORIGINAL POEM AND ILLUSTRATION

stored up. The latter type does best with a model. The sight of a beautiful form and color in the outer world stimulates her to her best work; through this she gets a sense of achievement and power, but this alone is not sufficient; it is well for her also to work from imagination, in order to develop deeper feeling and her own center.

Many people may question the validity of my view that such work as this may change the life of the child. At the Walden School we have so many examples of it continuously that we hardly realize that any proof is needed. Of course it should be emphasized that the point of view expressed herein is not confined to the special teachers in the arts and sciences, but is the point of view of the Walden School. Each teacher in his or her own way develops an individual technique. The balance between individual freedom and the quiet needed for creation is a difficult task. Its solution, I think, lies first in the teacher's having learned to find that balance in herself, before she is able to help the student find it. Brancusi, the sculptor, said, "It is not so difficult to make things; it is difficult to achieve the state where creation is possible." If the teacher is strong, and clear, and still enough, she may find the necessary wisdom to teach, just as the student, if he achieves this state, may find the power to create. In searching always for the child's deepest center and in assisting him to draw from that ever-living well, lies the one essential service from which all others come almost of themselves. It is like first seeking the kingdom of God and His righteousness, for "all other things shall be added unto you."

HOW CHILDREN DECORATE THEIR OWN SCHOOL

Margaret Naumburg

FROM its inception the Walden School has belonged to its children. An attempt was made in the beginning to break the traditional formality of school interiors by developing an intimate and childlike atmosphere. Gay print curtains, vari-colored tables and chairs, odd bits of pottery, Indian baskets made each room distinctive in color scheme and arrangement. And the children of every group then went ahead, added, improved, and changed the rooms, with paintings, wood carvings, pottery, and so on, of their own devising.

As the children of the school matured, a more systematic coöperation about the care and decoration of the school became possible. On one occasion a class of nine-year-old boys and girls, feeling the monotony of their cream-colored dining room, offered to design appropriate door, fireplace, and window panels. The result was a series of bright flower garlands and prancing wild creatures that gave life and accent to the room. Another group of older boys and girls heard that new nursery screens were in need of decoration and undertook a series of screen designs of boats, rabbits, and fairies, to delight the youngest group in its nursery.

Last year the growing esthetic consciousness of the older children led to even more serious undertakings. Usually the repairs and redecoration of the school are done in the summer when school is closed. This time the work was begun in the spring. A professional plasterer was called in to teach the children how to do the work themselves. He was amazed to find a ready group of eager boys and girls in business-like smocks climbing up ladders to clean down the walls. He was followed by a painter who instructed them in the next phase of the work. The children had decided to carry out a completely fresh color scheme for the two rooms and staircases that they were to decorate. A committee consisting of the best artists of each class was chosen and placed in charge of the work. When the plans and fresco designs were ready, they were submitted to both classes and some of the teachers for consideration and suggestion. These discussions brought out the necessity of relating the degree of room light to the intensity of color scheme chosen as well as the need of selecting colors that were simultaneously serviceable and beautiful for the wear and tear of school activity.

THERE CAME WISE MEN FROM THE EAST

Carson College, Flourtown, Pa.

IN THE MANGER

In one room the children frescoed life in the sea, in the same blue-green and orange color scheme of the adjoining hall. Here, in luminous tones were panel arrangements of seaweed, fish, and iridescent foam. In the other room a countryside with peasant girl and high arched trees appeared. The frescoing of each room went ahead under the direction of the chief designer, each child undertaking to carry out a special part of the work. Once the technic of the great sweeping arm movements necessary for fresco work was understood, the frescoes were carried to swift completion by the children themselves without further instruction.

FREEING THE CHILD THROUGH ART

Ellen W. Steele

FREEDOM for the individual is a relationship between himself and other people—the group—the rest of the world. It has two sides. Educationally speaking, the two aspects of freedom are working out the relationship for any given individual between the development of his powers so that he expresses himself through them, and the place that his expression takes in the group. The unadjusted individual is the one whose expressions have no place, no appreciations, who feels he can make no desirable contribution to other human beings, and he is the least free being on earth.

The reason why art is an easy and natural channel of development is that, for reasons that perhaps go back into the history of the race, art expression is valued and appreciated by the group. Children get great joy from each other's work. It takes form under their eyes and they like it. They even get the particular flavor that is originative in each other's work. A school, therefore, in which art is a vital part of the life of the children provides opportunity for the development of freedom, for it offers a condition under which the kind of freedom I am talking about can grow. From the point of view of teaching art, however, this is not so simple as it sounds. I mean just having art work going on in the school is not necessarily going to bring this thing to pass. The way the art life is lived within the school has everything to do with the point.

With very young children practically all the teacher has to do is to give them art materials and plenty of time to paint. They are fearless with color. They need no technique. They have much to express pictorially and, above all, they have perfect unself-consciousness, since no adult standards have as yet interfered with their ideas. "See my boat," they say of a few straggling lines, feeling perfect satisfaction. And, indeed, artistically, their work is interesting because of its vigorous freedom, its really unconscious originative quality. This unself-conscious work seems to continue for several years, through the first few grades of school. This is because through experience the child develops a kind of method of technique which is satisfying to him since it serves to express his ideas and because his mind, more concerned with ideas than with the means of expression, is not blocked by the difficulties of "how to do it."

It would be a comparatively simple matter to teach art to children of all ages if this condition kept up indefinitely. My experience, however, convinces me that this is not always true. I find that there is a point somewhere after eight or nine years of age at which the child's ideas are perhaps ahead of his technique and he begins to say, "How do I draw a horse to look like a real horse?" or, "I could never draw a man!" Or perhaps he says, "I have nothing to paint!" And when you ask him about expressing some of his recent experiences he says, "That's too hard!" I have even known some children to say, "I haven't anything I want to paint, I'm tired of painting." They seemed to have "gone stale" on the expression that came easily to them in their earlier years. A boy of nine who loved boats and had always painted them freely insisted on using the ruler and making careful tight drawings of boats with every detail in shape, rigging and nautical equipment put in. He had no interest in coloring them. His passion was for accuracy in detail and I think he felt this of anything which interested him, and where he formerly would have painted vigorously and pictorially bridges, trains, skyscrapers, and all the vividly impressing objects of New York life, he now wanted to put down only his observations accurately, or to do no art work at all. I believe many children at this stage observe and appreciate form and detail far beyond their power or technique to set them down with satisfaction to themselves.

This seemed to me to point to the teaching problem of finding some way to meet the difficulty and in some way to preserve the former freedom, else, I feared, inhibitions might be set up and the children might lose the great fun of expressing themselves in line and color and lose out on growth in art conception which is due one at any age. This growth best comes through the free and joyous trying and expressing on the part of each individual after his own desires and interests. I came to the realization then that the children must be given the feeling that they could use the art mediums, that they might attain a technique or method of work that would express their ideas, and further, that they could have the fun of this kind of creative play. I have grown to feel that a policy of non-interference is in itself not quite adequate. In some way I must enrich the child's experiences: First, that he may have ideas to express which seem within his scope, and second, that he may live in a situation where these are greatly valued. In this I have found history a great help. I have found that a dramatic living through the experiences of other times and places and getting into the spirit of another period through its own literature and art and architecture and daily life, furnishes an imaginative environment where the material is simple and easy for the child to use. This is because he can build up a castle or a Greek landscape, and so on, imaginatively and artistically. He will easily then eliminate nonessentials because he has no object present with which to compare, whereas if he tries to paint the Brooklyn Bridge he may be dashed by his inability to have the cables absolutely accurate.

Also in living through a period, dramatic situations come up. A group of children who know the daily life of a people and become filled with their legend and lore and their great pieces of literature, usually create naturally dramatic expressions of this in the form of dance or plays. Sometimes this calls for stage-sets, costumes, properties, and all sorts of materials which are easily decorated in the spirit of the period. Usually a group of children begin to express in such a situation, to decorate their things, and the old freedom comes back and a new freedom is attained. They swing into this expression without fear and without thought of technique. But this does not take place except where their minds are filled with images and ideas about those times. When this is true, expression happens naturally and spontaneously.

A group of eleven-year-old children illustrated this point most convincingly in a Greek experience which culminated in their creating an autumn festival of song and dance. Their interest centered on the early or archaic Greek period. They studied the daily life of the people, and they looked into facts about their houses and their costumes, and the processes of weaving and spinning and other forms of daily work. They filled their minds with myth and legend, and read parts of the Odyssey, and they gained a real imaginative conception of those early Greeks in the different settings of their activities. Early in this experience they had laid out a Greek farm in plasticine, with hills and plains that led down to a sea, and they peopled it with Greek figures and farm animals in clay. Very crude and archaic these were, carrying out all the activities of a Greek farm. Then, too, the children expressed in words—what they call "word pictures"—these scenes, and had each other act them out in pantomime. We tried these pantomimes to music, and they took, we found, definite rhythmic form which it seemed might be like the Greek dance as it had first arisen with the Greek people. We decided to present these to the rest of the school as a harvest festival to Dionysus in much the way the early Greeks would have danced and sung their harvest celebration with their chorus and chorus leader, as the villagers gathered on the hillsides. So the class picked out four scenes of daily life on a Greek farm to present. This required a stage set and costumes in the spirit of this period.

Our first art problem was the stage set. For this a number of children made a painting of their idea of a Greek landscape. First we had discussed the Greek contour and had seen some museum slides of Greece, and I had read the children a most interesting chapter called "The Soil" from Zimmern's *Greek Commonwealth*. The class chose parts of each person's painting, things he or she could do best, to go on the big backdrop. It was decided that one was to sketch in hills and rocks, another a vineyard, another fields and sheep, others sea and boats, and so on. In working at so large a picture, it became very important to have variety in color and to break up the space into interesting shapes and to have them take related form. In this we often appealed to group judgment. Certain children became expert at color mixing, and decided what colors would balance and what colors were needed in the composition. The costumes the children decorated with Greek borders, using as nearly as they could the colors the Greeks might have used, each child cutting his own stencil, and painting on the border with tempera color.

To me an interesting feature of this experience was the way in which one art reinforced the other. The spirit of the Greek landscape found expression in the action, and the action called for some explanation through words, and these gave in another form the same picture again. The children felt they would need to tell the audience what to look for in each scene. And since I had earlier read them a number of Homeric Hymns, the suggestion came that each scene should be described by a hymn the children should write to the patron god of each activity. Thus the scene of the shepherds seeing their god Pan dance into their midst was announced by a *Hymn to Pan*.

> Hail to Thee, O Pan!
> Hail to the one who doth help us and
>   putteth heavy fleece on our sheep!
> Thou, who with fleet hoofs, doth dance on rocky crags,
> Thou, who hideth in shaded groves and
>   playeth sweet tunes on thy merry pipes,
> To Thee, O Pan, I sing and give prayer!

The Hymn to Demeter which followed foretold the action of the second scene.

> Oh, thou Demeter,
>
> Goddess of both grain and fruit!
> Be with us in our harvest
> So our grains may be prosperous!

Our heavy oxen will draw the plow
Which turneth the dark soil.

Our slaves will sow the seed.
Then will our oxen tread the ripe grain.
Beg Æolus to send strong winds
To blow the chaff away,
And leave us the golden kernels
As we winnow the grain.

To Thee, O Demeter,
We will give our thanks,
And then we shall sing to another god!

Then came a scene of the women in the courtyard spinning and weaving before the queen, announced by a *Hymn to Athene,* and this was followed by a spinning song written by the children which they acted as they sang. The children had pictured in words the processes of the weaving and spinning, and when they came to act them out to the music, they recast these word pictures into a rhythm that fitted with the music, and thus made a song:

All the maidens come in,
All the maidens come in,
With their spindles a-twirl,
They come in!

Slaves are beating the wool,
Slaves are beating the wool,
Bending bodies so brown—
Arms so strong!

Women washing the wool,
Women washing the wool,
Squeezing, pounding the wool,
In the stream!

Maidens carding the wool,
Maidens carding the wool,
Fluffing, rolling the wool,
On their knees!

Now we show the fine thread,
Now we show the fine thread,
White and strong, the fine thread,
For our Queen!

The last scene was the grape harvest where the slaves picked baskets of grapes and emptied them into a wooden trough where other slaves trampled out the wine. While the workers rest, a bard tells them the myth of Dionysus and the pirates, and as he speaks, the scene he describes comes true before their eyes. This action was suggested through the *Hymn to Dionysus:*

> To Thee, O Dionysus, we sing songs of praise
> For the plentiful harvest of grapes
> And for the rich-flowing purple wine:
>
> On land hast thou endured great dangers
> In thy travels among mortal men so that
> Thou couldst teach them to grow the winding vine.
> On the sea, thou hast fought the foaming waves,
> the angry storm and the cunning pirates,
> Pirates who would steer thee far from
> thy course and sell thee as a slave!
> But Thou, who hast come down from Olympus,
> Thy power is great!
>
> Thou didst change thy form to that of the
> King of Beasts and roar angrily.
> Thou didst grow the winding vine about the mast
> Of the ship whilst all beheld in wonder!
> Whereupon the savage pirates ever after
> Obeyed thy word.
> This hymn to Thee, and one more, O Dionysus!

It is this kind of experience which provides the situation that places a value on art expression. It gives the opportunity for such a vital and desired use of art that it makes a working that centers on the ideas and takes away from consciousness of technique. No one stops to debate whether or not he can do it, but just helps do the thing every one wants done. In the Greek work described, the facts with which the children dealt were few, but the vividness with which they selected them and the variety of meanings which they built from them made the experience a rich one.

From this particular experience I noticed a great gain on the side of technique for the children. We had a discussion of the stage set and they talked of balance both in the composition and the color, and showed an advancement in their understanding of composition. Their understanding of color as a problem that requires extreme care, was greatly increased and I felt that every child went forth renewed in art interest, and in technical lines turned with increased power into other art work. I think that using art through history in this way does not mean turning one's back on the present but, on the contrary, it offers opportunity to make the stride forward in technique that will tide the child over

A PUPPET SHOW—HANSEL AND GRETEL

MAKING COSTUMES

THE STORY OF LAND TRANSPORTATION RESULTED IN THE CONSTRUCTION OF THE
COVERED WAGON AND THE FIRST RAILROAD

A MODEL OF THE SANTA MARIA

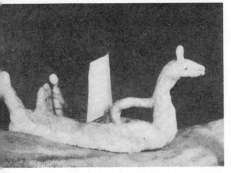 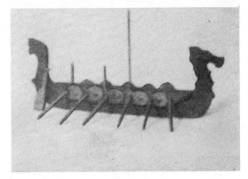

STUDIES OF PRIMITIVE BOATS

THE CITY OF HAPPINESS

A miniature city—the city of the future—with all the things necessary to make people happy. Conceived, built, and gaily colored by a group of children.

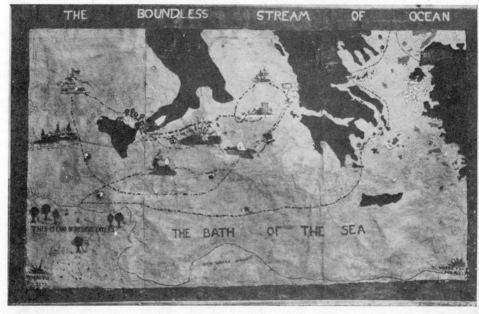

MAP OF ODYSSEUS' TRAVELS

Showing where his various adventures took place. Made by a group of children after studying the Palmer translation. The original is quite large and charming in color and detail.

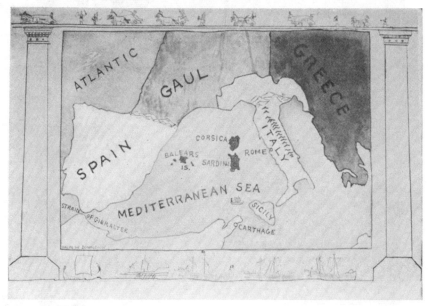

(Age 10 years)   *City and Country School, New York*

A MAP MADE IN CONNECTION WITH THE STUDY OF WRITING AND RECORDS

(Grade IV)   *Lincoln School, New York*

A MEDIEVAL CASTLE

Carson College, Flourtown, Pa.

WEAVING

Community School, St. Louis, Mo.

SEWING, DYEING AND STAMPING COSTUMES

(Grade II)   *Hubbard Woods School, Winnetka, Ill.*

(Grade VI)   *Hubbard Woods School, Winnetka, Ill.*

Rosemary Junior School   *Greenwich, Conn.*

Lincoln School, New York

(11th grade)   *Lincoln School, New York*

his period of self-consciousness and send him into the expressing of any ideas he chooses.

The place of the special art teacher in any work of this kind is to bring an advanced experience to bear upon the problems that arise that are too difficult for the children to solve alone with a group teacher, such as just the right color to go in some part of a stage set where one wrong color may spoil the beauty of it, how to break up a canvas with interesting shapes, how to enlarge a small sketch for a large canvas, how to eliminate nonessentials, and similar art problems. These difficulties are discussed and the children have the benefit of contact with the point of view of a real artist. From this contact their art ideas are greatly enriched and very often their technique visibly strengthened. No formal art lessons are given, as the emphasis is placed on each child's learning to attack his own art problem and on his working out his own technique. Any help from the real artist, then, merely serves to further each child in the direction of his own growth, thus preserving the individual differences which the children manifest.

A great help with children about eleven and twelve is painting in oils. Children like painting with oils very much because they have outgrown crayons which are too harsh, and water colors which often lack solidity to them, whereas oils give them depth in color and at the same time a chance for variety which is easily attained. Then, too, they permit a great individual difference in handling. In oil painting I believe in allowing the children to choose whether they want to go outdoors and sketch some real object, or stay in the studio and do what they call a "make-up" painting. I think they get a sense of developing their technique out of either. I have had an interesting experience, however, in having a child who had become quite skillful for one of her age, work with oil sketches mainly out of doors until she came into the studio one day and said, "I'm tired of making just paintings of things I see. I want to make something different. I want it to be some kind of a design, but I don't care whether it's real things or not." And so she sat down and thought out and planned a painting that was purely imaginary of a woods with tall trees and deer in the foreground. These forms she arranged into a most creative relationship, showing that she had come through to a new art understanding. She felt that she had the power to use oils for originating. She was now freed from the necessity of objects that were before the eye, and yet she embodied in her imaginary work skill in her arrangement of forms and use of color that she had gained from sketching out of doors.

This is, I think, the last development that will come out of art experience in the school. First, there is desire to have new experiences, next unconscious development of technique through doing and through having the chance to do things one's own way, though sometimes for a common cause, and lastly, the consciousness that one's own power is strengthened and may be carried into a use that is creative art in the fullest sense.

To my mind, the school that offers these opportunities can enrich the child's life so that he will have untold material to create with; it can set a great value on the particular quality any one individual can contribute; it can provide situations in which shared experiences offer opportunity for art expression, and through which the child comes to a consciousness of his own power and a fearlessness in the application of his own technique to new situations; it can provide him with a deep appreciation of his creative work, giving him a happy environment for growth. Not every child is an artist, but through art every child can have, not only the joy of doing the thing, but also the experience by which he can see more deeply into the art expression of others.

INFLUENCES IN THE CULTIVATION OF ART APPRECIATION

Helen Ericson

THE parents of a distinctly gifted thirteen-year-old daughter, seeking the advice of an eminent artist concerning her future training, exhibited to him a treasured collection of her artistic productions covering a period of some seven years. These creations had been entirely spontaneous with no special art instruction or criticism either at school or at home. The artist, accepting the rôle of the kindly critic to the fond parents of a child prodigy, was arrested by something he had not anticipated in these childish efforts. After thoughtful scrutiny he said, "This work shows a technical skill common to native talent but nothing out of the ordinary other than in its content. The variety and scope of the subjects and imaginings, the sincerity, vitality, and vividness of expression are, however, outstanding and truly remarkable! Where did it come from, what brought it about? How can she know all this?" It was readily explained by the parents as due to her school, since practically every impetus for art expression sprang from some interest or activity of her school life and studies.

The naïve imaginings and richness of subject content which so moved the artist (who perhaps received his first glimpse of a modern-school curriculum through this child's creations) are characteristic of all the art expression produced in the "Schools of Today." The art work of present-day school children reflects the new orientation of art training and appreciation. Every collection of children's creations bears witness to the richness and fullness of the school program.

And how is it done? Not by formal appreciation courses, not by copy book exercises, nor drill in art formulas. Children produce their creations under the same impetus which has moved the great artists of all times, which is having something of importance to say which must find expression.

The use of literary and historical subjects as the inspiration of art expression need not be repeated here but they are without doubt the richest field in which to mine throughout the entire school course. However, every subject has inherent some art aspect which may yield its contribution to a full art knowledge and experience. Even the higher mathematics course, the apparently arid plane and solid geometry, furnishes invaluable grist, and the general mathematics studies of the Junior High School place emphasis upon the application of principles of geometry to architectural art forms. Experiments in type forms are made in the construction of arches, rose windows, arabesque decorations, domes, bridge spans, and so on. Special projects are undertaken, such as a Gothic window cut from heavy card board and the tracery of patterns filled with translucent colored paper. Such a construction was used most effectively as the dominant feature of a medieval stage setting in one school for a high-school play. A Junior High School class miraculously transformed a regulation stage "set" with rectangular door and window spaces into a beautiful Moorish palace by inserting typical arches which they had designed constructed of beaver board. A beautiful Renaissance portico to frame a reproduction of an Italian nativity scene proved an interesting and valuable experiment in the construction of arches and rectangles in perspective.

In the yearly celebrations of the harvest, spring, and Christmas festivals fundamental and renewed understanding and a joy in the beauties of the world about us are gained. Picture an autumn festival—a stage setting, with a cyclorama backdrop of an elusive blue color, a figure draped in warm purples, flaming reds and gold, suggesting Keats' "Autumn" or a Greek Goddess of the Harvest, who sits enthroned above a simple earth-colored mound. A central flight of steps leads up to the stage; a procession of children forms in the outer aisles of the auditorium; the procession moves forward to stately music and ascending the central steps each member lays upon the improvised altar the wealth of the harvest, the choicest of fruits, vegetables, autumn leaves and flowers. Having made their offerings, parting to right and left, they gather below the stage and in chorus render thanks and homage to the giver of life and beauty. To this the presiding goddess responds in the words either of some great poet or her own. The entire scene has the quality and spirit of an ancient Panathenaic ceremony. The movement and scenic effect of massed color of fruits, leaves, and flowers, impress themselves deep in the emotions. The inner significance and outward appeal to the eye unite a religious and an esthetic experience.

Such ceremonies and the ideas contained in the great universal anniversaries of mankind make possible in their celebration an infinite variety of experiences which develop and train the esthetic sense. Year by year, under the leadership of a person endowed with a sincere and true understanding, who is as well an artist, the children who participate in, and those who look upon such celebrations may penetrate ever deeper into the secrets of beauty. In addition the inspiration which comes to a child in feeling himself one with all mankind brings an even greater impetus for a true and adequate expression of the underlying thought.

The spring celebration and all it signifies of the renewal of life and joy lies close to a child's instinctive reaction to the world of nature. The occasion described below has always been eagerly anticipated by all the children of the school from the youngest to the oldest. It is the poets' day—nature poets. For this occasion each child seeks to express in words, a creation of his own, some aspect or experience in nature which has been to him one of a special beauty or joy. Each class group has heard and enjoyed the creations of its members and has chosen one which it deems the best. Its author is "their poet." A faculty committee selects one composition among these which is outstanding in quality and idea. The author so chosen is to be recognized as the "Meistersinger" of the occasion, a poet of poets.

On the morning of the day selected as the May Day the children come to school laden with flowers and leafy boughs from garden and woods. The school stage is transformed into a Flora's bower, with a flowery throne for the Queen of the May. Some of the most perfect blooms of purple Iris are set apart and near the throne in readiness is placed a laurel wreath.

At the appointed time the children of the school and their friends gather. And to their joyous singing of an old song of the May, the Queen and her train take their places. The picture is one of loveliness— an embodiment of eternal spring and youth. The Queen of the May, dressed in gleaming samite, with flowing train of green (a robe of honor kept and worn each year upon this occasion), crowned and girdled in garlands of flowers, a blossoming bough her emblem of majesty, greets her subjects.

So begin the ceremonies. Then the maids of honor, themselves as lovely as the Queen, in quaint medieval gowns of spring colors, lead the Queen to her throne. She receives the poets, one by one, who come before her to recite their songs of the spring. Each poet presents a scroll whereon is inscribed his verse which is to become a part of the book of the Golden Treasury of the school. Each receives from the Queen the poets' coveted award, a purple Iris blossom, token of his achievement. Conducted to places of honor near the Queen by her attendants, they await the moment when one of them shall be called forth to receive highest honor.

When all have paid tribute, the Queen, according to custom long established, reads the roll of the poets laureate of former years and makes gracious acknowledgment of the achievement of the poets assembled before her. She then names the new recipient of the special title. He comes and kneels before her and is crowned with the laurel.

Each year this part of the May Day ceremonies is repeated with little or no variation. Upon occasion other festivities and features of old English or Medieval European spring celebrations are added, especially such as take place out of doors.

The central thought of the spring festival embodies the joyous response of humanity to the renewal of life and the beauties of nature. All old customs dear to the hearts of the race have their place and will bear endless repetition since they deepen the understanding and love for the simple eternal things of life. Such active participation by children in festivals giving opportunity for the use of beautiful color, pageantry, and movement is of basic importance in forming esthetic attitudes. Children instinctively respond to the inner meanings of these occasions because they are of a kind that have originated in the childhood of the race. They may be used to lead them to ever finer expression.

The Christmas anniversary is another deep source which may supply other inspiration and insights. The symbolic aspects give spiritual values in relation to art. With its past rich in lore and traditions of a noble kind, the celebration of Christ's Nativity offers an unlimited scope for presentation of sublime and uplifting esthetic feeling. In one way or another the naïve beauty of the works of the master artists of the Renaissance may be revealed to the children and in addition contribute a definite art knowledge. A vastly worth-while project was undertaken by a Junior High School group in the production of the Nativity play. The costuming and setting of the play were made from the study of pictures of certain early Italian artists. This necessitated a careful study of the pictures. A thorough acquaintance and a great fund of knowledge of the art of the Renaissance was thus gained. One group, with the aid of their experience in geometry, executed and applied to their costumes designs which they found in the pictures of Fra Angelico angels. Another interesting development carried out in another department was the study of musical instruments which had been inspired by those in the hands of the angels. The chorus which this group sang was a traditional melody which originated at the same period as the pictures. This gave added interest as the reason for the quaintness and peculiar quality of the music.

To expand by descriptions of Christmas festivals, of masque, play, pageant, and tableau would overreach my allotted space. In the main the manner and type of presentation are similar to that of the harvest and spring celebrations.

Another phase of the cultivation of art appreciation is concerned with the influence of good pictures. Children should live and make personal and intimate relationships to works of art. It is the privilege of the children of some schools to have brought to them from time to time

Edgewood School, Greenwich, Conn.

Lincoln School, New York

VIKING BOAT

(Grade IV)   Lincoln School, New York

(Age 10 years)   Francis W. Parker School, Chicago, Ill.

some great work of art which is placed in a much frequented part of the school building where its presence will arrest attention and interest. From time to time this is replaced by other examples of fine art. The circulation of great masterpieces in this way—where he who runs may read—may play a tremendous part in the growth of art knowledge and appreciation.

Such ingenuous day-by-day experiences with beauty as have been here presented are perhaps by their very nature the most potent influence for the cultivation of the esthetic sense. It is the conviction of the writer that they are fundamental in the establishment of true art standards.

Perhaps the greatest influence of all for the cultivation of art standards and esthetic appreciation is to be found in the school surroundings themselves. The beauty and taste which should be there manifested are more often conspicuous for their absence than their presence.

How many thousands of adults of today hold in their memory this almost identical dreary picture of the schoolrooms of their childhood: row upon row of rigid two-in-one iron-bound yellow maple forms— oceans of gray-streaked blackboards exhaling an atmosphere of stale sponges—bare windows, high along one wall, janitorially banned never to be opened, grimy gray floors—why continue? A sensitive child seeking healing for his wounded spirit in this dreariness could sometimes perhaps find relief in a bit of sculpture, perched high in the offing, or a photographic reproduction of some artist's dream, a bright chromo, perchance, or, and a rare event, a flower on a teacher's desk. At a magic moment a bell frees the little regiment to the measure of "one, two, three—turn, stand, pass." Through gloomy halls and worn stairways they pass lockstep to cinder-patch play-grounds. The entire picture bears evidence of the then prevalent idea of the practical exigencies and economy in school surroundings.

What a contrast to the schools of today—rooms flooded with sunshine, low windows framing the skies, tree tops and green lawns, opening in sections, free to admit the freshening air, simple, strong, movable furniture, pleasing in line, healthful and comfortable, often painted in glowing colors, suited to the age of the children in class and the general lighting of the room. No two rooms alike. Blackboard, so-called, of green, brown, blue, soft hangings at windows and cabinets decorated with designs, made by the children themselves, some well-chosen pictures, a vase lovely in color and form, blooming plants, the entire impression one of order and charm, looking its part as a work and living room of live, happy children. The halls lighted all the way; along the wall, cases and cabinets, filled with interesting exhibits, museum collections, picture exhibits, delightful places to linger and gather. Out of doors—spacious grounds, shade trees, grassy play-fields, the buildings beautifully set in the midst, the whole perhaps bordering a woods or a brookside.

And here in the words of John Drinkwater we find the answer as to which is the best environment for our school children.

> If all the carts were painted gay
> And all the streets swept clean,
> And all the children came to play
> By hollyhocks, with green
> Grasses to grow between,
>
> I think this gayety would make
> A spiritual land.
> I think that holiness would take
> This laughter by the hand
> Till both would understand.

FOR FURTHER READING

BARNES, ALBERT—The Art in Painting. Barnes Foundation, Merion, Pa., 1926.

BEMBRIDGE SCHOOL, Woodcuts by the Children, Cambridge, England, 1926.

BEST, MAUGART ADOLPHO—A Method for Creative Design. Alfred Knopf.

BOAS, BELLE—Art in the Schools. Doubleday, Doran.

CANE, FLORENCE—Teaching Children to Paint. The Arts, August, 1924.

CHENEY, SHELDON—A Primer of Modern Art. Boni and Liveright.

CIZEK, FRANZ—The Child as Artist. Cizek Exhibit, Greenwich, Conn.

CUSHMAN, LILLIAN—Principles of Education as Applied to Art. Elementary School Record, No. 1 (out of print. May be had in libraries).

DEWEY, JOHN—Art in Education. Cyclopædia of Education, Vol. I.
Imagination and Expression. Kindergarten Magazine, September, 1809 (out of print. May be had in libraries).
Individuality and Experience. Journal of the Barnes Foundation.
The School and Society. University of Chicago Press. Chap. II. The School and the Life of the Child.

ECKFORD, EUGENIA—Wonder Windows. E. P. Dutton & Co., 1931.

FURST, HERBERT—The Modern Woodcut. Dodd, Mead & Co.

HARTMAN, GERTRUDE—The Child and His School. E. P. Dutton & Co. The Relation of Art and Science to Occupations, page 34. Art Activities, page 77.

HINKLE, BEATRICE M.—The Re-creating of the Individual. Harcourt, Brace & Co. Chap. VII. The Psychology of the Artist and the Significance of Artistic Creation.

MAHONEY, BERTHA E., and WHITNEY, ELEANOR—Contemporary Illustrators of Children's Books. Bookshop for Boys and Girls, Boston.

MATHIAS, MARGARET—Art in the Elementary School. Charles Scribner's Sons, 1929.
The Beginnings of Art in the Public School. Charles Scribner's Sons.

MEARNS, HUGHES—Creative Youth. Doubleday, Page & Co. A School Environment for Creative Writing.

OVERSTREET, HARRY A.—Influencing Human Behavior. People's Publishing Co. Chap. XIII. Training the Creative Mind.

OZENFANT, Foundations of Modern Art. Brewer, Warren and Putnam, Inc., New York, 1931. 323 pages.

WILSON, FRANCESCA—A Lecture of Professor Cizek. Cizek Exhibit, Greenwich, Conn.
A Class at Professor Cizek's. Cizek Exhibit, Greenwich, Conn.

WOODBURY, CHARLES E., and PERKINS, ELIZABETH WARD—The Art of Seeing. Charles Scribner's Sons.

Creative Effort. Francis Parker School, Chicago, Ill.

The New Era Magazine. 11 Tavistock Square, London, England.

Abstract Art for Children. C. Fleming-Williams, April, 1923.

Creative Art in Childhood. Franz Cizek, October, 1923.

A New Approach to Drawing in Vienna Schools. Hans Gunther, April, 1926.

Musical Design. Muriel Mackenzie, April, 1926.

CREATIVE EXPRESSION
THROUGH MUSIC

A GENERAL VIEW OF MUSIC EDUCATION FOR CHILDREN

Thomas Whitney Surette

IN ITS relation to the teaching of music in schools the term creative expression has, in this country, an altogether too limited meaning. Schools sometimes seem to consider the term as signifying only original work, so called, either in the form of melodies invented by the children or of instruments made by them to play upon. Now while both these are, in a sense, creative, it is, I think, a grave error to stress them as they are being stressed in some schools. It is an error because neither one of these projects is important in the training of children in music, and because each takes too much time. Every moment of a liberal music schedule can be employed profitably in teaching children music itself and in developing their capacity in it.

Making melodies is quite a different thing from creating in the graphic arts or in poetry. In the former the children have their own experience in the visible world to draw on; in the latter they have a common language. Without the experience of these it would be impossible for them to create in either medium. In music, on the contrary, there is no storehouse. Home music is almost negligible, and the school at its best is not able to provide an experience at all comparable to that provided in the other mediums. Should not the creation of melodies await then some stored-up experience? Now and then one finds an exceptional child who might well be encouraged to make up tunes. Communal-melody writing is interesting; that is, making up melodies with the whole class at work at it, making suggestions and criticisms, accepting or discarding phrases, and so on. This practice gets the children familiar with the manner in which good tunes are formed.

Absurd statements are made in justification of beginning music with playing instead of singing, such as that the untrained child is by nature in the drum stage of music. It is true that young children have a sense of rhythm; they walk in rhythm, and more subtly, they see and hear in rhythm. But they have a highly developed sense of pitch. They can sing with ease melodies in the folk idiom; they can even sing chromatics, and they learn songs with the greatest eagerness. And singing is, of course, a much more intimate form of self-expression than is playing an instrument.

There is a lure in these forms of creative expression. A tune made by a child seems quite wonderful. A musical instrument made by a child is a delightful accomplishment in manual training, and does stimulate his interest in music. Are not the real questions, however: "What is the best possible use of the time devoted to music?" "What are the most important things to be taught in relation to the whole life of the child, as well as in relation to his immediate situation?"

Is there not a wholeness in music both in itself and in its relation to ourselves? Is it not an art that offers delight to our souls, our minds, our hearts, and our bodies? Is music in school merely singing, making up tunes, reading notes, playing the drum, the violin, or the piano? Or is it what happens to the children? Is creative expression so narrow a term after all? Is it confined to inventive activity either of mind or hands? Is it skill? Is it entirely an effort of the individual child? A child in a group singing happily a beautiful song into which he throws his whole being is creative in the best sense of the word; a child sitting in a group listening intently to a beautiful composition is creative in proportion to his capacity to feel vividly, to hear accurately, and to think the music with the composer. We are all creative when we look with the inward eye, or when we hear with the inward ear. In fact the visible world is what we make it with our creative imagination. Without that it is merely monochrome, its shapes and forms nearly meaningless, its significance almost entirely so. Looked at creatively, that is, looked at with the inward eye, the window of the soul, it is an everlasting marvel and an unending delight. What does Blake say in his *Vision of the Last Judgment?*

"I assert for myself that I do not behold the outward creation, and that to me it is hindrance and not action. 'What!' it will be questioned, 'when the sun rises do you not see a round disc of fire somewhat like a guinea?' Oh! no, no! I see an innumerable company of the heavenly host crying, 'Holy, holy, holy is the God Almighty!' I question not my corporeal eye any more than I would question a window concerning a sight. I look through it, and not with it."

You can look without seeing, you can listen without hearing, you can perform without making a note of true music.

What is this wholeness of which I have spoken? It is that form of music education which brings the whole child into action, which gives him an infinite opportunity for self-expression and, at the same time, makes it necessary for him to submit to discipline. The self-expression is attained chiefly through singing where the *self* and the *expression* are really one rather than through playing where they rarely are because of the complexities of the instrument which impose themselves between the two. It is attained because it permits freedom of feeling and temperament under conditions of joyfulness and pleasure; because it induces a kind of physical freedom so that the whole being finds issue. The discipline is attained through the necessity of producing a good tone, of using good diction, and of singing with others; through the concentration and mental effort necessary in reading music notation (when a child sings a second part even greater discipline is necessary and even greater pleasure is attained), and through the fascinating demands listening to music makes on everyone who listens intelligently. The wholeness of which I have spoken means, then, giving a child as much of music as he is capable of absorbing in each stage of his development. Instrumental playing should come after a long experience of singing; composition (creating melodies) after a long experience of music as an art.

Anything that takes away this wholeness is a detriment to the child, and his earliest years are the most important. You can teach very young children to read notation; but why should you do so? They are too young to deal with it. They need the experience of the music itself not only as a basis for the notation but as a natural method of expression and a natural means of happiness. "Shades of the prison house"; let them have their childhood.

Listening should be a part of the music program throughout the school life of a child. The objective is that he should be able to enjoy intelligently fine music suitable for his years. This implies cultivation of the memory, of the power to discriminate and to compare and the exercise of the reasoning faculty comparable to that exercised by the composer himself. In short the object of all this is that kind of creative listening which is a correspondence between the composer and the listener. Would it not be worth while to train children in music so that when they go out into life they will have had a full measure of self-expression through singing, and so thorough a training in listening as will make them capable of re-creating in every detail, when they hear it, a great symphony? Is not the average adult almost hopelessly confused when he hears one? Both things are needed, singing and listening; the former awakens the sensibilities to music; the latter, superimposed on the former, awakens the intelligence and stimulates the imagination.

Listening intelligently, then, consists in being moved by the music but also in exercising your intelligence over it, and above all your imagination. This is axiomatic. If the composer has put into his music feeling, mind, and imagination, it is obvious that you must apprehend it in those terms. This, it may be added, makes it unnecessary and futile to try to read "meanings" into it. It has no meaning other than itself.

I have carried through this listening argument because the technique of teaching remains much the same throughout. Perhaps I should point out, however, one or two fundamental principles. The chief of these is to let the music, as far as possible, do its own teaching. It is a disadvantage to tell the children about it beforehand. The best way is to play the piece through and let them get what they can, because the very first necessity is that they should like it themselves quite independently of your opinion about it, and that their impression should be original. How much better and happier we should all be if we got continually first-hand impressions of life, of books, and of art in general instead of continually stultifying our capacity by taking other people's opinions about them. When they have heard a composition enough to like it (play it through more than once if necessary) you may profitably ask them what they noticed in it, going on trying to get their original impressions. Always remember that it is a work of art and not a diagrammatic design to be examined like a blueprint. So finally you will have achieved a more or less complete re-creating of the music itself. The children will have responded to its meter, will have seized upon its salient rhythmic figures and observed how they expand, contract, fly off on tangents, tumble over each other, and so on. They will also have felt the ebb and flow of the melodic line, and the harmonic color, and will have grasped the form of the whole piece and seen how well ordered it is, and how satisfying to their natural sense of proportion and balance.

There is another important matter connected with this sort of teaching. All children should hear a certain amount of splendid music quite beyond their powers of comprehension. Such music should be played to them occasionally just for the hearing and not for study. These pieces should be repeated at intervals. A convincing argument for this, if any is needed, may be found in *The Art of Reading* by Quiller-Couch in the chapter called "Reading for Children." Care should be exercised in the selection of music for this purpose. Certain compositions are too complex; none is too fine.

But to return to our singing lessons. I have spoken of giving the children beautiful music, and I must take space to say what the term, in my opinion, means. In actual practice it means, in the early years, folk songs and not much else. Why? Because we are certain about them; they have survived centuries of use, have been incorporated by great composers in their works, and are acknowledged by musicians generally; because also they were conceived by simple people in terms of their own childlike feelings, thoughts, and aspirations; because they exist independent of all modern diffusion, confusion, and sophistry; and finally because they are, as works of art, quite perfect. Contemporary songs for children fall far below this standard.

If the children are taught simple songs during the early years (this implies characterization of the songs, dramatization of some of them, marching, skipping, running, and so on, these latter serving as a preliminary to seeing notation, marching for quarter notes, running for eighths, and so on, as well as preliminary to observing pitch distances) they will meet the intricacies of notation well prepared, and reading will not present serious difficulties. They should learn to read by reading. Assistance from the teacher, using numbers occasionally, will enable them to meet new problems and to overcome special difficulties. Arbitrary syllables, such as *Do, Re, Mi,* are quite unnecessary. May I add that in schools like the Beaver Country Day, Brookline, Massachusetts, the reading of the older girls is not only entirely adequate, but exceedingly musical; that is, they read the music and not merely the notes. In this school there is a glee club, of girls only, whose singing is good enough to be listened to by anyone anywhere.

From grade three onward, if this way is opened, the path is clear. The natural love of children for the best music carries them on irresistibly. Rounds and chord singing in three parts prepare the way for part singing which should begin in grade five. By this time the children will have heard a little simple polyphonic music and be able to see into vocal part writing. From almost the beginning of their school life they will have been singing the chorales of Bach, for even in the first grade they will have taken part at Christmas time in "Hush, my Dear, Lie Still and Slumber"; or at least let us hope so, for every child should know it. So now they may well try singing the chorales in two parts, the advantage being that the second part is "real," and not an undistinguished part running along in thirds or sixths below the upper part.

In what is now called the junior high school special stress should be laid on appreciation and on the historical aspects of music. All through the grades there will have been association of music with other subjects, but during this period the children will perhaps be doing less singing, and it is therefore possible to increase their knowledge of music. Theory may be stressed and the foundations laid for a much wider view of the whole subject. In the high school, where the college entrance examinations impose themselves on the curriculum an adequate schedule for music is difficult. The chief purpose here should be to keep the young people constantly in touch with music through some singing and much listening. A glee club for the more expert and mature pupils, an orchestra for those capable of taking part in it, and a general period for singing at least once a week, are really necessary.

The foregoing, it seems to me, constitutes a reasonable and comprehensive program. It is not by any means as detailed as I should like to make it. More should be said about instrumental playing, about the beginnings of the orchestra, about pianoforte lessons, and so on. One of the gravest mistakes in the education of children is to give them pianoforte lessons before their ears are thoroughly trained. A child who cannot sing should not begin lessons on any instrument, least of all the piano. The ideal arrangement is that the pianoforte lesson be given in the school where some coördination between it and the music classes can be secured.

The home is the place to start music. As far as I am able to observe few families sing together. Did they do so they would pretty certainly be better off as individuals and as a family. What a solvent it might be in family life. It would be especially valuable to the little children. Could they but sing just before going to bed, learning almost in infancy some beautiful folk songs, would not some hidden alchemy take place? Some awakening of that mysterious heritage of theirs which you, yourself, had in childhood, but have perhaps lost? Some exquisite harmony of the whole being? Music belongs specially in their world for it is a thing of fancy, unreal as a dream, fragile as a bubble, created for a moment and then gone.

Finally, I urge school heads and music teachers to forget theories, to forgo specialization and to deal broadly with music as an art native to all children. Our administrators may well observe that as mental activity, music stands on a par with any other school subject. Professor Hocking, in his book, *Human Nature and Its Re-making*, says:

"It has become a prevalent doctrine in educational theory that skill acquired in one department of knowledge is not transferable to another; and this is likely to be true if we deprive the mind of all esthetic interest in the activity in question. But interest in beauty reaches the central current of the will, and when this interest is awakened all transference of skill and discipline becomes natural. It is the nature of beauty to overflow departments and make the man of one piece."

Music, it may be pointed out, is the one form of activity in which a whole school can take part while at the same time creating something beautiful. It is like play minus the exuberant physical activity but plus an exuberance of the spirit. It requires the most accurate "teamwork," it is unselfish, it awakens sympathy, creates joy, frees the soul, and subtly harmonizes the physical being. What school can afford to neglect it? What school can afford to offer its children anything less than the whole of it?

EXPERIMENTS IN MELODY MAKING

Katherine K. Davis

IN DISCUSSING creative music for children as part of a general school music course, we must first agree to leave out all consideration of the child with a real creative talent. Such a child, possessing all the qualities that a composer needs—a gift of spontaneous expression, musical sensibilities, patience, industry, a good brain, and, above all, imagination—such a child is rare indeed. The curriculum need not be planned for him. He will go his own way if he is made of the real stuff. I have never had such a pupil; I have had many who had two or three of the necessary qualities, but they all lacked something essential.

Narrowing the subject then, let us consider creative music for the average child. Let me speak of the average child as I know him at the Shady Hill School. There we are very busy singing folk songs in the Kindergarten and lower grades, and later the songs of Schubert, Brahms, Mozart, Bach, and Beethoven, with a few more modern ones such as Parry's "Jerusalem," or part songs by Gustav Holst. Besides this, we have musical games, plays, and pantomimes; ear training, free rhythms and eurhythmics, theory, and enough sight singing so that the children understand the process, though we do not strive for perfection or lightning speed; and a great deal of listening to music of all sorts and analysis of the form of the folk tunes and dances. Creative work is not planned as part of the program, but occasionally it happens.

The latest of these occasions arose last month when I found the twenty little girls of the fourth grade busily reading and writing poetry. One of them suggested that I make a tune for the poem, and was amazed when I assured her that she could do it herself. She felt that she might need the assistance of the class, so we decided to use a poem that they all knew, instead of her verses. The process was simple. We chanted the first stanza, very rhythmically, and found that we should need four musical phrases. "Who will sing the first phrase?" A tense moment, each child doubtfully searching her soul for a tune. Then Polly sings a phrase, and Helen has one as well, and the class prefers Helen's, so I record it in my private notebook. "Now the second phrase! Shall it be like the first?" "No! The words don't fit!" Pause. Then Dorothy— "If you'll sing the first part, I'll sing the second," which she does; and I record it, while the class questions whether to make phrase three like phrase one. We try it; it seems good. We have three phrases, A B A. I sing them again, to aid weak memories. "Now for the last. Shall we have A B A B?" "Perhaps." We sing it. "No! It isn't finished!" Then

it must be A B A C. I sing again A B A and Polly finishes it for me.
A B A C, duly recorded. When we come to sing it again, however, we
are not pleased with B. "It jumps so!" Helen gives us a new B which
is better, we sing it all again and vote it finished.

"Now," they say, "let's do another. Let's do this poem." It is a charming one of Walter de la Mare's. "I can sing it all," says Ann suddenly;
and after a moment's thought she does—a tune continuous in form,

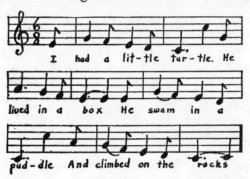

as the words seem to require, and showing real spontaneousness. It
delights the children and we learn it by rote at once.

The next day we sang Ann's song again and I asked them whether
they'd like to see it in notation. "Yes." So I put on the board a staff,
with the words below. First they worked out the pitch notation, by
means of numbers; then the rhythmic duration of the notes, this by

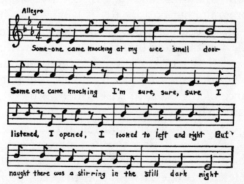

"stepping" the tune in the Dalcroze manner; by singing and "beating"
they discovered the meter; and by noting the down beats they were
able to put in the bar lines. Of course this work represented the combined efforts of the class and not the individual achievement of each
child.

Other classes, hearing of this song, wanted to make one as well. The
sixth grade, with profound cerebration, made one tune and then con-

demned it because "the poem is staccato and the tune is like church."
So we examined other tunes with quick, lively words and got some ideas
from them. "Two notes to a word!" "Repeat the same note, staccato!"
Then we tried again, with much discussion of the disadvantages of a
finished cadence in the middle of a song. "Go a note lower!" says Dora.
When the second tune was done they were only mildly enthusiastic

Of speck-led eggs the birdie sings And
nests a-mong the trees — The
sailor sings of ropes and things And
ships . u - pon the seas

about their achievement, recognizing that the material was borrowed
from familiar sources; and next day when I asked them whether they
wanted to sing it again, they voted heartily against it and in favor of
three Scotch songs about Prince Charlie.

The fifth grade, amid great turmoil, evolved the following: but they

Little In-dian, Sioux or Crow,
Little frosty Eskimo Little Turk or
Ja-pa- nee O don't you wish that
you were me!

were not sufficiently pleased with it to be interested in working out its
notation. The third-grade song, however, was such a simple, uninspired
little tune that they were able to put it all down on the board. When
it was done they looked skeptical, being new to such matters, so we sent
for a fourth-grade child to come and sing it at sight, just to prove that
it worked.

The second and first grades also built tunes, phrase by phrase, but most of the children were happier in improvising little songs, words and music, as the Kindergarten did. No record was made of these, for they are simply part of the natural language of any young child—formless musical speech, quite untouched by thought, but sometimes achieving an accidental charm. All little children make up such songs; even children with defective pitch will improvise on two or three tones.

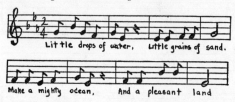

For the past week there have been individual flares of composition. Ann, inspired by her first success, composed a tune on the piano, but its complicated mechanism put chains upon her fancy and the result was disappointing. Betty, in the third grade, blushingly asked permission to sing "a tune I made to go with a poem that I read in several books at home." The poem proved to be "Where the Bee Sucks," and the tune,

which had definite form, she sang three times exactly alike, showing that she had constructed it with real thought. Her tonality was a bit vague in spots—she was a monotone in the first grade—but she says the following version is correct.

Patsy, in the same grade, with no thought at all will sing a charming setting of some verse; and when asked to repeat it will sing an equally charming and utterly different one, and perhaps even a third, all more musical than Betty's but all continuous in form, showing no feeling for structure.

In this class work all the children had opinions, and half of them contributed material, but of course there were always four or five who had the best ideas. A few years ago I did the same sort of work with these children individually and found that even the least musical ones could be led to evolve something, while some really good tunes were constructed by older girls. But with individual work a certain egotism crept in—an undue sense of the importance of the thing produced—

which vanished entirely in the wholesome atmosphere of concerted effort and criticism.

This work seems to me valuable only as a means—not as an end. Too much of it would take up time that could be spent in singing far better music; and might furthermore give a child the impression that music centered in him, when he should be learning to lose himself in it. But a little of it serves to make vivid in a new way the necessity for structure, contrast, and repetition, and the relation between poetry and music, in rhythm and spirit. It is also valuable as a means of teaching notation, and it is a sure way to find out how a child's taste is developing. When children invent music in healthy folk-song style, untinged by cheap Sunday-School songs or sentimental piano pieces, they are on the road that leads to Haydn, Mozart, Beethoven, Brahms, and Bach, chamber music and symphonies, a world where they may find lifelong solace and delight.

Perhaps the best proof of good taste, in this instance, was given by the children's own recognition of the fact that these tunes of theirs, though they were good fun to make, were not so satisfying to sing as

Hark, Hark, the Lark, or the *Skye Boat Song.* And when the sixth grade sang *Bonnie Charlie's Now Awa'* each child alive with the emotion of that song, faces tense and wistful, so that more than one listener confessed to a lump in her throat, it seemed to me that here, after all, was the best sort of creative music.

CREATIVE EXPRESSION IN MUSIC

Harriet Ayer Seymour

THE mention of music lessons recalls to most people weary hours of thumping out scales and five-finger exercises, of tears over the practice hour and agony over playing for friends and relatives who really didn't want to hear us play. Ask an audience of grown people whether they have ever studied music and then given it up—two thirds of them, at least, will say that they did. Then if you carry your investigation further and ask why, the answer will invariably be "I got so discouraged with the technical exercises and scales and never could really do anything so I gave it up." It is true that in the past, years of study on the part of the average person brought literally no results, yet everyone admits the need of music and almost everyone loves it. Then what has been the matter?

Let us take the title of this chapter and analyze it, *Creative Expression in Music*, what does it mean? In reality there is only one Creator, or Creative Power. Each person represents that power in his or her own way. When human beings become creative in a great artistic sense, they really "tune in" or re-create.

All great teachers, seers, sages, and successful people of every kind have used this Power, consciously or unconsciously. In music this invisible creative force has been acknowledged by all the great masters. Beethoven tells us that through silent hours spent alone with nature, he was able to hear and remember the motifs which have comforted and inspired thousands of people. Every creative artist will tell you the same thing. Painters, sculptors, architects, and masters in any art, inwardly see what they are afterward to express visibly on canvas, in marble, or in edifice. Composers inwardly hear the music they afterward write down. Greatness consists very largely in attention; the ability to pay attention, or to listen attentively, excluding everything else, is the key.

To be trained to use this power consciously is to be educated. The mistake we have made is that we have not adopted simple enough ways of culturing the creative faculty, for no matter how apparently dull or inert the child may be, it is possible to awaken that spark of creative power dwelling within him. This is rapidly being discovered and the teaching of music is now undergoing great changes. We are swinging around from the mechanical to the creative. What everyone is asking for is a simple way of accomplishing this reversal.

The study of music establishes the habit of quiet listening if it is taught creatively. So studied, it leads not only to hearing clearly, but to clear, easy, and unself-conscious expression. The playing of children so taught has a certain unmistakable charm. The children themselves are at home in music. They inwardly hear it, write it, and play it in a natural way. There is no forcing of any kind.

From one musical experience to another children grow to hear tunes, very short at first, longer and more complex ones later on. They have learned to be relaxed and quiet and to really hear the designs in sound which constitute music.

Music presented creatively furnishes its own discipline. Sometimes friends of progressive education are fearful of too much freedom which may develop into license. It is true that a certain lack of order and discipline is often apparent in experimental education, but in classes of children learning music "the new way" the listening is in itself a discipline. The difference between the old-time five-finger exercises enforced by a nagging mother, and the voluntary attention given by children who are taught creatively is the difference between external discipline and self-discipline. Children have often, under the new musical education, begged for lessons on holidays and tried to bribe their teacher to stay longer than the lesson hour, and have even practiced on the wall when no piano was at hand.

This process of inward listening, which means stillness and relaxation, and of expressing what is inwardly heard in this inward way makes an art of life. A full life, with health, peace of mind, success, and happy human relationships—this is what we want for our children. When children are led from one conscious musical experience to another through first listening, then thinking, and then playing, they are not only gaining in a musical way, but they are developing the creative power which will help them to lead happier lives. They have tapped the very source within themselves and, as they play more and more consciously, they write or play what they hear, they learn to have faith in this inner creative power and to use it. A tiny child, five or six years old, will sit with eyes closed listening and then give very definitely the tune he hears, repeating it correctly over and over. He has inwardly listened and inwardly heard. If we give music to children through experiences fitted to their age and ability in the creative realm, we shall not only be giving them a kind of musical education that they will continue in after they are grown, but we shall also be giving them a principle by which they may grow and live in all ways. Right education in its true sense is growth.

Not only the exceptionally musical, but all children positively need music of some kind to harmonize the hardness of this Iron Age. They may not all want to play upon an instrument, but they can all learn to listen creatively and so gain, not only an appreciation and understanding of music, but the ability to listen and create through listening.

The following little tunes, inwardly heard and written down by children, are a few selected from hundreds; for most children, as we all know, are at home in the creative realm and love to do anything that exercises the imagination and produces honest results.

The earth was dressed in brown last night, This morn-ing, See! Tis all in white.

(Age 11 years)   **Windy Nights**

When ev-er the moon and stars are set, When ev-er the wind is high.

All night long in the dark and wet, A man goes rid-ing by Late in the night when the

fires are out, Why does he gal-lop and gal-lop a-bout?

(Age 10 years)

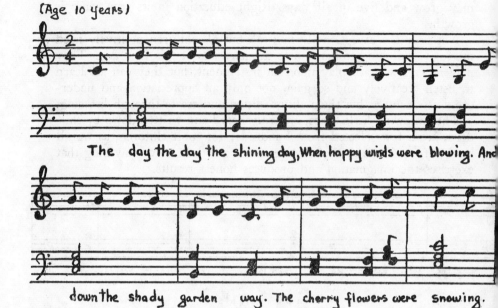

The day the day the shining day, When happy winds were blowing. And
down the shady garden way. The cherry flowers were snowing.

The Wind.

I saw you toss the kites on high, And blow the birds a - bout the sky;
And all a - round I heard you pass, Like lad-ies shirts a - cross the grass
Oh, wind a - blow-ing all day long, Oh, wind that sings so loud a song.

Cherries are Ripe

Composed by a child age 6½ years

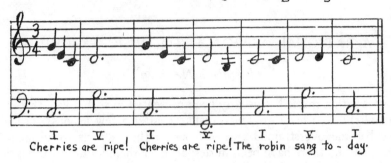

Cherries are ripe! Cherries are ripe! The robin sang to-day.

Time to Rise

A bir die with a yel-low bill, Hopped up-on the win-dow-sill,

Cocked his shin-ing eye and said, "Ain't you 'shamed, you slee-py head!"

A RATIONAL APPROACH TO MUSIC TEACHING

Elizabeth Newman

WHY is it that music has usually been presented in such a way that even musical children have grown to dislike it after a few lessons? Teachers have become overstrained and nervous in their efforts to awaken interest, and mothers have been in despair over their failure to force their children to practice. We all know that musical instruction in the past was aimed mostly at making performers, that stress was laid upon the cumulation of knowledge from without, and that the creative impulse was rarely if ever encouraged; now it is rather a liberation of music from within by means of delightful work and play, and musical feeling and knowledge are developed by a process of growth from within as life from a seed. In short, the child's emotional nature and sense of music precede, dominate, and preside over the later skill and technique on instruments.

For successful results in this work, it is necessary for the teacher to keep the vision constantly before her of the ultimate goal to be reached, and to guide the children logically and continuously through every progressive step, from the simple to the complex, without omitting any of the essential links. To do this requires versatility, adaptability, and imagination. New possibilities will constantly unfold for the teacher, as they do for the children, because music, like life, is always in the making, never completed. Perhaps a better word than teacher would be guide, one who leads the children on a journey of exploration, as it were, and with hints here and suggestions there, enables them to make their own discoveries of every new principle introduced.

If the lessons are made simple, practical, and logical, the inevitable results for even young children are: the correction of monotones, the ability to play rhythmically, transpose, and harmonize the songs that are inwardly heard, the development of the imagination in endeavoring to "sing the songs at the piano" with the same expression, rhythm, and mood that was felt in the singing, and the ability to modulate and to create their own songs.

For making the lessons joyous, and for sustaining interest until each step is thoroughly understood before being applied at the keyboard, games may be used. There are games for rhythm, which include folk

MAKING PITCH PICTURES

A RHYTHMIC GAME

STEPPING THE NOTE VALUES

ONE CHILD PLAYING THE CHORDS AS THEY ARE SUNG AND WRITTEN BY
A CHILD AT THE BLACKBOARD, ANOTHER PLAYING THE MELODY AS IT IS
SUNG AND SWUNG BY THE REST OF THE CLASS

dances, folk games, original games, and a play orchestra. There are original games for creative work, for the scale, melody (including transposition) and harmony. Each game involves an important principle and should be introduced at the logical time, so that the children discover the principles that are hidden within the games.

Rhythm is the very life and soul of music. It is inherent in every child, and music is a natural means of awakening the rhythmic sense. The first expression of rhythm may be given by means of songs for dramatic action, to which the children react as the music or words suggest. Folk songs are the best for this purpose because they are the most valuable material we have for beginners. Such songs are the result of natural feeling and express the primitive emotions in which the great law of rhythm never fails. As the teacher plays with well-marked rhythm and expression the children are quiet and listen, then when they feel the rhythm, they sway back and forth, or they march while playing imaginary instruments, or they run, skip, dance, clap, and gallop to match the music with satisfying motion. If they are unable to feel the rhythm the teacher asks them to tell of something they have seen or felt that moves rhythmically. Such answers have been given as the flying of a bird, the swimming of a fish, the running of a rabbit, and the beating of the heart. Helpful illustrations for the teacher to use are the rocking of a cradle and the swinging of the pendulum.

Children are born actors; their interest is maintained as long as their imagination is fired. The following songs suggest some form of dramatic action which the children themselves can devise while singing; this develops freedom, originality, and rhythm:

> Pretty Little Blue-bird
> Little Shoemaker
> The Blacksmith
> Dancing Fairies
> I Had a Little Nut-tree
> How Many Miles to Boston Town?

The following games have been found helpful as a means of interesting the children while a feeling of rhythm is being developed:

The children form a circle about one child who holds a cane which is to be used for tapping the rhythm of any song that has been used in class work. While the child in the center is choosing a song, the children in the circle sing:

> Let us sing around our play-mate,
> Till he taps his mag-ic cane;
> Guess the song, then we will hum it,
> As he taps it o'er a-gain.

The child in the center then taps the rhythm of the song chosen as the others listen attentively to be able to name it. After it is known, all sing to the tapping. The child who first guessed correctly is in the center when the game is repeated.

Each child may be given opportunity to create a dance composed of one or more rhythmic phrases, to swing and hum it for the teacher to play and for the rest of the class to sing, swing, dance, and write.

After a feeling of rhythm has been established by means of songs and music not intended for the children to play, and the simple movement of melodies is heard up and down and along the same line, and a musical consciousness and interest have been awakened, the special songs that are intended for the children to play are introduced.

To keep them simple and to make transposition easy and possible, folk songs are given that are arranged in groups according to the number of scale-tones they contain, and for a gradual development of rhythm and harmony. The first group includes only two tones of the scale, the next three scale-tones, the next four, and so on until all are included both above and below the keynote. By this arrangement the children are readily directed in hearing the exact tones and in becoming as familiar with them as with separate colors. And a tone consciousness is developed which to the majority of children is an entirely new realm.

Here again, games may be played so that the children will not become discouraged by any involved effort. One such game is Blindman's Buff. The teacher blindfolds one child in the center of a circle formed by the rest of the class. All except the one in the center skip around while singing a song with the following words:

> In the ring we're skipping lightly,
> Keeping out of blind-man's way,
> Tell us, blind-man, can you rightly
> Guess the tones that we will play?

When the song is ended, one child leaves the circle and plays on the piano the number of scale-tones that are included in the group of songs they are becoming prepared to play, and as each tone is played, the blindfolded child is to recognize and sing it by number name. After several repetitions another child is blindfolded and the game continues.

After the tones contained in a group of songs are perfectly heard, the songs are played for the children to swing, sing, phrase, step, and clap for a feeling of the rhythm, and for the drawing of a "rhythmic pattern" on the board. (See illustration below.) Songs are played for the children who indicate by motions of their hands up and down and along the same line for the movement of the melodies which they illustrate on the board in the form of "Pitch Pictures," and again for the children to listen and to sing the roots of the chords underneath the melodies for the basis of the harmony.

The following is a combined "rhythmic pattern" and "pitch picture" of one of the simplest songs contained in the group of two scale tone songs:

Far a - way the rob - in sings

The scale-numbers and letter-names of the first two tones of a scale are sung and written above or below the pitch lines, as:

1 1   2 2   1 2   1

c c   d d   c d   c

Far a - way the rob - in sings

After which the duration and pitch picture is changed into written music:

Far a - way the rob - in sings

The song is then fingered and sung away from the piano, and since it has become subconsciously registered, the children are equipped to go to the piano and play it as it has been sung and felt immediately, and without any practice in the old way. Before they attempt to play, however, they are given to understand that the piano is never to be touched except to "make music"; that every sound is to mean something, and that they are to listen and decide for themselves whether they are giving the tones the same meaning or feeling they expressed while singing; that when they play, they are to feel the same rhythmic swing that impelled them to move their arms as the songs were heard and sung; to feel each phrase to the end, and to realize that each tone is but a part of the whole, which is moving forward toward some definite goal. The result is relaxation and complete concentration. By means of other games they are prepared to sing and play each song as readily in any and all of the other keys.

For harmonization the chords are as simply presented. The first large group of songs is harmonized with the I or Tonic and the Dominant

V or V₇ chords. The next group includes the Subdominant or IV. The next the Supertonic or II, then the Submediant or VI, and finally the Mediant or III chord. The purpose of this arrangement is to give sufficient material for practice in singing and applying each chord as it is introduced underneath a variety of melodies. As a melody is played, the children listen and determine by hearing inwardly and then by singing, the roots of the chords that will harmonize with each measure. These are sung by chord-names and written on the board or in their music blankbooks in the form of what is called a chord pattern, as:

$$\| \ 2/4 \ | \ I \ | \ V \ | \ I \ | \ I \ \|$$
Far a-way the robin sings

To sustain the interest of the children in repeating the singing of these chord tones as a preparation for playing them later with the melody, and for increasing their sense of harmony, sometimes an "orchestra game" is introduced. In this game the class is separated into two divisions, one of which sings the melody while pretending to play solo instruments, as the violin, and the other the roots of the chords while pretending to play bass instruments, as the double bass. The teacher intones a new key for each repetition.

In order to develop freedom of expression and originality from the very beginning the teacher encourages the children to create their own songs, both words and melodies. They are asked to sing about anything that interests them and are led to realize that music cannot come from any one of them or be played upon any instruments until it was first imagined and shaped in the mind of the one who gave it musical expression. The children's original work is also written, played, transposed, and harmonized. They enjoy this, particularly when they can hear their melodies played by the teacher and sung by the class.

As this study continues, greater and greater delights are unfolded. The children play chord accompaniments while singing the melodies; they harmonize each tone of the melody with a part of the chord to which it belongs with an accompaniment in the bass, and are able to pick out and harmonize any melodies they hear. Thus is the musical consciousness gradually developed. And as the psychology of creative playing is the native impulse of the child, he is caught joyfully in the work by the law of life itself.

FOURTH GRADE MAKING DRUMS

GATHERING MATERIAL FOR MAKING WIND
INSTRUMENTS

JUNIOR HIGH SCHOOL CHILDREN MAKING VIOLINS AND CELLOS

CREATIVE EXPERIENCE THROUGH MAKING
MUSICAL INSTRUMENTS

Satis N. Coleman

No FIELD of learning is richer in possibilities for the development of the creative powers than is the field of music, and none offers more appropriate material for children. Everything that is rhythmic and everything tonal furnishes a starting place that will lead on and on in an endless variety of ever-widening interests, and the acquirement of many skills and appreciations that make children's lives richer, broaden their outlook, and enhance their happiness. If we take the field in a broad sense, it is easy to make music study conform to those processes by which we believe real education comes—easy to guide children into experiences that stimulate and exercise the creative impulse. But if we consider music training as merely the acquirement of a technique on some special instrument, we greatly limit the educational possibilities, and greatly increase the chances of failure.

Everyone knows of attempts at music study that have resulted in failure and disappointment. The custom of having children attempt to play instruments that are too complicated and difficult for them is one of the main causes of the frequent disappointment in their music study. For many years "music lessons" have meant either piano or violin lessons. The piano and the violin are the two most complicated instruments ever invented by the ingenuity of man, and yet these are the instruments we expect a little child to wield in his first attempts at instrumental musical expression. It is too much to expect of children of ordinary musical ability and even talented children often become nervous in attempting the difficult feats and the fine muscular adjustments that are required of them.

There is a wealth of musical material and different kinds of simple instruments suited to the varying capacities of all children, far better suited to many of them than either piano or violin. I do not refer to those unmusical toy instruments that are to be found on the market, but to those almost forgotten instruments of the olden days—those that have contributed so much in the past toward the development of musical people on other continents. How sad it seems that all this rich field has been of interest heretofore only to collectors and history students! What an opportunity the educator has lost! The music of the childhood of the race belongs to the little child. This is the time he must sing and dance and play upon instruments that make no technical demands, and only such melodies as his small brain can understand. As the simple elementary capacities of his mind are enlarged by experiences suited to those capacities, we can gradually lead him to larger and larger musical experiences.

Many years ago, in the beginning of my experiments with simple instruments there were practically none to be had, so the children and I attempted to make some; and thus from necessity, we were driven headlong into the application of an educational principle, and the discovery of how it worked. Great joy attended their experiments, and as in a vision, a complete picture flashed before me. "The children shall build up their own art, and experience the development of music from the beginning," I said to myself. "I shall find the child's own level, and lift him gradually to higher levels, with the natural evolution of music as my guide in leading the children from the simple to the complex. Primitive man made his own instruments, and so shall they make theirs. We shall study and make all types of instruments—wind, string, percussion, and what not! They shall not only sing and dance, but they shall also play and improvise upon the instruments which they make and upon other simple ones until finally they are able to select the modern instruments that appeal most to them, and each child will then give special attention to his chosen instrument. If a child lives the art of music from its primitive beginnings, makes his own instruments and plays upon them, and discovers for himself each stage in the development of musical instruments, how can he help being musical?"

An undertaking was before me: to bring the whole history of music within the reach of the child; to find out how to make and how to use all these instruments; and to arrange material suited to children's hands and minds that would give them the actual experiences of developing a complete art of music. Before me was endless study and research, experiments with children in the field of primitive music and in music's later development, trying out, sifting, testing, exploring my own way through an untried forest of thousands of years' growth. Stimulated by the vision of all this for children, the undertaking, however great the problem and however arduous the task, seemed worth trying. Thus it came about many years ago that I added a workshop to my studio, and there children of all ages experienced music from many angles. They sang and danced, investigated the musical life of primitive man, and lived the early history of music for themselves.

It would consume too much time even to outline all of the experiences included in creative music education for children. You are already familiar with various phases of singing, dancing, poetic expression, improvisation, playing by ear and by note. I will therefore write especially of the making and use of simple instruments.

Drums were already within the children's experience, and someone expressed a wish for one. The suggestion that the children might be able to make drums was received with delight, and they began at once to investigate materials to use. As a result of that investigation and of the industry that followed, we soon had a marvelous collection of drums. One child made a kettle-drum from a chopping bowl, another from a cocoanut shell; a spice box proved the right size for a tabor. We used gourds, butter tubs, and even stone bowls from the kitchen, covered with sheep-skin or heavy paper. The children made many uses of their drums—uses that meant interesting play to them, but were nevertheless musical experiences of definite value.

By this time the children had had some experience in tone as well as rhythm, had sung many melodies and were ready for tone experiences in their playing. Their experiments now turned to the pitch and tone quality of different objects—pieces of wood, metal, china, bells, pitchers, bottles, glasses—striking everything they could find. We discovered that some drinking glasses gave clear, bell-like sounds. We also found by experiment that we could alter the tones of these by putting water in the glasses. This gave us an idea. We took three ordinary drinking glasses, put different quantities of water in them, and by regulating the amount of water, found that we could tune them to our three-note scale and, by merely striking the side of the glass with a pencil or stick, could play our three-note melodies on them.

One day a little girl brought me a musical instrument of her own invention. It consisted of three silver spoons of different sizes, suspended with strings from a wooden rod; by striking them, she played a melody. This was only the start, and various other original contrivances for tune playing were soon brought in.

The experiments with wood led the children to develop a wooden instrument of the marimba type. They were led to discover that different pieces of wood differed in tone quality and pitch, and their experiments showed that the tone of a piece of wood was affected both by its length and by its thickness. These discoveries enabled them to plan a definite instrument of three notes, to tune the wooden bars in unison with the glasses and spoons and to set this new instrument up in proper form to use in our gradually enlarging orchestra. With a little wooden hammer each child played a three-note melody on the instrument he had made. To have made an instrument producing different tones—one on which he could play a real tune, and one he could use in our orchestra—seemed too good to be true! The scope of the instrument made by each child varied according to his age and development. The youngest children made those of three notes, and some of the older ones extended the scale to six, eight, and twelve notes.

In the fall the children went with me to see the plants of the hollow reeds that grow in the park, and to cut the dried stems. They discovered how a tone could be made by blowing directly across the open end of the reed, and they also found by experiment that the tone of the reed was affected by its length. So they cut long pipes for the low tones and shorter ones for the higher tones, and did not stop until each child had tuned a set of three pipes. Of course the legend of Pan was told at this time.

Just as they had experimented before by striking things, the children now tried blowing everything that could be blown at all, and their experiments revealed many facts. Bottles, test-tubes, and jugs of different sizes offered material for experimentation. Even the clock key was found to possess a musical tone, and the long valve cup of an automobile tire was a very good pipe of Pan. Other kinds of wind instruments were evolved quite naturally, and the older children made trumpets, horns, fifes, flutes, and various other types.

To make a bow and arrow and listen for the sound of the string as the arrow was shot, was our first work in strings. Then we found a thin board like a barrel stave, fastened a string to one end, bored a hole in the other end, and fitted a peg into it. The free end of the string was fastened to the peg so that the string could be tightened by turning the peg. By means of this simple device, the children made many discoveries about the sound of strings. Upon the rim of a cart wheel three strings and three pegs were fastened, and the field of primitive harps was entered and explored. As an example of our harp contrivances, a folding coat hanger of wood furnished us the frame for the triangle harp, and showed very clearly the effect of the length of strings. A wide board and a few strings became a Chinese kin, tuned by pegs fastened in the board.

The story of Mercury and the invention of the lyre stimulated the wish to make a lyre. A real tortoise shell was found somewhere, and after many experiments, the lyre was made, but it was afterwards found that a cigar box was more easily managed and furnished a better sound box for the lyre than the tortoise shell. From lyre to lute seemed but a step, now that cigar boxes were brought into use, and a three-stringed cigar-box lute gave us, perhaps, the sweetest tone we had yet made.

A hollow cocoanut shell offered tempting possibilities, and without ceremony there was soon developed a kind of three-stringed banjo, with skin stretched over the cocoanut shell. By chance one day, someone drew the hunter's bow across the strings of the cocoanut banjo. A new kind of musical tone was the result—one the children liked. Now the way was open for investigation in the field of bowed instruments, and the natural result was the desire to make an instrument especially for bowing. This new instrument was destined to be a monochord. We used a large, deep cigar box, put a strong stick through it, made ƒ holes (like those in other bowed instruments we had seen) and stretched a violin D string over a high bridge. Inspired by the success of the monochord, a nine-year-old boy wanted to go even further and make an instrument with three strings to be played upon with the bow. He would make a cigar-box cello out of the biggest cigar box he could possibly find! The cello proved as satisfactory as the monochord. Many three-stringed cellos were made in the studio, of varying sizes and with great varieties in tone. The violin too came in for a share of attention, and several were made to be played at the shoulder, as a real violin is made.

As soon as there were two instruments to be played with a bow, the children were eager to play them together, and by the end of the second year of the experiment, we had a delightful quartet of home-made stringed instruments. This quartet played folk songs in unison and in four parts, classic melodies, and original compositions.

On and on the children went in the field of the evolution of musical instruments as they have been developed by the race. There seemed to be no limit to their interest in exploring, experimenting, and making instruments. With all the main types of percussion, wind and stringed instruments, they had definite and vital experiences. They played on glasses, bottles of water, bells, piano, and all other instruments they could find; they made drums, rattles, tambourines, Pan-pipes, trumpets, shepherd's pipes, oboes, clarinets, tches, neys, fifes, flutes, harps of various kinds, lyres, kins, lutes, psalteries, banjos, and fiddles of all sizes, thus building a broad foundation to which could be related any musical experiences that might later come into their lives.

Something over twelve years ago I began a series of experiments in the Lincoln School of Teachers College to see whether it would be practicable for large groups of children in school situations to make musical instruments as the studio children had done, and to see if all the children in a grade could also learn to play these and other simple instruments with brief class instruction. These experiments have covered a wide range of instruments, and have dealt with children of all ages from first grade to junior high school. The results of these and the reports from other teachers who have been induced to try similar experiments in various parts of the country, have been very gratifying, and I am more than ever convinced that this type of work contributes to real and basic musical development, and to the child's broader education as well.

Every normal child has the healthy, natural desire to make things; and his mind is never so active as when his hands are doing a piece of constructive work that interests him. Every strip sawed to the right length and glued where it belongs, every surface sandpapered, gives the child a realization of something accomplished. I have never seen children show greater delight in any constructive work than in the making of a musical instrument. The eagerness to know how it will sound, and the creative joy of making something with a voice—something that will "talk back" to its maker—cannot accompany the making of many other things. It seems to me that the educational value of constructive handwork reaches its height in the making of a musical instrument which the maker will use.

By the time the child has made all types of instruments he knows their mechanical construction, and also the principles of the construction of all modern orchestral instruments, and how they were developed; and knowing them, he values, appreciates, and enjoys them more. But this is not all. The making of musical instruments leads on into other interesting fields of knowledge, and directly correlates art, science, and industry. The craftsman who would make a musical instrument must know something of the art before he can plan the style and capacity of his instrument; he must know something of the different kinds of woods, strings, and so on, before he can wisely select his material; he must know how to use his hands, and tools also, before he can construct it; and he must know something of science and must apply its principles before he can "make it work." Is it not the natural way of growth and real education, in music as in any other field?

The thrill of successful accomplishment in instrument making stimulates other creative work to a remarkable degree. Since the child has made his own instrument, how natural to want to make up his own tunes to play on it! Thus a subtle intimacy is established between the child and his instrument that goes over into all music, for his work covers all types of instruments. One of the most characteristic results of this plan of musical training is the impetus it gives toward original work. Since the creative power is exercised from the beginning, and in every phase of the work—in dancing, singing, language, in the construction of instruments, and in playing them—the child forms very early the habit of improvising, and is not daunted by a suggestion to improvise upon any instrument that he knows how to use. Improvisation, like singing and other powers which many people consider as special gifts, is the outcome of early habits; and the child who begins in the earliest stages of his musical development to improvise songs and dances and instrumental melodies, will grow in ability naturally. It is much easier for young children to improvise than to learn a set melody,

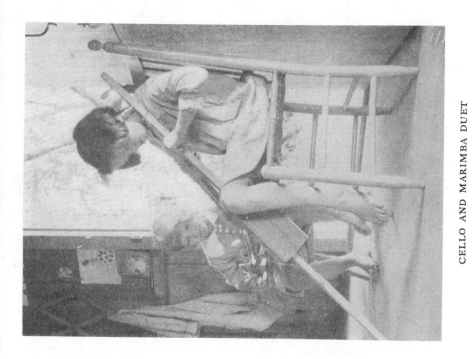

CELLO AND MARIMBA DUET

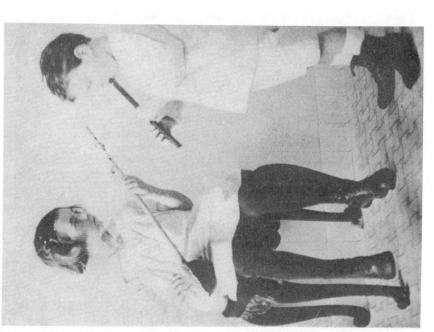

THE SHEPHERD'S PIPE AND COCOANUT BANJO

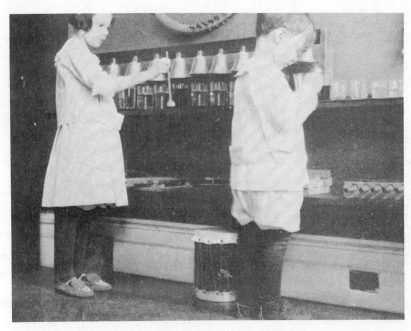

THE YOUNGEST CHILDREN PLAY BELLS AND GLASSES OF WATER

A QUARTETTE

and it is a very simple matter to guide their haphazard experiments into tuneful form.

By the use of these simple instruments, such as glasses and marimbas, very young children can have experiences in ensemble playing. (Of course these instruments, which must be very accurately tuned, cannot be made by very young children; they may be made by older children or by the teacher.) I find that some children as young as four years of age adjust themselves well to the playing of others, and all children enjoy playing in combinations. Few activities are more potent in the development of the social qualities than children's ensemble playing. This form of musical expression requires a fine adjustment to others, and at the same time, the more careful individual effort. It makes the child stand on his own feet and preserves his independence, while it fosters the idea of unity in common achievement. He realizes his obligation to the group when he hears the discordant effect which results from playing carelessly or inaccurately; but when he plays correctly, he feels the joyous and wholesome thrill of taking part in the making of something beautiful. When a child can play even a simple melody with a group of other children, without a single note out of tune or out of time, using his eye, ear, muscles and brain in perfect coördination in contributing his part toward the creation of something beautiful, who can estimate the mental, ethical, and social value of it?

One's real development always comes from experience. Those of us who merely listen are not the musical ones; we must handle the materials and make the sounds ourselves to be musical. But, of course, so long as the piano and the violin are the only instruments we teach our children, then the very young child—excepting, of course, the especially gifted one—must stand outside the pale of instrumental experience and look on with hungry, longing eyes. But if we give him music which is within his own grasp, instead of expecting him to understand ours, we shall find him an enthusiastic player. And he needs to play while he is yet too young for the difficult instruments. Psychologists attach much importance to the influences of the first six or eight years of the child's life, for during that time is shaped the pattern for many of his emotional reactions. These influences determine—perhaps in greater measure than we like to think—the things that will move him most and stimulate him most; they determine his mental habits, and his attitude toward things. This is the time to form habits of musical expression, to establish associations, and give experiences that will link up with other fundamental experiences, to make music something vital and tangible for him, and a helpful resource throughout his life.

The type of work here described is not a "method" or "system." It is rather a point of view, an attitude, a philosophy, if you please, of music education which attaches great importance to the teaching of music to children, but is much more concerned with the growth of children. It stands for experiences that not only develop the child's musical sense, but also stimulate adventure and discovery in all fields related to music; that make use of the constructive tendencies of children to enhance their interest, knowledge, and skill; that lead to free and original self-expression with both hands and mind, offering all children—whether talented or not—the opportunity to share in joyous creative experiences that lead to habits of creative work.

RHYTHMICS

Ruth Doing

WHEN a great musician and teacher visited one of my classes in rhythmics she said, "Ah, I see, one reveals oneself in this work," and then with a gleam of the eye, "How I should love to see some people whom I know doing it!" After all, what educators need as a point of contact with children is that the child reveal himself spontaneously without fear of adult disapproval, for then the real opportunity of the educator appears.

When we consider, as has been pointed out by an eminent psychologist, that "the mind works rhythmically and that the body consists of nearly four hundred organs of motion whose action is rhythmic, that rhythm has been a factor in the development of the race, and that probably the development of the race is in many ways repeated in that of the children," it follows that rhythm is fundamental, and that a system of rhythmic training should call into conscious activity this wealth of untapped rhythmic resource.

The observation of several hundred children a week over a period of school years engaged in creative rhythmic activity, has made me humble before the wealth of educational implication which has accrued, the significance of which calls for a readjustment of our valuation of the child's rhythmic relationship to the present-day world.

It is still generally believed that the child needs to be fed on the rhythm of the lullaby and the rhythmic patterns of folk songs, when even a little boy of six knows many of the intricacies of electric motors with their alternating currents, and the fascinating counter rhythms of machinery, the rhythms of transportation, the truck, the barge, and the train. The greatest misconception is that he chiefly perceives musical rhythm and expresses it through steps and beating of time, when the

truth is that his whole organism responds with creative energy to the pulsation of forces around him.

Many of the problems of behavior have their root in maladjustment of rhythm between child and adult, and child and child. The behavior patterns of an individual are noticeably good if they are balanced and flexible in rhythm, and are disturbing if the rhythm is either broken or tensely set into molds. The training for war is essentially metric and allows of no fundamental differences in individual temperament and rhythm, so that mass psychology and performance rule out imagination, beauty, and spirit. Competition, which is so much to be deplored, will disappear if true creative impulse is liberated and fostered. If skill in the mastery of the tools of expression is seen to be another aid to self-realization and not as an exhibition of prowess in which one's competitors are laid low, the testing of the individual will be made through his own growth; it will be made by him and not through contests with others. Can one imagine a great creative musician, sculptor, painter, writer, artisan, or thinker, competing with another for first place?

We must furnish an environment of freedom in which the child may exercise his fundamental potentiality for rhythm, wherein he may clarify his rhythmic images and develop his latent powers through bodily activity for service and efficiency.

Music, since it contains so many elements which find resonance in the organism, furnishes an effective experience in rhythm. We observe that when a child comes into a space which is greater and less hampered with furniture than he is accustomed to, he generally springs into some free movement such as running, jumping, or skipping. He rarely begins to move in measured or balanced walking; therefore I do not agree with most teachers of rhythmics that this is a spontaneous starting point with a child in his consciousness of musical rhythm. While engaged in this free rhythmic activity which he motivates, a pianist plays music appropriate to his mood and movement, the composition chosen depending on his relative attention span and age level; vice versa, he responds to the mood and movement of music when it motivates him.

Rhythm is contagious, and it is seldom that all children in a group are not drawn into active response. When a certain amount of fatigue is experienced in various locomotor activities, the children usually rest on the floor; this leads naturally to some experience of torso propulsion, stretching the spinal column, rotating and flexing articulated parts, dramatization of animal life, swimming, crawling, and moving about on all fours. With older children these torso evolutions eventuate in a sequence of movement through which the body becomes the vehicle of emotion, imagination, and will, capable of many nuances of gesture and attitude.

The use of the big muscles of the body and the spinal column is basic for physical coördination, and to a sense of dynamics, symmetry, unity, balance, and relaxation. When music which contains these elements is played, organic hearing and execution synchronize.

Musical rhythm arranges bars of notes of long and short duration into groups such as four-bar rhythm, six-bar rhythm, three-bar rhythm, and the more unusual five-, seven- and nine-bar rhythms, therefore the pulse or beat of each bar is not rhythm but is contained in it. To constantly stress the metrical beat is to produce an unrhythmic effect in music. In relation to the child in his "motor attitude" towards musical rhythm, the accentuation of the metrical beat produces an automatic response which is at once uninspired and lifeless. To comprehend a rhythm as a whole involves the comprehension of its units of measure, and rhythmic precision would be impossible without it. The child will respond with precision if the rhythmic stimuli be vivid enough and related to his own experience. As he dramatizes it, the train does go choo-choo-choo-choo, but first of all it is going somewhere. It obeys the signal man who starts and stops it; it is an express or freight, has a crescendo of speed and an accent of vibration and finally comes to rest at its destination. The run that leads up to the jump is important, but the jump is the climax of the rhythm and carries one lightly over into the next running in preparation for the next jump.

Why do composers sometimes write music without indicating musical bars? Obviously because rhythm is larger than meter and falls very often into unequal patterns in order to express the content desired. And why is blank verse a natural medium for the poetic conceptions of children? Because of this larger sense of flow and unity, which will not be compassed by meter.

Children are given every opportunity through the use of simple materials to construct their own rhythmic patterns. This lets the child into the freedom of its individual rhythm and reveals many interesting differences in type and temperament.

Too much cannot be said about the proper selection of music for progression through the different age periods, or the purity of tone or musicianship required for the execution of it. Improvisation by most pianists is so monotonous and unmusical that it is wiser to draw on the musical literature of the masters in order that the child's musical growth and appreciation be not retarded and vitiated. Perhaps we shall have some appropriate musical literature from the child if we help him find tools for the job, the first and most important of which I believe to be his own pulsating and vibrating organism. One such musical example I have in my possession, sung by a group of children while they were engaged in a skipping dance and taken down and harmonized by a

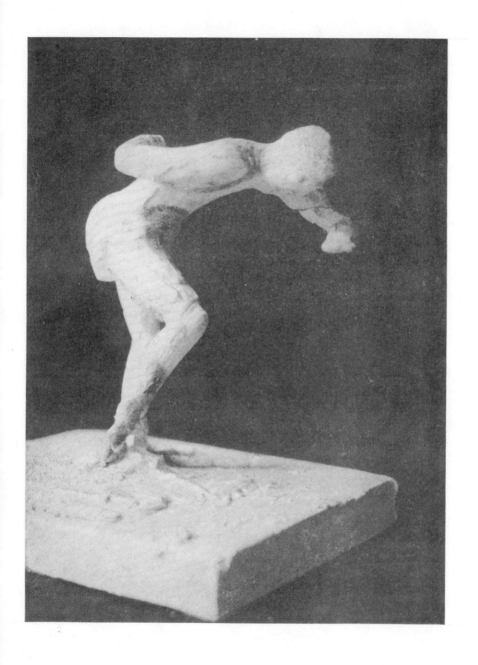

splendid musician. When this is played for children, the joyous response elicited is identical with that of the composers when the melody sung itself out of their happy mood, quite different from the usual laborious method of extracting original melodies from children based on words or poems.

Many of the plays based on subject matter with which the children are occupied in their classrooms are correlated with the rhythmic work. As children are living vividly through these dramatizations, it is most natural for them to continue to live even more largely in them where they have space and freedom for their dramatic set-up, where bodily movement and gesture are encouraged and where music is theirs for the asking. This presents a valuable opportunity for the teacher of rhythmics, if she is willing to undertake a considerable amount of musical research in her collaboration with them. One meets early settlers, Indians, Vikings, and Greeks, and lives and moves with them through epoch-making events. I have even been party to The Dance of the Solar System, the sun whirling with terrific velocity through space, throwing off bodies which traveled at different rates of speed, with comets and meteors bursting at my feet.

On the other hand, some very moving dramatic moments which children have realized have come out of music of a dramatic character. A poetic conception of a boy of eight, of a musical composition based on Indian themes, called *The Mysterious Story*, which was played when the class asked for Indian music, was made the central theme of their play, with the customs and rituals of Indian life surrounding it. His story was of the supernatural appearance of his chief in the form of a wonderful and beautiful bird which he killed; on discovering it was his chief whom he had killed, he was filled with remorse and fear and fled the encampment. The children accepted this mystical interpretation which he had made so vivid through his accuracy in musical hearing, pantomime, and mood, without a question.

A group of children in my summer camp, ranging from twelve to fourteen years of age, wrote a play, the plot of which concerned the coming into being of creatures called *The Cloudies*, who passed from one country to another seeking the Light. In each country they encountered creatures apparently unlike themselves, the Jerkys, the Happys, and the destroying Birds. Some of the Cloudies shedding their cloudy robes revealed themselves dressed and moving in the manner of the people whom they encountered and with whom they remained. In this way their number gradually became less and less, until finally only the leader and one or two of his followers found the Light. No adult stimulation was provided and no adult help was asked, except in taking down and harmonizing the music which they composed, and in meeting with them when they held discussions. These discussions were reported verbatim and are revealing as a glimpse into what is called the subjective life of the child. Much beauty and wisdom is held in abeyance there because of our fears and lack of confidence in him. Some pictures of this play are shown here but they are static, while the play moved with a rhythm which made the climax, the finding of the Light, a veritable *Te Deum.*

Some examples of sculpture made in the clay room of The City and Country School by eleven- and twelve-year-old children, photographs of which are reproduced here, show what seems to be an indication of a transference of their experience in rhythm to a concrete representation in clay. This sculpture illustrates, as no photograph could, some of the things the children actually do in the rhythm class, as they have captured the complete moment of climax without giving one a feeling of arrested movement. This, then, is a true expression of rhythm. Each has brought into plastic form a figure portraying mood, rhythmic sequence, equilibrium, and proportion. They have not worked from the nude, but have clarified their images of the body as it appears to them in their experiencing of it, as an instrument of feeling, thinking, and volition through their representation of it.

These few accounts of the efforts of children along creative lines indicate that training in the rhythmic arts furnishes the groundwork for independent creation.

The growth periods and the consequent psychological states accompanying them, would be passed over with less strain, and the personality would be strengthened and harmonized if the rhythmic training were continued into adult life. If we were more alive to the deep significance of rhythm in its service to the race, we should observe with more clarity the growing organism with its pulsating and vibrating life and render it more understanding service.

TEACHING INSTRUMENTAL MUSIC THROUGH MUSIC

Norval Church

IF WE date music as a part of the school curriculum from 1837, when Lowell Mason began class instruction in the Boston Public Schools, school music has been organized less than one hundred years. This work which Mason started is significant for two reasons; first, it emphasized the fact that children could be taught music, while prior to this time only adults had received systematic instruction; secondly, it introduced the idea that this instruction could be given in groups as well as individually. While vocal music has carried on the idea of class instruction, instrumental music has suffered because of the conception that it could be taught only to individuals. Up until the last ten years practically all of the instrumental instruction has been on this basis.

It is quite natural that when instrumental instruction entered the public schools the problem of class teaching should appear. The first solution was the attempt to carry on class teaching as expanded individual instruction. The great difficulty with this conception is that it makes no appeal to general or group interest. Good class work must always be interesting enough to hold not only the attention of the individual but also that of the entire group. Attention to this idea has led to advancement in general education and also to the more recent developments in instrumental instruction. For example, in reading, this adaptation has led to the use of selections which have a hold on the pupils' imagination for its own sake, so that while following the story for their interest in it they get control of the technique of reading. In the same way that children are taught reading by reading, we must seek to teach music through music. Not only is it necessary to use improved methods in teaching music with music as the end but it is also necessary to adjust the approach in such a way that it will realize many aims of education which are too often neglected by instructors in music. This is probably due to the fact that the demand for instrumental teachers has exceeded the supply to such an extent that many school systems in their desire to introduce instrumental music were forced to engage instructors who were fine musicians but rather poor educators. The writer knows of no subject in the curriculum today that has in it more possibilities for realizing the aims of education than has instrumental music.

It offers unusual opportunities for the development of group coöpera-tion, creative thinking, and leadership. While education in general has not been able to solve completely the problem of individual differences, it is conceded by many that music when properly taught has met this problem with as much success as other subjects in our present curriculum.

If instrumental music is to become a vital part of the school curricu-lum, it must provide opportunities for the less as well as the more musically gifted child. This wider participation will mean the inclusion of a larger percent of the student body, thus increasing its usefulness to the school. While no small part of music contribution is that of giv-ing the child a fine musical experience and opportunity for self-expres-sion in music, a great many advantages may be realized from group participation that would be of definite value to the child who probably would never continue with music. In order to encourage this wider par-ticipation in instrumental music, we have been working at Teachers College on a type of approach which attempts to do in instrumental, that which is already done in vocal music, namely, permitting children to become members of the group without previous technical skill. In con-trast with the usual method in which a certain amount of performing ability is required for entrance, the child is now invited to join the band or orchestra whether he knows anything about music or not. That is to say, we place the function ahead of the technique and let the child acquire the technique as the need of it arises while playing in the band or orchestra.

Let us first consider the organization of a beginning orchestra which consists of those who already play and those who do not. The usual procedure is as follows: A talk or a demonstration is given to the chil-dren in which they are acquainted with the nature of various instruments, but are also invited to join an orchestra even though they have no pre-vious training. All children interested are asked to attend the first rehearsal. At this rehearsal each child is given a definite seat in the or-chestra even though he has no instrument. If they have no instruments they are seated in the section with which they hope later to play. After the general work of organization is over, beginners are instructed in the manner of holding the instruments. This is quickened by the help of those who can already play, and are now ready to assume responsi-bility and leadership. The need for coöperation is very evident to the group in a situation of this kind, and they immediately respond with whatever they are able to give. Those who have instruments are started in to play at once while the remainder are given the same instruction and go through the drills on imaginary instruments. The arrangements include graded parts ranging from those suitable to the beginner to those difficult enough for advanced players. The object of this is to make the first tone a child produces on his instrument a contribution to the organization of which he is already a part. The more advanced parts are included because of the desire to keep each child working up to his full capacity in order that he may more effectively serve the group.

The first selection requires for the beginners on strings but one open-string tone. Beginners on wind instruments are also required to play but one tone in this first composition. This first number is quite short and permits one sustained tone to be played or held throughout, which means that it could be played with the beginners using various rhythms. If enough advanced players are present, the orchestra may be emancipated from the piano at once and in case of the lack of advanced performers the piano must be added to supply the missing parts. The first lesson is so arranged that the beginning strings will have learned to play upon three of the open strings in that many compositions. The wind instruments have learned to play three of the easiest tones that can be produced on their particular instrument. It is significant that no attempt is made to teach those facts which are not necessary to the child's participation in the group.

As the work progresses greater allowance must be made for individual differences. We now use material in which the beginning violins have the melody but require the use of only the first finger. The advanced violins play either an obbligato or play in unison with the beginners. Other numbers of this stage should be ones which will give all advanced players plenty to do and should be arranged to involve the use of the first finger for advanced beginners. Open-string parts should still be available for those who still need to play them; first, because some children are slow and need more open-string work, and secondly, because their contribution to the group will be greater if they play a part which is not too difficult for them. This process is carried on until all fingers are in use and they find themselves playing parts similar to any standard orchestration. While the wind instruments have easy parts in the selections designed especially for beginning strings, other pieces are included which give them the responsibility of the lead and involve not only the notes they have already learned, but additional information essential to this section. For the ambitious beginner home-study material is included which consists largely of easy melodies with piano accompaniment. The differences in musical ability of the children are so great that we soon find beginners representing every stage of development. Those who have ability and are willing to work are soon rewarded by the opportunity to assume a responsible position in the orchestra.

Many of the problems occurring are taken care of by student assistants both during the regular rehearsal and also in sectional rehearsals which they themselves conduct. One beginner made such rapid progress that she not only finished a six-weeks' summer session playing first violin, but when she joined another orchestra in the fall she was chosen as one of the four assistants to the director in charge. All of the other assistants had studied privately for a period of three years or more. She had some five or six beginners assigned to her for whom she was responsible. Any help she gave them was aside from the regular rehearsal period and was to be arranged for without the help of the teacher. The interesting part of this particular case was that when a group of children was tried out for advancement some time later almost every one of her pupils was chosen. This of course was not intentional as the one examining the children did not know with which assistant they had been working. This may be only a coincidence and therefore unimportant. However, it seems to show that the girl, having started in the same manner herself, has caught the spirit of coöperation and is now developing real ability in leadership.

The band is treated in much the same way and, while I shall not attempt to describe it in detail, the result of an experiment carried on at the Horace Mann School for Boys may be of interest to you. This school of about four hundred boys never had a band and out of the two hundred who signified their interest in one, we found one baritone, one flute, one clarinet, and about four or five saxophone players. This heterogeneous group consisting of almost all beginners was assembled and was able to play an introduction and two strains of a march at the very first rehearsal. They rehearsed once a week and after eight meetings played an engagement using standard first- and second-grade marches and a Christmas carol. The enrollment of the band at that time was forty, which has since increased to over fifty members. The band is rapidly gaining a good balance and the offer is still open to any boy who wants to join at any time.

While certain beginning books were recommended for individual reference, the band never played from a so-called beginning band book. After the first appearance a bass player, in discussing the band, made a remark that is interesting. He said, "You know this band was handled in a different way from what I supposed music would be taught. I thought that in order to play music one would have to spend hours on scales and exercises. But you know we were just given an instrument and told to play it, nothing being required. Pretty soon I noticed we were learning about music and scales as we went along." This boy had just begun to realize that in this band the function had been placed ahead of the technic, and while it had been a real organization from the first, the technic was being developed as the need for it seemed to arise. In sight reading a new march, the boys meet many new problems which must be solved at once. For example, when the band is stopped after having read a new section, many hands go up. The alto player wants to know how to finger G sharp, the bass player an A natural, the cornet player a D flat, the clarinet player F sharp, and so on around the band. The director must have this information at his tongue's tip, the total time consumed in answering these questions not to exceed one minute. The alto player's question answered, he is concerned with nothing more. He immediately fixes his eyes on the music and is ready to play that G sharp correctly the next time. On the other hand suppose we say to him, "This is the way to make G sharp—use the second and third valves. Now please remember this, for some day, perhaps a year or two from now, you will be playing with a band and will need to know." The chances are he would take little interest in this particular problem and in many cases music in general. It is quite essential that, in order to handle a situation of this kind, the person in charge must have a knowledge of the instruments. While it gives a teacher a great deal of power to be able to answer all questions without referring the players to other sources, this should not be used to the extent that it serves to militate against the development of initiative and the desire for research.

It is quite evident that we have in instrumental music a subject which is unsurpassed in its ability to realize the aims of modern education. Our duty then is to see that this subject receives as truly a pedagogical treatment as any other subject in the curriculum. The above method was designed to give instrumental instruction this treatment and to give every individual the opportunity for musical expression as well as an opportunity to belong to a real live organization without setting up standards of technical requirements. Due to the fact that we have such a wide range of ability, our instruction must provide opportunities for the less as well as the more gifted child. It should not only include those who have interest in music but also those who seem at first to have little or no interest in it. In work of this kind there is distinctive value in terms of a true socialization of the members of the group. Qualities of coöperation, responsibility, and initiative are exhibited and promoted to a marked degree. While this method is not the only way to develop bands and orchestras, it seems to maintain interest, to facilitate normal technical progress, offer excellent opportunities for development of leadership, and in general meet the needs of modern education.

THE PLACE OF THE FESTIVAL IN MODERN LIFE

Peter W. Dykema

IT IS a commonplace observation that often the most precious elements of life are least treasured. Probably most neglected of all is the potency of joy. What does it mean to have a joyful attitude toward life? The answer would include such terms as courage, inspiration, peace, brotherliness, willingness, to meet the problems of the day. It would mean appreciation of life, the readiness to use the arts, to welcome courtesies, in a word, to participate in that fuller life which is itself an expansion of a joyous outlook.

Joy is not a subject, a definite fact which may be tabulated and measured. It is a by-product which may come with many other subjects but which does not necessarily accompany any subject or any experience. Educators are able to measure knowledge and to a less degree power, but they have still to learn how to measure that which to a great extent conditions the amount of knowledge and the amount of power; namely, the attitude toward the acquisition of these.

The festival in its essence is an embodiment of joy, as the adjective "festal" well suggests. In every manifestation there appears the essence of joy, that permeating content, that being alive, that desire to have more and more of life, that hunger for experiences which will perpetuate this feeling of well being. So the term festival must include not only the great celebration of large groups for which long and arduous preparation has been made, but must run the gamut down to the humble celebration of the birthday of a little child in a family of three or four; yes, indeed, the festival of one person alone who celebrates an event which possibly for him only has significance.

Likewise, there may be involved in the celebration any or all of the arts: the stately pageant, the poignant drama, the involved dance and the simple measure, the mighty chorus, the tiny song, elaborate staging and costuming, or the improvised suggestion of the moment. Through it all, art appears both for its own lovely sake and for the purpose of ministering to the exaltation of life.

In calling upon the arts to assist in the celebration of a festival we are simply repeating the processes which gave them birth. Every art is the result of an expression of that inner joy which could not be satisfied

SCENE FOR A GREEK HARVEST FESTIVAL

(*11 year old group*)

Rosemary Junior School, Greenwich, Conn.

MUSICAL PLAYS IN THE ETHICAL CULTURE
BRANCH SCHOOL

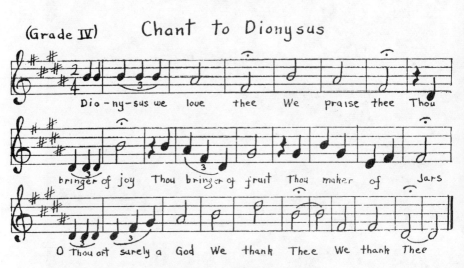

(Grade IV) Chant to Dionysus

Dio-ny-sus we love thee We praise thee Thou
bringer of joy Thou bringer of fruit Thou maker of Jars
O Thou art surely a God We thank Thee We thank Thee

The children composed the words and music of the chant for their original Greek play "The Feast of Dionysus."

A processional in the play gave opportunity for what might be called creative listening. Through this the children gradually came to hear and to express with their bodies the phrase and rhythm of the music.

until it appeared in outward form. Upon no other art has the festival made such extensive and constant demand as upon music. Music, the most social of the arts, because most readily admitting large numbers of participants in its production, has seemed the simplest and most natural medium for the expression of the feelings of festive groups of people. Again, music has been closely associated in its origin with the labor of groups of men. One of its earliest uses was as an aid to rhythmic movements, such as rowing or reaping, and it has remained as an instinctive expression of man's delight in his labor. But it has gone far beyond this, and has interwoven itself with all human experiences. As far back as our records go, we find music utilized at gatherings of people when joy, praise, thanksgiving, sorrow, supplication, or any general feeling was to be expressed. By all peoples, untutored or cultured, music has ever been cherished for its rare emotional qualities. Both means and end, it serves as a stimulant to deep feeling and hence to action—and as an expression of the aroused being. Old as man himself, music has shared his lot, now heightening, now tempering, his joys and sorrows, his loves and his hatreds, his memories of the past, delights in the present, and hopes for the future.

Thus it is that a nation's folk culture is the lovely, imperishable flowering of centuries of the people's thoughts, dreams, and aspirations. For no song or story that lives long can be merely the passing fancy of any individual; it must be the carefully nurtured child of generation after generation. A forced hothouse process may produce a novel exotic, but if the air into which it is born affords it no nourishment, no encouragement, it must soon wither and die. Such material, serene and secure after the lapse of centuries, has frequently been loved and cared for by every succeeding generation since its birth. To know the art and music of a nation, therefore, is not merely to add to one's store a few more trifling fancies; it is to touch the embodied national ideas and ideals of ages. Well may Carlyle be quoted, "To know the old Faiths brings us into closer and clearer relation with the Past—with our possessions in the Past. For the whole Past is the possession of the Present; the Past had always something true, and is a precious possession."

In a composite civilization like ours, much of our life—our laws, language, and customs—can be understood only by slowly unraveling the twisted threads that lead back into older civilizations. Acquaintance with the tastes of peoples of other days, knowing the music they loved, often sheds a bright clarifying light upon our actions and sentiments today.

There is no more significant movement in the educational processes of America than the growing use of the drama, and especially the dramatic spirit as exemplified in the festival or pageant. In thousands of schoolrooms, though the open space be restricted to a few narrow feet, enthusiastic teachers are experimenting with the dramatic method of presenting salient facts in various subjects. In country schools the playground becomes the scene of many a little pageant dealing with the history of the locality. In the most modern school buildings an auditorium with a stage is included by the architect as a matter of course. More and more the churches are forming dramatic clubs among their young people, and in several places the regular Sunday services are replaced, especially at the great holidays, by reverent presentations of some old mystery or morality play or a modern masque. At great conventions the pageant has become an acknowledged means of symbolizing the salient epochs, past, present, and future, of the world's important institutions.

There is great need of material which by its beauty shall charm the youthful mind; by its poetical fancy shall stimulate the imagination; by its essentially dramatic nature shall lead to a greater use of impromptu or prepared little plays; that shall, in a word, preserve to us some of the charm and culture which has come down through the ages.

Music has a peculiar power as an expressive and fusing agent in the festival. The part assigned to music varies with the type of the celebration. Through the principle of association of ideas it may be used to create local atmosphere of time and place. In this it is allied to scenery and costume. Frequently the emotional appeal may be intensified by appropriate music. Skilfully introduced, it strengthens the dramatic force of an event; it makes pathos or grief more appealing, joy more exuberant and contagious, and adds to the impressiveness of any ceremony or ritual. The appeal of speech and action is broadened and deepened by music because, transcending the exact and hence limited suggestions of the definite arts, it conjures up possibilities which are beyond the limits of the known and expressible. Often, however, a song may serve to render concrete the general idea of a scene, may focus or summarize a situation, and long afterward recall it, both by the text of the song and by the feeling which the music carries with it.

Sometimes a musical prelude serves not only to suggest the mood of what is to follow, but also its historic period, locality, or characters. We expect to be greeted by quite different personages and places according as the prelude takes the form of a solemn ecclesiastical chant, a rollicking old English ballad, a lilting Irish ditty, a dreamy Italian boating song, a monotonous Indian war dance, or one of our own national hymns. It may be an incidental diversion introduced to vary the uniformity or lighten the heaviness of the proceedings; it may be introduced for its own sake as contrast and relaxation, with no relation to the central idea; it may serve to accentuate or reinforce certain climaxes of

Drums

Indian Lullaby

(Grade I)

Sleep, sleep, my little pa poose, The camp fire flames are red; — —

Sleep, sleep, my little pa-poose, Fire flies are over — head.

Park School, Baltimore

THE BELLS

Original three part song. Words and music by two 6th grade boys, age 10 and 11 years

Tower Hill School

Hear the bells, sil-ver bells, They are ring ing loud and clear,

Ding — Dong — Ding Dong bell,

Sound-ing far, far a — way, then so near —,

Ding Dong Ding, Dong, ding.

Hear them chime, hear them ring, While to all they bring

Ding Dong Ding, Dong, Ding.

Mes-sa — ges of joy and cheer.

Ding Dong Ding Dong.

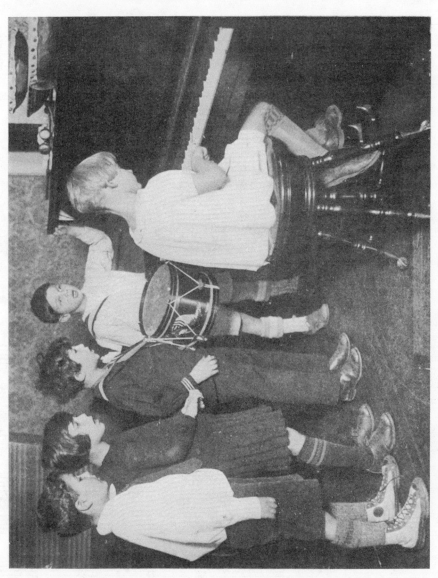

A QUARTETTE OF CHILDREN FROM THE FIRST GRADE SINGING HOT CROSS BUNS TO THE PIANO
ACCOMPANIMENT WHICH THEO HAS PICKED OUT BY EAR ON THE PIANO

the festival; it may assume the dignity of the central and overshadowing factor in a great religious ceremony, such as the solemn mass; or, aided only by poetry, it may itself become the entire festival.

Because of its very indefiniteness no other art is so universal in its appeal, and hence so susceptible of being variously employed and interpreted. It is only in connection with the other arts, such as poetry, pantomimic dancing, painting, and sculpture that music becomes definite, and hence limited in its significance. Alone, and in connection with these, it covers the full sweep of human and superhuman emotions, creating, intensifying, varying, transfiguring the moods of man.

Today mankind is seeking for still greater mastery and still wider use of the most companionable, the most intimate and open, and yet the most fleeting and inexplicable of all the arts. The festival offers a fruitful synthesis of the arts of civilization. Its wise use in school and community means an awakening of youth to the humanizing arts of life.

THE CREATIVE ASPECT OF A MAY DAY FESTIVAL

Helen Goodrich

THE idea of a teacher of the seventh grade many years ago, who first recognized the springtime feelings of her children as basic racial experience which needed natural and lovely expression, was a fruitful one which has eventuated in our May Day festival.

The festival in which the queen is crowned and in which she is to hear poets and minstrels and give a reward for the best poem and the best song, was entirely "spontaneous" at first. One teacher had the plan of the exercise in mind and prompted all the action. Now the organization into a coherent, semi-dramatic whole is in the hands of the head of the dramatic expression department. He has developed the exercise in vital ways. For the crude dialogue, written by teachers and children, the exquisite words of Milton, Spenser, and Shakespeare have been substituted. Ease and simple charm are brought into the exercise by expert handling of rehearsals of procession and stage pictures. The part of it which is "spontaneous" in the sense of "left without training or direction" has been abandoned. The outcome of many years of working to free our children for expression has brought us a sense of the necessity for a right balance between spontaneity and conscious direction. We give the children not only occasion and stimulus, but we provide the kind of training which they need in order to express themselves in the best possible way at any given time. We have lost some of our fear of interfering with their freedom of expression, because we can now recognize surely the difference between a technique which frees and an imposed formalism in expression.

When May Day arrives the stage is a bower of springtime flowers. The orchestra plays a loud, joyous march as the school comes into the auditorium. Presently this changes to a lighter, more graceful type of music as the Queen's procession starts down the aisle. Following is a typical program:

MAY DAY

1922

PROGRAM

March "Norwegian Dance"................Grieg
Queen's Processional.............Franz von Blon
Crowning of the Queen
Greeting to the Queen
The Queen to her subjects:
Song: "Grasses Green Are Growing".....Caesar Cui
First Group of Poets.................First Grade
                       Second Grade
                       Third Grade
                       Fourth Grade
Round: "The Spring Has Come"............Hayes
Second Group of Poets...............Fifth Grade
                       Sixth Grade
                       Seventh Grade
                       Eighth Grade
Round: "Come, Let Us All a-Maying Go"....Hilton
Third Group of Poets................High School
Song: "Now Is the Month of Maying".Thomas Morley
Original Melodies
Queen rewards the Poets and Musicians
The School's wishes for the year's planting
March: Followed by planting of trees on either side of
      the gateway

Spring has always moved the poet, and even a city spring stimulates the writing of verse in school. Of course poetry is written all the year round. Some is given school publication and much more is produced with no thought of a possible hearer or reader. But the multitude of "spring poems" provides annual embarrassment for the committee choosing which shall be recited before the Queen. Last year the plan was tried of printing in a little pamphlet issued on May Day worthy verse which found no place on the program because time was limited or the verse was in some way unsuitable for a place in the ceremony.

MUSICAL PLAYS IN THE LINCOLN SCHOOL, NEW YORK

THE ROOSTER

The children of the First Grade made up several plays: The Milk Play, a Chicken Play, The Apple Tree Play. Various songs were composed by individuals and a number were chosen by the group to be woven into the plays. As the plays developed, different movements such as plowing, watering, the train, and so on were preceded by appropriate songs.

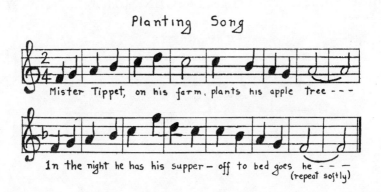

Planting Song

Mister Tippet, on his farm, plants his apple tree ---

In the night he has his supper - off to bed goes he - - - -
(repeat softly)

Through their original songs and rhythms the children wove together their feelings and knowledge of people who plow and plant, those who drive the big trucks and engines, and expressed in a dramatic way the relation of these workers to their own lives.

Only a very occasional bit of our original verse possesses ultimate value, but a considerable fraction of all that is written contains genuine merit.

Here are a few of the poems which have been spoken before the Queen:

> O lovely mountain!
> With Winter on your head
> Spring time at your waist
> And Summer at your feet.
> O lovely mountain! (Grade IV)

> In the Spring, in my heart
> I can hear river waters
> Rush and babble, to part
> At some stone in the flow.
> I can see green moss cling,
> And ferns bending over,
> And the snake grass spring
> In slow, shallow places.
> The yellow water lily
> Is blossoming once more,
> And the mud turtle wakens
> And scrambles to shore. (Grade VIII)

THE LOVELY MAIDEN "SPRING"

> Through the barren forest glade
> She came, the lovely maiden,
> Golden-haired and fair arrayed,
> Wind-wafted, flower-laden.

> Light was her step on the frozen ground
> And gay her carol clear.
> Earth in its dreaming heard the sound,
> And felt her presence near.

> Stooping low she would gently press
> Her lips on each sleeping thing.
> Earth awoke to her soft caress,
> And called the maiden Spring. (Grade XII)

The interest in writing melodies to be presented to the Queen is often keen, especially among those who have already tried it. It is of course voluntary work. Two or three congenial girls make a very good working group. Some must work alone. A few make their tunes at home and bring them to the teacher ready to sing, and even written out more or less accurately.

We have made a small collection of lyrics for the use of our budding song makers. This little booklet contains some of the finest English short poems, some less fine but good as texts; also poems by pupils on various subjects, including prose poems of former years which are regular in form.

So then the song makers begin. They may go with a teacher to the group room and sing their melodies to her, or work in some quiet corner alone. The teacher's function is to write the phrases as they present themselves, and when the song is finished to have it sung until the children are perfectly familiar with it and can keep it in mind as a whole. A simple accompaniment is usually supplied by the teacher after the song is finished, subject to the taste of the composer.

The next step is for the song to be written on the board in the music room. It is sung by the composers and is learned quickly by the rest of the class. Then begins the stage of criticism. A fairly solemn air pervades the group. Tentative suggestions begin to come: "I like it," "It fits the words," "It has a monotonous rhythm," "It seems to be too much like" another tune. A failure in the coherence of the melodic line is always noticed, or the lack of a climax, or of a satisfying close.

A few examples of this song making follow:

9th girls, 1925, ½ period

The great point in directing this song making is in our opinion a process of clearing obstructions away. Timidity and self-consciousness are to be overcome, vague and uncertain criticisms are to be interpreted, some light is to be let into questions of form, and there is need of help in the final rendering of the song by the class. This is always subject to the taste and feeling of the composer. The places at which suggestion and criticism shall come from the teacher are impossible to state. They depend largely upon our knowledge of the pupil.

It may be added that though the interest and joy in these songs are often intense, no unhealthy self-satisfaction is encountered in the children. The teacher's reserved pleasure in a song may be quite overborne by the fervid admiration of the group for it, but a little calm analysis restores the balance. In a few cases a child may need unreserved praise, but usually we think a somewhat tempered expression of pleasure is most useful. The little songs are, in some cases, of the sort that sound better than they really are to the uninitiated audience.

The growth of the May Day festival from a perfectly "spontaneous," that is, pleasant but loosely-planned, unskilful type, to a more definite, though still easy-going style, came partly as a result of our having acquired a larger auditorium with its increased requirements in the performer, and a larger and more critical high school; but chiefly it developed with our growing recognition of the need of the children for a better technique; that is, more command of their bodies as means of expression, and a better understanding of form in poetry and in music. We still have funny contretemps, as when the crowning of the Queen goes wrong, or a group on leaving the stage realizes tardily that it has neglected its obeisances, but we can laugh easily and go on without much embarrassment.

The day is one of the happiest of the whole year. Each return of springtime gives us a little glimpse into its eternal meaning and purpose.

THE DEVELOPMENT OF MUSICAL CONSCIOUSNESS IN THE YOUNG CHILD

Edith Potter

TODAY is a day of revelation to many who are for the first time becoming interested in the problem of education. Everywhere one hears questions asked as to the reason for the tremendous changes going on in the school curriculum. Children are learning to read before they know their "letters"; they are using addition and subtraction in making a box or a table before they know the "table of twos." In music, too, they are being given a chance to love and experience it before they are asked to dissect it. The problem of giving music to very young children has become an entirely separate problem from teaching them to read it. This problem is being met later when the joy and love of it has been so instilled that even the monotonous singing of Do-Re-Mi will have no disastrous effects.

The kindergarten and primary teachers have opportunity to carry out this purpose of giving the young child a fund of experience in music. Moreover, these first years in school are the years in which to develop in him every spark of originality, and we find there is much when he is not hampered by the ideas of his elders. It is in the nature of the child to create and nothing brings him as much joy. So we let him create bits of music. What if they are not good enough to be used by the group? They have given the child who created them a feeling of confidence which is invaluable. Or perhaps some bit of true melody may be expressed through "one of the least of these," and should we scorn such

AN INDIAN DRUM FROM A SECTION OF A HOLLOW
TREE CUT DOWN IN THE SCHOOL YARD

THE CHIMES

Thus our present orchestra had its start

AFTER FOUR YEARS OF MUSIC EXPERIENCE NO CHILD OF THE FIFTEEN IS ANYTHING BUT EAGER TO TAKE PART

a melody or its use? In the Junior Elementary School, which is, as its name implies, a school for only young children, the creating of melody is encouraged, for it is an integral part of the free spirit of the school.

The first experiences in music in the kindergarten are innumerable and ever variable. Those in our school of which I shall tell you have spread over a period of eight years and may or may not have been used in any one year. There has always been the informal singing of Mother Goose songs and folk tunes at the piano during the free-work period. Some child is sure to ask for this every morning, and there is never a time when two or three at least do not respond to the call of music within themselves, and soon there is a little group about the piano eagerly listening to the songs and enjoying the illustrations.

Another experience which is part of the year's program is the period of creative dance rhythms. We find that every child responds naturally to rhythm, but in some children there is a much stronger subconscious rhythm than in others so that their response to a rhythm given by us may result in awkwardness or seeming lack of rhythm. This makes a strong argument for individual and creative dance rhythms rather than those of a stereotyped order in a large group. A child who cannot follow a given rhythm in a large group forms habits of careless listening which is the worst of all evils and the most difficult to overcome. We begin then with simple rhythms which individual children may desire, such as stepping, skipping, galloping, running, or hopping. The first step in originating is brought about by asking the children to think of different ways of doing these things. A response to this has never failed and many members of the group are always eager to attempt the new way of skipping or stepping or hopping. Sometimes small groups like to be tested by having various rhythms played in succession to see if they can be puzzled. Some child may like to suggest a rhythm and ask others to join him. Or he may make an entirely new rhythm of his own and ask if others can do it. We may ask him to make something that has never been done before and once this is started there is no end to the different ideas the child will have. Often a child will say that he has made a new rhythm at home and wants to try it out. Along with this individual and creative work, new music may be played, and the children invited to make dances to fit it. Sooner or later as the social consciousness develops they will be led into the folk-dance forms. It is interesting to note that the little dances in circles of four or more children, in lines or in groups, partake of much of the true folk-dance form of the past.

Another popular experience in music on the rhythmic side is the use of percussion instruments in connection with the dancing. Often some child will bring the drum to the rhythm period or to the piano in the free period and want to play for the other children to run or gallop. The use of familiar music with this instrument has brought much better results than the typically band music formally played. Sometimes this may develop further with a few children, and a more advanced orchestra may be formed.

In developing the singing side of the musical consciousness, there are also many devices and games. In this field, too, we must take the child where we find him, and we find each child in a different stage of development. Before he can be expected to sing he must have a singing vocabulary, just as he must have a word vocabulary before he can be expected to talk. At least one third of the children entering kindergarten do not distinguish tonal differences as they appear in a song. Children are still asked to join in group singing which is entirely beyond their comprehension. If a child is tone deaf, or even partly so, group singing will never remedy that trouble. It is better then to put off the singing of group songs in kindergarten as long as possible and to sacrifice the pleasure it gives to adults for the good of perhaps a dozen children who may suffer by attempting the impossible. We can substitute for it with equal pleasure to the children individual singing in small groups of two, three, or four, or as many as are actually equal to the song. There are endless devices. Most children find it a pleasure to imitate single tones. These tones should usually be high, though there are some cases in which it is better to start low with the child's voice and lead him gradually to a higher pitch. The day a so-called monotone gets his first tone "up in his head" is a red-letter day, for from that day a new field is opened to him. He suddenly finds himself in a beautiful, unexplored country. He can experiment with his voice. He can try imitating two tones in interesting ways as singing "Good-morning," names of birds, flowers, activities, such as running, jumping, animals in a circus or any of the interesting things that come his way every day. Counting napkins for the luncheon table in his singing voice is good. Other interesting ways of giving the child a tone vocabulary are games in which one child blinds and another stands behind him and repeats an interval sung by the teacher, the child who is blinded trying to guess the singer; or the child who sings hides somewhere in the room and the child blinded tries to locate him from the sound of his voice. This is a good game for the shy child who dreads singing alone. The game of checking with a colored crayon each successful attempt to reproduce a single tone or interval draws some backward child into the fold.

During this time of individual development there should be much singing of beautiful but simple songs to the group. Whenever and wherever possible they should listen to the best music, which for them is undoubtedly the folk music of all countries. Thanks to Mr. Surette and others, we are able to give it to them in simple and childlike form. This is an opportunity for the more musical children as they can soon learn these songs and sing them to the group. Children should also hear simple instrumental music every day with much repetition of the selections they like best. Violin music is perhaps the most appealing. The folk melodies played beautifully are the most appreciated by the children. Much music played to them is either too difficult or too long really to enter into their experience. Often the melodies later to be taught them as songs can be played as music for appreciation.

Lastly, a child often gains deeply in experience by the creation of

Catherine's Shepherd Song (age 6)

The shepherd is making a tune on his pipes

melodies of his own which in their very making build up a control of melodic interval. This is a way also to give the child who is not equal to group singing a chance to express himself musically.

A child who has had these experiences in kindergarten is ready for new and more difficult problems in the primary. He is ready to do more correlating with the subject matter of the group. He is ready to learn many songs quickly and easily which pertain to the particular interests of the group as a whole. There is a certain control and understanding of melody which gives a background for the use of music of other

Betty Jane's Melody for Indian Verse

Ko Ko shens, doo wee jee wah Mis go wah Bo ya nee da

Mab jee doo Ah qua quaq Da ee jah men

countries. In our study of the Bedouins and of Shepherd Life some of the children were able to give the atmosphere of the Bedouin music, as in Catherine's song, "The Shepherd Is Playing a Tune on His Pipes," which she made on the harp using the interval of the minor third because she thought it had "a sound of music you would play on the desert."

Betty Jane brought back an Indian song from the Chippewa Indian Reservation this year, and this was learned with great interest by the Second Primary Group. The melody was so truly Indian in its rhythm and atmosphere that it was with surprise that we found it had been made by Betty Jane herself to go with the verse taught her by a little

Indian girl. This melody is being preserved in the hope of comparing it with the real Indian melody on her next visit to the Reservation.

The First Primary Group was much interested in making short rhythms on the drum and having them written down in quarter and half notes to indicate fast and slow counts. If the rhythm was an acceptable one some children were asked to make a little dance to it or to step to it. By repeating the rhythm four times a simple folk dance could be made, especially if some tune could be harmonized to go with it. This game was so popular that individual books were made containing all the different rhythms of each child, some of the children even attempting to copy the music themselves so it would be "all their own." A book was also made by the First Primary Group containing all the

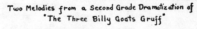

Two Melodies from a Second Grade Dramatization of "The Three Billy Goats Gruff"

The Troll's Song

Who's going ov er my bridge?

The Smallest Billy Goat's Song

'Tis 1, the smallest Billy Goat.

songs which had been made on the Chimes, a series of eight pieces of gas pipe, which will be described more fully later. This was called the *Chimes Book* and many members of the group participated in its making. Writing music had all of the joys and none of the sorrows sometimes connected with that task and has probably given the children a pleasant feeling toward it which will be lasting.

The Second Primary Group continued this work by making orchestra books which contain all of the pieces played by the group. These books were decorated and made into gifts for the parents and incidentally to be kept as very pleasant reminders of the Second Primary Orchestra. Through this writing of notes and their connection with familiar music this same group is reading the notes used in the Third Grade Orchestra with no difficulty at all.

The Secondary Primary Group of this year is working on an entirely new project, that of composing music for a "little opera," using for the libretto the story of the "Three Billy Goats Gruff." There has been much interest shown in the kind of voice necessary to distinguish the Troll or Big Billy Goat Gruff from Little Billy Goat Gruff.

This "opera" will be given later in the year to the kindergarten at the

Friday assembly. All of these and many other experiences add to the fund of musical knowledge which is being stored up in the consciousness of the child to be used many times as he advances into the realm of beauty which constitutes our heritage of the music of all ages.

The orchestra of the Junior Elementary School has come about through the intense interest shown by the children in the playing of the instruments in preference to music of any other kind, a greater interest even than is shown for dance rhythms when the child has reached the First Primary. The development of the orchestra has not been forced but there has been an effort made to provide material which will meet the growing consciousness of the children's power to use more difficult instruments. There have been three direct sources which have contributed to the interest and development of the present orchestra. These sources in terms of subject matter are: Indian Life, Fairies, and Primitive Man.

The discussion of typically Indian instruments was started by trying to think what Indians would naturally use to keep time for their dances. Many things were suggested both by teacher and children, such as the beating of a tree with a stick, the beating together of stones, sticks, or shells, the shaking of gourds, the making of clay rattles, the rattling and beating together of bones. This was followed by the actual making of an Indian drum from a section of a hollow tree cut down in the school yard. The kneebone of a calf was found in a field—the holes closed up after inserting small stones—and was used as a rattle. The hoof of a horse was found and used by tying dried beans into the holes at the edge and shaken as a rattle. The jawbone of some animal was found and used by drawing a thin bone across the teeth.

The orchestra played with great joy the accompaniment of several Indian songs which were learned with much interest and ease. Only the actual songs of the Indians were used in this connection and these did much to create the true atmosphere of Indian life. The children were divided into tribes and each tribe made a song for itself using a favorite Indian melody.

> Ah ha! Hi ya ha! The eagle is our friend.
> Ah ha! Hi ya ha! His claws are very sharp.
> Ah ha! Hi ya ha! He flies high through the air.
> Ah ha! Hi ya ha! He can carry baby sheep.

Sometimes the instruments were taken out of doors and played by some of the children while others danced and sang. Some dances partaking of much of the Indian spirit and rhythm were made to the accompaniment of the orchestra.

The Fairy orchestra of the kindergarten was much more simple. The children were greatly interested in fairies during one springtime and were making fairy dances. They were asked to find things in the woods which the fairies might use for their dances at the Fairy Ball. The result was much like that of the Indian orchestra in the primary though not so elaborate. Folk melodies were used for the music and the fairy musicians were soon playing for the fairy dancers with shells, sticks, stones, and other findings from the woods. New dances were made and were used for an outdoor festival and bazaar at the close of school.

The orchestra of *Primitive Man* began in much the same way but grew still more interesting when the children began bringing things which made tone as well as kept rhythm. Stringed instruments were added after the story of Ab's Twanging Bow. Experiments were made with loose and tight strings. A cart wheel was made into a sort of harp. This orchestra was used in the same way as the others with the added personal interest of their friendship with Ab.

Thus our present orchestra had its start. The first real instrument used in this orchestra was the chimes. These were made from a number of gas pipes of different lengths brought by several members of the class. The first attempt at an instrument resulted in a chord made of five or six pieces, then the scale was tried but it was difficult to find enough pieces to make the eight correct tones. It was finally suggested by one of the class that her father who was a plumber could supply the needed pipes and cut them in exactly the right lengths. This was done and we had an instrument which has been a general favorite from kindergarten to third grade. It might be added that a friend with the gift of absolute pitch helped in the tuning so that the tones of the scale are true.

Other instruments were added in quick succession. A marimba was made to match the tones of the chimes. One day a boy brought a zither from the attic at home. Anything played on the chimes or marimba could be played on this instrument because the numbers were there beneath the strings. A harp was made of wood after the pattern of the zither and is still a favorite instrument. A violin was bought by the school and is used intelligently by many of the children. The free use of this instrument seems to engender an easy movement which often results in a really good tone. In many cases the children who were especially interested in the violin became eager to take lessons and did so with most excellent results. Other instruments brought were: ukuleles, a guitar, and a banjo, all of which have been used exclusively in a melodic rather than harmonic way. Just now a third-grade boy is engaged in making a large, stringed instrument which will make a deeper tone like a cello. Another boy is trying to make a flute out of a reed. A cornet has been bought which is taken home each night by some child hoping that he will be the one to conquer it. The xylophone has been a great source of pleasure also and has been the cause of much experimenting with familiar melodies and those of the children's own creation. The scale is familiar ground to all from five years on and will make sight reading a much less formidable field.

Miss Ruth Laighton's *Tunes and Technique, A Beginner's Book for Violin,* has been the chief source of material used for the orchestra. Starting with the single tone A or 6, she presents a very pleasing harmonization of an old folk tune all on that one note. The next little tune uses A and E and so on until combinations of all the open strings

MELODIES MADE ON THE CHIMES

are used. These tones are easily found on all the other instruments and there is enough material in the book to carry through many months. The introduction of fingered strings is also made a very easy process, and in the third grade the first position is being used with some success by several of the children with no more help than the instruction of one or two other children in the class who are having private lessons and are eager to pass on their knowledge. This class consists of fifteen boys and girls and they have two orchestra periods a week. Every day in the free-work period two or three or perhaps more gather together for a special practice, perhaps to work up something for the morning assembly. After four years of orchestra work no child of the fifteen is anything but most eager to take part, which is perhaps the greatest argument for its place in the elementary school.

So day by day and year by year goes on a feeding of the fire within which means beauty, health, and a power to meet life's experiences with joyful courage and a singing heart. To the melodic folk song and the music of the masters, continually introduced into their environment from the first, these children who have experienced this kindling fire bring a lovely warmth of response and appreciation which has in it something of kin to kin. Real music has taken on to them a meaning, because through their own primitive efforts at melody making and the mastery of musical instruments there has been created in them an understanding consciousness.

CREATIVE MUSIC IN THE GROUP LIFE

Ellen W. Steele

In coöperation with Rosemary Lillard, Director of Music

FOR some time people have been interested in the free art expression
of children in painting and drawing. The child, if left alone, has something to say, live and colorful. And letting the child be free has made a
great contribution to art, because the directness of the child is a much
better illustration of the primitive in art than some of the sophisticated
attempts of adult painters. We have a great respect for children's art
and, in experimental schools, we have freed the child from the imposi-
tion of adult ideas.

In music, however, we do not dream yet what may be the result if we
assume the same attitude that we have now in art—the idea that children
have something to say in their own idiom. We are just at the beginning
of this realization and we shall probably have to live through all kinds
of experimental stages before we, as teachers, have the understanding
to deal with the child musically. We are ourselves filled with musical
preconceptions. It is easy for us to say that something is "not musical,"
unless we have a very advanced musical viewpoint. There is apt to be an
insistence, or at least an assumption, on our part of usual forms. And
until very recently we have not had any forms other than the classic to
think with. The modernists, whether we enjoy their music or not, have
at least torn our minds open to new musical conceptions, new intervals,
new scales, new rhythms, new relationships. To me the realization that
atonality breaks up our old dependence on tonality, that one does not
need to end on a note or chord that resolves what has gone before, means
that one may let his musical imagination out on to distant planes, just
as the modern artist does in spatial relationships. By this I do not mean
denial of beauty in the great music of the past. Nor do I mean over-
praise of contemporary musical expression. I mean, merely, that from
the music experts of today we, as teachers, may get a new attitude musically, or rather a new attitude toward music and the child. I think we
must assume with music the same attitude we do with painting and
with language—that the child be observed objectively more than we
have done. We must provide an environment where his musical concepts, at any point in their development, may come forth freely and

joyously and can be received naturally and with respect, and not make the child feel that his technique must be developed before his creative power.

In music it is almost more difficult than in any of the other arts to give the child free growth, because music in its conventional forms comes to him on all sides. The radio pounds tonality into his ears, his teacher drills him in his cadences and usual intervals and extols the virtues of the classical masters. However, recently in the use of old folk music we have provided the child with modal music and freer rhythms. But even in experimental education, when we let a child create, usually we expect him to create in the usual modes and meters. Thus, so far, most of us know scarcely anything about the real music world of the child, and we do not always discover his impulses toward musical creation, or often

provide the stimulation or opportunities for these. A big field opens for him whose musical knowledge includes not only conventional forms but whose imagination has widened to see new possibilities, and who is interested to find out about the inner musical life of the child. It must be one who is sensitive to the child's creative impulses, and able to take an experimental attitude toward the child in his musical development.

In my experience, so far as musical expression has occurred, I have found, in music as in art, that children give the best expression out of an environment where they have absorbing activities of their own. Such activities have phases that call for musical expression. The children find that they need music to express these in a satisfying way. When this happens I find that there is no holdback on the children's part. They go, as a matter of course, to the music room to compose the music they need. There, however, they must find someone who has the belief that they can create and the ability to help them get their musical thoughts into whatever form they take.

A group of eleven-year-old children, who were deep in the Early

Medieval period, decided to write a play of an amusing legend of Charlemagne which we found in a collection of source material, the story of Charlemagne and Rauf, the Collyer. The story seemed to the children to suggest a puppet show. They had made a study of the life of the people of the period, and we had read together, in translation, the *Chanson de Roland* and they were filled with all kinds of medieval language expressions. So they proceeded to write the play, build, and decorate the puppet theater, and make and costume the puppets in the medieval spirit. When it came to putting the play together, they found a number of places where music was needed. They were not able to find music that suited them, so there was nothing to do but make the music they wanted.

For the Rauf song, the children had the idea of expressing the character of Rauf, a rough peasant who poached on Charlemagne's preserves and was overheard by Charlemagne himself singing this boasting song. In writing the music for the words the children quickly caught the spirit of the folk song. Making the song was play. The whole group was present. Someone sang one phrase, and then another person sang another, the music teacher recording these, until what they had suited the group, except the last line. A committee went back later and worked on this line until they were satisfied with that.

RAUF'S SONG

I'm a poacher brave and bold,
All men fear me, young and old.
I shoot deer and I shoot doe,
Leaping rabbit, quivering fawn,
And all the gentry feast upon!

If I were knighted fair to see
Charlemagne would fearful be!
All his countries I would take,
England, Spain, and fairest France,
And hold in fief with my good lance!

When it came to composing a song to Charlemagne, the children planned to start the work with a committee because, as they said, "It works better not to have so many people around." So a small group of children worked with me on the words. Then they went with these to the music teacher. The deep impression made on the children by the *Chanson de Roland* appears in the allusions to Charlemagne's sword, "Joyeuse" and to the Saracen King, Marsila. In this song in accordance with their words they wished to have a spirit of dignity and an expression of allegiance to the Emperor. The song is in the style of plain chant. As an ending for the play it was very impressive dramatically.

SONG TO CHARLEMAGNE

Oh, Charlemagne weareth a crown of iron,
    And ruleth with scepter of gold,
And Joyeuse flashes a glorious light
    When he striketh Marsila the Bold.

O noblest of monarchs, thy vassals so strong
    Will follow thee hard to the foe
O'er snow-capped mountains, through passes so deep,
    Till they scatter the paynims to woe!

For the "Jester's Song," the children chose to use the music of a little old French song, "La Polichinelle," and in this case they merely wrote new French words to fit the tune, trying to express gayety and play.

JESTER'S SONG

Pan! qu'est-c'qu'est la?
    C'est les marionettes,
      Mes amis.
Pan! qu'est-c'qu'est la?
    C'est un cocasse cheval.
Il est villain
    Et aime vous deplaire.
Comment s'appelle-t'il?
    Le diable Lucifer!

They had another experience of a different sort with "The Song of the Bard" which was recited at Charlemagne's court. The music teacher brought them some medieval French music and played it for them several times. They listened and discussed the feeling this music gave, and two children wrote a story for the Bard to recite, using this music as a background. Here the children found a language expression for the mood of the music, a kind of musical narration very much in the style of modern recitative.

THE SONG OF THE BARD

It is night time. Thick are the heavens studded with stars.
Pale is the moon as it sheds its silvery light over the dark waters.
A long shadowy boat slips softly by.
'Broidered is its sail, and carved its prow.
Now comes the soft strains of music from the harp strings of a wandering
    bard.

The bard on deck sings while many a man crouches listening with eager ears to the wondrous tales of heroes.

Now we see a brave knight struggling with a scaly dragon,

Fire is pouring in hot flame from his gaping mouth, and black smoke gushes from his nostrils.

Now as the music grows softer we see a lady fair waving a silken scarf from a narrow window in a high tower.

Softer and softer grows the music as the boat vanishes in the mist.

These experiences exemplify music meeting a dramatic need that came from a background of history and literature. The dramatic use of music is, however, only one of the many ways that group activities seek musical expression. Pantomime dance and play naturally require it also.

Sometimes this demand arises in connection with other subjects. The study of other countries and times arouses an interest in the music and the musical instruments of a period or place. And the children like very much to experiment with these instruments and improvise in the spirit of this music of other places and other times. Some twelve-year-old children who are now at work on the geography of China are doing this with Chinese instruments, and have made a coolie song of the workers on the Yangtze-kiang.

Industrial arts offer all sorts of opportunities for expression in music. Tools used by workers give beautiful rhythmic patterns. Processes suggest expression in rhythm and song. After an experience in making pottery last spring which extended over several weeks, the classes in the school were sharing with each other in assembly the story of pottery through the ages, each group taking some different phase of the development. The sixth grade, which had previously studied Greek life, had the story of Greek pottery to tell. They planned a series of scenes which would show the various processes of the potter's work with his clay, from the time it was dug from the ground until it was sold in the market place in Athens. They decided that a good way to show the potter working at his wheel was to sing a song of the potter at work. The spinning of the wheel gave them their rhythm, and they wrote words to this rhythm which expressed the potter, his work, and his feeling. The children worked with the music teacher until they got the music that expressed the wheel rhythm, and they made their music change as the processes changed. The mode and rhythm both change freely to suit the spirit of the words and the rhythm of the process.

THE POTTER'S SONG

Round and round goes my wheel.
Kick! and it spins and whirls.
Soft is the clay in my fingers,
With force, I throw to the wheel!

My whirring wheel sings to me,
As I thump, and shape, and mold,
Tall grows the clay in my hands,
Like magic, it winds itself down.

Still spins my wheel so fast,
I press into shape with my thumbs,
Till smooth and stately it stands,
My vase, so slender and strong!

The group teacher has a function in building an environment in which music has a natural place. The musician's part lies in helping the children's desires come true. Such music experiences greatly enlarge the child's appreciation, so that he takes back to any further study of music a keener understanding, listens with a more intelligent ear for artistic mood and musical form, and carries with him, too, the feeling that he can create, and that he desires to create, as well as to listen. This provides the natural quest into the underlying technique of the musical art.

FUNCTIONS OF THE CREATIVE PRINCIPLE IN EDUCATION

Calvin B. Cady

THE effort of this paper is to present a conception of functions of the creative spirit in education, a conception which is the result of more than thirty years of work with children of all ages from five to sixty—not a simple task in limited space.

Since the art of music was my specific field of work, quite naturally application of the creative principle began with the music education of the child, especially of the little child. The results of this application and their far-reaching effects in general education, not only revealed the function and the necessity of creative imagination in all forms of art education, fine and industrial, but led to its recognition as the vital principle of all phases of educational processes.

If in this article the art of music serves as opportunity for analysis, it is not because music is any more important as a subject of thought, nor because it offers a greater incentive to creative imagination than does any other subject, but (a) because it has served as an opportunity for study of child education, (b) because the function of the creative principle in music is not generally understood, and (c) because its integrations are not realized.

I

The common conception of creative thought in music is concerned solely with "original composition." Almost from the beginning of my own study this aspect of creative imagination played an important rôle. This fact, however, is not of so great moment as is the occasion which led to the discernment of the real nature and function of the creative spirit and to its recognition and adoption as a primal factor in general education.

It was contact with the mental state of the alleged "unmusical child" which led to the discernment of the nature of creative activity and its basic function. It is said of such children that "lacking the musical faculty, it is unwise or useless for them to spend time with the subject." If it be true that a child lacks the musical faculty, the deduction is necessarily sound, but it is a question of fact. Why are these children thus judged? Because, forsooth, they do not seem to be able to differentiate the pitches of tones. Coming into educational contact with children of this class whose mental state, musically speaking, had not been bettered by ordinary processes, the question arose: What is the fact concerning these children? Are they really deficient in capacity for music conception, or has the process of awaking this capacity been wrong? Being of that philosophical persuasion which rejects the dictum that all knowledge is derived from without and through the physical sense, it occurred to me that the failure to reach the child might lie in the process; that the appeals had not touched the intuitional power of mind.

Quite naturally, this state of mind would seem to be the farthest removed, psychologically, from the possibility of creative thought in music. There is, however, a super-psychology revealed in this scientific principle that "the kingdom of God is within."

Fortunately, not a part, but the whole of the kingdom of intelligence, knowledge, power of knowing, understanding, and expressing, is the lordly heritage of every being. Not by external means, therefore, but by touching the hidden springs of intuition, is it possible to lead the child to discover and organize himself—the prime aim of education.

The application of this creative principle has never failed to result in the child's purely intuitional discovery, conception and voicing of melody; still further, he has reached most quickly the realization of the "kingdom of music within"—usually during the first or second effort, rarely more.

Again, intuitional development of melodic conception has never failed to evoke a pure voice; a demonstration of the fact that intuitional activity of thought in its discovery and conception of the beauty within, also intuitively creates its own modes of incarnation. "Truly," says Mazzini, "all action is the incarnation of idea."

As early as 1903, a volume * was published containing original melodies, accompanied songs, and instrumental compositions—the work of children of ages from three and a half to ten years. This material, even at that period, represented the fruit of at least fourteen years of practical application of the creative spirit by teachers of music education in all parts of this country.

The testimony of the teachers gave sufficient evidence of the value of the awakened creative spirit (a) in arousing interest in the study of music and (b) in leading hundreds of alleged "unmusical children" to find their God-given musical heritage and the "voice of melody." Most significant, however, has been the testimony that in many cases the discovery of the creative spirit in music has changed the entire mental

* *Music-Education, an Outline,* Vol. II, Teachers. Material. Clayton F. Summy, Publisher, Chicago, Illinois.

status of the child toward his power of study in general and has led him to rise from a low to a normal power of intellectual activity.

II

Two aspects of the teacher's relation to the creative activity of the child need consideration.

(a) For real and effective work it is absolutely necessary that the child be left unqualifiedly to himself in his within-search for melody. Nor should there be any effort to awaken melodic conception by audition in any form. It is not imitation that should be sought from the child, nor "invention of melody," but the spontaneous expression, in melodic form, of an inner urge that may be awakened.

(b) The teacher must not tamper with the fruit of the child's imagination. The irresistible tendency of the teacher to impose his own notions of the child's conceptions, arises from failure to recognize the fact that to him the child's conceptions are as great and beautiful as the conceptions of Bach and Beethoven were great and beautiful to them.

The teacher should not make his cultured experience the criterion for the primitive ideas of the child. Because of this misunderstanding of development the teacher assumes the necessity of injecting into the child's imagination what he may conceive necessary for true creative thought. This occurs all too often and the result obtained is not the work of the child and savors of invention rather than intuition or real creation.

If there be any comparative rank among the capacities of mind, that of judgment is the most precious, yet in too much of our educational work judgment is the most neglected and almost discouraged activity. Aside from mathematics, in no realm of child thought is judgment so positively passed into discard as in the realm of art.

The failure to appreciate the child's primitive art intuitions leads the child to a false estimate of his function as judge; therefore, all judgments and decisions in respect of the child's art imagination are made subject to the knowledge and taste of the teacher. This is wrong, because it smothers the free play of the creative spirit and precludes the educational use of such primitive intuitions for awakening the child's inherent power of esthetic judgment.

III

As an ultimate principle of education, the fact of the withinness of the "Kingdom of God," the whole kingdom of infinite intelligence is scientifically sound. It is a necessary predicate of all intelligent minds, since every individual involves the whole potentiality of the one genetic force; not as a possession, but as a complete manifestation of that force.

The child, in his conception of music, therefore, is not creating anything or any idea as the term "creating" commonly signifies; he is simply discovering and outlining or imagining in thought a part of the infinite content of his own individuality as the manifestation of the one genetic intelligence. Creative activity may be predicated of the child, therefore, only in the sense that each individual mind, of necessity, forms its own identity, or definite image of every idea or experience and thus may be said to create the images which represent or embody the idea or experience present in consciousness.

In this sense, then, the vital function of creative thought lies not in its evidence for "self-expression" but in its revelation of the nature, capacities, and content of individual being and in the opportunity it offers the child for the true discovery of individual selfhood.

The revelation of the creative spirit in any one subject of thought is the demonstration of its application to all ideas—the whole content of mind. Every subject, therefore, may and should serve the purpose of awaking creative thought and its influence will necessarily be felt in the general mental activity of the child.

This conception of the function of the creative spirit develops another deep and far-reaching effect upon the individual mind. The child who, by intuition, has been led, for instance, to break through the barrier called "lack of musical faculty," thus discovering himself, has reached a basis for realizing a just attitude of mind toward his fellow humans, for he knows that no virtue or praise is due him more than other children since the same potentialities are seen to exist in each and all of his fellow beings. Thus he has reached a sound basis for fulfilling the law: "Thou shalt love thy neighbor as thyself."

IV

"Original composition" is not the only nor the most important field for the exercise of the creative power. Quite contrary to the common notion, both appreciation and interpretation demand a high order of creative activity and it is this aspect of the subject that should be better understood.

In 1904 the real significance of appreciation of art was recognized during efforts to secure from a class of adults absolutely *de novo* impressions of painting, sculpture, and architecture. Such works of art as were chosen for study were unknown to the class and no comments of any character were made concerning them. Furthermore, the members of the class were requested not to consult one another but to write (in the class) his or her own impressions.

When a digest of the papers was made the impressions were seen to fall into certain general classes, a lesser or greater number of which appeared in each individual report. These general classes were applicable to all the arts. Poetry and music were then subjected to the same constructive appreciation and the same general classes of experience again appeared in the reports. The most illuminating aspect of the papers was the constructive, the creative imagination displayed in efforts to convey inner esthetic, emotional, or spiritual experiences resulting from impressions made by each and all the arts. Appreciation was thus seen to be the temple each mind forms of the material involved in all the various classes of experience. Mr. Robert Schauffler's sententious designation of appreciators of music as "creative listeners" may be made applicable to appreciators of the visual arts by the paraphrase "creative see-ers."

More significant from the point of view of creative activity was the revelation of the absolute oneness of art. The roots of all forms of art are the same and the fundamental significance in human life is the same, the arts differing only in material or in structural and plastic form.

However interesting may be the adult process of thought evoked by any subject of investigation, the child's mental and spiritual response to the stimulus of the same idea is of far greater interest.

In large classes of music appreciation at the Speyer School (the former experimental school of Teachers College, Columbia University), and in small classes in the Music-Education School in Portland, Oregon (an academic, not a music institution), plus innumerable demonstration classes in connection with summer normals in various parts of the country, the children revealed not only a keen appreciation of the spirit of music, but with great joy expressed their impressions in many forms of art—crayon drawing, painting, dance, pantomime, drama, poetry, and modeling.

From the point of view of child education and the creative spirit the important aspect of these experiments is appreciation of the oneness, the integral unity, of the arts in relation to the child's inner life and imagination.

v

To objectify or to incarnate thought and the experiences of life in visible or audible forms is the most operative urge and primitive necessity of the human mind. Out of this primitive need has developed the various forms of the art of expression or interpretation, with their respective techniques.

In the arts of language and music, two primitive arts, with voice and fingers men create "castles of the air" for the expression of thought and feeling; castles that vanish in building but which become the sweetest of memories to him who has ears to hear and heart to cherish. Child and adult alike shape these castles out of the evanescent but plastic sounds of oral melody, rhythm, and harmony and call it language and speech. Out of the equally evanescent but more plastic tones of melody, rhythm, and harmony, child and adult alike create other castles of the air—"Temples built to music," glorious in beauty and power of incarnating the innermost thought and feeling of individual being. If anywhere, in these two modes of the art of interpretation the child should be allowed opportunity for the free play of his creative imagination. Unfortunately, it is in respect to this art of interpretation, with its wealth of opportunity for creative thought, that the general, but most particularly the music, education of the child is sadly deficient, for it fails to awaken if it does not discourage the free play of the creative spirit.

This is too large a subject for discussion in the limits of this paper, but the time is opportune for calling attention to this most important aspect of "creative education."

A SELECTED BIBLIOGRAPHY ON MUSIC

CADY, CALVIN B.—Music Education. Clayton F. Summy Company.

CANFIELD, JULIA—Original Composition. Francis Parker Year Book, Vol. I. F. W. Parker School, Chicago.

CHAMPLAIN, DORIS S.—Music and the Child. Child Study Association of America, New York.

CLEMENTS, KATHERINE—Music Moods in Pastel and Charcoal. Francis Parker Year Book, Vol. VI.

COLEMAN, SATIS N.—Creative Music for Children. Putnam.
Creative Music for Schools. The Lincoln School.
Textbook 3, Creative Music in the Home; Volume III of the Massachusetts Library. Lewis Myers & Company, Valparaiso, Indiana.
Creative Music for Schools; "The beginnings of music: the making and use of instruments for entertainment," special manual edition, 1925. "First Steps in Playing and Composition," special manual edition, 1926. "The Marimba Book," special manual edition, 1926. Lang School of Teachers College.
Bells. Rand McNally & Co., 1928. The Drum Book. John Day Company, 1931. Children's Symphonies. Bureau Publications, Teachers College, Columbia University, 1931.
The Gingerbread Man and Other Songs. John Day Company, 1931.

COLEMAN, SATIS N., and THORN, ALICE G.—Singing Time: Songs for Nursery and School. John Day Company, 1929.

CORNISH, LUELLA—Creative Effort in Melody. Francis Parker Year Book, Vol. VIII.

DICKINSON, EDWARD—The Spirit of Music. Scribner.

DYKEMA, PETER W.—Festivals and Plays. Harper.

GORDON, DOROTHY—Around the World in Song. E. P. Dutton, 1930.

GOODRICH, HELEN—Creative Effort in Melody. Francis Parker Year Book, Vol. VIII.
Music in the School Community. Francis Parker Year Book, Vol. I.

GREENEBAUM, SARAH—Creative Effort in the Morning Exercise. Francis Parker Year Book, Vol. VIII.

HALL, G. STANLEY—The Psychology of Music. Proceedings of the National Education Association, 1908.

KERN, M. R.—Song Composition. Elementary School Record, No. 2.
Elementary Music Teaching in the Laboratory School. Elementary School Teacher, September, 1903.

KINNEY, CHARLES M.—Work with Children Backward in Music. Francis Parker Year Book, Vol. I.

MACPHERSON, STEWART, and READ, ERNEST—Aural Culture Based on Musical Appreciation. Boston Music Company.

NEWMAN, ELIZABETH—How to Teach Music to Children. Fischer.

PALMER, WINTHROP B.—American Songs for Children. Macmillan, 1931.

SCHOEN, MAX (Editor)—The Facts of Music. Harcourt, Brace & Co., 1927.

SEASHORE, CARL E.—Psychology of Musical Talent. Silver Burdett.

SEYMOUR, HARRIET A.—How to Think Music. Schirmer.
    The Philosophy of Music. Harper.

SURETTE, THOMAS WHITNEY—Music and Life. Houghton Mifflin Company.

TROTTER, T. H. YORKE—Making of Musicians. Dutton.
    Music and Mind. Doran.

UNTERMEYER, LOUIS (Editor) and MANNES, CLARA and DAVID—New Songs for New Voices. Harcourt, Brace and Co., 1928.

CREATIVE EXPRESSION
THROUGH LITERATURE

CHILDHOOD'S OWN LITERATURE

Hughes Mearns

I have a secret from everybody in the world-full-of-people
But I cannot always remember how it goes.

I

As soon as children begin to speak they attempt the language of literature. During those early months and years, when they are struggling
with the difficult medium of language, come occasional flashes of achievement. Parents have always known about this; but outsiders make it the
subject of their jokes. Anything under the heading, "bright sayings of
childhood," is always good for a laugh. Our jokes, however, exhibit
our natural antagonism, or rather our lack of understanding. Literature
is simply unique self-expression; yet at the start we strive for conventional self-suppression and laugh away, or scold away, that individual
utterance without which literature is not.

In a short time, under our loving but ignorant drive, the native gift
of language may hide itself away in private dialogue with doll or toy, or
carry on solely in the spirited domain of silent dream life—out of
which the child comes stumbling and awkward to receive our chidings
for stupidity—or it may die out and seemingly be lost forever.

Mothers have been aware of this more surely than teachers. Each
mother knows that she has a wonder child, one who talks to her in a
language adequate for every need, who inquires with intelligence, whose
reasoning is direct and well-nigh miraculous. She cherishes the startling
beauty of every casual utterance, but she learns early not to speak of her
wonder aloud. That bored look, the smile of cynicism, the jest that labels
her as "proud parent," these and other manifestations of an unbelieving and prejudiced world soon silence her.

Lately, however, an international interest in the unique contribution
of childhood has brought courage to mothers; out of secret drawers have
come the precious baby books which record questions, fancies, soliloquies, indignations, and protests even. I have only to mention this in
public and then, when the lights are being turned off warningly, they
wait in the darkening hall to tell me, with a wistful and timid eagerness—so few there are who will listen to mothers—of this and that
startling expression of their very own. I urge them to keep careful

notes. "The child," I tell them, "is now expressing his real self; so you may find out much about him now which will serve later. Later he may not believe in himself; you it is who must give him the strength of self-faith, for you know—you have seen and heard."

My mail is full of such records. One night, just before tucking in, Bunnell says,

> "Mother, did you see the sun go to bed? . . .
> He pulled the woolly white covers
> Up over his head. . . .
> Are his blankets soft and white and warm
> Just the same as mine?"

"At another time," writes Bunnell's mother, "he asked me if the clouds in the sky were the people who had gone to God"—this in a family where there is no attempt to inflict upon childhood any theological theory, gruesome or otherwise—"and at another time he said, 'Do you know what the stars are, mother? They're the lights God puts out so I won't be afraid of the dark.'"

To childhood the life within is one of the sure realities. Gretchen, thinking of clouds, says, very, very slowly,

> I see the white clouds floating low
> As though sheep in a meadow
>
> I see a man wave his crook
> In a deep blue shadow
>
> I see the house
> Where the shepherd lives

This, of course, is literature. What else? All the elements are here, rhythm, design, unique insight, and the perfect picturing of thought and feeling. Some of us have tried to teach these children language! They already possess a language adequate for all the purposes of their little lives, but we do not often discover it; nor do we always recognize it when it appears right before us.

In the high-school classes Sandy had begun suddenly to weave a strange pattern of words; it was, really of course, an old gift that had disappeared into the depths of personality until aroused and brought to the surface by a school environment which welcomed and paid high prices in social approval for genuine self-expression. He surprised himself, I think, for the voice of his inner spirit was unlike anything that he had ever sounded before, but he must have drawn strength and confidence from the delight of those around him; he seemed to grow visibly into manhood before me.

There was another result, however. I may be wrong in tracing it to Sandy, but I have always felt that the strong home interest in the boy's new development was caught up by the little brother Jack. In those confidential hours at eventide he began to talk to mother in a new way. One day she came to see me with the story of the awakening in Jack of a self-expression totally different from Sandy's but like Sandy's in that it was all his own.

Although it was winter and the family were in the city, Jack talked exactly as if he were back in the summer home, in his bed from which he could look out of a window.

Children, of course, do not give titles to these quiet pictures but when the mother wrote it out for me she called it

SUMMER LIGHTS

I love to see how many kinds of lights
I can find on a summer's night

I love the white spots of phlox
In the gardens
With the moon shining on them

I love the white spots of stars
Twinkling in the black sky

I love the white spots of fireflies
Sparkling
On the edge of the woods

And then, besides,
When my brother goes out to see that the
    chickens are in bed
I see his lantern
Bobbing in the garden

And when I go to bed
I like to see the light, way off in the woods,
That comes back from the windows
Of the old stone house

And, last of all,
I love my mother's candle light
On the little table
Beside her bed

Mothers have given us our best revelations of the creative spirit in the young. I pay my tribute here, as I have done elsewhere, to one mother who listened to the beautiful voice of the child artist and had the fine courage to give the result to all of us.* Hilda tells us much of the reality of that inner life when she says, in one of those quiet moments beside her mother,

> I have a secret from everybody in the world-full-of-people
> But I cannot always remember how it goes;
> It is a song
> For you, mother,
> With a curl of cloud and a feather of blue
> And a mist
> Blowing along the sky.
> If I sing it some day, under my voice,
> Will it make you happy?

II

Most of the speech of children that we hear is not their own language but an imitation of the forms, thought, and imagery of their elders. The adults who surround a young child go in eagerly for teaching their own speech; they ignore the native gift or drown it out with doggerel rhymes, set phrases, adult polite idiom, and verses and prose made for children by adults. School readers, Mother Goose, and books such as the exquisite *Child's Garden of Verses,* have their place in childhood education, but these excellent materials, wrongly used, may really deprive the child of certain valuable experiences in self-expression.

So children talk like their primers, saying "See the," for instance, an infantile idiom that is simply bookish to Americans whose phrase is "Look at that"—or they bang out bad rhymes that obstruct their clear and beautiful thinking, or they force their language into imitations of Robert Louis Stevenson. Now imitation, however excellent, is never art; and proof is ample that even very little children have a language of their own, the outcome of which is undoubtedly art.

For, notice in the illustrations already given that children speak naturally in a form that we adults are accustomed to call poetry and without any searching for appropriate use of the medium. That is because their mind is wholly intent upon something real within them; the language is instinctive and really of secondary consideration; they fashion it to the significant form exactly as other artists handle their medium, swiftly and without disturbing thoughts of standards outside

---

* *Poems by a Little Girl,* by Hilda Conkling (Stokes).

themselves. The child poet—without ever knowing that he is a poet—
"weaves to his song the music of the world and of the clouds," as little
Elizabeth so wisely phrased it when she wrote of

THE PIPER

The sun shines on the brook and makes it look like silver
And in a cave where the winds are all asleep
A piper plays a tune;
He weaves to his song the music of the world and of the clouds.

Elizabeth has other lines which I never read without thinking that
she, all unwittingly, is giving us the picture of the real voices of youth
which are lost because of the storms we elders set up in the name of
education!

The sun is leaving the heavens and the wind is waking
And the music of the piper
Is fading
Like a shadow

Only the artist may appreciate the work of an artist; and adults are
standardized persons without that gift of language that marks one's
speech as unique. Our chief aim—reflected in textbook and curriculum—
is to become expert copyists. We go to the length of studying the exact
phrase to use in the meeting of *any* friend ("How do you do!" we cry
out in unison, like a species of cuckoo!), or in writing *any* letter, be it
of affection or condolence; it is the public demand that has forced the
telegraph companies to supply us with the wording of the only seven
ways to express our congratulations or seasonal wishes!

Yet, sad thought, the unstudied naturalness of the early "poetry" of
childhood will thrive among those only who have ears to hear and judgment to approve. It is a terrible law of training that we shall have
whatever we approve. If our standards are conventional the artist child
in our care will surrender his most valued possession with hardly a mis-
giving. Only through constant exercise in a favoring environment will
the artist nature survive. The rare rebel, of course, is of different mold;
he fights and suffers but remains an artist, mainly, I often think, because he refuses to give up his gift of seeing and thinking and feeling
as a child.

III

Let me show how the literary gift was preserved and kept alive in
one school environment.

I had taken upon myself to find that lost personal voice of childhood in the eighth grade where usually, it is agreed, it has gone completely; Nell C. Curtis was finding it abundantly in the third grade.* Hardly a day passed in those early years that we did not contrive meetings to show each other this and that discovery of the strange, powerful speech which children rarely disclose to others but which they have "under their voice," as Hilda tells us so unerringly, "a secret from everybody in the world-full-of-people."

But one day she met me with disconsolate brows. I believe she had just come from an informal conference of teachers and parents. We walked along the halls in silence until she said with a kind of mournful humor, "They have called me—a gifted teacher!" It was an accusation, and she took it indignantly as she knew I would. That is the excuse they give for not finding what we experience daily. "Gifted teacher" always ended the argument, we knew, and sent them back with renewed strength to their everlasting struggle to make inartistic and conventional adults out of children. We hated the phrase.

"I want you to come with me," she said firmly, "right now; I am going into the third grade for about thirty minutes. I want you to stay with me and watch me, to see," she smiled, "if I have anything up my sleeve, any 'trick' that anyone else couldn't have."

I agreed to go and to watch. "Of course I know what I am going to get," she turned to say at the door. "Thanksgiving will soon be here. They will tell me about it—in their own way; and of course I know it will be good—because their own way is always good."

She walked in thoughtfully but did not once eye the class professionally or call it to attention. She seemed really to be looking out of the window while, musingly, she let fall the word Thanksgiving.

Then she wondered—really wondered—as if to herself, what she, Nell Curtis, should be thankful for. It was so well done, the simulation of genuine inquiry—so different from the conventional mastery of a class by means of the drawing-out question—that it took me completely off guard, stopped me in an awkward position in front of the group, where I had not meant to stay, and sent my mind wondering too; while one could almost feel the thinking going on in the little bodies before us.

Then she just said nothing at all, while she continued to gaze thoughtfully at the bare trees and grassy hummocks of Morningside Park. With the children who knew her she was not afraid of silence; rather she comprehended its great value for little bodies. They thought slowly; and, so great was the spell of the moment, I thought too.

I was thinking, I remember, how thankful I was that at last I had

* See her *Boats* by children of the third grade and their teacher, Nell C. Curtis (Rand McNally).

reached the age when I could afford to be honest with my own thinking; I was amusing myself with the thought that I no longer needed to try to be anything; that I could, for instance, cease trying to write and speak correct English, or even cease trying to be a gentleman; for, I was saying to myself, so long as one needed to *try* to be a gentleman, that was a sure sign that one wasn't one—when a boy spoke thoughtfully "under his voice"; and another followed, and another.

They were not using the accustomed speech, I noted instantly, that high-pitched monotone of children reciting before other children. They were conversing in the low, contented, slow-measured syllables of self-communion. Miss Curtis could do that to children; cause them to lose the conventional pose of being other than themselves—if that be a gift, make the most of it!—but I hasten to say that even she could not do it at the first meeting. Many previous hours had gone to make them accustomed to her; little by little, as she accepted (and so approved) the voice of their secret and seldom heard personality, they lost their fears of alien standards, strengthened the deep feeling of contentment with their own sure ways of speech. And then one day, as on this day, her casual appearance in the room would be a sign for the shy self to speak out.

She had moved so shadowlike to the blackboard that no one was disturbed; they continued to speak on slowly, with easy long silences in between, while, with her back to them, she scribbled an illegible shorthand of her own concealed from the children.

During the fifteen minutes or so that followed she never turned to face them. Once she grimaced over her arm to me, a brave attempt, I guessed, judging from my own feeling, to stay unaccountable tears; and then I turned my back too, for those mites would never understand how the simple beauty of their speech could affect us elders.

A whirr of buzzers off somewhere in the school and she stopped and moved quietly away from the board. "I shall need guards," she said. Two girls came forward understandingly and stood beside the welter of unintelligible chalk marks. In another moment someone appeared at the door, and the class filed out for the roof playground. The guards produced apples and munched them; they knew they were to keep watch over the blackboard until Miss Curtis could have time to get notebook and make a complete copy.

The next day, according to agreement, I went in to watch for "tricks." In clear manuscript writing Miss Curtis had placed all their statements on the board, naming the author in each case. Among repetitions they proceeded to choose the best; decided which should be combined with others; elided and amended here and there. Hardly a word from Miss

Curtis. In an exercise in taste she was not one to impose judgment. I wish I had space to record their quiet acquiescence or cool disagreement and final compromise.

Eventually, it became the following Hymn of Thanksgiving. The phrases are the work of children unaided by adult suggestion but, on account of time, the parts that belonged naturally together were combined and grouped by Miss Curtis and two other teachers, the whole being used by the third grade as their contribution to the Thanksgiving Assembly.

A HYMN OF THANKSGIVING

1

We give thanks for the beautiful country that lies around us
We give thanks for the grains and vegetables and fruits prepared for us
And we give thanks for the growing trees and flowers about us.

2

We give thanks for the rain that falls and the sun that shines down upon us
We thank God for the mountains that tower above and for the rocks that
    give us shelter and beauty
We give thanks for the sky above us and the earth below us and the birds
    that fly between earth and sky.

3

We give thanks for the cloth to make sails and the wood to make boats that
    sail on the water
We give thanks for the little streams that flow
We give thanks for the tide that rises and lets us go out in our boats
We give thanks for the sea with fishes in it
We thank God for all the living creatures on the earth.

4

We give thanks for the fire that warms us
We give thanks for warm clothes and beds and houses to live in
We give thanks for the schools to learn in.

5

We give thanks for the beauty and love all around us
We give thanks for all the things that the Lord has set upon the earth.

A week or so later in the elementary-school Thanksgiving Assembly, two tall candles burned at each end of the curtained stage, otherwise bare of ornament; a selected group from the third grade came up one by one and told us these their own words of thankfulness. It was powerfully effective, religious, if you will.

IV

Childhood will have no difficulty with literature if it has a chance to develop its own native gifts in language. This, of course, is not the whole story, but it is one of the most important chapters.

ADVENTURES WITH PUPPETS

SEVERAL summers ago, while walking down the Merceria in Venice, I noticed in a toy shop, a bunch of little puppets dangling by their heads. They were gayly dressed in the costumes of the characters of the classic Italian comedies and were offered at the attractive price of seven cents each. I purchased the entire company and it has reposed in a cupboard of the school studio and has been exhumed occasionally to illustrate various pieces of literature. The exhumations have always been accompanied with exclamations of "Aren't they darling?" from the girls and "Do they work?" from the boys. Of course they are darling and they don't work, being of the most primitive construction, the only string being attached to an eyelet in the top of the head. At the writing of this article, they are no more, having been literally used to death but they have left behind dozens of descendants and a method of playwriting which has seemed to me quite unusual and that may prove interesting to others.

The classes that originated the method were two groups of boys and girls, one group averaging ten years and the other twelve. In the ten-year group, boys predominated and in the other, girls. They discovered the puppets and immediately asked if they could have a show. The teacher, being in a constructive mood, built and painted a gaudy proscenium and presented the children with show-card colors, tag board, a box of scraps of colored cloth, wire, porcelain bases, plugs and bulbs, and told them to go to it. The result was a bitter war between the boys and the girls. The girls were all for doing a play about a princess and the boys wanted one about pirates, in spite of the fact that none of the puppets resembled pirates in the slightest degree. All attempts at arbitration failed and the result is that the studio is the home and workshop of four rival producing companies.

At first each company divided into committees, one for costumes, one for lighting, one for scenery, and the last chosen to write the play. The whole company outlined the play in general so as to know what scenes were to be needed, and how many characters used. The costumers, scene painters, and electricians set busily to work while the literary members sat in the corner racking their brains and watching the other workers with envious eyes. The puppets were immediately disintegrated, heads were switched, blond hair was painted black, costumes were exchanged, and new ones made. Finally the completion of scenery, costumes, and lighting was announced and the writers were ordered to produce the play. It was produced, a version of "The Sleeping Beauty."

AUNTIE KATUSHKA DISCOVERS ANDREWSHEK BOUNCING ON HIS FEATHER
BED INSTEAD OF SLEEPING

ANDREWSHEK REMONSTRATES WITH THE WHITE GOAT FOR RUNNING AWAY

ONE OF THE REHEARSALS

GIVING THE SHOW FOR SOME OF THE KINDERGARTEN

FINISHING THE MARIONETTE THEATER

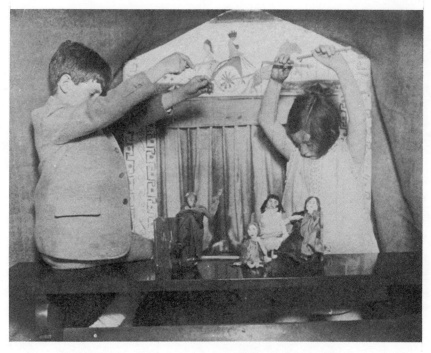

MANIPULATING ONE OF THE SCENES IN HADES

SOME OF THE PUPPETS AND THE PAINTED CURTAIN
DEPICTING THE FATE OF THE PICNIC BASKET

THE PUPPETEERS AND THE ANIMALS THEY MADE

The manuscript was quite imposing, but the actual reading of the five scenes occupied less than three minutes. After stormy discussion, the company rejected the play on the grounds that the waits between scenes would be longer than the actual scenes themselves. The playwrights asked to be allowed to make up the play as they went along, the point being that they had plenty of ideas but it took so long to write them down. This was considered fair enough so the opus went into rehearsal. Each rehearsal found the play growing more and more elaborate as to lines. The principal puppeteers, being protected from stage fright by a curtain, grabbed the center of the stage and held it as long as possible. Finally the craft members rebelled and demanded healthy pruning. To do this, the thing had to be put on paper, so it was written, edited, re-rehearsed, and so our first original play was born. It was tried out on the kindergarten with great success, then performances were given for forms one and two, and as they seemed to enjoy it, the other forms were included, until now audiences are drawn from the entire school including the faculty. Needless to say, "The Sleeping Beauty" was a feminine production. The boys had already started a pirate play and as the girls had monopolized all the puppets, they made some of their own, constructing wire armatures such as sculptors use, padding them with paper and cloth and dressing them in crude but effective pirate costumes. They learned by observation and did not commit their play to paper until after the first performance.

Since then we have proceeded gayly, our productions are becoming more and more elaborate and our kind audiences—we prefer the kindergartners because they always laugh in the right places and become absolutely terror stricken at the cap-pistol shots—are becoming more and more enthusiastic. The girls stick to stories containing a princess who absolutely must have golden hair. Long descriptions of things are considered quite smart and a little chaste love making is allowed. The boys on the other hand are all for action and they prefer plays without feminine characters. All of our puppets are frightfully modest and go about simply buried in elaborate clothing. In our masculine plays pirates are the first choice, Robin Hood second, and characters from the newspaper comic strips, third.

The school considers the experiment successful for quite a number of reasons. It was initiated by the children, it provides a creative outlet, is a good means of giving instruction in diction, develops imagination, encourages teamwork, and is unlimited in subject matter.

At the present time we have produced "The Sleeping Beauty," "Aladdin," two pirate plays, a play about Robin Hood and one about Krazy Kat. To those interested it might be well to give some idea of the equipment. The proscenium frame has an opening of three by four feet, the lighting is taken care of by a row of foots and an overhead flood over which gelatine screens can be placed. The curtains are of brocade running on a curtain rod and are operated by hand. The whole thing is set in an opening of the regular stage curtain. The puppets are about eight inches in height. As the object of the experiment is to get the original play from the children, we have not gone in for the construction of elaborate and beautifully made puppets. Realism has no place in our scheme, and if a man wants to shoot a dozen people with one cap, it is allowed. In closing I should like to confess that I really cannot say who is enjoying the experiment the most, the pupils, the audiences, or the teacher.

L. YOUNG CORRETHERS.

THE puppet idea, on this particular occasion, flashed out of a clear sky, with no warning other than the fact that a number of interesting puppet shows had recently been given in the city and some of the children in a certain third grade had been introduced to puppets for the first time.

At the outset the idea was vague, intangible, and refused to be crystallized into definite thought. But, finally, the crucial day arrived when the important decision was to be made. For some in the group this was to be simply another interesting school event, full of fun and frolic, but to others it was destined to develop and unfold within themselves imagination and creative ability to a degree hitherto undreamed of. An experience was to be lived through, the warmth and afterglow of which was to remain with them as long as they should live.

The final decision, actually to produce a puppet play, came at the end of a reading hour when Marsden closed his book and remarked that the story just finished would make a fine play. Soon after this a group conference favorably voted upon Marsden's suggestion. Directly the following committees were appointed:

> Story Committee
> Purchasing Committee
> Building Committee
> Properties Committee
> Publicity Committee

The idea now quickly took shape and form. All vagueness of thought was dissipated. Constructive thinking and creative imagination grew by leaps and bounds as the plans unfolded. There seemed to be no dearth of suggestions as to what might be done, but only a question of eliminating all but the most helpful and those pertinent to the success of the undertaking.

Before recommending the book suggested by Marsden as best adapted to their needs and purposes, the Story Committee read others, always bearing in mind the limitations of a small puppet stage and the desire for interest and effect. Many heated discussions ensued as to the relative merits of more than a dozen stories. Advocates for one or another warmly discussed the arguments in favor of their choice and sought to convince the remainder of the committee as to its value and worth. At no time during the progress of the undertaking was better thinking done or discussion held more rigidly to the subject at hand, than just at this point. However, after all the evidence had been weighed and measured, Marsden's original suggestion, "The Poppy Seed Cakes," stood approved, because it seemed to furnish the best material from which to make a puppet play.

The story was read and reread many times until the different characters became living personalities. Russian folklore and pictures of Russian peasants in striking, gay costumes at once became source material from which to get helpful suggestions.

Two boys in the group so caught the spirit and atmosphere of "The Poppy Seed Cakes" that they wrote additional episodes to those already in the book. These proved to be so full of dramatic possibilities and interest that they were at once accepted by the group and incorporated into the puppet play.

The next step in the evolution of the play was to secure the coöperation of two special teachers, namely, the art teacher and the shop man. It would be impossible to overestimate the kindly, sympathetic understanding with which these experts responded to the children's invitation. As advisers, they were always eager to carry out the wishes and plans of the group, following their lead and offering suggestions only when needed. They not only supplemented the children's knowledge and skill with their own but they contributed something even finer and more inspiring. It was the genuine interest which they found in the work and joy in the undertaking which made for unity of purpose and a fine *esprit de corps* between teacher and child. In fact, the art teacher developed such enthusiasm over the play that when an enforced absence for a number of weeks became necessary, she was delighted to learn that the children had voluntarily delayed the completion of their work until she should return.

Meanwhile the Building Committee was busily concerned with the puppet stage. Before beginning its construction an excursion was made to see one that had been already finished and set up. The dimensions of this theater were taken as well as other data which seemed likely to be helpful later on. Requisitions for wood, beaver board, hinges, and angle irons were then immediately passed on to the Purchasing Committee. These demands had been somewhat anticipated by this committee and consequently there was no delay in assembling the building materials ready for use.

The actual building of the stage lasted for several weeks. Much ingenuity was exhibited by different members of the group in adding labor-saving devices such as hooks, shelves, and lights for the convenience of the puppeteers later on. The theater when completed was painted and then decorated with the silhouettes of the various characters in the play. With this the work of the Building Committee was finished.

If the children at work upon the stage seemed to show increasing ability to meet difficult situations and overcome them, even so to a greater degree did the members of the group who were engaged in making the puppets, the house, fence, animals, and other properties. They knew that their puppets were to be gignols, but how should they be made, that was the question. Celluloid dolls were suggested. These were purchased at the five-cent store. The heads were cut off and used as foundations for paper pulp which was easily molded into such features as the children desired. This was accomplished with admirable success. A hunt was then instituted for suitable materials, sufficiently bright in color with which to clothe Andrewshek and his Auntie Katushka in a manner appropriate to their nationality. The final gay and festive effect could not have been more strikingly typical of a Russian peasant woman and her small nephew if in some mysterious manner they had been suddenly transported from the mother country especially for the occasion.

With the theater completed, it was a silent reminder that the property makers should hurry with their part of the program. It was, indeed, a happy day when the first experimental play was begun. As if by magic a pasteboard hat-box was quickly converted into Andrewshek's house and the various animals sprang to life from some odd bits of beaver board. Day after day this preliminary play went on with different children manipulating the puppets and choosing their own conversation. By this time all the members of the group had become thoroughly saturated with the story. They had lived so long with Andrewshek and Auntie Katushka that they knew exactly what each would do in any situation. Never was any particular part of the play learned verbatim. The spirit, general plot, and most important episodes always remained the same, but each time it was given, something new was evolved, and an unexpected interest was always sure to be introduced. For that reason the children never tired of the thrilling "Adventures of Andrewshek."

Finally, Christmas was approaching and this particular group of children wished to assume its share of responsibility in helping to provide a Christmas celebration for the little children in one of the city's day nurseries. They determined to give a performance of the "Adventures of Andrewshek" and charge a small admission to the other members of the school and their friends. Accordingly, this was done, and through the efficient efforts of the Publicity and the Ticket Committees, the net proceeds accruing from the play were sufficient to fill to overflowing the stocking candy bags for the nursery children.

The Museum of Art in our city provides Saturday afternoon programs for children. Late in the winter the puppet theater manager was invited by the Museum, to give another performance of the "Adventures of Andrewshek." This was done with the same freshness and joy as had characterized the previous productions. The play met with favor; the youthful audience applauded loudly, and at the end of the performance made the special request that Andrewshek's episode at the circus be repeated. Behind the scenes at that point, the following remark was overheard, "I hope they don't expect us to repeat it exactly as we gave it before for we never do it twice alike, you see." So it may be seen that from the beginning the puppet play furnished rich opportunity for a fine type of free oral expression. It was always interesting and childlike but at the same time rich in content and full of meaning.

Never once did interest flag during the many weeks of preparation, even though scores of discouraging events conspired to thwart and disrupt the children's plans.

It would be extremely difficult to estimate accurately just what this rich experience contributed to the lives of those children, for who of us can tabulate or measure the far-reaching results of work well done, carried on through many happy days, filled with the joy of achievement?

However, there were some more or less tangible results, quite apparent and worthy of note. These were listed as the puppet theater was folded away and Andrewshek and Auntie Katushka passed on to their reward.

Question: What did the children get out of the Puppet Show experience?

Arithmetic:

Experience with actual money.
  Many different kinds of money.
  Counting receipts.
  Simple bookkeeping.
  Selling tickets.
Measuring and counting tickets.

Geography:

Something about Russia, its location, peasant life, and mode of dress.

English:

Many stories read before one was found suitable for puppets.

Poppy Seed Cakes read and reread. Careful selective reading done to choose the best parts of the story for the play.

Written English:
Original adventures were written.
Ordering committee wrote requisitions for all materials bought.

Excursion:
To see another Puppet Theater.

Shop Man's Coöperation:
Much measuring.
Use of many tools.
Actual building of the puppet theater.

Handcraft:
Sewing—puppet clothes, bed coverlet.
Making of properties:
Beaverboard furniture.
Beaverboard animals.
Cardboard house and small properties.
Clay properties.
Paper tickets.
Making of pulp for puppet heads.

Art:
Commercial advertising, posters.
Scenery and background for the acts.

Writing:
Printed matter on the posters.
Copy for the mimeograph.
Letter written to the Museum.

Organization:
Committees appointed—Story, ordering, building, properties, puppet making, ticket, publicity, puppeteers.

Social and Intellectual Gain:
Genuine interest in story writing.
Rich content and atmosphere.
Excellent thinking manifested in planning and organizing.
Ingenuity developed.
Imagination strengthened.
Division of labor when many worked together.
Much weighing of judgments and discrimination shown.
Joy in the work.
Joy in service for others (Day Nursery).
Recognition of individual abilities.
Perseverance (Lion was made five times).

Fine spirit of coöperation.

Unusual amount of initiative shown.

Sustained purpose. Interest carried over a long period of time.

Satisfaction in success attained in the face of many difficulties.

Steadiness and poise when appearing before a large number of people.
Lack of self-consciousness because of greater interest and absorption in the work itself.

EVA LOUISE WILDE.

AT A recent Parents-and-Teachers meeting, the children of the seventh year presented a puppet show, using as their motif their own adaptation of the well-beloved Pinocchio story. The children of the group had taken a trip to hear Tony Sarg describe the mysteries of the puppet stage. This stimulated in them the desire to make their own puppets and on their return to the studio enthusiasm to organize their own puppet show pervaded the entire group.

Their interest manifested itself first in a natural curiosity to learn how and where and under what circumstances puppet shows had been presented in the past. We learned how in other countries in other times and in other climes puppet shows were presented amid varied surroundings. In China and Japan of ancient days, in the Italy of the Middle Ages, and from there, together with the other cultural revivals of the period known as the Renaissance, puppet shows spread throughout Europe. In America, too, the Indians used articulated dolls during their ceremonial dances.

After some discussion the children chose Pinocchio as the subject of their puppet show. In their English periods, they worked out and adapted the dialogue to suit their purpose; namely, to keep the play simple and within their capabilities. Each puppeteer selected his own character and set about the creating of his own puppet. The puppeteers had studied their characters and decided just what they ought to look like. They made their working drawings. With these they went to the pottery room to model the heads and then to the shop to make the jointed body, later to various stores where they bought material for the costumes, and to other sources for wigs, shoes, buckles, and so on. Into this creation went many, many elements: appreciation of color, of proportion; mechanical smoothness of execution; strict adherence to detail; efficiency on the practical side; and a conviction on the part of the child that success is possible only through sustained concentration and application to the work in hand. The accompanying diagrams are reproductions of some of the children's preliminary sketches and give an idea of the amount of detailed work necessary even in the early stage of the project.

The children toiled manfully, loyally, conscientiously, and through it all, joyously. They lived in this happy atmosphere for a period of nearly three months, during which time they enjoyed the rare pleasure of seeing painstaking efforts result in successful achievements. They tasted the joy of the artist in contemplating the object of his creation.

It wasn't all smooth sailing. In the attempt to overcome their obstacles and their difficulties, they faced many real problems. These problems, however, were not so difficult but that thinking and planning overcame them. How to get the proper designs and costumes; how to get wigs

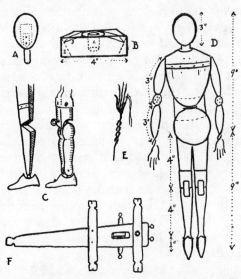

A, Head showing cardboard tacked to doweling and cloth stuffed with cotton sewn over it. *B*, Shoulder-piece; *1*, hole to mount head. *2*, side cut off. *3*, whittled down. *C*, Legs showing jointing. *D*, Showing head attached to shoulder piece; cloth tacked on wood to form body. *E*, Fingers of hand, made of wire. *F*, Controller to which working strings are attached.

to fit the various-shaped heads; how to procure the proper lighting effects; how to control the strings of the puppets: to solve these questions, and a myriad others, called for much sustained effort. While some of these solutions to problems were quaint and comical (such as cutting one's own hair for the puppets' wigs), in larger terms these situations made for the development of fine coördination, for appreciation of what goes on behind the scenes on the real stage, and for dexterity in the simultaneous use of hand, eye, ear, memory, and speech.

It is the natural desire of the craftsman to use and play with his handiwork; to put life, as it were, into his creations; so, too, our little craftsmen took upon themselves the rôles of puppeteers and in their guild worked toward the common goal of seeing how their puppets could talk, live, and act with each other in a puppet show. The educational forces of the studio, the pottery room, the kiln, and the classroom were augmented now by the use of the stage.

To some of the children whose dramatic instincts had hitherto been dormant, the new rôle of puppeteer brought a strong challenge to rise to greater heights, so that they could most fully express all the quaintness and charm of their created work. For the others who had already been successful in dramatic expression, this new medium had a stronger appeal than anything that had ever been done by them before. The usual things staged by children or adults aim to dramatize some character created by another, while here the situation meant dramatizing the character created by the actor; the little artist was living and acting through his own creation.

The audience, too, senses this unique appeal of the puppet show in contrast to other forms of the drama. Indeed, who can fail to be charmed with the puppet—its quaintness, its absurdity, its exaggerated gestures, its refreshing simplicity, its uncanny power of being almost human, and its bewildering knack of apparently doing so many things that it really does not do. It would be fatal to leave one's imagination at home when going to see a puppet show. In this instance, the parents responded to the universal appeal of the puppet show by enjoying it as whole-heartedly as the children.

Staging our play presented an entirely new project involving innumerable details. The scenery, lighting effects, costumes, properties, and all the other necessary appendages to the staging of a dramatic production required patient and conscientious attention. Committees chosen from the class were held responsible for the various phases of the work and the children's own stage manager supervised all the details. The counsel of the art director was sought only when an immediate situation seemed to be technically insurmountable. Throughout this period the status of the art director was that of pilot or adviser in chief. The children did the work and solved their problems with many startlingly original and excellent suggestions, so that ultimately, in overcoming the obstacles through real thinking and planning, they derived the deserved satisfaction of those who see a piece of difficult work carried through to a successful conclusion. This result is, of course, one of the basic aims in the learning process. The marionette stage, it is true, is entertaining; but just to be entertaining is not sufficient reason for giving a puppet show in a school.

It behooves the educator to take an inventory at the conclusion of a project and record, as far as he can, the concrete evidence of gain to the children in terms of mental, social, and esthetic growth. We know definitely that concentration, perseverance, loyalty to the task, necessary social coöperation, all resulted in good habit formation. We know, too, that the need for muscular coördination, the handling of various tools, the construction of stage properties, the modeling, painting, experimenting with colors and designs, resulted in increased skill and keener esthetic appreciation. Then, too, working with and for others, planning together, and mutual appreciation of tasks well done, resulted in finer social concepts.

To appreciate fully just what was accomplished would require a searching appraisal of all that this project meant to the children who participated and to the group, as a group. No written or oral report can adequately record all the elements that went into the piece of work. We must content ourselves with the justifiable conclusion that this project was a definite and long stride in the general direction of a many-sided, well-rounded development in child growth, and a keener and deeper understanding and appreciation of the good, the true, and the beautiful in the world about him.

Rose Khourie.

This puppet play had its genesis in Child Labor Day. The boys and girls in the fourth grade of the Ethical Culture Branch School decided to raise some money to send to the Committee on Child Labor. After all sources of income had been examined, the idea of giving a play and charging admission remained as the most attractive and surest way of getting the money. Then came the idea of a puppet play, and actually making everything that was to be used, even the puppets, which eventually were made in the form of marionettes controlled by strings.

Searching for material for their play, the children came upon Jenny Hall's *Four Old Greeks*, Hawthorne's *Wonder Book* and Kingsley's *Greek Heroes*, which were conveniently at hand in the classroom library. After many stories had been read, they finally selected *The Pomegranate Seed*.

Earlier in the year the class had dramatized *Alice in Wonderland*, following as nearly as possible the actual forms from the book, the scenes, the conversations, even the colors and designs of the costumes. So in the new piece of group work it was especially desirable to encourage something more original instead of depending upon material already formulated.

Many versions of the story selected were written by each child, and the final draft was arranged from this material by those especially interested in completing it.

After the stories had been written and the important incidents grouped sequentially into six scenes, the children met in small groups to reread and discuss them. Such lines as, "I am Mother Demeter, who looks after the grain and harvest," and "I am Persephone who looks after the flowers," became the one speech for Persephone. "You have to be away and work all day, attending to the harvest, and insuring people their breakfast cereals while I have only the care of the flowers." Not content to have Persephone alone register her grief, the servant in Hades was given these lines, "I wonder why this fair maiden is not happy," and "Why dost thou weep, beautiful Persephone?" When Pluto ordered the servant to bring "rich dainties" he helpfully suggested, "Your Majesty, how about pies?" To which Pluto replied, "Fine, bring the best the cook can make." But Persephone, having been correctly reared, refused the food, saying, "My mother would never allow me to eat such rich desserts."

Several visits to the Metropolitan Museum with the art teacher to sketch figures and designs from vases and other exhibits suggested ideas for original Greek designs which were used on the costumes and in the decoration of the theater. Greek influence spread to each department in the school, as experiments with the theater, the puppets, and their costumes continued. In this way the study of Greek life, usually included in the year's work, was developed through the medium of a puppet show.

The work of making the puppets was carried on experimentally. Three girls, after working unsuccessfully in the shop on wooden puppets with cloth joints, resorted to a marionette of cloth after a model discovered by one of them in a current magazine. They dressed her up as Persephone and put her on display before the group, who chose her as a model for the women of the cast. A wooden model with modolith head appeared later for the men. Those who wanted to sew made the women, and those wanting to saw made the men.

The standards of work of different children varied widely. One boy quite early in the work came into the shop, hurriedly sawed out a small doll, found a pasteboard box, and collecting an audience of some third-grade children made a crude play for them. Working at the same bench with this youngster was another who sawed and filed and sandpapered, examined minutely, and filed again, and before he showed his results to anyone had a marionette body with arms and groove for the head, the joints neatly fitted and ingeniously devised.

The two boys who volunteered to make the theater thought up some elaborate devices which they discarded in favor of simpler schemes as the work developed. A third boy, who joined them when anything especially pleasant was going to be done, added his critical voice and found flaws everywhere. To this, one of the original workmen constantly retorted, "Oh, the proscenium will cover that all right," and these words became the catchwords for the entire work.

To avoid the use of any complicated system of shifting scenery, the children ingeniously made two curtains in the form of "cycs," and tacked them around the back, one on top of the other. The top curtain was blue, representing the scenes on earth, the curtain underneath was black, and was used for all the Hades numbers. When the characters descended, the top curtain was just turned over the back like turning the page of a tablet and the other scene was revealed. In the last scene painted flowers on a long cardboard were pulled across the back of the stage to make realistic Demeter's words, "Didn't I command that nothing should grow until I find my daughter, and more and more flowers are growing?"

The crafts teacher directed the general discussion of colors and fabrics and had samples of many colors and types of material. The colors ranged from pale yellow, green, and lavender chiffon for the sea nymphs, through orangey pink georgette for Persephone, autumn golds and brown crêpe for Demeter, gray and silver silk for Hermes, to purple and gold for Pluto, with the servant in a green velvet chiton over an undergarment of tan to hide his joints.

While the puppets were being made in the shop, there sprang up entirely without prearrangement a complete set of furniture just their size, a unique little throne carved and decorated, tables, chairs, stools, couches, and bookcases. Shields and crossed swords were made for the background. The servant in Hades alone benefited by the chairs. He slept a good deal, too. This seemed to be a part of his character, for the moment attention left him, he slumped and nodded and looked sound asleep.

Pluto was by far the favorite doll and the most versatile. His dramatic possibilities were limitless. He took on a different character at each performance, a courtly gentleman at the hand of one lad, and a cunning scoundrel when another pulled the strings. The sea nymphs waved realistically, and Demeter's head and right arm seemed to be her principal means of expression. Hermes in flight, equipped with his silver wings, sounded and looked very like an aeroplane.

Beginning as one group, the organization changed gradually from group to individual or small group work until rehearsals began when the whole class worked together for a time, then divided into two casts, each of which gave two complete performances of the play. The stage manager worked with both groups, looked after all the properties, set the stage, and drew the curtains.

The original purpose of the play, to raise money, was soon lost sight of in the interest of production, which took so long that the contribution for child labor had to be brought from home, and the play was finally given at the close of the year for the parents and the various groups of children in the school. IDA RHEA PEARSON.

A SELECTED BIBLIOGRAPHY ON PUPPETS

ANDERSON, MADGE—The Heroes of the Puppet Stage. Harcourt, Brace & Company.
> Descriptive matter on puppets. Exhaustive bibliography.

BUFANO, REMO—The Show Book of Remo Bufano. Illustrated by the author. Macmillan, 1929.
> Seven plays for marionettes and how to stage them.

CHUBB, PERCIVAL and OTHERS—Festivals and Plays in Schools. Harper and Brothers.
> Although written in 1912 this still remains one of the richest source books on playmaking in schools.

GRANDGENT, CHARLES HALL (Editor)—Punch and Judy. Illustrated. Washburn and Thomas.
> Follows the version of the puppet play now more than a century old. Cruikshank.

GRIMBALL, ELIZABETH and WELLS, RHEA—Costuming a Play. Century.
> Directions for making and dyeing costumes followed by a series of historic costume plates.

JASSPON, ETHEL, and BECKER, BEATRICE—Ritual and Dramatized Folkways. Century.
> "A source book for creative people." Scenes from Japanese life, Russian folk lore, French ballads, Bible stories. Designed to fill the need for simple, direct dramatic material suitable for school, camp, settlement or club.

JOSEPH, HELEN HAIMAN—Ali Baba and Other Plays for Young People or Puppets. Harcourt, Brace & Company.
> Three plays and brief directions for giving them.

McISAACS, F. J.—The Tony Sarg Marionette Book. Viking Press.
> How to make marionettes and two plays from home-made marionettes.

MILLS, WINIFRED, and DUNN, LOUISE—Marionettes, Masks and Shadows. Doubleday, Page Company.
> A beautiful and comprehensive book just published, giving a wealth of information for every phase of puppet making. Pictures of actual puppet plays.

MITCHELL, ROY—The School Theater. Brentano's.
> Costuming, make-up, stage lighting, scene building and painting.

PETTEY, EMMA—The Puppet as an Elementary Project. Pioneer Publishing Company, Fort Worth, Texas.
> This looks like a very useful little book for a teacher. Relates the puppet show to actual school-room activities for making and working mario-

nettes. Suggestions for Musicians of Bremen, Little Black Sambo, and other favorites as puppet plays.

PLIMPTON, EDNA—Your Workshop. Macmillan Company.

This is an attractive little book very simply written, designed for children, giving directions for making boats, toys, etc. Chapters on puppets and marionettes.

ROSE, A.—The Boy Showman and Entertainer. E. P. Dutton & Company.

Another new book giving directions and practical suggestions for putting on marionette shows, peep shows, and shadow pictures.

SMITH, ANDRE—The Scenewright. Macmillan Company.

The making of stage models and settings described in detail. Five chapters on scene painting and stage furnishings.

STEWART, MARY—The Land of Punch and Judy. Fleming H. Revell Company.

Punch and Judy and several other puppet shows.

STODDARD, ANNE, and SARG, TONY—A Book of Marionette Plays. Greenberg.

Contains five plays.

CHILDREN'S EXPERIMENTS IN LANGUAGE

Lucy Sprague Mitchell

CHILDREN are born into a talking world. Language as a fully evolved adult activity greets them and follows them in a peculiarly pertinacious way. Probably there is no other elaborate and perfected adult performance which they are so early urged to share. For adults are continuously hammering even at infants, trying to make them "understand" language and rejoicing when they take on adult forms of speech or adult attitudes towards language. One of the commonest measures of maturity used unconsciously by parents and consciously by psychologists is the degree to which children have taken on adult forms of language. And there is no gainsaying that it *is* a measure of one sort of maturity. The degree to which a child uses the sentence, for instance, or any grammatical structure, measures his receptivity along this particular line of stimulus. Receptivity is a part, and an important part, of the maturing process in language as in other performances. But it is by no means the whole of the process. Though the stage is not set for experimentation in language so far as the attitude of adults is concerned, yet we find ample evidence of the experimental attack here as in all activities in which children take part. This experimental aspect of activities in general has received many names according to the value placed upon it by the interpreting observer. Some call it "creative" or "dynamic," some call it "art," some call it "play," some call it "practicing." Children's early experiments in sounds and language occasionally are dignified by these names, but more often called "babbling" or "nonsense." I prefer to avoid the connotation which these names bring up and to designate such efforts in language merely as "experimental."

It is this experimental attack on language that I want to illustrate. And I must be content if I do nothing more than show that children do spontaneously experiment with language. I have drawn my illustrations from any recorded speech ready to hand—some from my own children, some from children in the Nursery School of the Bureau of Educational Experiments, some from the City and Country School, a number from scattered published sources. I do not believe that these illustrations are the average language of children of the ages represented (twenty-three months to nine years). But I believe them to be the language of average children. I have neither the time nor the ability to make an intensive scientific analysis of these illustrations. But certain outstanding characteristics are easily noticed.

In the first place, early experiments with the speech mechanisms have little or nothing to do with conveying ideas. Whatever the urge, it is not the urge to communicate. If we go back to the stage before infants have any idea that the flow of sounds with which they are surrounded is "language" in our sense of the word, we find them making sounds of their own in a fashion quite independent of the talking adults around them. Very likely their own first experiments are purely muscular and the sound produced is a by-product so to speak. It does not matter. The point is that this laryngeal activity is carried on for its own sake and not as a means to an end. It is interesting to note that Piaget thinks 47 per cent of the language of the six-year-olds he studied was still egocentric—that is, required no audience or at any rate no response. It was not genuine "communication."

In the second place, the young child seems to get satisfaction from his sound productions, just as he seems to get satisfaction from his kicking or other experimental use of his body. I know that those who are chary of interpretation must disregard this point since the data are not objective. But I for one cannot even read the babies' remarks in the Nursery School, for example, divorced as they are from the situations which occasioned them and divested of the gusto with which they were uttered, without being convinced that the children were getting something out of their utterance over and above the content value. Indeed, for some years the fun of talking seems to be a more dominant urge than the desire to communicate. The six-year-olds whom Piaget studied had taken over much of the structure of adult language. Yet in half their language no aim was evident beyond the pleasure of the activity.

In the third place, early language takes place during activity. A two-year-old tends to say what he is doing as he is doing it. This tendency appears in Piaget's six-year-olds as well.* Whether such speech which announces the action as it is performed heightens or reënforces the experience, or whether it indicates low degree of inhibition so that the word associated with the action comes out more or less automatically, I cannot say. A fourth characteristic of much of this talk-to-oneself suggests an intensification of experience, but whether speech is the cause or effect I do not know. I mean its rhythmic character. Even the "pre-speech" nonsense syllables are very often rhythmic. This should not be surprising. The infant's leg activities are rhythmic. Why should not his

---

* *The Language and Thought of the Child*, by Jean Piaget. Harcourt, Brace & Company.

laryngeal activity be rhythmic? Practically every activity that Miss Johnson has recorded of the babies in the Nursery School is at times performed rhythmically and at times is accompanied by rhythmic sounds.
Children tend to rhythmic expression in all their activities. They repeat
themselves. And repetition is the simplest form of a pattern. Run
through the illustrations looking for pattern irrespective of ideas con-
veyed. Can we not trace a maturing in the technique of experimentation
as evidenced by the elaboration of the patterns? "Giddy, giddy," example 1, at twenty-four months and "Rain," example 24, at nine years,
have a common element. "Giddy, giddy," is a very immature pattern
as we should expect from the general immaturity of twenty-four months.
"Rain" is a pattern mature even for nine years. This nine-year-old boy
was unusually sensitive to word pattern. In this stanza, for instance, he
originally wrote the gutters were "full." But as he remarked "That
word didn't go with gutters. A barrel could be full, but a gutter would
be running." It was the rhythm and the sound quality of the words that
he was pursuing rather than their meaning. In the same way, the three-
year-old in example 8 was in the grip of a pattern rather than in the
grip of an idea and when no idea came to him to complete his pattern,
he improvised with pure sound and was content. The maturity of example 23 cannot be measured exclusively by the extent to which adult
structure of language has been taken over or the efficiency of the language as a tool for communication of ideas. We have here a maturity
in pattern not measured by language tests and not taken into the reckon-
ing of most grown-ups. This kind of language maturity is not due to
receptivity—to the taking over of adult forms. Rather it is due to experimentation. I know of no way of answering the question why a child
experiments with sounds and later with language except in terms of
his other activities. He seems to be an experimenting animal. Experimentation seems to be the method by which the complex organism
called a human child grows. He lies on his back and experiments with
his leg muscles. He experiments with his back muscles until he rolls
over. He experiments with leg, arm, and back muscles until he creeps.
He experiments again and he walks. So in his experiments in language
I believe we can trace the maturing of certain spontaneous language
forms which seem to proceed along their own lines in some kind of
rough age progression.

There is still another—a fifth—characteristic of the early language
of children which these quotations illustrate. The reports of children
have the first-hand ring. Children report in terms of actual sense or
motor experiences, not in terms of the generalized or the inferred. For
example, the ordinary adult, when he looks out into the darkened world,
says, "The sun has set"—an intellectual observation based on memory

of a past condition, not a report of what is in front of him. A four-year-old confronted with this situation once said to me, "The big shadow is all around." That is a statement of the Homeric order—direct, sensory, first-hand. It is a child's native method of speech.

I have saved the quotations to put them together as a group. The characteristics seem to jump out when the quotations are read one after the other. I have not attempted to place these particular quotations in a general language study. Nor have I tried to weigh rhythmic language as compared to language for communication at any given age or for a particular child. These are many quotations chosen more or less at random to illustrate (1) that children talk to themselves without need of response; (2) that they seem to get satisfaction from such use of language; (3) that they talk what they act; (4) that much of their speech is rhythmic, often to the point of genuine patterns; and (5) that they report their observations in direct, concrete, sense or motor terms.

Harriet M. Johnson has let me take illustrations for the youngest children from her book, *Children in the Nursery School*, published by the John Day Company. The following are excerpts from her records:

1. Geordie, 24 months

"Giddy, giddy, giddy"—repeated seven or more times back and forth, from chute to slide steps.
"Demme, dem-me, dem-me."
Laughed over the top: "Dub-dee, dub-dee, dub-dee."
Then, "Wuh, wuh, wuh," "Duh, duh, duh," a throaty sound.
As he ran, "Bee, bee, bee: lee, lee, lee: Dub, dub, dub."

Miss Johnson adds that usually there were more than the three repetitions she has given.

2. The same child at 27 months stood at top of the slide chute, a hand on either post swinging the left leg out, and in a deep throaty voice chanted, "ma-wee, ma-wa, ma-wee, ma-wee, A-a."
These are genuine, if embryonic, sound patterns.

3. Matthew, 27 months

"Dee dee doo dee, scrap a row, scrap a row, scrap a row, scrap a row," chanted with no apparent reference to activity.
Seized a wooden peg from the settle, and beating the air with it, chanted: "Wing a dong ding, wing a dong ding."

4. Jean at 25 months stood at a low table with a scoop and a little pan containing a few pebbles and said, "Shavoo" (shovel) twenty-two times in succession. Tipped stones out of the pan saying, "Stones, stones, stones," etc. Picked them up and put them back saying ten times, "Put it in, put it in." Spilled some water: "Spill it. Wipe it."

5. One day an adult was speaking to Rab of the approaching taxi trip and said, "Soon we'll go bumpety bump to your house." Frieda Mac, at her table drinking her milk, set down her mug, and eyeing the adult solemnly, delivered herself as follows:

> Bumpety bump to *my* house,
> To *my* mamma,
> To *my* daddy,
> To *my* ba-lamb,
> To *my* table,
> To *my* chair.

The pattern is approaching a stanza.

6. Carter at 26 months charmed us by this lilting refrain apropos the Nursery equipment:

> We've got just *one* cariole at home,
> And that's *all*,
> We've got just *one* waste basket at home,
> And that's *all*.
> We've got just *one* kiddy kar at home,
> And that's all.
> And that's broke.

This was delivered in a monotone except for the "one" which was chanted on a higher note, and emphasized each time.

7. Caroline at 37 months was throwing and chasing a ball. She shouted as she ran:

> Oh, inda, nida, ginda, go
> Da, gane, da go.

All the above quotations are taken from Miss Johnson's records. It will be noticed that the language accompanies action and is not in any way connected with the function of communication.

8. Three-year-old boy while riding through the country in an automobile:

> The cows b'long in the pasture.
> The hay b'longs in the big red barn.
> Walla walla, lo lo lo.
> This is a nice nice song.

9. Same child at three lying in bed in morning turning on and off an electric torch which had been given him to keep him quiet and which he played was a traffic light on Fifth Avenue:

Green light it can't go
Yellow light it can go

Green light it can't go
Yellow light it can go.

This he varied by saying:

Big bus come,
Green light it can't go
Yellow light it can go.
Big bus it go.

Big auto come,
Green light it can't go
Yellow light it can go.
Big auto go.

He and his four-year-old sister worked out about twenty stanzas with different vehicles on Fifth Avenue, ending with themselves.

10. Story told in class by four-year-old:

One day a tug boat went out in the river and a steamer came out and passed it. And then a ferry boat came along and passed the steamer, and then a row boat came out and didn't pass any of them.

Here the pattern is one of motion.

11. Story dictated at home by four-year-old:

All About the Outside
   All about the Sky,
Little birds are flying in the sky.
The birds are all flying.
The eagles are flying.
All different birds are flying.
And trees, and trees, and trees,
Over the mountains
And over the mountains,
And over the mountains
Grass is growing around and around,
And the sky is all around.

12. Story told in class by five-year-old:

In Atlantic City we went out on a long thing over the water. We walked and we walked and there was a great big net. Soon it got closer and closer and the fish in the net splattered around and splattered around and splattered around and jumped around and the net came closer and the fish splattered around and splattered around and splattered around on their brothers and sisters. How would you like to be a fish in a net and splattered around on your brothers and sisters?

Stories told in class by six-year-olds in City and Country School

13. Told to go with picture of a locomotive:

A TRAIN STORY

Bingety bang, bingety bang, a train going fast!
The green lantern is at the left, and the red is at the right.
Pretty soon we come into the forest dark and green.
There are cedar trees and branches.
Then before you know it we are out of the forest into a lovely field.
The children are playing ball and the big men are playing baseball and football.
Then we get to the Pennsylvania Station in New York and then we stop—bingety bang, shsht—All off! Amen.

14. Told while playing harbor with blocks:

SONG OF THE BELL BUOY

Ding, ding, ding, way in the water deeps
I hear that bell so far away, ding, ding, ding,
In the deep, deep waters of the ocean it tells all different ships
To not go near that bell, ding, ding.
Each day we hear it far way in the distance of the ocean.
Boats go sailing by, but not so near that bell,
For rocks are underneath, you see, and that is why we have that bell.
Ding, ding, ding.

15. Told after a visit to the docks:

THE GIANT SHOVEL

The Giant Shovel takes a bite of coal and he spits it down into another boat.
Then the coal wagon comes and takes his breakfast away from the boat.
The giant shovel takes a bite and chucks it down into the coal wagon.
Then another bite and then another bite until the coal wagon fills up.
Then chunk a chunk chunk, away goes the bingety bang bang truck.
And then comes another truck and gets some more coal.

Then when the whole boat gets empty a tug boat comes and pulls it away and it goes back to get more coal and it does that until the end of the day is over.

16. Told after seeing the Aquitania sail:

THE AQUITANIA

Who-o-o, whoo-o-o, whoo-o-o, the big Aquitania ship going and all the people hurrying down to see their friends off.

The sailors were all letting down the ropes from the big ship and hoisting up the anchor and the little tugs were pushing and pulling and pulling and pushing.

And the people were still waving their handkerchiefs to their friends, little white things, and all sorts of flags too.

Way, way up on the top, the Captain was up on his bridge guarding the wheel and the band was playing on the docks and the little tugs were pushing the boat around, and then the boat was off out into the open seas going for distant lands far away.

Whoo-o, whoo-oo.

My fog horn!

17. ### AN OCEAN LINER

Toot, toot, toot
The ocean liner
Toot, toot, toot
She's out of dock.

Toot, toot, toot
She's down the river
Toot, toot, toot
She's down the bay.

Toot, toot, toot
She's in the ocean
Toot, toot, toot
She's in the dock.

18. Story told by seven-year-old to entertain his little sister in bed:

Once there was a little girl and her name was Marni Moo. She was sleeping in her bed on the porch. She heard some little feet walking and she thought, "That can't be Mary because it is not big enough." Then up got Marni. She got out of bed and looked around on the floor. And there she found a Daddy-Long-Legs. She took the Daddy-Long-Legs into bed with her. She held him tight. Daddy-Long-Legs did not like it. So he tickled Marni. Marni did not like it so Marni threw him out of the bed.

Then she heard a little noise. She looked and there was a little fly buzzing. Then up got Marni. She got out of her little bed and she caught the little fly. She took the fly back into bed with her. She held him tight. The fly did not like it. So he bit Marni. Marni did not like it so Marni let the fly go. He flew away.

Then she heard something come bz-z-z, b-z-z-z, b-z-z-z. And there came flying a big bumble bee. Then up got Marni. She got out of her little bed and she caught the bumble bee. She held it tight. The bumble bee did not like it and he stung Marni Moo on her hand. Marni Moo cried. She let the bumble bee go and he flew away. Then Mary came. Mary said, "Little girl, do you want to get up?" So she took Marni up and she said, "Now you can run in to mother." So Marni came running, running, and here she is!

19. Sad Deer Story by seven-year-old.

Little Lightfoot was traveling in the forest when he heard a gun go off. Quickly he ran with his head back, horns shining, feet springing into the air with every jump through the dimpling sunshiny forest. Soon he felt a pain in his back leg, and it was struck lame. Then another pain in his stomach. And he fell over dead.

20. Story by eight-year-old in the City and Country School:

On Brooklyn Bridge facing city. White smoke and black smoke and blue smoke and chimneys and big high buildings everywhere, windows, roofs, points of towers sticking up. One looks like a volcano with smoke coming out at top.

21. Story written jointly by eight-year-olds after visiting a paper mill. A striking case of excitement being expressed in rhythmic language:

THE PAPER MILL

Boom s-z, boom z-z
The dynamo goes whizzing around.
It turns the wheel which beats the pulp
And makes it finer and finer.

In goes the blueing
And makes a purple track
All around the tub,
The bubbling foam goes round and round the tub.

Little knives go up and down
Chip, chip, chip
They cut the wood pulp finer still.

Zip, zip, zip
The shaker shakes the water out

Sh, sh, sprinkle sprinkle goes the spray,
The water it goes curving up.

R-r-r-r-r
The rollers go round and round
They squeeze the paper and roll it up
And then it's shipped away.

22. Stories written by nine-year-olds in City and Country School:

SEA PICTURES

I am a diver;
I go down, down to the floor of the sea through the green water—
For a Spanish frigate.
On the way I see a red jellyfish, many starfish.

I see many different kinds of shells.
I could not find the Spanish frigate,
But I came up and told my story!

23. THE FERRY BOAT

The poky old ferry boat goes poking along
Over the river and back again.
The bell rings dang! and the whistle blows,
As the boat comes coasting in.

Notice the long O's and the slow rhythm.

24. THE RAIN

The rain is falling very hard.
The streets are wet and the gutters are running.
The toys are out and all over the floor.
I play all day till bedtime comes.

It seems to me no one can read these children's language unmoved.
Yet I am aware that most of those who read them will be concerned
with the pedagogy of the situation. And surely, if my analysis is right,
there is an implied pedagogy. If it is true that children spontaneously
experiment with the quality of sounds and rhythm before the adult
conception of language is clear to them and if it is true that in their
early use of words they continue this play attitude and build sound and
word patterns for themselves with the same feeling for pattern and for
design that they show in block building or in crayons or in bodily movements, then it would seem up to the adults with whom they are in contact to allow this experimentation with language to proceed unimpeded
along its own line. The least that adults can do is to keep "hands off."

They can stop their attempt to hasten the process of acquiring adult forms along with the adult attitude that language is merely a tool for communicating ideas. It may be that if grown-ups put their minds on to the problem, if they listened attentively to the small children around them intent to find the urges to speech and the quality of children's speech under differing situations, that they might discover a more constructive pedagogy than merely "hands off." They might work out a language environment both in stories and in their own speech with children which would utilize the close connection between speech and muscle activity and give a better chance for the pattern sense to mature. Anyone who will conscientiously record and study small children's language from the point of view of the experimental attack will find ample suggestions for a language pedagogy.

ACTING THINGS OUT

A Group of Teachers of the Shady Hill School

THE morning at the Shady Hill School begins with the informal gathering together of all the children for what is known as Assembly. It is the time when one group shares with the rest some interesting piece of class work they have done. Often the medium of expression is a dramatic presentation. Such an important sounding term, however, does not at all represent the spirit in which these Assemblies are prepared and given. Carried over from classroom work, the costuming is often simply a spear or a crown, and the setting merely one end of the Assembly room, helped out by properties and burlap covered screens. We try to do away with a curtain and to make as few shifts of scene as possible, and these quite openly.

One of the rich fields for dramatization is poetry. This year two interesting and very different things were done by the children of the seventh grade (eleven years old). The idea of acting out certain poems in *Now We Are Six* came from one of the girls. So I brought a copy of the book to school, and in our hour of poetry time, read aloud. The book was just closed when the silence of rapt attention was broken by the many eager suggestions the children had for "illustrating" Milne's poems. Different ones told their choices for the different parts and then these were assigned by thoughtful voting. The next hour that the children had for English, they spent on their dramatization, learning the poems by heart and acting them out. They worked individually or in groups till they felt they had something to present to the rest of the class from whom they asked and accepted comments. Such real people were Christopher Robin, Poole, Alexander Beetle, and the rest, that not a thought was given to costumes or scenery, those more artificial things which help heighten illusion, till the very morning of the presentation to the school in Assembly. Then there was a brown fur coat for Poole, two hats and school bags for doctors, a bench and blanket for a bed, an empty bottle and spoon, a gray wooden box and a broom handle for a fishing pole. Nor was anything more needed, for the members of the grade were really living in the book. Now they were ready to give to their audience the same joy as they had had when first they heard the poems. In all they spent two hours in preparation for a twenty-minute assembly, that has not yet been forgotten.

This same group of seventh-grade children did a second and very different piece of work in dramatizing Masefield's poem, *Spanish Waters*. I read this to them because they had asked for another poem that they might act out. Listening carefully they realized that there was only one real play character, the old tired man who was remembering back to the days when he had been a pirate, seizing gold on the ships that sailed through Spanish Waters. And it seemed to him that again he heard the waters;

> Like a slow sweet piece of music from the gray forgotten years
> Telling tales, and beating tunes—

The children were able to enter into the old pirate's mood, seeing with him his pictures from the past. It was their suggestion that, besides showing the old man, they could act out two tableaux, the landing of the pirates at sunset and the carrying the treasure inland, and the burying of these chests by the moon's ghastly light. These pictures of necessity required action, and it was planned that all motions should, as much as possible, be in accord with the rhythm of the poem.

Because so much of the beauty of *Spanish Waters* lay in the pictures, the children wanted to have some suggestion of costumes and scenery. To create the semblance of pirates they all wore bandannas, gay belts, and neckerchiefs. They carried chests in which they had stowed a string of beads, a few coins, or a silver cup—the treasure. Yet these chests so weighted them down that their steps were slow and their bent backs ached. They stumbled over imaginary tree trunks and plowed their way through sucking quagmires. In the background, "a mile off Nigger Head," lay a large model of a sailing ship.

Certain devices were necessary to keep the whole piece together. The remembered music of the Spanish waters suggested to the minds of the children that two of their number should play off stage, one at the piano, the other at the 'cello. So there was music before and after each picture, making possible the drawing of the gray blanket curtains, behind which electric light bulbs were changed, from red to blue, and pirates shifted places. Meanwhile the worn old man, his head in his hands, listened, as he sat on a box to one side of the closed curtains. The music over, they parted, and once more the old pirate saw his visions of the glorious days on Spanish waters.

The fields of history and literature are closely connected, and much material available for dramatization may be found therein. The fourth grade of last year, in preparation for a study of Homer's *Odyssey*, had parts of the *Iliad* read aloud to them. The swing, and forceful simplicity of the language, fired their imagination, as they followed the Greek heroes through the battles of the Trojan War. Each child identified himself with one of the characters and lived with him his adventures.

Particularly vivid is the incident of the Trojan camp when Odysseus and Diomedes creep spying to the Trojan lines to get information and hostages. On the way they meet Dolon, one of the enemy, who is out on a like reconnoitering expedition for the Trojans. They kill him and after a sudden, swift visitation on the enemy the two Greeks return unharmed to their own camp.

The dramatic suspense of the whole scene was intense, and as the reading stopped, there was silence for a moment. "I wish I could be Dolon," "Oh! I want to be Odysseus," "Let me be Diomedes," came in quick succession.

The room was at once converted into an imaginary plain in Troy; the watch fires of the Greek camp flickering in opposition to the dull glow of those of the Trojans on the other side. Each character took his place and the group started in to reënact the scene, extemporizing where memory failed. The rhythm of the language had fixed itself in the children's minds so that it carried over almost entirely. There was no costuming; a book served for a shield; invisible swords were brandished and sweaters were heavy armor.

After the initial attempt there was a storm of criticism, each child suggesting action and words to be substituted or speeches to be entirely changed. Certain parts were read again, the children listened intently and reconstructed their own ideas.

The next time the character's parts were reassigned. New interpretation brought new problems. With a unified group conception acting as the driving force, the class demanded the reading over once more. When several more such trials had been made the children who had best taken their parts were chosen and the incident was acted for the final time to everyone's satisfaction.

The whole dramatization took perhaps an hour. It was done without preparation for an audience and so impelling was the children's desire to give this scene that the result reflected the vividness and strength of the original. Also the whole historical incident was impressed on each individual in a far more real and lasting way than any objective presentation could have done it.

This year's fourth grade found dramatic possibilities in their study of Egypt, which served as an introduction to the story of Greek civilization. For three weeks they became archeologists and excavators. With the help of a book of photographs the class would approach the outside of a tomb, choose the place to dig, and, as the pages turned, bring to light one treasure after another.

One day the teacher suggested acting what they had been pretending. The children were delighted and went into the study to make their own plan. Everyone began to tell what he would find. After a noisy half hour they returned having decided in what order each would come and what he would find. So far the finding of the tomb was to be all imaginary. The teacher suggested the possibility of making an actual tomb enclosed with the burlap screens. This idea was seized upon. For several days, about three and a half hours in all, children, without any outside help, worked over large sheets of brown paper with brushes and paints until they had made the decorations for the walls of the tomb. To dress the mummies who were to be inside the tomb, they copied from a book headdresses, the costumes of two guards, and a little mummified monkey they found.

Since the first day of planning the class felt this scene should be shown to the rest of the school, so one morning exercise was set aside for "The Discovery of an Egyptian Tomb." The school was informed that Grade IV had gone out with some of the Harvard unit and hoped to discover something of importance. These searchers were now before the school, with real picks and shovels. Pretending to dig, they unearthed an imaginary scarab, a bit of a broken tear bottle and jewels. Then a hole led them to pull away some rocks, and screens, and there, in the stillness of centuries, stood a silent group surrounded by a blaze of color. On the walls in red and blue and yellow were obelisks, river boats, desert scenes, hieroglyphics, and real Egyptian numerals. Two rigid guards stood faithfully watching over the prostrate mummies of a Pharaoh, his Queen, and son. The royal family were tightly wrapped and wore brilliant headdresses. Beside the boy squatted the mummy of his pet monkey. After a long look at these riches the tomb was covered up again until the archeologists should return to remove certain treasures to the school museum.

I feel sure that almost every kind of class work may be illuminated by dramatizing. Most little children act things out quite naturally and if they are encouraged to keep it up they are spared self-consciousness in acting, even at the self-conscious age in living. When a class acts for itself there is of course no audience. That is the time when most creative things are done, before repetition has established a way of doing. At this stage the play is an experience being lived for the first time, not a known thing being shared with onlookers. Once a form is established, however, it seems to kindle the actors to have an audience. The bothersome conventions of having to speak louder at assembly than in the classroom, of having to keep from standing behind each other and so forth, seem to be more than compensated for by the heightened excitement of having more people to draw under the spell of the situation. All the above examples are of rapid dramatizing, where the purpose was to make vivid a piece of class work. There is another kind of acting experience that we try to give our children once in a year—that is, taking part in the production of a play that is as finished in speech and action, in costumes and setting, as they can make it. A sense of workmanship comes from such a long-time piece of work, where the best skill of grown-ups and children is requisitioned, that sometimes lasts as an unforgettable experience. By their nature, however, these great events can happen only very seldom. Meanwhile on any week day, in almost any classroom, one can be acting things out.

NURTURING THE CREATIVE SPIRIT

A Symposium of Teachers

A YEAR ago a thirteen-year-old girl brought me a group of stanzas, some of which had been printed in newspapers and some of which had been freshly written. She offered them with high expectations. Most bore such titles as Hope, Truth, Death, Sunset. Except that they showed the impulse to create, and some ability to handle rhythm and rhyme, they were valueless. A few days ago the same girl offered me a bit of poetry called "A Prism," with this illuminating and, to me, extremely satisfying statement, "I spent a solid half hour looking at that prism, first with the sun on it, and then in shadow." The lines, as was to be expected, presented fresh observations of color, light, movement, and sound, with three original and apt similes.

This illustrates what at present seems to me the most liberating concept for a young writer to grasp. All material for creative work must come through the senses. Bits of this raw stuff may be later combined and recombined, but the process of the imagination is impossible without the results of keen sense experience.

The knowledge of this fact heartens the girl who has felt that what the brighter student writes is the result of a Prospero's wand which she can never wave. She looks with attentive eyes at the lake which she has hurriedly passed every day, and strikes out in her next written work, "On a gray lake the sun suddenly squandered his beams." From the moment when she has received recognition for this fragment of accurate writing she becomes in her small way a self-confident creator. To the talented girl it brings the steadying knowledge that her only opportunity for growth lies in increased sense perception of the world immediately surrounding her, passed through the dome of many-colored glass which constitutes her personality. More fundamental, then, than the increased appreciation of the fine distinction in words, or the ear for sentence variety and rhythm is this sharpening of sight, smell, hearing, taste, and touch.

While this type of work is being done, which is in the first two years of the upper school, instructions are given that no written work should be more than two hundred and fifty words, thus emphasizing quality rather than quantity. During this period also she is reading, during the first year, modern poetry and novels, and during the second, narratives of various types and times. Up to the third year the emphasis is on description and narration, convenient labels for the teacher.

Now the essay writing begins. A solid foundation of observation of men and things has by this time been laid. Longer themes, in which more attention is paid to the planning of the whole, are now required. But over and over is reiterated the principle that there is no creative writing without creative living through the senses. Good familiar essays are suggested for reading, modern at first and not too far beyond the girl's ability, later the masters. Of course, there is no rule that one type of writing shall not be done while we are studying another. Arrangements by which a girl may work on anything which she is eager to create are always easily made, provided she does not deprive herself of the opportunity to try out all sorts in order to find her own line.

Since we are primarily a college preparatory school, the régime is less flexible than that in Utopia, both in the matter of themes and works studied in the classroom. However, the disconcerting thought often obtrudes itself that pupils who have the creative impulse will create without a régime good or bad, provided only they are encouraged. Therefore, I submit this brief account of my method for exactly what it is worth.

Lulu M. Hood.

No TEACHER is directly responsible for outstanding creative work on the part of his pupils. If he seems successful above the average, he must be unusually fortunate in the material which comes to his hand. He may help or hinder the development of those in his charge, but he will find it difficult to hide the light of genius under a bushel, and impossible to reap masterpieces unless there are imaginative minds to sow. At his best, he is only a catalytic agent to bring about desired results.

I have no classroom method for the encouragement of creative work. If the writing of an individual interests me, I make some written comment to that effect, and take the first opportunity thereafter to speak to him privately on the subject. Occasionally I read to the class some particularly interesting bit of work. If the pupil shows an inclination to keep to or improve his standard, I think myself fortunate. If he shows himself uninterested, I reluctantly let the matter drop, for a forced interest will get nowhere.

Some of my best contacts have come with people who are no longer in my classes. There are always a faithful few who come as friends after they have ceased to be pupils, and a number of those have been interested in writing. One girl, whom I had in class for two years, and whose written work I commended highly, never hinted to me that she cared for poetry particularly, so I was taken by surprise when she won the first national poetry contest conducted by *The Scholastic*, in 1925. She has ever since come to me for advice and encouragement. But I can take no credit as a teacher for that or her subsequent successes, for our relations have long since ceased to be those of pupil and teacher, and have become those of intimate friends. I may have helped her by my interest, but any other friend who loved poetry would have done as well.

There are always a few spontaneous poems every year—usually after a study of poetry has been for months a thing of the past. I have yet to require of any of my students a poem. The very nature of poetry demands that it be called forth by some need of the writer, not of the teacher. I can recall only five or six students, all girls, who have brought to me anything worth attention. I gave them such encouragement as I could, but half of them have lost interest, and I suspect will write no more. One of the exceptions, though no longer in my class, brought me three poems that I think much the best work she has done.

With a few exceptions, I receive much better prose than poetry. There is always someone who can handle words cleverly. Out of the one hundred and forty people in my classes this year, I have four or five who will bear watching, and a number who are distinctly above the average in ability. We require a great deal of written work in our school, and by Junior year we expect fairly mature original work—and usually get it, although we have to keep an eye out for selections (clandestine, of course) from magazines and books.

I must not give the impression that my classes do nothing but write. We read, and we talk about our reading. We are not slow in finding out what others say about the things that interest us, yet we are fondest of forming our own judgments. In one of the courses which particularly interests me, we study Untermeyer's *Modern American Poetry*. I have to divide the semester to cover it, three other classics, the text, and the numerous small things that arise, but I am afraid I scant the others shamefully in Untermeyer's favor. Of course he is just a starting point, and we branch out in all directions. Our library is fairly well supplied with modern poetry; usually I find a considerable impetus towards checking out these volumes follows our study, or rather accompanies the

BLACK AND WHITE

I met a man along the road
  To Withernsea;
Was ever anything so dark, so pale
  As he?
His hat, his clothes, his tie,
  His boots
Were black as black
  Could be,
And midst of all was a cold white face
And eyes that looked wearily.

The road was bleak and straight and flat
  To Withernsea;
Gaunt poles with shrilling wires their
  weird
    Did dree;
On the sky stood out, on the swollen sky

    The black blood veins of tree
After tree, as they beat from the face
Of the wind which they could not flee.

And in the fields along the road
  To Withernsea,
Swart crows sat huddled on the ground,
  Disconsolately,
While overhead the seamews wheeled and
    skirled
    In glee,
But the black cows stood, and cropped
    where they stood,
  And never heeded thee,
O dark pale man, with the weary eyes,
On the road to Withernsea.
        —H. H. Abbott.

TWO ORIGINAL ILLUSTRATIONS OF A POEM.

STAR TALK

"Are you awake, Gemelli,
　　This frosty night?"
"We'll be awake till reveille,
Which is sunrise," say the Gemelli,
"It's no good trying to go to sleep;
If there's wine to be got we'll drink it
　　　deep,
But rest is hopeless tonight,
But rest is hopeless tonight."

"Are you cold too, poor Pleiads,
　　This frosty night?"
"Yes, and so are the Hyads;
See us cuddle and hug," say the Pleiads,
"All six in a ring; it keeps us warm;
We huddle together like birds in a storm;
It's bitter weather tonight,
It's bitter weather tonight."

"What do you hunt, Orion,
　　This starry night?"
"The Ram, the Bull, and the Lion,
And the Great Bear," says Orion;
"With my starry quiver and beautiful belt,
I am trying to find a good thick pelt
To warm my shoulders tonight,
To warm my shoulders tonight."

"Did you hear that, Great She-Bear,
　　This frosty night?"
"Yes, he's talking of stripping me bare,
Of my own big fur," says the She-Bear;
"I'm afraid of the man and his terrible
　　　arrow;
The thought of it chills my bones to the
　　　marrow.
And the frost so cruel tonight!
And the frost so cruel tonight!"
　　　　　　　—Robert Graves.

latter part of it. It takes time to convince the majority that it will do neither them nor me any good to have them parrot my likes and dislikes; that I want them to form their own opinions, regardless of orthodoxy. The course is the hardest I teach—not from the standpoint of preparation, but from that of teacher effort. Every year I am tempted to cry and throw poetry books at the lumps of ice that occupy my thirty chairs; but presently the thaw comes, and the library is flooded. There are always one or two who come through unshaken in the belief that poetry is not for them. My faith in my knowledge of human nature would be unsettled if all were converts; but on the other hand there are the few who get something from the course which they keep with them always.

Another course which gives us ample fields in which to browse is devoted to a study of world literature in translation. We can do no more than open the gates and let the children wander, for a four-year course would not do justice to the subject. It is amazing to see the pleasure with which they find something new in literature which they can like. Their comments are surprisingly mature, and the influence on their writing is apparent. I'm sure many of them never knew that there was any work worth reading written in any foreign language.

Our principal asked the faculty the other day whether they thought our school was average or superior in mentality, and surprised us very much by saying that the mean was very close one hundred; but it will take more than a few statistics to disprove to me that the children who are really creative will write, teacher or no teacher, and the others will not go far, for all our urging. We can guide their reading and give them sympathetic criticism, but in the end we must stand back and watch them strike their stride.

RACHEL A. COOGLE.

ANTHOLOGIES of children's verses are perhaps less common in Great Britain than in America, and although the writer is an editor of *Public School Verse*, which is the only regular series of volumes devoted to anthologizing school verse in that country, he confesses to considerable relief that its publication has not started a fashion. The itch for publicity is a dangerous disease in the young, and the word "poet" turns more young heads than any other. The real poet, it is well known, thrives on discouragement; the poetaster is a doubtful blessing, and only too often needs no encouragement, and deserves none.

This may sound a curious creed on the lips of the editor of a school anthology; but it is a sincere one, and the purpose of this article is to show how he reconciles his profession with his practice. This is most easily done by first explaining what *Public School Verse* is and is not, and by then outlining what it is trying to do, in the interests of boys, of literature, and of the healthy reaction of one upon the other.

Throughout the secondary schools of Great Britain (and it must be remembered that a "public" school with us is a secondary school of a particular kind and in no respect equivalent to the "public" schools of America) a mass of verse is being written every year—most of it deliberately fostered and guided by competent teachers, much of it doubtlessly scribbled anyhow in out-of-school hours. A great deal of this verse finds its way into school magazines, where it secures for the authors a certain measure of fame or notoriety (it depends on the school) and gives them that indescribable pleasure of a first appearance in print. Since school magazine editors are not infallible, and since personal reasons sometimes govern their selection, it not infrequently happens that good verse is rejected and bad verse welcomed. And there must be, in such cases, a comparatively low standard of acceptance, and a lack of adequate criticism of the right kind; hence the young versifier imagines himself a poet, and acquires all the disagreeable symptoms of precocity. Now, *Public School Verse* aims at collecting the work of all the best writers, of an age from about 14 to 18, in the big schools of the British Empire, whether they be the darlings of their school magazines or not, of subjecting the material thus collected to careful criticism, and of selecting from it those compositions which approximate in part or in whole to poetry. These are then issued in a modest form to a small public, chiefly composed of critics, boys, and schoolmates. It is not claimed that these volumes contain poetry, nor that their contributors are poets; as far as possible the editors try to prevent the wrong kind of appreciation as well as the misunderstanding type of criticism. Above all it is our heartfelt prayer that we may never be patronized by the "My-dear-how-wonderful" and "How-too-sweet-for-such-a-child" school, which would make a swan of every duckling, the uglier the duckling the better, in these *vers libre* days.

It is time, perhaps, that I said something to conciliate those whose belief in the value of verse writing by the young may have been offended by anything I have written. Let me hasten to assure them that my belief in that value is as deep as their own; both as an assistant master and later as a head master I have aimed almost beyond all else at fostering and inspiring the desire to write, to create, to give "To airy nothing a local habitation and a name." Other writers in this volume will tell, better than I can, how this may be done. I would agree with them all that few things are more vital, more akin to real education; but not with all perhaps would I agree when we come to consider the purpose and the result of this noble art of creation, though I trust there are some with whom I could keep company to the end. Let us consider the matter more closely.

The great poets write because they must, and all poets, great or small, are justified in proportion as they ennoble or console or enrich the mind of man. But only one in a thousand is a poet; yet nine hundred in a thousand should try to write poetry. A few hours digging in a clay soil gives us a new respect for gardeners; and only the student who has hammered out his own halting sonnet can catch the full glory of "Shall I compare thee to a summer's day?" This, to my mind, is the first great argument for teaching the young to write; they must learn to write in order to learn appreciation of their great heritage, the literature of the English language. Without such exercise in creation they may learn to admire the thought in a poem or an essay, to love personalities, to worship ideals; but never will they learn to admire, love, and worship great literature, which is all of these and yet more than these. What were the soliloquies of Hamlet without the immense store of vivid and potent words which make them immortal, what *The Eve of St. Agnes* without the romantic richness of its language? We know that Shakespeare stole his plots from others; tell that to a boy and then give him a plot for a scene and bid him write it, and he will soon learn how to appreciate Shakespeare.

I would therefore make boys write in the first place in order to teach them how to value the writings of others. But of course, this is not the only fruit of such training, else there were little excuse for *Public School Verse*. In many cases boys will never be enough interested in creating verse or prose to travel beyond this stage. But some will go further, and write in order to write better. Here perhaps we must deal faithfully with those who believe that "self-expression" is the end of all education; to these the extravagant poem, the highly colored essay, the *tour de force* in one medium or another, is valuable in itself, as emanations from and evidence of the personality of the writer. They are more concerned with the "expression" than with the "self," that self which they should be educating to aim ever at higher things than it has achieved. And just as we should never let the promising boy think that his ideas are either particularly unusual or original or final, so we must always add as. epilogue to the praise of his poem or essay the warning that perfection lies some distance yet beyond the mountain ranges. And then, if he is worth anything, he will go back and try a little harder for the right word, the fitting cadence, and his literary soul will come appreciably nearer salvation.

It is with this minority that *Public School Verse* has to deal. School and class magazines are legion, and the more of them there are the better. But there should be in every country one, and only one, anthology of the type of *Public School Verse*. The great majority of our contributions are rejected, only about thirty poems out of many hundreds are printed each year, and this means that the facile verse writer is put in his place and the real trier spurred to greater efforts. Those that are accepted are for the first time brought together, so that writers and schools can see what others are doing. The authors get a certain amount of sane criticism (though the gushing reviewer is not yet obsolete) and are encouraged to go on and become—if not poets—at any rate decent writers of prose.

These are our aims, this the idea behind our work. If much that I have said is tedious and obvious, it is only because we have been so often misinterpreted that I thought it worth while stating our position from both sides; for not once or twice in our short career have we had cause to send heavenward that most heartfelt of all petitions, "Defend us from our friends!"

P. H. B. LYON.

IF CHILDREN are exposed to literature early enough they will surely catch the taste for reading, provided only that the literature is vivid, genuine, and presented with variety. Let them have it in its first form, and let its appeal be not primarily for children. Chaucer himself has an infinitely greater zest, for young readers, than any retelling I have ever discovered. And let them meet as many experiences as they can. When a child who had been carefully fed a diet of New England poets, and no others, came into a class of children who had browsed through several of our excellent modern anthologies, the difference was marked. His written style was monotonous, his judgment was sentimental, his taste in general was limited, but after a few months of wider reading he was as discriminating as anyone in the class. I believe exposure to good poetry, old and new, is the first step toward deepening appreciation.

The seventh grade at Greenwich Academy begin the year by selecting their own books of poetry. All of the best collections are available for their choice and they take great interest in this process. When each has chosen her own, after frequent consultations with teacher and classmates, the children compare books and exchange them, or borrow favorites from the teacher's desk, and so a class library of poetry is actively circulating. Once a week they have a poetry hour, eagerly anticipated. The most successful device for sharpening their powers of discrimination has been an anthology compiled by the class. Every child recites the poem she has selected and the class solemnly passes judgment upon it, while its sponsor awaits their verdict.

"It's a good poem, but our standards are getting higher this term.

We'll take only *very* good poems," says one kind but firm critic. "Isn't it just a little 'pink and white'?" asks another. But when, as more often happens, they like the poem, they burst into spontaneous applause. And they know exactly what they like about it. When a poem is honored by these severe critics, the sponsor may print and decorate it for the anthology. The children display great ingenuity in making these "illuminations," and the resulting book, which they ultimately bind, is usually charming. They take a great interest in each other's treatments, and read the poems over and over.

Sometimes the poetry recitation is restricted to a definite topic, or a search for certain rhythms, or a survey of some one poet's work, but more often the choice is left freely to the children. They select their poems at least a week before they recite them, and the learning, in this leisurely way, is rarely a task, particularly at this age which is so apt at memorizing. Sometimes two or three will combine "for a surprise," and share in reciting a longer poem, such as *The Forsaken Merman* or *A Song of Sherwood*.

In this process several things have happened. Their minds have been stored with lovely images, they have learned a great deal about poetry, they have exercised their powers of judgment and expression, and they have been happy.

This same class is studying English history, and the subject matter is closely bound up with their English. *Beowulf* comes first, and its appeal to eleven-year-olds is strong. Their compositions bristle with "misty moors," "foamy-necked craft," "fearless ones," and "grim demons" for several weeks. It is ideal for dramatizing, and nothing proves too difficult to represent. When it was suggested that the fight under the sea was not feasible, they were surprised, and concocted, with a mosquito netting drop, dyed blue and green, and realistically undulated from the wings, and a slow motion hero, a watery, hair-raising spectacle.

The ballads, which come next, are always successful, and two or three weeks at these are sufficient to steep the class in medieval feeling. They keep bringing in new ones, adding to their own *Representative Ballads* from many sources, and using the delightful Arthur Rackham illustrations for inspiration. They beg to read them, recite them from memory, and best of all sing them, sometimes solo, sometimes with the class joining in the "lillie-gays," and sometimes all blithely chanting. Then they act them in teams, alone, with an audience, and without. This gives endless opportunity for imaginative detail. A footstool, it is explained to the waiting audience, is a milk-white steed, a golden-oak chair is a lady's bower. While one classmate reads the poem, the lady emerges from the bower, jumps on the milk-white steed, Sir Ronald MacDonald holds seven imaginary brothers at bay with brilliant sword play, and they all "rive their hair" at the unhappy *dénouement,* while the class watches sympathetically. At the close of this study they present their various ballads to the school assembly with costumes from the property closet, and with choruses singing or minstrels reciting the ballad, but their horses, their castle walls, their swords and loudly clicking keys are still in the mind's eye, and all the more satisfactory.

Miracle plays and mysteries here help to present the middle ages. Some of the nativity plays, that of the Chester cycle, and the Noah's Ark scene can be adapted.

Almost every week sees a dramatic moment interpreted in the classroom or on the school stage. Thomas à Becket before his altar, Harold swearing on the sacred relics, the Roundheads in session, all are presented with intense feeling. Ten-minute whispered conferences in the far corners of the room, and some hasty grouping of tables and chairs, and before the eyes of the class come riding Richard the Lion-Hearted and all his followers. But to make this scene instantly possible, they have called on their knowledge of a score of books. The feudal system is more than a generalization when vassals kneel before their lords, the clod of earth is exchanged, the accolade is delivered, and all march off on the King's service.

Here again illustration serves, and all of these scenes are drawn or painted or charted, so that each week the walls are covered with a fresh crop of bright episodes. Most of this work is voluntary, and the desire of children of this age to create things with their hands seems to be unlimited.

They like to tell stories, too. The class soon falls into the habit of pretending, the classroom is a great hall, the members range themselves above the salt, one of them is a King, very kingly, and the story-tellers are minstrels who strike their harps and quite forget to be stilted as they almost sing their stories.

Writing is an important factor in increasing appreciation of literature, for the more children write, the more interested they are in other people's writing. While they are reading so much narrative their writing reflects this same form, and I find this the most natural medium for this age group. The other natural outcome is poetry, which to some children is the simplest and surest form of expression.

To start them off music is often helpful, particularly played on a Victrola, which can repeat endlessly without effort. The children listen silently absorbed, then seize their pencils and write down words, snatches of ideas, prose at first, which with some of them shapes itself into poetry. They never try to reflect the beat of the music, but they are very sure of just the rhythm they need to express their images. The music creates a feeling, and their imaginations race away with it.

Of course, no children are ever required to write poetry, and many, after one offering, are firmly turned back to prose. In any case the only way to induce them to write fluently with real enjoyment is to give them ample time and unlimited scope for developing their ideas. A class which took "Color" for its starting point for their next week's theme responded eagerly with suggestions. And they were eager to work out those suggestions. "Yellow makes me think of a wheat field, and a hot day, and lemonade, and Rapunzel's hair. I know exactly what I want to write. Please, let's not talk about it any more." The results were delightful— thoughtful essays, unusual stories, and several poems, of which I can quote only one, "Scarlet and Green."

An elf left his shoes in my garden,
　　A green garden in a woody glade,
Delicate shoes with crimson toes,
　　On a bed of green moss they were laid.

The elf had been in swimming
　　In my cool, green, shadowy pool;
I saw his little brown body
　　As he sunned on a red toadstool.

He dried himself with an emerald leaf,
　　And wiggles and shivers he made,
And from the leaf hung two cherries
　　Of a brilliant crimson shade.

He donned his tiny green jerkin,
　　He set his cap on his head,
And dragged home to his oak tree
　　His towel and cherries red.

But he left his shoes behind him,
　　In my cool, green, shadowy glade.
I think he had forgotten them
　　As he played by himself in the shade.

HELEN W. LEET.

Two articles in my creed as to ways of helping the student of today to self-expression seem to me each year more vital.

Success, I think, comes partly from the teacher's own attitude to what is written. If she can see each work, and get the class to see it with her, as a worth-while effort, however crude it may be, to express one's ideas, observations, or emotions; if she can take every feeble effort as worth serious consideration and exhaustive work to perfect—she is on the way. She needs time to talk with individuals over their experiences, time for group discussion in which all can contribute ideas, time for individuals to come to her with difficulties as they arise. She needs, too, sympathy and judgment to know when the result can be looked at objectively and frankly criticized by a group; when it is wiser to treat with protective care confidential revelations so that the shy half-seeing may not take to cover. I have poems or other personal revelations that I never reveal tucked shyly into my hand; I have others that can be brought to the open, looked at impersonally, frankly discussed. Always the problem here seems to me to be to get the self-expression open to critical judgment without the atrocious self-exploitation that destroys life and beauty. "Every man," says Keats, "has his speculations, but every man does not brood and peacock over them till he makes a false coinage and deceives himself."

The second article in my creed seems to me of vital assistance to the first. The attitude to what is read is of supreme importance. One may not "brood and peacock" if one sees one's own effort as a part of a great whole. As I think it a real danger to see our age disconnected from the past, I think each child is given a more sane perspective upon what she is feeling if she is in intimate contact with those through all the ages who have given us their best. New life seems to have come to literature in the ages in which the past could live, not as a model for the present, but as an illumination of it. And I have much of the same feeling as to the forms of the past. I do not wish them to think of originality only as something different, but as also, and perhaps more truly, new life in the old. I should not expect a miner to work with no equipment that the ages have secured for him; I think the young are due an intimacy with what has already been secured. It is the emphasis upon only one form that seems to me dangerous, or the attitude that all truth has been finally revealed. They can have, I find, their adoration for passages in Shakespeare, for *L'Allegro*, for Shelley's *Night*, for Keats's *Autumn*, without thinking that there is nothing left for Amy Lowell to give them. When a girl is feeling for her form, I try to make few specific suggestions to limit her; I try to keep before her the need to be clear and coherent, and then I try to make her intimate with greatness of the type she is feeling for. There is a wealth to help her: Herrick and Robert Frost if she wants emotion over her objective world, Poe and De la Mare if a sense of mystery about a place, Mrs. Battle or Gabriel Oak or a Katherine Mansfield if portrayal of an individual, Carl Sandburg or Mrs. Dalloway, if impressionistic effects.

I am sure that I succeed best when I can get a class to care greatly for their heritage, but to see it as living truth of which their own efforts are an integral part; when they can see the work of each age as the expression of the life and thought of that age, and as needing the expression of the thought of today for its completion. I think the enrichment of their imagination from intimacy with the great gives them an enlarged life. I think, too, a sense of kinship in their struggles gives them a new freedom. Remarks of the last few days seem to me illustrative. A class reading the *Sir Roger de Coverley Papers* came in excitedly: "Why, the things need saying today! Look at the one on party spirit!" The class reading Burke declared, "We like him. Why does he seem so modern?" The difficulties in the growth of an empire are, they see, of the same sort as those found in the development of internationalism. A girl meeting Tolstoi came with much emotion to say: "He is saying things that I have been thinking; I did not know other people had these same thoughts!" And in every case I think a resulting freedom has come as truly to these girls as to the girl who is working out an expression of the noises in her city in a queer Vachel Lindsay fashion.

FLORENCE S. HOYT.

POETRY parties were usually held at four or five o'clock in the afternoon, round the old fireplace in the English room at Manumit. Anybody could come who would bring a poem to read. Such browsing in Anthologies!—such demands, "Who's taken *The Home Book of Verse?*" "Where's *The Singing World?*" Then, "You'd better choose either Joe or me to begin, Aunt Sally, for we're supper cooks, and you know we have to leave at half-past five!" And when the supper cooks had had their turn, they chose the next reader, and he chose the next, and there were invitations frankly proffered to "Choose me next—I've got a beauty to read!"

The poems were perfectly miscellaneous, and humorous ones, like Daly's Italian dialect pieces, and the *Thundering, Blundering Irishman*, were popular. Sidney won great applause with his reading of *Darius Green and His Flying Machine;* but at every party some great and famous poem, that would touch the deep places of the spirit and fire the sense of brotherhood, was sure to be read by somebody. Eugene would throw real power and passion into *The Man with the Hoe*, or Hilda would read with a quietly thrilling enthusiasm Keats's *Ode to the Nightingale.* Gussie loved mystic poems, and would often choose something by Æ. Benny could read De la Mare's *Listeners* beautifully. Ralph had a genius for Kipling, and was great in the *Ballads of East and West.* I shall not soon forget how electric it was when Elsie read her favorite child-labor poem from the *Cry for Justice*, and how hushed it was when Sidney Gaft read Longfellow's poem on the hunted slave.

Portrait parties were very popular too. Anyone could come who would bring a written sketch of a member of the community. We sat in a ring, and each read his portrait, and then each of us had one guess who it was. In the end, the author announced who it was; but in most cases it had been guessed by a majority. These portraits were brief, cool, frank, unsentimental, often really discerning. No single instance of unkind or embarrassing personalities ever occurred at a portrait party. What has always surprised me most was the guessing. Interpretations of each other's traits made by the children, though often puzzling to me, were usually swiftly recognized by them. On the other hand, my own portraits of the children were usually soon recognized, too.

Definitions parties were very lively too. We each brought a word to be argued about, a student acting as chairman. Sometimes we have taken half an hour over a word, anybody who chose offering his ideas and attempting a definition. The sort of words it interested us most to work on were great words like "freedom," "religious," "create." Sometimes I could hardly keep from exclaiming at the originality and depth of the children's thinking.

The younger ones loved imaginary speeches parties. In these I almost always acted as toastmaster, jotting down beforehand a list of subjects so that I could be ready to introduce without previous warning, one after another as "Mrs. Spoopendyke," or "Mr. Featherhead," "who will give us an account of his seven years' work exploring in Mesopotamia, and the ancient Hittite tombs he discovered," or "will give us an account of how she came to found the Society for Furnishing Hoopskirts to Elderly Gentlemen." Or perhaps, "We will now hear from Dr. Doolittle," or "Huckleberry Finn." We had a (not too rigid) time limit of two or three minutes. The children proved highly inventive and droll; and I found that if eleven- and twelve-year-olds attempted this in small groups, they liked very much to have me take notes of their sentence arrangements (featuring, of course, their best points and their improvement).

We have had at Manumit miniature Shakespearian plays: *Five Scenes from Julius Cæsar*, taken very often from *Lamb's Tales*, and using the children's own language, except for the very thrilling passages, where we used the great original. We thus gave a modern language version of the *Winter's Tale*—a plan two of the children made, which I at first didn't encourage, because I foresaw difficulties they didn't see, difficulties which proved in the end not to exist! A nine-year-old girl came into the English room one morning and told me she intended arranging four scenes from the *Taming of the Shrew*. These scenes she sketched out in writing and succeeded in manning with five or six boys of about her own age, one of whom, with infinite gusto, and a voice inconceivably honeyed and delicate, assumed a lady's part. But Tessie was a child of somewhat petulant temper, and when this plan of hers had proceeded so far as the second or third rehearsal, there was such intolerable bickering among the cast that I refused any longer to stage manage it. That evening Tessie hunted me up and said, "I've seen all the boys, and we all think we'll go ahead with the play. We really think we can do it just as well without you—and maybe even better!"

This was really thrilling; and, much electrified, I said I would help to any extent wanted with the costumes, and if they wished me, I would come to the dress rehearsal. This arrangement was triumphantly carried through, and the play was produced with immense spirit and considerable éclat.

We have had a great many plays at Manumit first and last. My own work with the children in dramatics has always involved spontaneous language on their part, rather than meticulously learned parts (which to my ear almost always produce a rather stilted effect). In this manner the Manumit children have dramatized *Tom Sawyer*, Masefield's *Dauber*, the assassination of Lincoln, the underground railway and Harriet Tubman's great adventures, the life of Manumit itself, etc. In these plays we never had a prompter. If anyone forgot his part, he either improvised something, or his fellow actors came to his rescue with something appropriate, and helped him back with an improvised cue. None of these plays ever suffered an embarrassing moment from such a cause.

Of course the children spontaneously wrote plays, and some of these they acted; one in particular was written, rehearsed, costumed, set and successfully produced within a single week's time, by two eleven-year-old girls. But this was a high-water mark.

I once assigned, to a group of twelve- and fourteen-year-olds, four-chapter autobiographies. The first chapter was to cover home, family, and childhood up to beginning school; the second, from the first day at school to some well-remembered event such as moving into a new house, the birth of a younger brother or sister, or something else that made, in the writer's estimation, a proper landmark. The third chapter was to bring the narrative up to exactly a year previous; and the last chapter was to cover the previous year.

These autobiographies aroused so much interest that children of all ages and dispositions began writing theirs. I have kept copies of a number of these autobiographies. Herman became so interested in his that he continued writing it even when ill in the infirmary. Gussie's ran to five thousand words, and hadn't a dull line in it. Of course the effect of the autobiographies upon bashful or repressed children was very releasing and expanding. And they were valuable, too, as guiding the teacher to a deeper acquaintance with the children. I joined with the children and wrote my own, and found it very good fun.

Two or three of the things we have done in grammar have been very successful indeed. Especially the students of all ages enjoyed the "Collections." The first of the "Collections" was—

> Collect fifty pairs of twins—nouns and verbs, like this
> A cook—to cook

The children flew at this with keen interest, and I heard with joy their spontaneous self-questionings, in which, without knowing it, they began investigating for themselves the deep logic of grammar. Next came "Collect thirty collective nouns." They were soon comparing lists and arguing "Is library a collective noun?" "If library is, then book is—a collection of pages!" These collections were made on paper, individually; but when we began collecting ten adjectives apiece ending with -al, -ous, etc., it was much more fun to do it *viva voce* (our groups being small), and I kept score of everybody while they triumphantly produced new specimens far beyond the allotted number. Sidney Goldberg, a Stelton boy, whose program didn't require grammar, and who had made up his mind that he didn't like it, laid down the tale of adventure he was reading at the other end of the long English room, and came and joined with us in collecting adjectives; and from that time on, he was a grammar enthusiast. This collecting of adjectives, or adverbs, or nouns, with special endings, like -ous, or -ly, or -ness, or -ry, seems to me immensely valuable, for the children, *con amore*, search and winnow out their conceptions of the parts of speech, until they have that thing so unspeakably superior to even a well-understood definition, namely, *a living and organic form* for language, firmly planted in their imagination. Aside from this, they unconsciously enlarge their vocabularies, unconsciously organize their notions of spelling, and begin with almost excited interest to discover how words are built out of one another. It constitutes a genuine exploration.

I haven't spoken of the things I devised and thought clever, which didn't capture the children's interest at all, or even of a majority of the things that did; but I do want to speak of two of our Manumit customs, which I think fundamentally valuable, even were it at some cost: first the community meetings, where everybody in school was certain sooner or later to be elected chairman or secretary or both, and where everybody learned more or less to think on his feet with the genuine object of influencing his colleagues and had a realistic reason for shaping his thought as coherently as possible. And then our fixed habit of making academic games and projects always coöperative, never competitive.

This seems to me sure to make discussions broader and more living in their demands upon the whole intellectual and emotional outfit of the children's minds, as well as to penetrate them with social inclusiveness— a feeling worth its weight in pearls.

SARAH N. CLEGHORN.

THE first step necessary toward a successful presentation of poetry is for the teacher, preferably by means of his own deliberate thinking, to come to a clear conception of the purpose of what he is doing. Granted that there is an intellectual approach to the "Ode to a Grecian Urn"; granted that the full emotional response is not possible without it; none the less the prime values sought are not purely intellectual. They are to be found in emotional responses to poetry similar to those which, in his own experience, the teacher recalls as crucial in opening up to him the esthetic values in life which it is the function of poetry to supply. If there are none to recall, he should not be teaching poetry.

The teacher must be very certain, therefore, to begin his work with such poems as will be sure to call forth a response. Here lies the value of the work done in recent years by Untermeyer and Forbes. But we must carefully gauge our group. In the case of boys, Service and the more bustling poems of Kipling never fail; our own critical powers need not intrude too soon. It was the meat that Cæsar fed on which made him great.

In the second place, I think that the teacher must consciously keep himself pointing toward the goal selected, even when this entails the rejection of traditional methods whose object is something else. These include analysis of a poem before the group is ready to analyze it; the assigning of poems and memory passages which don't call forth a response, because teacher thinks they should; the confusion resulting from the teaching of vocabulary and of poetry at the same time; the obsession that a thing must be old before it is good.

I think that the third element necessary to success in teaching poetry— it cannot be called a step because it is the result of a number of suggestions by the way—is to make boys gradually aware that poetry is not the artificial and feeble thing they have imagined, but a great lifting force in a man's life; not a matter of long-haired rhyme-hounds prowling by moonlit brooks, but natural, intimate, universal. Let the lad feel his own pulse, count his breathing, watch the waves, the planets, and the constellations, think of his dances, imagine the invisible forces at work in his radio, and he becomes aware that rhythm is built into the very fabric of his life. Let him remember that this sense of rhythm, which makes his foot beat to the passing parade, probably had its beginning when his mother's blood began beating through his own half-formed body.

He is then ready for further readings in poetry, and these may be largely left to take care of themselves. That is, so long as we have at hand books—piles of them—to refer to, to finger, to read from. Responses are individual. Let him read, learn, and finally write what he wants. When, with a mumbled apology for being a fool, he shuffles his first copy of verses under a pile of our papers, no need to disguise delight. We shall read it with wide human sympathy and build on whatever is there. For now and then there will be something which will bring a little gasp of amazement from the teacher, and a slight chill traveling up toward the back of his neck. He will forget what is happening in the room, and will go over to the window to read it again to himself slowly.

JOHN A. LESTER.

No ONE who teaches English, I think, enjoys writing about teaching it. It seems so presumptuous to imply that any method of teaching has had much to do with that natural and strange force, the creative urge of the child. In so far as the creative spirit is simply one which sees the world in a new way, a fresh significant way, that spirit is an integral part of any childhood that is natural—not inhibited too soon by conventions. Not to inhibit is a harder matter in any scheme of education than first appears. It means a kind of tolerant patience on the part of managing elders which is unnatural to us. We know that however freshly a child is seeing or feeling, the little-mastered medium of expression is a difficulty. Too much interference with the manipulation of the tools in the process will inevitably make the child disconnect what has just been seen or felt vividly and freshly from the expression of it. We have all seen the great danger in making skill in expression seem to be something valuable in itself. It seems much safer to let the expression fumble and fumble rather than interfere too soon and break the connection. The child must realize first of all that what the teacher really cares about is the observation, the idea, the truth which the child is struggling to express, and that the teacher is willing to be patient, interested, and tolerant while the child is trying to make the bridge to language.

Because we believe this, we are starting in the teaching of composition to ten-year-old children by focusing the attention on perception, not on expression. We have a series of problems for eyes that see, ears that hear, noses that smell, mouths that taste, hands that touch. A kitten playing on the floor, a budded branch in a jar, a car coming in the subway, the smell of baking gingerbread, may serve as starting points.

In the words that convey the fresh, accurate impression of the child there is frequently unexpected beauty. After a few weeks we notice usually a heightened awareness of the world about that is, after all, the beginning of all creative writing.

In another way, we think that our Poetry Group in the Winsor School does something to foster the creative spirit in the older children—not that we think we can teach girls to write poetry; we know that in any real sense we can not. We do believe, however, that we make the attempted writing of poetry a possible pleasure to more and more people each year by making it seem a more natural creative activity. This volunteer group which meets for an hour once a week is made up of people who have written verse. Last year the ticket of admission for every meeting was an original poem. This year the ticket of admission for every third meeting is a poem. Anyone may come from the youngest to the oldest in the school, if she comes bearing a poem. As a matter of fact the age range has been from thirteen years to about forty. Several teachers, including one of the science teachers, usually come, and graduates of the school return occasionally. We hear that several parents are preparing to come, but they have not appeared as yet! As last year the most creditable poetry usually came from one of the youngest members of the group, the idea grew that age had no overwhelming advantage. The leveling process produces a salutary humbleness on the part of the older members, and the younger members tend to think more highly of the pleasure and dignity of an activity entered into so seriously by their elders.

Our procedure is simple. The reader for the day collects the poems at the door. We take turnabout as reader. The poems are read anonymously. The first reading goes straight through, taking them as they come, without comment. For the second reading and careful discussion sometimes it seems obvious that certain poems should be grouped together. After the second reading of each poem, criticism bursts from every quarter. Value of idea, clearness, beauty of expression, rhythm, and everything else, is attacked and defended. It is a Stoic author who can keep her anonymity under fire. It was pleasant to find, however, after the first few times anonymity concerned very few people, for a fine objective critical spirit seemed to be one of the best by-products. No one has been so discouraged by this free criticism that her first appearance has been her last.

That we may help to encourage the blossoming of a poetic power that otherwise had lain dormant, or that we may bring to a finer blossoming a poetic power that gains in its early growth by the light and air of criticism, we sometimes timidly hope. With more assurance, we believe that by this participation in a creative activity we are helping to create a more intelligently appreciative public for great poets of the future.

FRANCES DORWIN DUGAN.

IT HAS recently been my fate to read a most naïve and, so far as I know, unparalleled disclosure of the creative processes at work in a young "poet." The author, a girl in her second year at high school, relates under the title, *My Autobiography on Poetry*, how she early discovered her extraordinary talent and proceeded to turn out "poems" to the amazement and delight of her family, her teachers, and even the school principal, who always thereafter introduced her as "the little girl who writes such beautiful poems." She was blissfully unaware of technique. No one had ever explained metrics to her, or the pattern of a poem. No one had encouraged her to see the world with her own two eyes and to report truthfully what she saw as she herself saw it.

In response to a hint of disappointment that she had not been progressing so fast in senior high school as she had hoped, I finally nerved myself for the encounter and talked to her. I dared to tell her that most of her poetry was pretty bad. I pointed out the triteness and the stale rhymes and the cheap sentiments. I told her that when she could see something as freshly and individually as my little nephew, who likened the new moon to a banana, she should catch her impression in a net of simple, colorful words that would enable me to see it through her eyes. Then I fortified her with some of Hilda Conkling's poetry and Untermeyer's *This Singing World*, and sent her on her way.

Celia was one who wrote without being urged. When it comes to stirring up enthusiasm for writing poetry, I cannot lay claim to any particular method. The few boys and girls who have slipped their verses under my blotter or ventured a poetic treatment of an assignment would probably have tried expressing themselves in rhyme sooner or later anyway; but I may have had a hand in steering them to more individual daring or a less artificial choice of words. I don't remember ever giving the general assignment, Write a poem, but I should expect an epidemic of acute poetic indigestion if I did. At the beginning of the term, however, I suggest that many assignments might be answered in verse form.

It has been my experience that modern poetry forms a very natural introduction to the reading of poetry and makes a more direct appeal, particularly to young high-school pupils, than older works. John Masefield, Edna Millay, and Carl Sandburg are alive and understandable. I shall never forget the fight over Carl Sandburg in a literature class of mine a year ago. Each member of the class had a day on which he read selected poems from some modern writer and told as much about him as he had been able to find out. The class split on their opinion of Sandburg; and for at least half an hour the reader who had fallen under the Sandburg spell defended her poet against all manner of criticisms hurled at him. It led inevitably to a discussion of what poetry is and what is expected of a poet. Very soon after, the Sandburg devotee began to bring me verses in which she tried to express her ideas as racily and vividly as the object of her admiration. Among these was one which she called *Words*.

> Some words are misshapen like trapezoids and rhombi;
> Others have the beauty of old English lettering or oval mirrors.
>
> Some words snarl like wolves or spit like angry cats;
> Others have the caged grace of lions and leopards.
>
> Some words are gawky and screeching like ostriches and cockatoos;
> Others flash the sunshine on the wings of orioles.
>
> Some words are offensive to sight and smell like stingy weeds;
> Others give us the cool joy of flowers.

Other boys and girls in the same class made attempts to express themselves in verse. One, in particular, was too shy to hand in her things; but I persuaded her to let me see her notebook one day in study hall, and after that she brought me her work. During the term she began to write more concisely and subtly than she had before, reflecting perhaps the influence of Emily Dickinson and Edna Millay.

QUATRAINS

> Love is a gaudy tissue-paper kite—
> The opal sky the height of its desire;
> It flounders futilely, and very bright
> And pitiful, it clings about a wire.
>
> God keeps a flower garden
> Of joys and loves and things like these;
> He has a kitchen garden, too,
> Of terrible necessities.

Some teachers I know have had very interesting results when they have asked for a fourth stanza to Masefield's *Cargoes*. Another teacher steeped one class in poetry for about two weeks, for the most part reading without comment. Then he asked them to write and they achieved some truly astonishing things. I think they liked it, too.

I think a teacher should ordinarily refrain from a too stringent criticism of a poem brought to her. If she emphasizes some of its best features and asks for more poems, succeeding efforts are likely to show the improvement that any amount of correcting would fail to bring about in the original piece. I think that above everything else a sympathetic interest in what each pupil has to say and in the most fitting way of saying it will stimulate the desire to create. I think, too, that many pupils write more spontaneously and freshly in free verse than in accepted standard meters; and any attempt to dogmatize or restrict the medium will bring about a corresponding restraint and reversion to worn-out, hackneyed language. After all, the boy who wrote,

> The forsythia
> By the gateway
> This morning
> Was a blonde laugh
> Echoing your loveliness,

whether he ever publishes a book or not, has felt once the joy of creation; he has approached poetry from the standpoint of the poet, and will, at least, make one in that enlightened audience which makes the writing of great poetry possible.

KATHARINE A. BARBER.

THE POETS' CLUB of Evander Childs High School was organized several years ago. Two girls who were writers of poetry had collected four or five others who were more or less interested in reading and writing verse, and they asked me to be the faculty adviser of their Poets' Club. Before this time very little verse had been written in school. The "Poets' Corner" in the *News*, our weekly newspaper, contained one poem once in two or three weeks. Since then the "Corner" has grown to a column which is filled each week. The *Bridge*, our school magazine, had printed only a few good poems in the ten years of its history. The Poets' Club has undoubtedly been responsible for the present growing and rather general interest in poetry in our school.

Each term, as the older poets have graduated, I have feared that the Club might become defunct, but each new term has brought forth new poets, among them always two or three really talented ones. We have never been large in numbers, our average being six or eight members. Any pupil may become a member by submitting beforehand work of his own that the Club considers as having poetic merit.

Our procedure is most informal. We meet once a week for about two hours. The members read their new poems, and each reading is followed by criticism from the others. They become very keen critics of their own and others' work. Sometimes another pupil will send up his poems by a member, who reads them and later reports the criticism to the writer. The poetry editors of the school paper and the school magazine are members of the Club, and they collect the best poems read for the next issue of their publications. Informal reports are frequently made on books the pupils have been reading or lectures they may have attended. They are all readers of poetry, and we have a kind of circulating library within the Club, including the best anthologies, some books of criticism, and all of the "Pamphlet Poets," both English and American. Sometimes we go together to poetry readings. Last year we heard John Masefield.

Each term the Club gives a poetry contest for the rest of the school, the members themselves not competing. Fifty or a hundred poems will be sent in, most of them bad, but among them a few excellent ones by hitherto undiscovered young poets.

I have been amazed by the quantity and quality of the writing that has been produced. It has ranged from humorous triolets to near-epics, centering around historical events or allegorical figures. After one particularly interesting meeting, I suggested to the Club that they make an anthology of their best work. They were delighted with the idea and began at once to work it out. It proved to be a very educating experience indeed to all concerned. They decided to include all of the good poetry ever printed in the school periodicals. This necessitated going through the older files of both publications. Several hundred poems were considered. These were subjected to rigorous criticism so that we might have only the best. Our final decision included sixty poems by twenty-four writers.

Then came all the harrowing and thrilling questions involved in making a book. We must have cuts—something to suggest Poetry! The members who were artists as well as poets made designs for cuts, and the two best were chosen. We decided upon the format after examining, from that point of view, Mosher books and other publications that we especially admired. We must have a printer who would give us the best work at the lowest possible cost, and various estimates were secured and considered. The wording of the title was another important matter. Finally, there was the problem of advertising and sales management.

Mr. Hughes Mearns, in criticizing our *Anthology*, said "The work is genuine and beautifully individual." His last word, I think, is very good criticism. The poems are quite different; each one writes from his own experience and like himself. Mary B. writes nature poetry almost exclusively—nature highly poetized, as in

DUSK ON THE ROOF

I journeyed to the roof one twilight deep,
To watch the weary world go hustling by;
There, thru the noise, a silence seemed to creep.
Its calm and balm gold-threaded with a sigh.

A few faint lights shone dimly thru the haze,
I saw the last swift swallow southward fly—
The trees and houses faded to a maze,
And trails and veils of smoke rose up the sky.

I stood and gazed until the evening star
Came stepping timidly into the night,
And thought I heard its music from afar,
That sings and rings thru firmaments of light.

When I asked her how she happened to write that poem, she replied, "I really went up to bring down the clothes, and Mother thought I was gone an awfully long time."

Herzl F., who is a violinist, uses musical images in most of his poems.

MORS VITAQUE

Men say that life is discord
And death is harmony;
Yet death is but a measure's rest
And life the melody.

Helen M. is our best love poet. Some of her poems are really exquisite.

PRUDENT APRIL

If I can only come safely through April,
And keep my eyes detached and cold,
And keep my dreams behind my lips,
And on my heart a firm, sure hold;

This would be different from other Aprils,
This would be peacefully quiet, and then
I could go softly the rest of the year—
But, oh, my heart is high again!

The "beautiful individuality" is due to the gods or the muses or whatever power it is that inspires poets. These youngsters poetize the life they live. A kind of negative credit may be due me in that I have never suggested subjects or required them to do definite assignments. I tell them about rhythms and forms and then let them do as they please. I feel that I collect poets rather than teach pupils to write poetry. But there are many poets in the world, especially among the young.

NELLIE B. SERGENT.

MY FIRST concern in teaching has been the developing of a love for poetry and for verse writing. I have felt it my mission to help my pupils to enrich their lives as mine has been enriched. I am a happy teacher because the world of poetry has made every day a strangely beautiful adventure, and I desire my pupils to be just as happy in their various future walks of life. My most interesting work has been done in connection with the Poetry Club in the Wadleigh High School. Here are students who will be stenographers, teachers, lawyers. Many have gone so far in their effort to interpret that they have developed their own idiom and a resulting confidence that is not misplaced. Moreover they have had to delve into the spiritual significance of many things in order to give their own ideas. Surely their present effort will help to build up a spiritual background that will not fade quickly, even long after they cease to write.

To tell just what is done at the meetings of the club would be impossible. This extract from an article written by a reporter for the school paper gives the spirit of any meeting as clearly as it can be defined:

"To attempt to describe a meeting of the Poetry Club would be like attempting to describe the vagaries of a blue-white cloud or the wanderings of a baby brook. All follow Fancy's dictates. Thus the meeting on Monday, October 10, touched on the intelligence of the Chinese, and the respective values of certain rhymes, the mechanism of poetry, and the uprisings in Armenia.

"But in spite of the seeming waywardness of the conversation, much is accomplished by the club. The girls learn to say the old, lovely things—old, yet new to us—in a fitting new way. They learn to form patterns of their own, to gain a firm touch that gives to the beauty of their lines a confidence as ballast."

A student may go away from such a meeting walking on air, and she may write a poem that night on "My Mother's Hands" or "Young Trees" or some other subject that received little or no attention at the meeting. However, we know that the poem would never have been written if she had not attended.

I believe that every faculty adviser of such a group should write verse herself. She should be a coworker. I frequently read my own verse at these meetings and, I am glad to say, receive frank criticism!

Because my own poetry group was a growing one, I decided some years ago to feel the pulse of interest in verse writing in other New

York high schools. Our girls invited representatives from other poetry clubs. Fourteen enthusiastic students appeared. Then and there the boys and girls decided to have two meetings a year—an open one for the discussion of work in their various groups and a competitive reading. Three prizes were to be offered at the reading: one for a boy or girl, and two of equal rank, one for a boy and one for a girl. Our first meeting was almost a catastrophe. Ninety-nine poets appeared! Since then we have had to limit the number to one representative from each school, who is allowed to read one long or two short poems. Twenty-five schools were represented at our last meeting.

Because the schools are so far apart, we have had to drop the open meeting, since it is impossible for a representative number to reach us late in the afternoon. For our annual competitive reading, principals excuse their students early in order that we may begin at two o'clock and that they may reach home before dark.

Professional poets have been most kind in consenting to act as judges. We have had Anna Hempstead Branch, Arthur Guiterman, Marguerite Wilkinson, Joseph Campbell, and several others, including Dr. Elias Lieberman, Principal of the Thomas Jefferson High School, who has shown great interest. It has been our custom to ask them to autograph copies of their own books, which we offer as prizes.

It is most gratifying that the Inter-High School Poetry League has encouraged the forming of poetry groups in high schools where there were none before. Prize poems have appeared in new school anthologies, and I dare to hope that we include in our number professional poets of the near future.

ETHEL M. ERICSON.

YOUNG PEGASUS

Lucia Burton Morse

THERE is no room left for doubt, as one views the mass of children's verse which may be assembled today by a call to schools and parents, that "all God's chillun's got wings." They are as various in their action as the many-winged things of earth; some, just carried off the ground, feeble and frail, and others possessing the strong, glorious wings of a future poet; but each flutter of any kind lifting humanity out of the commonplace into a freer realm.

It is no new thing for children to essay poetry. The thing that poetry is made of has been always there in the race since time began, beating against the bars of inexpression, or dumbly sitting behind them because there was not strength or knowledge enough to break through, except in the case of genius.

Not one of us of the older generation but has covered sheets of paper, or filled up the blank pages of old notebooks with secret efforts to get into words the elusive something which wells up in the heart when beauty, or joy, or sorrow, has entered into our experience. As life goes on, and we find in its satisfactions other mediums of expression, more amenable to will and inspiration, and more acceptable to a conventional society, we cease, even secretly, to use our own wings, and take our flights vicariously with the poets.

Not so this group of children of the last decade. Psychology and understanding have taken away the bars of timidity, self-consciousness, and self-depreciation, and everywhere young lovely thoughts fly forth in flocks like the swallows of one of their own poems.

SWALLOWS *

The air is thick with swarms of swallows
    High among the clouds,
    Flying all in crowds;
Up the hills and down the hollows,
Swarms of swooping, swerving swallows,

Burnished, dark blue, darting swallows,
    Sailing o'er the sea,
    Flying blithe and free;
Every bird the next one follows,
Swarms of flying, floating swallows.

GEORGE R. (age 12).

Reading through the verses *en masse*, good and poor, those which are commonplace and those with touches of genius and a forecast of real poethood, one can only be glad beyond words that universal verse making has become a legitimate and dignified procedure, and that the fine thought, the feelings of ecstasy or pain which surge up in the mind of the growing boy and girl, may find this wholesome outlet through trained and open ways, in forms of beauty. We may not have greater poets than the past has given us, but we shall have more poetry in the daily outlook of men and women, which will be a saving grace to this materialistic age.

It is a temptation, in looking over the pile of material before me, to generalize somewhat, and many questions arise:

* *Homework and Hobbyhorses*, Perse Playbooks, No. VI. Perse School, Cambridge, England. E. P. Dutton.

How much should the little snatches of poetic expression of younger children be preserved in print?

How many of the things so printed are absolutely untouched by the artistry of the adult?

Should the child be unconscious of the form of his expression, or are these telling little touches of an artist aids to him?

Is the free verse of the newer schools a more legitimate avenue of expression for a child than freedom of thought clothed in the poetic form of sonnet, quatrain, villanelle, or what not?

If such a questionnaire were sent to those gifted men and women who are cultivating this new field, it is evident that opinions would be varied and conflicting, for, after all is said, it is true that the verse making of any group of children is, in the main, reflection of the ideas of the leader of that group on these points.

The generalizations present themselves as book after book, sheet after sheet of verse is gone through, written by both boys and girls, from public and private schools, in every English-speaking country; and by all ages of children, from the four- and five-year-olds lisping rhythmic repetitions, to the serious college youth, finding expression for his struggling thoughts of life and love and death.

The geographical distribution of this work is wide and the results, from a standpoint of merit, unaffected by mere location, though the subject matter is influenced by environment. Note these verses on Spring from two high schools, the first from mellow California, the second from eastern city surroundings:

SPRING DAY

Lavender rain from a shining sky,
Lavender, white, and shadow blue,
Gently falling the whole day through.

Silvery mist on the apricot trees,
Low and soft, though the sun of spring
Should be teasing and tearing the whispery thing.

And who could tell from a distant hill
That the mist and rain through the frail sunshine
Could be apricot bloom, and wisteria vine?

JOSEPHINE M.
Los Angeles High School.*

* Anthology of Student Verse.

SPRINGTIME

Oh, it's springtime in the city,
  And the skies are turning blue,
And a bit of green is showing
  With a freshness ever new.

There's a sparrow in a tree top,
  Who must surely burst his throat,
For he's glad, glad, glad,
  With the warmth and joy and hope.

The dingy streets are brighter
  In the tumble and the roar,
And the ragged children babble
  Of the play that is in store.

And Tony has his hurdy gurdy
  Singing up the way,
And you know for sure that
  Spring has come—it's in the air today.
            ELIZABETH R. S.
            West Philadelphia High School.*

This from a girl of the Chicago Latin School visiting in Rome:

CITY ETERNAL

Marble, warmed by the hot sun of centuries,
Stained by rain,
Worn by wind;
Color, mellowed to a softness unbelievable,
Bits of columns,
Statues, cornices,
Steps of yellow and pink marble.
And all alone, three slender, fluted shafts
Of dazzling white,
Aloof, serene and perfect.

Two fountains, each a surge of rainbow mist,
Reaching
Toward a sky of infinite blue,
Falling back upon a pavement of pure gold.
The Cathedral,
Domed and low;
Long rows of pillars outstretched on either side;
And beneath them

* *The Torch Book of Verse.*

Alternate streaks
Of cool, black shade,
Of hot, yellow sunshine
On rough and dusty cobblestones.

Patiently switching off the flies, an old nag
Bowed, dejected,
A fitting steed
For the dusty "carozza," awaits a passing fare.
Streets gay with laughing, jostling crowds,
Officers in uniform
With clinking, shining spurs and sabers.
Children with their noisy clamor
Playing in the teeming streets;
Sunlight, shadow,
Beauty, squalor.

VIRGINIA S. (age 17).

and another from an English public school:

THE RUSTIC PATRIOT

The hills dark-cloaked by the plantation,
The dove-soft grass in Oxted fields,
A sweep of down, the village street,
The cowslips yellowing the wealds
Where hills with hills and valleys meet—
This is his England, this his nation.
By Titsey woods, by Titsey hill,
By all the stiles which mark the way
From Limpsfield over to Woldingham,
By Grub Street, by the ruined mill,
By half-a-dozen Charts,—the dam
That blocks the stream, and by the may
That blooms beside his cottage door,
The mosses on his garden wall,
By three old cherry-trees or more
He is a patriot; for all
Are his, and he is well content
To call them England; there is furled
His battle-flag, beneath, his sword,
His ancient shield all cut and bent,
For all of this, without a word
He'll guard the land which gave him birth,
Though Oxted valley be his earth,
And Titsey skyline bound his world,

And going home once more, will say:—
"For England have I fought this day."
JOHN H. B.
Bradfield College, Berkshire.*

Free poetic expression of the very young children seldom has rhyme, and most frequently partakes of the form of a song or chant with many repeated words. Here, however, is a four-year-old from the Park School of Cleveland, Ohio, who did find a convenient rhyme:

The sun is shining very bright,
I wonder will it rain tonight?
Maybe it will
Maybe it won't
Maybe it will rain.

FRANCIS (age 4).

Here is the repetition but no rhyme:

Dark, dark, come dark,
Rain, rain, rain hard.
When it comes morning
Rain stops, dark goes,
Flowers look pretty.

DENNISON (age 5½)
Park School of Cleveland, Ohio.

It is possible, in the collections at hand, to trace the growth of power in expression in an individual child.

Kenneth S., of the Ethical Culture Branch School, New York City, wrote in Grade III:

HALLOWEEN

Halloween is here tonight
The witches will go crazy
All the night they'll dance and fight
And at day
They'll go away
They're lazy.

In the fourth grade we have from him:

A WINTER MORNING

Everything is beautiful
From trees to housetops

* *Public School Verse: An Anthology.* Vol. III, 1921-1922. Wm. Heinemann, Ltd., London.

White forms
Towering up into the sky
Whitened wind
Blowing everything about
Not a sound
All the earth seems dead
All is white
This is the work of the snow.

Spontaneous group records may produce lovely and original results, and prove an inspiration to the child who hesitates to try his powers in a full poem.

Here is the work of a group, nine and ten years old, at Carson College for Orphan Girls, Flourtown, Pa.:

MOTES

A little straight hole in the roof with the sunlight peeping through
When you look you saw all pretty colors.

They were dancing.
One would chase the other.
The hole looked like a little window.
The motes looked like birds flying back and forth.
They fell over each other.
They were bright colors.
They looked like tinsel on a Christmas tree.
They got scared when we blew them and went back to the hole.

One day in the attic there was a little hole and when the sun was out little
    colors would shine through and dance.
I wasn't there but I asked these things:—
Did they look like the colors on Mother Goose roof?
Did they look like the colors like sometimes the leaves of trees look in the
    beginning of Spring—like they dance coming down from the trees?
Did they look like butterflies—like the big and small ones?
Did they look like sometimes the children's dresses are?
Did they look like some china and all kinds of countries' dishes?
Did they look like some of the shells at the sea shore?

MARIE H. (age 9),
ALICE W. (age 9),
EDITH D. (age 10).

The Lincoln School, of Teachers College, New York City, has a beautiful illustration of this form of procedure. Dr. Caldwell's introduction explains the form of the offering and its purpose:

"After we had considered in a general way the meaning of the Disarmament Congress, we asked the younger children to tell us what they thought would be the meaning of peace to the whole world. They told us directly and simply in these unpremeditated words. . . . Each sentence is the utterance of a single child. The arrangement into groups and the selection of the refrain, however, was done by a committee of the teaching staff. . . . Given as a tableau play "The Meaning of Peace" was appropriately our Thanksgiving offering to the school, as it is now our Christmas greeting and our message to all our friends."

IN PRAISE OF PEACE

A Child Said

Peace means the beginning of a new world
Peace means a whole world like one country
It means that all nations are friends
It means joy to the world

Then All The People Said

The Lord shall give His people the blessing of peace

A Child Said

Peace is quiet and calm. It is rest
It is silence after a storm
It is love and friendship
It is the world's dream of dreams

Then All The People Said

The Lord shall give His people the blessing of peace

A Child Said

In time of peace the strong respect the weak; the great respect the
small; the many respect the few
Peace brings comfort and happiness
It brings bread to the hungry
It brings prosperity to nations

Then All The People Said

The Lord shall give His people the blessing of peace

A Child Said

Peace is like a mother to those who have suffered
Peace after war is like a sleep after a long journey
It is like Spring after Winter. It brings sunshine into the world
It is like sweet music after harsh sounds
Peace is a dream that someone dreamed would come true
We wish that peace would come and stay with us forever

Then All The People Said

The Lord shall give His people the blessing of peace.

In the same way a group of second-grade children of the Junior Elementary School of Downers Grove, Illinois, reflected at Thanksgiving time the spirit of St. Francis' *Canticle to the Sun:*

> We thank Thee, Lord, for our happy days
> For our food and clothes and our eyes to see;
> For the rain, the flowers, the snow, the sun;
> The stars that shine through the dark dark night;
> For our Sister Moon that shines so bright,
> For the earth we play on and the grass so green.
> Oh Lord, we thank Thee for everything.

Poems of the "Littlemen" (as all under thirteen are called in the Perse School of Cambridge) are numerous and varied, and with a sincerity and charm of their own as the following selections show:

SHELLS

> Shells on beaches.
> Waves adashing on the shore—on the nice smooth sand.
> Birds aflying above and singing,
> Sea gulls and water birds.
> Pelicans on perches
> And diving for the fish.
> The sky is blue when the water is blue.
> The sky is gray when the water is gray.
> Picking up shells are all the people,
> And the dashing tide comes in toward evening.
> When the tide goes out
> It leaves a little pool of water,
> And star fish all alive.
> Then the water near the sand bars,
> As the shifting waves come in,
> Leaves the shells for little children.
> > JEAN W. McK. (age 5)
> > Edgewood School, Greenwich, Conn.

BELL BUOY

> Ding, dong,
> Hear my song,
> Hear my voice
> Far away
> In the sea.
> Far away
> Deep down
> In the sea.

Ding, dong,
Ding, dong,
Hear my song.

L. (age 6)
City and Country School,
New York City.

In the city.
When April comes the streets look cleaner.
Apartment houses seem much redder.
Cement sidewalks shine in the sun.
So do roof tops after rain.

.   .   .   .   .   ꓹ

In the country.
Spring is here!
Soft rain comes down and wakens flowers.
Red, lavender, and pink crocuses peep up through green grass.
Yellow daffodils sway in the breeze,
And tulips will soon be red.
Spring is here!

HARRY (age 5½)
Park School of Cleveland, Ohio.

THE LILAC BUSH

I love the lilacs.
Their leaves are like hearts;
When I go near the lilac bush, they bow to me,
And I bow to them.

AIDA F. (age 8)
Public School No. 45, Bronx, New York City.

THE TREE

There was a tree;
It stood by many other trees
All of beauty;
But it was the loveliest.
It had great gold and yellow leaves,
And through the moss
That dropped about it,
It looked at me.
With moss like knitting thin and fine,
All thin and fine.

EVELYN W. (age 10)
Luther Burbank School, Santa Rosa, Cal.

RAIN

Rain patters on the attic shingles,
And the drops run crooked down the window pane,
You look out into the warm grayness of the world,
Of dripping leaves, and drops falling into puddles;
And you wish you were out in the woods,
To dance naked on wet pine needles.
Rain pours in torrents down your roof,
And lightning flashes past the window pane,
Shutting out your view of the wild world outside,
With trees tossing to and fro, and the branches
      creaking against each other.
(It's good to be safe in your cosy house,
Watching the pine cones being tossed about.)
            MARJORIE W. (age 11)
            Ethical Culture School, New York City.

DUSK

Into the sleeping garden creeps the dusk
Downward wreathing.
Stray wisps of mist behind her waver
And drift away
To hide beneath the tiny bridge.

The darting dragon fly that swirled and swooped
Above the brook
Has gone to rest among the lotus blooms
All dew misted.
            PEGGY P. (age 11)
            Phœbe Anna Thorne School, Bryn Mawr, Pa.

THE RAIN

I am alone, alone. The great sun frightens me, that ball of fire. The lone moon chills me, the stars laugh at me. But the rain, the little drops of spring rain! They fall into my heart and soothe it, quiet it. They bring me peace from the sky.
            WILMA S. (age 11)
            Walden School, New York City.

English poems come to us redolent of literary traditions, mature in thought, and evidencing a richness of experience and background which is the inevitable outgrowth of an older civilization than ours.

The great English Public Schools have been the pioneers in this particular phase of creative work, and since 1920, have published yearly an anthology of *Public School Verse* which "aims primarily at bringing into a larger circle of criticism, whether kind or harsh, and of a wider competition, those writers who are most likely to take advantage at a critical stage in their development of such an opportunity."

Selecting at random from some of these small volumes, we have from Rugby School:

ARCHÆOLOGY

To dig from mounds of Nineveh
Old fragments of forgotten things,
To catch some fragrance of the past, .
Some warrior's ardor for the long-fought fight,
Some dark-haired princess' deep, sweet love of him,
To feel the life of ages dead and gone and dead,
  That dream for me.

To finger treasures of Tyrinthian kings,
Stand where they stood, and watch the same green bay
Where golden galleys of Phœnicia rode
Bearing their purple dyes and robes for queens,
Their jeweled sword-hilts and their gilt-graved blades
And Nubian slave-mined gold from Mizraim,
  That dream for me.

From some dim figure swathed in mists of time
To snatch the hiding veil, and greet as friend
A man who dies six thousand years ago,
Menes the Tinite, or Semiramis,
Those whose great kingdoms, more than passed away,
Have crumbled dustward out of memory!
  That dream for me.

       D. R. G.*

And this from Tonbridge School, with its vivid picture of the horror imprinted by war on a young mind.

KEEP TO THE LEFT

Keep to the left and tread your hobnailed lightest;
There's someone underneath—no! not alive—
He's only one of those who broke their necks,
Thought it was fine—or otherwise—and fell,
Shuddered, lay still, sown in the ready soil!
The bursting shells had plowed it up already
. . . Just one of those who melted in the smoke,
He cried, "That does me!—ugh!" then plunged and sank

* *Public School Verse,* 1919-20.

Into a sloppy crater and arous'd
The musty things that curdled on the bottom . . .
Till choking bubbles giggled to the surface,
Smiled there and spat in fragments—so his life,
Smiling, had shattered into shards uncounted,
To scud in darkness on the gale of time,
Unknown, unseen, forgotten. . . . Mind the hole!

D. J. M.*

Bedales, one of the great pioneer coeducational schools of England, has in its printed collection poems from both boys and girls, and one of the latter has contributed this vigorous and interesting villanelle:

CAIN

I shall go down to dust again,
My soul disperse like some dark cloud;
I cannot love my fellow men.

Until I love all men, till then
I have no reason to be proud;
I shall go down to dust again.

No prayers of mine have meaning when
I cannot love an alien crowd,
I cannot love my fellow men.

Yet some I loved, indeed some ten
Who laugh not now my head is bowed;
I shall go down to dust again.

I lied, I lied with tongue and pen,
But in the end I cried aloud;
"I cannot love my fellow men!"

Yet some there are, beyond my ken,
Whose love remains by doubt uncowed;
I shall go down to dust again;
I cannot love my fellow men.

PHYLLIS W. D. (age 15).†

The Perse Playbooks, from the Perse School in Cambridge, are another series of yearly publications from a single school, the last being the sixth in their series. These include the work of younger boys, but keep to the same high standards.

* Public School Verse, 1919-20.
† Bedales Poetry, 1927. Bedales School, England.

"Imitation of good models has always been a part of the method,"
says Mr. Cook in his introduction, "and these boys have got by heart
literally scores of poems. Yet there is no sign of slavish reproduction
in their work."

Note this tender thing from a group of carols.

THE FLIGHT TO EGYPT

One day the word was given,
    That all the babes should dee;
But Joseph had a vision
    Telling him to flee.

They took an ass to ride on,
    Across the desert land,
And so our Lord was saved
    From Herod's cruel hand.

HAROLD R. (age 12).*

And this gay little rhyme:

THE NEW PENNY

One day my mother gave to me
    A lovely bright new penny;
I ran off to the shop to see,
    If ships they had got any.

I asked if I might have a look
    For ships if they had any,
But suddenly I saw a book
    Better than mine by many.

I asked if I could have the book
    For my bright and lovely penny;
He gave it me with a smiling look,
    "It's the cheapest I've sold by many."

LESLIE MACA. (age 12).†

Humor is not as prevalent as pure sentiment, but here and there are
found nice touches of it.

TO A GAME BIRD ON THE TABLE

Little wild fowl,
I would mourn you,
Small brown denizen of the fragrant wood.
Life should be tender

---

* *Homework and Hobbyhorses,* Perse Playbooks, No. VI.
† *Homework and Hobbyhorses,* Perse Playbooks, No. VI.

Of a small brown bird
But—with a sauce of herbs and a little salt
You are very good.

SARAH S. (age 15)
Tower Hill School, Wilmington, Del.

JOHN PURSE

He was an old crank, was old John Purse.
He never felt bad, but he always felt worse.
He never ate little, tho he always ate less.
Tho he never was thin, he grew thinner in stress.
He never held tight, tho he always held tighter.
He never was right, but he always was righter.
At ninety he died—like him none such.
Tho he lived more than most of us, he never lived much.

HELEN G. (age 17)
Chicago Latin School.

It is in the High School, however, that we begin to find the real out-
pourings of youth, confronted with all the burning questions of life and
death, love and war, in their first seriousness. Here, in a flood of singing
verse, we find expression of every feeling humanity may have, much of
it startling in its depth and understanding to those who have not yet
accustomed themselves to thinking of these maturing souls as other than
the "children" of but a year ago.

A LONELY CHILD

Once when I was a lonely child,
I stood upon a hillside wild;
The world stretched out to meet the sea,
Then sank into eternity,
Unsolved. . . .

I stood upon a dismal street;
A lonely dog was at my feet;
A man tapped by, he could not see;
Dear God, the world is yet to me,
Unsolved. . . .

DOROTHY M. P.
High School, Chester, Pa.*

THE FATHER

Hearing his son and daughter
Laugh, and talk of dances, theaters,

* *Glimpses: Anthology of Secondary School Verse.*

Of their school, and friends,
And books,
Taking it all for granted—
He sighs a bit,
Remembering wistfully
A certain mill-town
And his boyhood there,
And puts his arm
Across his son's broad shoulder,
Dumbly, as fathers do.

JOHN H.
High School, Somerville, Mass.*

WAR

Onward the ominous footsteps go,
Clinking, scraping, sucking in the mud.
All day long they go past.
Ever the same. Faces . . . set hard. . . .
Young, tremulous, unknowing.
Faces grim with the grime of a thousand such roads.
Overhead, the sky—a huge wispy grayness—
Hovers, all wings, jealously waiting.
Miles yet from the front when
Out of the stillness streaks a river of living fire;
It crashes to earth, seering, up-rooting,
And in its wake, so many more lie by the road.
Stop them—stop them! Ask them where they are going.
Do they know?
Do they know who sent him and why?
Dear Father, before it's too late
Turn them back.
My three went like that—marching
Straight ahead, and where are they now?
Marching still, straight ahead, somewhere . . .
Tell them; and cannot they see
Those shadows laughing at them from the side of the road.
Those shadows—men who
Have gone by once and returned to mock.
Thousands and thousands of lives.
Where are they going? . . .
Cannot . . . they . . . see . . . ?

BARBARA B. (age 17)
Beaver Country Day School,
Chestnut Hill, Mass.

* *Dawn: Anthology of Secondary School Verse.*

ON THE G. A. R. FIFE AND DRUM CORPS

As They Stood Playing in Front of the Court House

We stand, three frail old men, and play faint tunes,
While thousands stare, or brush us by in harsh, bewildering haste;
We play the songs which stirred men's blood to fire,
We crack the whips which flicked a nation's ire,
On our lips is the taste
Of battle; dimly these great crowds which press
So close on us with half-pitying scorn
Are hazy figures on a blood-crazed plain
Smoke-swept; convulsing in wild din and stress.
The brawn of youth has not been spent in vain,
In union of our making—these were born.

BEATRIX M.
Central High School,
Omaha, Nebraska.*

TO ALICE

When I was working in the garden
Near gentian buds and daisies red,
My sister came across the grass
To tell me you were dead.

And when she turned and left me there
Alone with red and blue again,
I shut my eyes to see the dark
That you were seeing then.

ANNE C. (age 14)
Winsor School, Boston, Mass.

I shall always wonder why it is
That you who are so delicately formed,
Will never see the curved throat of a bird,
And feel a swift delight and ecstasy.
That you who have been wrought with perfect grace,
Will never understand the subtlety
Of swiftly moving limbs in careless play.
I shall always wonder why it is
That you whose eyes are timidly afraid,
Will never keep wise silence in the midst
Of passing beauty, longed for, aptly caught.
That you who have been colored with such art
Should never, gazing at an Autumn leaf,

* *High-School Poems.* Collected by the Script Club. Harcourt, Brace & Co.

Wonder at the scarlet miracle.
It is so hard for me to see you fair
Yet ignorant of all that beauty means.

YETTA G.
Wadleigh High School,
New York City.

EBONY ORNAMENTS OF NIGHT

I took two slabs from the skies;
I took them and carved my castanets
To click me a song
                on joyous nights.

I took two slabs of ebony from the skies,
And carved rods
To beat a bastinado on the drum skin of the moon
                on tearful nights.

I took two slabs of ebony from the skies,
I took them and shaped handles for my moon-plow,
For me,
Plower of stars,
                on silent nights.

FRANCIS W.
James Munro High School,
New York City.

TERRA COTTA

Out of earth a bowl was made.
My own hands made it.
My own thought formed it.
And it grew full and round like a fruit,
And was rich with the redness of earth.

Candles I fitted to it,
Curved like branches.
And I laid it in a crown of fire.
The flames attacked it
With sharp swords and bright spears,
But it stood white-hot, unharmed.

When at its base
The angry coals had cooled,
I took it out and painted in black upon the surface.
Figures of gods and heroes.

The labors of Herakles
And the wild creatures of the woods.

STEPHANIE P. (age 16)
Sunset Hill School, Kansas City, Mo.

SPRING FEVER

I want to get out in the country
Away from the dust and grime;
And wrap my arms 'round a crooked tree
And climb—and climb—and climb!

I want to get out in a new plowed field—
Where the world and sky are big;
And fill my hands with the steaming earth
And dig—and dig—and dig!

I want to get out in an open place
Where my soul can see the sun;
And drink deep draughts of the scented air
And run—and run—and run!

I want to get upon a high, high hill
Beside a bubbling spring;
And lift my arms to the God of Life
And sing—and sing—and sing!

I want to get out 'neath a forest's dome
Oh, far and far away;
And kneel beside a purple pool
And pray—and pray—and pray!

WILMA E. (age 15 or 16)
East High School, Rochester.

KING DESIRE (A PROLOGUE)

O, it was spring that morning, there was dew,
And magically the mist still veiled the trees
Curtaining in the mysteries of night
Within her forest-temple, while the East
Flushed with the virgin-birth of a new dawn.
Then at the birth of light, the birth of day—
Then as the mist shifting unhid the river,
And the cold water in its ceaseless flow
Caught the new sunlight, as it swelled on pebbles
Or swept the brown banks grass-rimmed—
Then, Glorious King Desire went riding by!
Could I then loiter, when a king rode by,
The royal king who bursts the bonds of age?

Could I then loiter, when the flag of youth
Flashed for a moment in the secret mist?
I followed and I heard a song of thoughts,
An intertwine and dance in the earth's soul.
Hope in a glorious swiftness flashed me past,
A fire-eyed runner; O his feet!
Flames from the smithy of the world's desires!
The hills swept naked heavenward in worship;
From all their sumptuous depths the lakes stirred secrets.
Streams poured their wealth into the lap of morning
With voices triumphing in the eternal.
The infinite broke through the glowing vault;
Winds from all quarters swept in harmony
Through all the shadowed alleys of my being.
O life, it seemed a wave that bore me onward
On to a shore beaten with silver foam,
Girdled with waves, flashing in armory
Of all their sunlit deepest-hued enamels,
And crowned by forests, flocked with singing birds,
That surge around the old eternal peaks,
White in untrodden snow against the blue!

D. R. G.
Rugby School.*

Again we are grateful for a fine and wholesome medium through which all these thoughts of youth may find expression, and for the strength and beauty of the poetry which strikes our ears with many notes of genius in its young harmonies.

With what exquisite reserve have these three written of love.

SHADOWS

The silver star-sheen
Lights the shadows of your upturned face . . .
Turns your hair from dusky night
To the shimmer of boatlights on black waters . . .
Turns your lips from sullen red
To the passion of a bleeding heart . . .
Even the dimple in your petal chin
Is a poll of light . . .
But the shadows in your eyes—
Eyes that once were mist of moons
When he came near—
And he has not come
For such an endless space of time . . .

* *Public School Verse.* Vol. 1920-21.

Not a thousand stars could set them shining,
Nor the gleam of all the flickering candles
In a world of candles . . .

DORIS C.
Los Angeles High School.*

SONG

O I had gotten me a love
    That was as fair as fair,
Her eyes were as the sky above
    And flaxen was her hair.

But, out alas! this love of mine,
    That now is gone away,
She loved not scented larch nor pine
Nor hollyhock nor columbine;
"The which," she said, "are loves of thine,"
    And so she said me nay.

And I will not seek after her,
    Nor any other maid,
But I will love the forest fir
    And sit beneath the shade.

And the green larch shall be for me
    A love that is divine;
And every other forest tree,
And columbine that blooms so free
And hollyhocks along the lea—
    These shall be loves of mine.

HUMPHREY J.
Perse School, Cambridge.†

THE DREAMER

He sits and hammers on the yellow gold,
And his eyes are weary and dim above his work;
Steps come and go before his door
But he heeds nothing;
His body is in Chinatown,
His soul is in China—China, the Everlasting.
His dreams are fashioned of jade,
Traced round about with royal blue
And scrolled with crystal dragons.
They are scented with purple jasmine and the lotus bloom;

---

* *Anthology of Student Verse.*
† *Public School Verse,* 1923-24.

Through his dreams there floats the plaintive wailing of the
  high, full-throated flute,
And the pattering of tiny feet;
In his dreams She is ever present—
Hovering with lacquered hair and almond eyes,
Vermilion lips and pale, pale pointed chin.
"Tap, tap," his hammer beats upon the gold,
But on his heart it is the beating
Of two dainty little scarlet, painted heels.

ELIZABETH P.
West Philadelphia High School
For Girls.*

Heritage has a lilt and charm which yet does not hide its deep
thoughtfulness.

If your father had walked on the cold coast of Clare
  With only the wind and the rain and a smile;
If he heeded the laughter in eyes that were fair,
  But thought of one woman mile after mile;

If your mother had danced in a sun-patterned patio
  With a rose in her hair and the sun on her throat;
If her eyes were the night, star-littered and slumberous,
  And her lyrical voice held the nightingale note;

You should have more than a failing for beauty,
  More than a smile for a star in the night,
More than a kinship to crimson and scarlet—
  You daughter of laughter! You child of delight!

HELEN M.
Evander Childs High School,
New York City.†

Woodsmoke is a rare picture.

In the gray chill of the night,
Through the waves of wood blue smoke,
Middle-aged trees cross slim, black fingers.
Always they whisper,
Come!
Our limbs are old
But our hearts still dance
To the dryad tones
Of windstrung harps.

KATHERINE C. S. (age 16)
Bryn Mawr School, Baltimore, Md.

* *Torch Book of Verse.*
† Evander Childs' *Anthology of School Verse.*

And perhaps most beautiful, most thoughtful of all is this:

RETURNING MOMENT

Returning moment, after centuries,
Lone and transcendent as an evening star,
Set high and fragile over reaching trees
That strive to touch the ecstasy you are;
Violet and rose and a soft-stirring dream
From some forgotten garden in old Thrace,
The blurring through the misty years that seem
But a dim shadow on a moonlit face.
Moment I knew in Greece and Babylon!
Silver and purple in a loveliness
That is not earth's, but whirling from afar
Lights for an instant, and the minute done—
Vanished its glory and its sharp caress,
And hands are trembling that had held a star!

WINFIELD T. S.
Haverhill High School, Mass.*

"Poetry cannot be taught," said John Masefield in an introduction to one of the volumes of *Public School Verse*. "Poetry is a mixture of common sense, which not all have, with an uncommon sense, which very few have. No one can 'teach' any such thing. But delight in poetry, one of the deepest delights of men, is in everyone and can be trained and encouraged to the enlargement of all enjoyment. By delighting in poetry, and by endeavoring to write it, men obtain keys to the universe and to themselves. They learn the language of their race, and the passionate thoughts of their race, to love the one and live the other. These are things well worth the fostering."

A SELECTED BIBLIOGRAPHY ON POETRY BY BOYS AND GIRLS

ADAM, HELEN DOUGLAS—The Elfin Pedlar and Tales Told by Dixie Pool. G. P. Putnam's Sons.
    Poems written by a little Scotch girl up to the age of twelve.
Bedales Poetry.
    An Anthology of poems by boys in Bedales School, Petersfield, Hants, England.
BENNETT, MARY A. (Editor)—The Torch Book of Verse.
    An anthology of the best poems from The Torch, the monthly publication of the West Philadelphia High School for Girls.

* *Saplings*, Second Series, 1927. Scholastic Publishing Company, Pittsburgh, Pa.

By Seven Singing Willows: Children of the Elementary School, Bronxville, New York. Bronxville Public Schools, New York City.

CONKLING, HILDA—Poems by a Little Girl. Frederick A. Stokes Company.
>Hilda's first book written at eight years of age. Preface by Amy Lowell.

Shoes of the Wind. Frederick A. Stokes Company.
>The poems written in the two years following the first volume.

Silverhorn. Frederick A. Stokes Company.
>A selection of more than a hundred poems from the other two books.

COOK, H. CALDWELL (Editor)—The Perse Play Books. Vols. I to IV (out of print).
>Mr. Cook was a pioneer in poetry work with school boys.

Homework and Hobbyhorses. E. P. Dutton and Company.
>Volume VI of the Perse Play Book Series, published in this country, and still available. Prefaces of great value.

CRANE, NATHALIA—The Janitor's Boy. Albert and Charles Boni.
>Poetry written at nine years of age.

Lava Lane. Albert and Charles Boni.
>Poetry written at twelve years of age.

The Singing Crow. Albert and Charles Boni.
>Poetry written at thirteen years.

DAYRELL, VIVIENNE—The Little Wings. Basil Blackwell, Oxford, England.
>Verses written between thirteen and fifteen years of age.

Fragments—Published by the Decatur High School, Decatur, Ill.
>A collection of verses written by the poetry club.

GILKES, MARTIN, HUGHES, RICHARD, LYON, P. H. B. (Editors)—Public School Verse. Vols. I to VI. William Heinemann, London.
>Yearly anthologies of the best poems written in the English public schools.

GRAVES, FREDERICK (Compiler)—A Book of Hill Verse. Macmillan Company.
>A collection of poems written by boys between the ages of fifteen and eighteen, in the Hill School, Pottstown, Pennsylvania.

HAPPOLD, F. C.—Two Plays from the Perse School. W. Heffer and Sons, Cambridge, England.
>The first play is written by one boy; the second by a group of boys.

HARRISS, MARY VIRGINIA—Blue Beads and Amber. The Norman Remington Company, Baltimore, Maryland.
>Verses written at the age of four, nine, ten, and eleven years of age.

High School Poems collected by The Script Club, West High School, Minneapolis. Harcourt, Brace and Company.
>Letters were sent by The Script Club to over a hundred cities asking for contributions from high schools. The best pieces selected. Introduction by Louis Untermeyer.

JENKINS, E. B. S. (Editor)—The Young Authors. Alexander Moring, London.

A book of verse and prose written and illustrated by children under twelve years of age.

JOHNSTON, K. M. (Editor)—Almond Blossom. Sampson Low, Marston Company, London.

A collection of verse and prose written by children of Tormead. A few copies of Almond Blossom have been sent to this country and may be had from Frederick Warne and Company.

LONGLEY, SNOW (Editor)—Anthology of Student Verse.

A collection from the Los Angeles High School.

MEARNS, HUGHES—Creative Youth. Doubleday, Page and Company.

An anthology of High School verse from the Lincoln School, New York.

MOUNTSIER, MABEL—Singing Youth. Harper and Brothers.

An anthology of poetry by boys and girls from four to eighteen years of age in England and America.

NICKERSON, PAUL SUMNER (Editor)—Glimpses. Published at Middleboro, Massachusetts.

A national anthology of secondary-school verse selected largely from The Gleam, a magazine for and by secondary-school students.

Dawn. Published at Middleboro, Massachusetts.

A second national anthology of high-school verse.

PATRI, ANGELO (Editor)—A Number of Things. Published by Public School 45.

Six volumes of verse written in Public School 45, Bronx, New York.

ROBINSON, MAURICE R. (Editor)—Saplings (2 vols). Scholastic Publishing Company, Pittsburgh, Pennsylvania.

Verse, short stories, and essays, selected from manuscripts written by high-school students in competition for the Scholastic Awards, conducted by The Scholastic, a high-school magazine.

SERGENT, NELLIE B. (Editor)—The Evander Childs Anthology of Student Verse. Published by The Evander Childs High School, New York.

A selection of the poetry written in the school over a number of years.

SHEEAN, GERTRUDE A. (Editor)—Anthology of Poetry and Prose. East High School. Published by the East High School, Rochester, New York.

A selection of poems written between 1914 and 1923.

Little Book of Original Verse, A, by children of Sunset Hill School. Compiled by Helen Ericson. Kansas City, Missouri, 1931.

A FEW REFERENCES ON POETRY FOR TEACHERS

AUSLANDER, JOSEPH, and HILL, FRANK ERNEST—The Winged Horse. Doubleday, Page and Company.

A new book which shows what a history of English literature may become in the hands of authors who have re-created the past through their own imaginative spirit.

CHUBB, PERCIVAL C.—Teaching of English in the Elementary and Secondary School. Macmillan, 1929.

CONKLING, G. H.—Imagination in Children's Reading. The Hampshire Book Shop.

COOK, H. CALDWELL—Perse Play Books. W. Heffer and Sons, Ltd., Cambridge, England.

Unfortunately out of print, but may be had in some libraries. The prefaces are full of suggestions.

The Play Way. Frederick A. Stokes Company.

In particular, chapters 4, 5, 7, 8, 9.

DOWNEY, JUNE E.—Creative Imagination. Harcourt, Brace and Company, 1929.

HARTMAN, GERTRUDE—The Child and His School. E. P. Dutton Company.

Art Activities, p. 77; The School Festival, p. 87; Linguistic Activities, p. 91; Composition, p. 99.

LOWES, JOHN LIVINGSTON—Convention and Revolt in Poetry. Houghton Mifflin Company.

A penetrating and balanced study of poetic tradition and modern forms of poetic technique.

MEARNS, HUGHES—Creative Youth. Doubleday, Page and Company.

The first fourteen chapters describe in detail "A School Environment for Creative Writing."

MITCHELL, LUCY SPRAGUE—The Here and Now Story Book. E. P. Dutton Company.

No one who is seriously interested in the spontaneous art forms of children's language can afford not to read the preface to this book. It offers a point of view not found anywhere else in print to our knowledge.

PIAGET, JEAN—The Language and Thought of the Child. Harcourt, Brace Company.

Actual records of children over periods of time, and an analysis of the author's findings.

WILKINSON, MARGUERITE—The Way of the Makers. Macmillan Company.

An examination of the various aspects of the craftsmanship of the great poets, taken from their first-hand accounts.

PROSE BOOKS BY YOUTHFUL WRITERS

Mabel Mountsier

Books by children, both prose and poetry, have been published in the last few years in such rapid succession that only he who runs may have time to read. In fact, most of the elders have not had time to make up their minds about this new phase of writing—the youthful works of youthful authors. So leaving to the child psychologists the question of the advisability of publication and to librarians and teachers the opinions of boy and girl readers, let us take the easiest way and look at the content of the books in prose.

When Daisy Ashford's *The Young Visiters* (1919) appeared, it aroused much discussion, partly because the public was unaccustomed to books by children. The letters and diary of Marjorie Fleming, the clever little friend of Scott, had been written more than a hundred years before and had come to be considered an isolated example of juvenile writing that by its quaint humor delighted the grown-ups. But here again in *The Young Visiters* (I still believe that it was not a hoax) was a book praised by everyone capable of enjoying the situations arising from a nine-year-old's disregard of social conventions. We hope she knew not what she was doing, for it would be sad to think of one so young as a novelist of the sophisticated school, or can it be that Ethel suggested Brett and Iris to their creators?

Later on appeared a number of books of travel, the first of which was *David Goes A-Voyaging*, by David Binney Putnam (1925). This would have been a great find for David's children or grandchildren if discovered as a diary in an old trunk, but if we really want to know about the voyage of the *Arcturus*, we go to the account by the head of the expedition. In *A Solemn Foreword* by William Beebe, author of *The Arcturus Adventure*, Mr. Beebe says, "Pragmatism alone was the stimulus of my suggestion that eleven-year-old David Putnam go on one leg"—he adds "of the journey," but it is too good an explanation of the limitations of the narrative to continue to the end. As to David's age, it is only fair to say he celebrated his twelfth birthday on shipboard.

The following year he published *David Goes to Greenland*, and as a third annual crop, *David Goes to Baffinland*. Each year the product improves, the account is less self-conscious and moves more rapidly.

A much better boy writer, who accompanied David on the third voyage, is Deric Nusbaum, who wrote *Deric in Mesa Verde* (1926) at the age of twelve, and a year later *Deric with the Indians*. The first is a lively account of a boy enjoying himself exploring Indian remains in the national park of which his father, an archeologist, is superintendent, and the second is the record of a trip among the Indians of the southwest. Both books are interesting and contain much valuable information about prehistoric and present-day life among the Indians. If their style is the boy, then Deric's writing has style, for the reader comes to know him and likes him immensely.

Another traveler in the north is Kennett Rawson, whose *Boy's-Eye View of the Arctic* (1926) shows the desire of a boy of fourteen to display his knowledge and indulge in "fine writing," but he is so wholehearted and serious about it all that the account is amusing and refreshing. It is no mean task for a boy of Kennett's age to write a hundred and forty-two pages in a boy's Johnsonese. *Vide* this example:

"A short time later after the excitement fomented by the berg had subsided, we began to notice signs of the proximity of land."

But of the making of these travel books there is no end. Another is Robert Carver North's *Bob North Starts Exploring* (1927). Bob is only eleven when he goes "with his father into the little-traveled bush of Northern Ontario, back-packing, sledding, canoeing," writing his journal as he goes along. He has plenty of courage in enduring hardships and proves himself worthy of his pioneer forebears, about whom he has a great deal to say.

Among the Alps with Bradford, by Bradford Washburn (1927), sixteen, is a record of thrilling sport—his own mountain climbing and also that of the pioneer climbers of the Alps. Unlike Bob North, Bradford seems to have unlimited means at his command, even to adding a photographer to his three guides. But we do not begrudge him the opportunity since the result is a book that can be recommended without making allowances. As they get older, they seem to do it better, a fact that should encourage the grown-ups.

The travel books, which represent an incalculable amount of work, show it is a good thing that the very conditions compel their authors to stick to their subjects and keep moving. Besides, they are fortunate in the matter of illustration, for the books have been made more attractive and surely much more valuable as sources of information by numerous photographs and drawings.

The child's garden of prose during the year 1927 produced also Barbara Newhall Follett's *House Without Windows,* a highly imaginative tale of the little girl Eepersip, who, refusing to stay in her parents' house went forth to dwell in the Meadow, the Sea, and the Mountain;

and *The Admiral and Others* by Peggy Temple, an amusing story of the crotchety old Admiral, who tyrannized over the Others.

In a class all of their own are the books in which the young authors give their opinions about life and about themselves. Among these *A Young Girl's Diary* (1922) was a simple, straightforward record of an adolescent's experiences, including her reactions to the information that came to her in regard to sex. The book is a valuable study of a girl's mind, and why it should have been suppressed is hard to say, considering the number of salacious books that pass unchallenged.

A more recent book, *Our Generation, by One of Us,* is the "effort of a Seventeen to give her point of view on life in general," but what a feeble effort. She explains, in an inane and innocuous manner, the meaning of such terms as a line of talk, and crashing a dance, and discusses proms, football girls, and other collegiate matters.

The Younger Generation, by Elizabeth Benson, age thirteen, now a sophomore at Barnard College, is an amazing example of a child's assimilation of varied reading that includes Casanova, Freud, the author of *Elmer Gantry,* Anatole France, the *American Mercury* and the tabloids. She talks of sex, prohibition, censorship, religion, night clubs, divorce, parents, and everything else, saying what we have heard many times before, but saying it in an entertaining way.

"We do love to shock you," she writes of the older generation, not realizing that we understand the pose and have heard so much of Elizabeth's kind of talk that we have become shock proof. Also, "So we swagger and bluster and talk a great deal of nonsense, but down underneath we are pretty much like any other crop of youngsters."

This book is surprising, not only because of its scope and daring, but because Elizabeth Benson handles her subject with ease and writes in a style so facile and so swift that the reader feels as if carried along in a flapper's Chrysler. But as soon as he catches his breath he asks, How can she do it? Is it because she has an I. Q. of 214? Is she a monstrosity, or is the coming adolescent to be a paragon of sophistication? (*Deus avertat.*) Let him who can answer these questions.

It is a relief to turn for first-hand experience to *Why Do They Like It,* a book of real value in showing what E. L. Black, a boy of fifteen and a half, has to say about an English public school in which he was incarcerated. Making all allowances for the fact that he was a poor little rich boy unaccustomed to the companionship of other boys, his indictment of the system is unanswerable. In his public school three or four boys were assigned to each small study, and the effect is similar to that of criminals herded together in a prison. No matter what the character of a boy, he might be compelled by circumstances to come in contact with certain vicious youths so cruel and immoral as to leave scars on any boy associated with them.

The disregard for the tastes and ability of the individual pupil as far as his recreation and studies are concerned is an old story, but E. L. Black's account of its effect on him is very impressive.

Why Do They Like It shows considerable feeling for style and unusual skill in revealing disagreeable situations, but a quality not so pleasing is the monotony that comes from repetition, a characteristic of the work of many other youthful writers in a long sustained effort.

Among shorter pieces of prose some of the essays and narratives based on experience are really good, but when it comes to the short stories, they are usually pretty poor stuff. Young people love to write stories, especially love stories, and they should certainly not be restrained from doing what is done with such zest. But it goes without saying that a high-school pupil is limited in ability to interpret character and to show action as the outgrowth of character and circumstances, and a little knowledge of the emotions and experiences that make life significant. So if his stories are to be put into print, don't tell him that his work comprises a cross section of American genius; rather, while he is having a good time contributing to the school magazine, help him to see its limitations by putting into his hands the work of such writers as Thomas Hardy, A. E. Coppard, and Katherine Mansfield.

When this new activity of young people in writing books is motivated by the desire of youth to express itself, the printing of their work may perhaps be justified, provided the attitude of others helps them to feel that writing is a natural, not a miraculous, means of expression. The printed page is not only a source of satisfaction in feeling that a piece of work has been completed, but it furnishes a better opportunity for self-criticism.

But the consideration of this subject must include, besides the effect on the individual author, the opinion of the readers. Judged from the point of view of adults, few of these books make really good reading, though they have aroused widespread interest, and have received praise from such discriminating writers as Amy Lowell, J. M. Barrie, John Masefield, Dorothy Richardson, William Beebe, and Witter Bynner, all of whom have written prefaces for the prose or the poetry.

The attitude of very young readers is a matter that has yet to be investigated over a period of time and among many groups. If such a survey should show that children find pleasure and profit in the work of their contemporaries, of more or less the same background and degree of development as their own, then in these printed books there has come into existence a new source of knowledge for them.

BOOKS MENTIONED IN THIS ARTICLE

ANONYMOUS—Our Generation, by One of Us. Century Company.
ANONYMOUS—Diary of a Young Girl. (Out of print.)
ASHFORD, DAISY—The Young Visiters. George H. Doran Company.
BENSON, ELIZABETH—The Younger Generation. Greenberg.
BLACK, E. L.—Why Do They Like It? Bookshop for Boys and Girls, Boston, Massachusetts.
FLEMING, MARJORIE—Diary. Thomas H. Mosher, Portland, Maine.
FOLLETT, BARBARA N.—The House Without Windows. Alfred A. Knopf.
NORTH, ROBERT CARVER—Bob North Starts Exploring. G. P. Putnam's Sons.
NUSBAUM, DERIC—Deric with the Indians. G. P. Putnam's Sons.
   Deric in Mesa Verde. G. P. Putnam's Sons.
PUTNAM, DAVID BINNEY—David Goes A-Voyaging. G. P. Putnam's Sons.
   David Goes to Greenland. G. P. Putnam's Sons.
   David Goes to Baffin Land. G. P. Putnam's Sons.
RAWSON, KENNETH—A Boy's-Eye View of the Arctic. Macmillan Company.
TEMPLE, PEGGY—The Admiral and Others. E. P. Dutton & Company.
WASHBURN, BRADFORD—Among the Alps with Bradford. G. P. Putnam's Sons.

RELATING ENGLISH AND ART IN A LARGE CITY HIGH SCHOOL

John L. Foley

WHEN the *Fort George Lantern,* a literary and art magazine, first appeared a few years ago, as the medium of the creative work of the boys and girls of The George Washington High School, New York City, it drew keen educational and artistic interest to the activities of the pupils in the new Georgian building, which, topped by a colonial lantern, looks off northwest from Fort George Hill to the Palisades and the Hudson. "You have a new school, a young spirit, and a fresh adventure," said the chairman of English in another high school. "The degree of coöperation between English and Art achieved in dramatics and stage design, and in your *Cherry Tree* and in the *Lantern,* is most remarkable." Hughes Mearns, author of *Creative Youth,* wrote of the *Lantern;* "I am astonished and delighted. . . . It is a mark forward in school magazines, and further proof that inartistic adults have alone prevented the right growth and right expression of art by children." Doubtless the teachers who coöperate in these creative activities would disclaim more than a share at leadership in work thus rated, and would point to the opportunities given their students for artistic expression. One significant living proof of their efforts, however, is that George Pierce Baker, of the Yale University School of Drama, accepted as a freshman last September Ronald Jones, directly upon his graduation from George Washington High School where he had done distinguished work in Shakespeare, Dramatics, Stage Design, Stage Craft, and in Fine Arts.

The beauty and finish of the *Fort George Lantern* inevitably called forth many questions like these which came from an educational magazine editor: Do the pupils determine the choice of paper, cover designs— inside and out—the stock used, the decorative elements, the layouts, captions, and type fonts? Do they choose, with faculty guidance, the articles, stories, and poetry? Do they make it pay? Briefly, yes, and although it carries no advertisements, and although it runs color plates, the *Lantern* at fifty cents a copy has paid for itself. Evidently, here was a group of teachers who decided that beauty and excellence with creativeness were possible to children in Democracy's high school. By what permanent committees, regular classes, plans, and methods, English and Art are related at George Washington in spite of a register of over six thousand students, this paper may serve to explain.

PROVIDING A CREATIVE ENVIRONMENT

Freedom, informality, and naturalness have been the spirit of faculty and students of George Washington High School from its inception some years ago. Before entering the new building in February, 1925, certain teachers felt the need for more abundant opportunities within class time for creative work, and for some medium which should stimulate boys and girls to their ablest effort. Accordingly, this belief was voiced when Mr. Edwin Van B. Knickerbocker, Chairman of the English Department, suggested that a literary and fine-arts magazine should be established for work done by the students of any department in the spirit of craftsmanship. Miss M. Rose Collins, Chairman of the Fine Arts Department, readily joined in this enterprise which in three years has enjoyed a remarkable development. Dr. Frank M. Wheat, Chairman of Biology, gave prodigally then and since of his time and knowledge, for having been trained as an artist and being an illustrator, he has expert knowledge of the photographic processes used in commercial reproduction. Three champions of creativeness were ready.

Fortunately, the Principal, Mr. Arthur A. Boylan, believed that youth should have happy and spontaneous expression, and that too often conventional routine and repeated methods preclude the natural surprise and pleasure attendant upon creation. It was fortunate, indeed, for this adventure in creative activity that the Principal was thoroughly in sympathy with such methods and aims, for it is a truism that in any organization, and certainly in all educational bodies, the policy and attitude of the executive head are reflected in the subordinates. Mr. Boylan believes with teachers interested in progressive education, that children learn best in a humane and creative environment.

STEADY GROWTH FROM SMALL BEGINNINGS

The conviction that boys and girls exert themselves agreeably when they work in the spirit of the craftsman found quick and sustained response in the teachers. Starting with the creative work done in only two English classes—those of Miss Cornelia R. Trowbridge, literary adviser of the *Lantern,* and of Mrs. Abby Forbes Chapin, the faculty members have watched the "copy" grow until every English class now submits its worthiest efforts to the editors. In art the same interest has been spread. Using the art work chosen from such groups as Miss Ann Bebarfald's in Design, and in Miss Virginia Murphy's in Stage Design and Stage Craft, the art teachers have seen material come from many classes covering a wide range of more than thirteen different electives, among which are those in Costume Draping, Dyeing, Etching, Woodcuts, and the Graphic Arts.

LIVING IN NEWSPAPERDOM

Journalism offers a natural medium in school for uniting the art of writing with at least one other art—cartooning. Art principles in newspapers also get emphasis in these directions: in headline writing, economy of style, symmetry, balance, and arrangement of values. Happily, Miss Mary J. J. Wrinn, adviser to the *Cherry Tree* and instructor of Journalism II, a writer of stories and poetry, is able by her experience with newspapers and magazines to re-create in daily classes some of the conditions of newspaperdom.

In these Journalism classes pupils may vary as to terms of English. In Journalism I you might find thirty-eight boys and girls who will get credit for English 4, or 5, or 6, because they have been recommended by their previous teachers as superior in ability and hence fit to elect newspaper writing. To meet their needs in literature, they go each fortnight to an assigned class in literature for their respective terms. Certain of these classes are taught by the teachers of Journalism. This method of programming has worked effectively.

Freed to do the daily writing for a school newspaper, the students get frequent opportunities in doing "leads," interviews, reporting speeches, "human-interest stories," feature items done in a "box," lines for a column of verse, and book reviews. That is not unique, to be sure, for other schools do similar work. What does strike one as unique here, however, is the kind of experience students get in being in the same class with those older and abler than they, and in the degree of achievement they reach often as a result of daily observation of effective writing of their fellows who may be more skilled or merely more accurate.

Examples of exceptional work which came in in the daily returns printed in the *Cherry Tree* biweekly are the following poems written by a sixth-term girl, Muriel Hochdorf. The first was suggested by the students' gift to the school of four Colorado silver spruce trees planted with ten oaks just before Christmas in a landscape architect's design contributed by one of the former graduating classes.

TO A CAMPUS FIR

Tall and serene,
And many veiled with dusk,
You stand like some proud queen
Wearing the moon, a pendant for your throat;
Your hair is star-powdered-white
And you sway proudly
Sheathed in blue velvet by the night.

The second poem is a Petrarchan sonnet.

YOU

You said I would forget and smile again,
And I have known the mellowness time brings
And I learned to treasure love of little things,—
Yet sudden beauty brings the old, old pain;
A blaze of sumach scorching autumn's lane,
Wind-music, and the bubbling song of springs,
The secret of the aspen's whisperings,
They bind you to me with a shining chain.

I think of you in every well-loved place:
Can I forget you while there flames the light
Of ecstasy in beauty's inner shrine?
All loveliness will hold your mirrored face,
There will be swift-starred moments of delight
To mind me of you, grown—at once—divine.

The same young poet startled the class with a lyric like this, in which a rarely beautiful impulse found fitting form.

FUTILITY

Every night I talk with you:
　Exquisitely I shape each thought
　To silver words, all finely wrought,
Beauty, Poesy are there too,
Garbed in star dust and in dew.

And you, you have not praise or blame,
　For you are far away and high,
　Clear against the midnight sky;
And even if you knew I came,
You would not answer to your name.

Surely, when such high sensibility can find space with the broad humanity of an issue publishing a fun column, as well as cartoons showing Mr. Pickwick coaching up the semicircular driveway to the classic portico of the school, or Santa Claus sleighing over the lantern top with gifts or quips for everyone, it is self-evident that Journalism and Art meet here effectively.

HOW THE CREATIVE SPIRIT MOVES IN ART WORK

In Design, the principles back of creativeness are stressed steadily, and originality, not technical skill, gets recognition. Here all class instruction emphasizes what goes into the creative act by an artist: organization, arrangement of ideas according to the laws of design, viz., rhythm, balance, harmony, coherence, dominance, and subordination. To any pupil who has studied or written verse, the universality of these laws is apparent. Teachers try especially in the first year to get work in training and in appreciation, because these pupils are having their first chance to express creative work. For the *Lantern*, all teachers of Art are asked to submit two or three examples of any class work to a committee of that department; after an elimination by them only the best goes to magazine board. Outside class as within, the aim is to let inspiration come from the mood of the pupil with no coercion. If a group take any material like a story to be published, as many as feel that they would like to illustrate it, may try to design the impression the tale makes upon them. Two arresting examples of work in design blending with English through a monster school project, Colonel George Wringling's Highflying Circus—designs which appeared effectively in color in the *Lantern*, were an almost life-size poster of a clown saying, "The Circus Is Coming" with the dates and the prices, and a double-page layout, gay with small drawings of every imaginable circus suggestion to frame the poem, written on his own perception that the show needed

CARDBOARD MODEL WITH FIGURES MADE OF CLAY FOR "THE GODS OF THE MOUNTAINS"

A MODEL FOR THE DRINKING SCENE IN "TWELFTH NIGHT"

ANOTHER MODEL FOR "THE BIRTHDAY OF THE INFANTA" SHOWING A
ROYAL SPANISH INTERIOR

STAGE MODEL FOR THE SAME PLAY

A MODEL OF A STAGE SET FOR "IN A PERSIAN GARDEN"

THE INTERIOR OF A WOOD-CUTTER'S HUT MADE FOR "WHY THE
CHIMES RANG"

A SCENE FROM "THE BIRTHDAY OF THE INFANTA" SHOW-
ING COSTUMES DESIGNED BY STUDENTS

A SCENE FROM "THE FLOWER OF YEDDO"

a verse for a sawdust princess to recite at the start. Theodore Nathan not only wrote this poem, afterwards reproduced in the magazine, but also did a special article, "Under the Big Top," to picture imaginatively the varied bill in which close to three hundred pupils were directly, or indirectly, involved, for five performances to crowded houses.

THE BALLYHOO SONG

Oh, roll back the curtain, and strike up the band,
Come here, all you Harlequins, lend me a hand,
Let's smooth out the tanbark and fasten it down
For everything's gay, there's a Circus in town.

Now everyone's happy, abandoning care,
Tomorrow comes sorrow, but we'll not be there,
And everyone's merry, sun bright and sky clear
A scowl is a traitor, the Circus is here!

Tomorrow comes sorrow and skies may be gray;
But what of tomorrow while we're here today?
There are pachyderms, pythons, freaks, funsters and fools;
Good cheer, all ye people, King Carnival rules.

There are ballyhoo barkers and bursting balloons,
And calliopes wheezing a wealth of old tunes;
Oh, time is a jester and fate is a clown,
And fortune's a fool when the Circus hits town.

Sweet Columbine's dancing on slippers of air,
So roll up the canvas and open the fair;
The calliope's rooting refreshing refrains,
The whole world is happy—King Carnival reigns.

We're here at the Circus, the Circus in school:
Time is a jester, and fortune's a fool;
Hide grief like a clown, paint a smile on your lip,
For life is a circus, and fate cracks the whip.

That mood also inspired the inside cover design of the *Lantern*, October, 1927, a drawing jolly in very grotesque clowns, all done in orange. Here were English, Art, and the folk-spirit in happy unity.

Less spectacular and likely more lasting in effect are the original designs done for initial capital letters of articles and stories published in the *Lantern*, not to add those for headbands at the top of, or including, captions furnished by the student editors who are themselves chosen after careful eliminations.

Illustrations for poems, sometimes of a full-length page, are noteworthy, as, for example, the poem by Erna Jonas with the stanzas placed above ocean waves from which a winged horse rises against a background of blazing stars.

STEED OF BELLEROPHON

Pegasus! It was he,
And I, affright,
Saw in my dream
His wing against the night.
I marked and marveled at
The feathered steed.
About him was
A ring of light. The freed,
The glossy creature. Ah!
To run my palm
Over that coat!
With that he fled. The calm,
Cool mead where fiery he flew,
Alas, too soon
Was left alone.
He, passing, pawed the moon.

A feather by my bed
I found next day;
No treasure that,
But how left—who can say?
Against all reason I
Have saved the thing,
From feather bed
Or from a heavenly wing.

EFFECTIVE POSTERS DISPLAY ART IN ENGLISH

The Poster Classes at least a month in advance of any large school project, such as a new issue of the *Lantern* or a dramatic performance, join in a selling campaign with the school newspaper. Information in poster form is indispensable to a financially successful result on any large venture. Here, as in the world of motor cars, the "teaser" advertisement skillfully prepares the persons to be persuaded by stirring anticipation and curiosity. The classes in major elective Poster Design and in minor elective take care of this need. The practical commercial use of such posters for sales promotion in business must be evident to any person.

DESIGNING AND BUILDING SETS FOR PLAYS

English and Art may obviously be combined with the strongest popular appeal and satisfaction in dramatics. At George Washington High

School, Shakespeare I and II, and Dramatics I and II, offered by Mrs. Helen Kenny, for learning dramatic literature by acting, often hold the same pupils as those registered in the classes on Stage Design and Stage Craft. In these groups students of terms four, five, or six are elegible. Perhaps some incidents would best illustrate the way these courses function.

When the Dramatic Committee two years ago voted to produce on one evening's bill three one-act plays, namely, *Cinderella Married, A Night at an Inn,* and *The Birthday of the Infanta,* these classes took over the complete production of the latter play. For that they made as a class project models from designs, one of which, made by merging two of the best models, was realized in the stage setting. One of the two students whose ideas were merged was Fred Cooper, who, now at Columbia College, is one of the runners up in a competition to write an original book and lyrics for the annual 'varsity show, for which he also offered stage designs. Mr. Cooper expects later to study architecture. From the English side it is agreeable to note that one of the two girls who played the Infanta—usually two students are given a chance to play each rôle so that each may get an opportunity to play at one of the performances—Miss Maxine Rothchild, now a freshman at Barnard College, was chosen to play Dora in the recent Philolexian production of *Fanny's First Play.* Meanwhile, when no project is afoot, these classes go along independently, or by special arrangement jointly. If, for instance, Dunsany's *The Gods of the Mountain* should be selected by the Dramatic Committee for one of the plays to be given this Spring, the designs and models made in class last year, possibly modified, may be worked out into the actual stage sets. Within the past three years these classes functioned smoothly in producing *The Flower of the Yeddo, In a Persian Garden, When the Chimes Rang,* given as a Christmas entertainment at three weekly assemblies, and scenes from *Euripides* given at assemblies last June. The same close coöperation was achieved in the Circus for which the Stage Design class planned and made the setting to suggest half of an arena. And at a costume show given by the class in Costume Draping, the spoken word functioned no less easily with the art in poster and on the models. It may be added that the design for *Twelfth Night* was done by Carmen Miller, '28, who has also revealed marked talent in the classes on Shakespeare and Dramatics. Science inevitably joins art here. With the lighting equipment worth over several hundred dollars, part of which was contributed by a former senior class, the class in Stage Craft learns to practice the science of lighting on the model stage as seen in one of the illustrations. Some members of the Stage Craft Club work on this stage, which has a fly gallery, adjustable border lights, and all the equipment of a professional stage. The switchboard, planned and made by one of the students, has sixteen controls for different lighting units. The stage is used by the classes in Stage Designing to experiment with illumination on the small models constructed by the students in class. Having watched the classes in Stage Craft and Stage Design in action, and being so impressed by the Stage Craft Club as to remain until four-thirty o'clock one afternoon, Dr. John L. Tildsley, District Superintendent in charge of High Schools for the city, exclaimed, "That is real education!"

Possibly a clew to understanding the effectiveness with which English and Art function at George Washington High School is the executive organization of the faculty and student standing committees, most of which meet one day a week. The Board of Publications, which acts as a central executive committee for all the school publishing, is composed of the faculty advisers of the *Cherry Tree* (the school newspaper), the *Lantern*, of at least one other art and one additional English representative, and two other members representing business and finance. Under a general chairman, who, as it now happens, is an artist, this Board has invaluable advice in regard to printing, particularly as to what kind of plates will reproduce best in the magazine. A similar representation of faculty members makes up a separate sub-committee for each of the publications, including those for the *Hatchet*, a year book, and the *Orange Book*, a volume of general information about school. On the Dramatic Committee with a general chairman and a large representation from the English and Art departments, there are also representatives of Music and Physical Training, and, when special productions require, of the Science Department for lighting.

Such correlation of English with Art, and Art with English as that secured at the George Washington High School, if extended to other subjects, might help to answer Thomas Arnold's query when, brooding on the Chartist Riots of 1837, he wrote at Paris in his Journal: "How can he who labors hard for his daily bread—hardly and with doubtful success—be made wise and good, and, therefore, how can he be made happy?" At all events, here there is proof that beauty and excellence are preferred by pupils when they are given a genuine choice. Even if creative activities should not prove of special use in life for the students, they nevertheless develop an intelligent appreciation of what is the best in literature and art, and fix deeply in their habits intelligent discrimination to serve them all their days.

CREATIVE WRITING IN THE COLLEGE

Matthew Wilson Black

THE traditional inaugurators of "courses" in writing in America, Dean Briggs and Barrett Wendell, were early forced to declare their faith in the face of a host of objectors. They believed, so we are told, not that writing could be taught, but that "under the right conditions something could be learned." Unfortunately, it is a declaration which has borne less fruit than it deserves. The difficulty, one supposes, is that "the right conditions" for the prentice writer seem less definable than for learners in other arts, such as music and painting. Young violinists, young etchers, young sculptors, seek in Vienna or Paris or Rome— what? Freedom, one supposes; a new and stimulating environment; the companionship and criticism of those who share their ambitions; the inspiration and standard of a master. But is there any real reason why these same conditions would not be helpful to young writers? And is there any real reason why anyone, even though he may not be intending to be a writer at all, should not enjoy the same conditions, if he so desires, and somehow profit thereby? It is with these two questions, which to some will seem trite, to others heretical, that I wish to preface this discussion.

In affirming, by way of answer, my belief that "the right conditions" of the atelier can be realized to a worthwhile extent for young writers, and in college departments of English, I am fully conscious that few writers of any rank have found such training in colleges. No one need be concerned about the supply of great writers. They produce themselves. The living memory of our department of English literature and composition in a great metropolitan university runs now to well over a generation, and within that time the tale of boys who later became great writers is naught; and those who became writers of any sort are just sufficiently numerous to prove that if we of the universities cannot produce writers, and perhaps not even discover them, neither can we do them any lasting harm. My present concern is with the rank and file of our college men and women, with those who intend to become mineralogists, and lawyers, and teachers of mathematics, and managers of trust funds, and bond-salesmen, and civil engineers, and husbands, and wives, and parents. I believe that for them training in creative expression should be offered, and even recommended, or required.

The conditions of the atelier are reproduced somewhere in the literature courses of many of our schools and colleges. A case in point is Dr. Hughes Mearns' remarkable creation in the Lincoln School, New

York City, of an atmosphere that drew forth from their hiding places in notebooks, parents' desks, and in the spirits of children, literally hundreds of poems, the best of which he has made into a substantial and delightful volume. Dr. Baker's workshop and the Carolina Players are already famous for their stimulation of embryo dramatists, and similar courses are being established everywhere. Attempts are constantly being made to induce poets of repute to lend their presence to this or the other campus, to be there, merely, and communicate themselves through informal and invisible channels. The lack of tangible results in the latter cases is in no sense discouraging. What counts is that in all of these experiments there has been a stimulus and an outlet for the creative spirit in writing; something, in fact, of the freedom, the companionship, and the inspiration of the atelier of a master. And these "right conditions" may be reproduced to some—and, I insist, worthwhile—extent, in "courses" involving the writing of original verse, essays, and fiction. I know that it is being done in many colleges, but I can only draw my illustrations from the department I know best.

It is necessary to man such courses with professors, since the supply of artistic luminaries, even supposing all of them stout-hearted enough to attempt such work, is readily exhausted. In our own department the bulk of the creative courses are conducted by the younger men, since it has been our experience that the students will talk more readily to them of their lives, and of what there is in those lives to write about. In truth it is not necessary that the "master" be a great master, but merely that he be a little more mature than his students in the ways of life and art. But it seems to me all important that he adopt toward them the attitude of an older fellow craftsman, explorer, adventurer, who communicates such theories as he has in terms of practice, and becomes the critic and arbiter of taste only on demand.

The arrangement of courses in writing at Pennsylvania is unusual in that it provides a continuous and increasingly creative training throughout the student's four years of college. The regular freshman course, which meets two hours a week during the first year, is designed to stimulate independence of thought, and a reliance upon original material for themes, while correcting any defects of technique which have survived the preparatory school discipline. The men are divided into groups of twenty or less, and each group meets with a separate instructor, who has full charge. In addition to this, however, an advanced course, English Three, is required during the sophomore year, which is given by practically all of the department under the grade of professor. English Three is a very adaptable course, but with a group of average ability it is our custom to devote at least half of it to creative experiments. This is followed, for those who wish it—and the number is surprisingly large —by an elective course in the junior year under the direction of an experienced and able assistant professor. Junior composition meets as a group one hour a week throughout the year, and each member of the class has a second hour of individual consultation each week with the teacher in his office. The traditional number of assignments during the year is ten, and they include verse, a short story, chapters of a novel, a piece of portraiture, a pastel, and other equally specialized and difficult forms. Finally, in senior year, the boy may spend two hours a week during the year with one of the older men, Dr. Weygandt, Dr. Quinn, or Dr. Mendenhall, and develop under his guidance that kind of writing in which he wishes to make himself proficient. The success of the almost unique required course in sophomore year, and of the later elective courses is attributable not only to the ability and willing expenditure of time on the part of those who conduct, but also to the interest which creative writing holds for all sorts and conditions of students, provided it can be pursued as nearly as possible under the ideal conditions of the atelier.

Practically all the courses in writing are concurrent with reading courses. And during the conference hours as well as in class every effort is made to stimulate the learner's reading. As will be seen, some creative assignments are given in connection with specific reading. But we have never been able to satisfy ourselves that a boy learns to write simply by reading, any more than he can become a musician by listening to music. As Dr. Schelling is fond of saying, "There seems but one way of learning to do, and that is, by doing."

The beginning of the writer's learning is his finding in personal interviews with the teacher of what in his own experience is worth artistic expression. And in these interviews lies the crux of the experiment. There must be talk, eager, impassioned, time-forgetting talk. That project, among many, must take shape which will fire them both with a faith in its possibilities and an interest in the technique of whatever handling seems most appropriate. Practical corollaries are, first, that the number of learners admitted to each atelier should be restricted in some way, out of consideration for the teacher's time and health; and second, that such interviews, already semi-creative in spirit, cannot be too rigidly scheduled or cut short. An ideal symptom it is to glance through an office door at one of these afternoon conferences, to see the instructor and a boy, their heads together over a project, too absorbed to turn on the lights or to look at the clock and see that it is time for dinner.

My own experience with creative assignments in the required sophomore course, English Three, has provided me with some most illuminating and exciting literary adventures. Very frequently one is asked, by men from other colleges or by friends, "How do you ever stand it? It must be awful truck!" Well, most of it is very bad, and at the same time surprisingly good. At any rate, my colleagues and I "stand it" because we are primarily interested for the time, not in art but in a process of mental and spiritual development taking place in the boy, in connection with art. Let me take for illustration the case of Anderson.

Anderson was a member of one of my groups in English Three. It was a group which consisted of a typical cross section of American life, and it was in consequence extremely stimulating and not too easy to handle. I remember that there was an engineer named Diggs, a quiet, shrewd lad with an unexpected vein of gentle fancy; Lewisohn, a brilliant, business-minded Jew, with a mastery, incomparable in my experience, of the argot and philosophy of the city "flapper" and her "gentleman friend"; a divinity student named Mather, whom for two years I tried to induce not to say things in the largest possible number of words; Tracy, an able but superior youth from private preparatory school, and a dozen others less distinguishable.

As it was a class of average ability I decided that they might profit by attempting a short story. And Anderson took it very seriously indeed. He worked hard, for a month, in the attempt to get into this art form his disillusionment over a girl, against the background of the inevitable disillusionment of youth in the later teens, and the accompanying longing for far-away, romantic adventure. (Disillusionment is, by the way, the most frequent theme among boys of Anderson's age whose creative impulses flow naturally and seriously. It is the ground current of their lives at the time; and their expression of it, however violent, must be received without prejudice and gratefully, for they show that the boy is doing what he *must* do, if his writing is to improve, that is, trying to seize and perpetuate *his* vision, his reading of life.) But Anderson insisted on using as symbols things he knew nothing about; and he imitated bad models in his style. I worked hard with him over these faults. I tried to lead him to see that what he really knew was the life of the up-state town from which he came, and to which in spirit he still belonged. I read with him Conrad's "Preface" to the *Nigger of the Narcissus*, in the hope that the dignity and beauty and genuineness of Conrad's ideal would help to set his feet on the highroad. I read with him Thomas Burke's *The Dream of Ah Lum*, which I knew he would like, and commented feelingly on it as an illustration of the fact that even a sentimental story gains something by restraint of telling. All in vain; I was a mere theorizer, Anderson was deep in practice.

And so I set aside an hour when Anderson should read his story to the class. The greatest advantage of the group method is of course that it provides the groping artist with his final touchstone, an audience, when he is ready for it. And it is an audience whose judgment is final with him, a jury of his peers. It is also, in my experience, an audience whose judgments are sound, so that it provides an ideal instrument for the enforcing of artistic theory.

Anderson's story told of a youth in a university not a hundred miles from our own, and in fact, surprisingly like it. Seized with an unconquerable wanderlust, the product of a vast satiety with city life, gay people, and endless dusty learning, the hero quietly disappears from the campus in the first term of his junior year. His friends, his fraternity brothers, remember him for a little while, but alas, he is soon forgotten when football season begins. There is a girl, who wonders too. The hero works his passage on a liner, jumps ship at Boulogne for a winter in Paris, re-ships at Marseilles on a steamer bound for India. In Bombay he joins an expedition northward into Mongolia in search of *ovis poli*. After facing death in several of its grimmest forms, he repossesses his soul, and finds a hero in the leader of the expedition. On the latter's advice he returns to the university town, there to prove to himself that all is not so stale, flat, and unprofitable as it had seemed. But he is hard now. He will not rush back expecting a welcome. He will appear cannily in some of his old haunts, watching, testing, waiting to be sure. On an impulse he arrays himself in faultless evening dress, and takes a table alone on the balcony of a fashionable restaurant. As he gazes down on the crowd of dancers, listens to the Ethiopian musicians, whose deep, care-free voices break out from time to time in a meaningless, fantastic popular refrain, he sees this side of life as it really is for him, a clamor raised by little, pitiful man to frighten away the in-creeping and remorseless silence of the great natural spaces of the world, that silence which he has felt at evening on the plains of Asia. Gradually he becomes aware of voices, a man's and a woman's, at the adjoining table, which is screened from his by palms. The woman's voice sets his pulses thudding. He suddenly knows what has really brought him back: the inner knowledge that one soul in all the vast, corrupt society from which he had fled, was vital, fearless, true. The voice of the girl at the next table is like Hers; less ringing, less sweet, but sufficiently like to send him instantly in search of a telephone, and Her. He rises, signals the waiter. As he does so, his gaze surmounts the screen of palms, he sees the couple at the next table. Can it be? It is. And as he gazes, shocked and unbelieving, then gradually stricken with certainty, her companion, a dark, red-faced old man of thirty-five reaches out a podgy hand and touches her with a possessive, too-intimate caress. Flinging wide his arms in a gesture of passionate renunciation, the hero rushes away, doffs once for all the detested livery of decadent civilization, and takes the first freight out of town.

I, who had read the same story in a hundred different guises, knew what was going to be made to happen. The boys, not knowing, or at least not sure, were interested to varying degrees in the outcome. But during the *dénouement*, snortings and the drumming of restless fingers gave proof that spontaneous criticism was imminent. Finally Tracy raised his hand. I nodded, and asked Anderson to pause.

"Look here," said Tracy. "You really can't say 'Flinging wide his arms.' "

"Why not?" Anderson scents snobbery.

"Well, it's too late in the world's history. Mrs. E. D. E. N. Southworth is dead."

Anderson, red and angry, looks around for support. I happen to be staring at the ceiling. The others are grinning or implacable.

"You wouldn't really act like that, would you?" suggests Lewisohn briskly.

"Certainly not, but I'd feel like that."

"Yes, but if you wouldn't do it, why put it in? That's probably why it sounds so phony." Excellent word, Lewisohn, I say to myself. It suggests the natural voice disguised by mechanics, which is Anderson to the life.

"The Indian part is phony, too," Tracy goes on, "and I read that article on *ovis poli* in the *National Geographic*."

"I don't think that all girls can be said to be inconstant, which I take it is the inference you would lead us to draw. I have more faith, in fact I know of a girl—girls—" Mather, of course.

"There was a bit there in the restaurant that I liked," Diggs puts in, dreamily.

The discussion outlasts the hour; and through it sits Anderson, angry and grateful by turns, and—learning fast. In particular he learns that the scene he really knew, that in the restaurant, the emotion that was really his, the hero's sense of the emptiness of a certain kind of pleasure, were the only things genuine enough to bear imaginative handling.

If the reader who has followed me so far now exclaims, "Do you mean to tell me that a college should actually give credit for the writing of such a piece of hopeless, melodramatic claptrap?", I reply unhesitatingly that it should, and for worse things than that, so long as they represent long and sincere effort. Looking toward the winnowing of ideals, the stripping of intellectual pinfeathers, the formation of taste, which is eventually the formation of character—toward everything, in short, which a cultural course in literature ought to give a man, I doubt if anything more important than that hour could happen to Anderson.

In the first place, why were Anderson and the rest of that group, to say nothing of the scores and hundreds of others each year, few or none of whom have literary aspirations, so easily led into the attempt at literary expression? Obviously because they enjoy it. Prizes, mentions, the hope of publication in the undergraduate magazines, are useful stimulants, but they are all unnecessary. The impulse is there, in nine out of ten youths of college age, and is readily roused into action. (One source of it, I have discovered, is the miscellaneous reading of periodicals which most of them do. This develops a genuine, however secret, conviction that given a little time they could do better stuff than much of what they read.) "The time went by like winking, while I was doing that," they will tell you. "Sir, I forgot an economics recitation because I rode in town and got started on that diary of things seen you asked us to keep." In my own experience with alumni, there is abundant proof that they remember their attempts at creation with pleasure and pride. And if these, then with profit, too. "The days that make us happy, make us wise."

Moreover, I should reply, the college, the broadly cultural institution, is exactly the place where credit should be given for such attempts, for that is the kind of benefit that is derived from them. As Dr. Spiller of Swarthmore, himself the master of a most interesting "workshop," remarks in a recent article,* "if the aim . . . be the perfection of presentation, professionalism is immediately implied and such courses belong no longer in the liberal arts or cultural college."

I have said enough concerning the influence of creative attempts on the morals and the philosophies of their makers. Let me hasten to add that original writing remains the most valuable adjunct to courses of reading. "I never appreciated Fritz Kreisler," Dr. Child once remarked, "until I bought a violin, and tried to fiddle for myself." That seems to me a fundamental bit of doctrine. My own teaching of the ballads and the eighteenth-century satire in the couplet has been most successful when I demanded of the students an original enterprise in each form. Simply to have attempted a character study, a bit of local color, a passage of dialogue, an episode, or a familiar essay will completely remake a student's attitude toward the masterpieces he reads, because for the first time he not only is told, but knows, how incalculable and wonderful are the elements of experience, feeling, and technique which enter into great art.

What is more, the elusive spirit of beauty hovers over all human moods, and all honest pens, and it is a rarely practical or clodlike soul

* "Drama and the Liberal Arts," Part III, by Robert Spiller. *Quarterly Journal of Speech Education,* November, 1927.

whose efforts she does not once brush with her wings. Fitfully, impermanently, but often enough to make the experiment eternally alluring, the rank and file write well. They even finish a few very nice things. And if the general level, to say nothing of the worst, is very far below the level of the best—still, art has a way of surviving.

CREATIVE EXPRESSION
THROUGH DRAMATICS

TO THE CHILDREN

With *you* rests largely the future of the Theater. We, who work in the Theater, can do very little without your help and encouragement. I will try to tell you what I mean:

In ancient times, the Theater was a part of religion; it was a sacred and holy thing, and was approached with reverence and awe. The actors were priests, and to the public these performances were as vital and necessary as the bread which gave their bodies strength.

Through hundreds of years of struggle, of wars, revolutions, massacres, and plagues, the Theater grew to be a different thing, and strangely, from being a part of religion, grew to be its enemy. The Theater was denounced from the pulpit as a thing of evil. Today, this phase has almost entirely passed but the Theater, with few exceptions, remains far removed from its lofty and beautiful beginning. It is looked on too often as a clown or a buffoon, something to make the hours pass easily, with false laughter.

If you will realize the possibilities of the Theater for beauty, truth, and inspiration—and demand of it these things—you will force the people working in the Theater to a wider vision. . . . To supply your demand of truth, beauty, and inspiration, they must of necessity become finer and nobler in themselves. They must increase on every side their wisdom and their *humanity*.

As a priest takes the vow to God when he enters the church, so must the actor take the vow to God (who is Beauty, Truth, and Love) when he enters the Theater. He must become the priest of a new religion— the religion of Beauty.

Do not misunderstand me. By all this, I do not mean there should be no joy, no laughter, in the Theater. It should not be a dismal, gloomy place, to be sent to as a punishment. Nature is made up of love and death, of joy and sorrow, of pain and ecstasy; all these things converge and mingle to form that curious and poignant rhythm which we call life. So with the Theater: it should be a place where all things can be found, transmuted and heightened in beauty through the medium presenting them.

And so I beg of you, let your ideals and hopes for the Theater be high, filled with reverence and tenderness, and the Theater will not fail you.

EVA LE GALLIENNE.

INTRODUCTION

School dramatics needs the new perspective on the play of children that is fundamental to the progressive-school approach. Progressive education begins with the child's play interests—with what the child normally wants to do—and bases its program squarely upon the child's play developments. The progressive teacher assists rather than directs the fulfillment of the child's purposes and emphasizes the process rather than the finished result. She has found that growths, educative outcomes, are the inevitable by-products of the whole-hearted play. Moreover, the school sees in play an invaluable opportunity to observe the child, to discover his possibilities, to learn how to provide an increasingly richer environment, one that will engage the child more fully in more play and better play.

In striking contrast is the meagerness of the approach stated in a recent study of the psychology of play activities: "The play life of children constitutes a significant part of their *leisure-time activity.*" Indeed, many textbooks of educational psychology for teachers entirely ignore this basic characteristic of child life. The occasional paragraphs or chapters devoted to ·play invariably proceed on the foregoing assumption that play is a necessary relief from the more important and serious business of work, an unavoidable concession to that childish weakness—short-attention span. Those holding this view of play would seek to *use* it by directing it to educative ends. These educators are fundamentally distrustful of the word *play*. It has a bad odor; it seems to connote letting the child do as he pleases, sugar-coating education, making things too easy. Progressive educators, in order to obtain a friendly hearing for their aims, have learned to avoid the use of the term. They speak of activities, units of work, creative self-expression. This mistrust of play profoundly hampers the spread of progressive principles. Witness the wholesale adoption of activities, units of work, creative expression as new subjects in the old curriculum!

The literature of children's dramatics also reflects this confusion concerning play. In the discussion of values, one may discover but slightly modernized rephrasings of Spencer's surplus-energy theory, the practice theory of Carl Groos—that the child through play prepares for life's demands by practicing his future functions—and adaptations of G. Stanley Hall's recapitulation theory. The imposing list of virtues ascribed to dramatics, however, indicates that educators are aware of its fundamental importance; but no one who is mistrustful of play itself can hope to deal effectively with children's dramatics.

Progressive schools see in dramatics activities as natural to children as breathing and as necessary. They can not use it as a study or an art form to which children are to be subjected, for they know that the richest possibilities that could be outlined in advance will fall far short of the actual results which children can achieve with the right kind of assistance. It has often been pointed out that dramatic activities offer a singularly fruitful synthesis of all of the arts, an integration of intellectual, emotional, and physical aspects of experience in an expression that is at once intensely personal and broadly social. On the basis of these rich promises, enthusiastic plans for a school organized around a theater are sometimes projected. But such plans usually overlook the fact that unless this integration takes place *within the child* himself, and not merely in the minds of the organizers or on school programs and reports, it will be no more significant for growth than the same number of activities studied as separate subjects.

As a matter of fact, the very wealth of possibilities inherent in dramatics portends danger, for the more basic the tendency with which one is dealing, the more serious may be the damage inflicted through misuse. Misdirected dramatics may actually force children to practice, under guidance and pressure, the worst sort of personality traits. Examine the photographs of children in a play. Observe the painful self-consciousness masquerading under a show of bravado, the insincerity. Amid stage sets and costumes that too often are adult confections of the most literal and unimaginative sort, young bodies are stiff with restraint, uncomfortably aware of alien trappings. Here is no freedom, no imaginative fulfillment, no real living. These children are not Vikings, nor Greeks, nor fairies, nor circus folk; they are merely John and Betty all dressed up and acting "cute."

Directors of dramatics make quite a point of enlarging the child's sympathies and extending his understanding by such commands as "Put yourself in Little Beppo's place. How would he have felt? What would he have done?" But if the child of his own accord would never have chosen to be Little Beppo, if he felt no inner identification with the qualities which that character represents to him, his attempts can amount to no more than shallow pretense.

Equally misguided are the recent attempts to use dramatics for emotional therapy. A timid child may be cast in the rôle of pirate or Captain Courageous in order to evoke self-assertive feelings, and conversely, the too aggressive child may be assigned minor rôles to make him feel a proper relation to his fellows. Needless to say, such therapeutic measures resemble bailing the sea with a spoon. They are not based on an adequate knowledge of motives underlying conduct and behavior. Directors of dramatics, like teachers of subjects, seldom possess analytic insight into child behavior. The very word "director" reveals that the emphasis is in the wrong place. Rarely have such directors realized that children's plays offer a unique opportunity for learning on the part of the director, a chance to find out important things about children. It is unlikely, for example, that girls of fourteen feel an inner urge to enact "Snow White and the Dwarfs," or that children of eight are emotionally responsive to the amours of "A Mid-summer Night's Dream"; yet such mistakes are frequent when plays for children are chosen by adults and directed by them.

The aridity of high-school dramatics bears ample witness to this overemphasis upon outside direction. Whether taught as a subject or permitted in dramatic clubs, the aims are too often extraneous; the emphasis is upon the mechanics of diction, the so-called principles of good acting. The occasional half-hearted attempt to evoke creative dramatics is doomed to mediocrity because the director's attitude is so charged with a lack of confidence in the students' formulations. Not until the emphasis in high schools shifts from subjects and preparation for college entrance merely—to permit some degree of consideration of the needs and interests of students as they are—may we hope for much vitality in any of the arts at this age level. The fact that high-school students flock to dramatics courses in spite of all this misdirection may well reveal the urgency of their need rather than its fulfillment.

We have been most successful with the dramatic play of children at the lower age levels, for we have had greater confidence in the younger child's play needs; indeed, we have been rather helpless before his insistent absorption in play. The noninterfering research techniques, observations, and records that are gradually being developed in nursery schools contain sound suggestions for research in dramatic play of older children.

The psychology of play that remains to be written will be based upon such first-hand observations of unhampered children working out their own purposes with all the assistance that coöperating teachers and a rich environment can give. To be truly fundamental, such a play psychology should take cognizance of the ethnological and sociological studies of the rôle of play in other cultures and of the recent findings of psychoanalysis, notably those of Jung, concerning the subjective intuitive processes which give rise to art.

Progressive schools are frequently criticized for their failure to test scientifically the propositions on the basis of which they are operating. While it is true that the progressive schools have been more interested in formulating these propositions than in testing them, it must also be acknowledged that the kind of testing most research scientists have in mind would fail to measure the outcomes toward which the progressive schools are working. A subject-matter specialist could easily determine the history facts gained through a play about Columbus, for example; but no battery of tests now in existence could isolate the values involved in the play about the miners which twelve-year-olds developed with Miss Leila V. Stott, or in the play described by Miss Berta Rantz. The new schools are establishing larger values than can be indicated by the scientific educational techniques now available. This does not absolve them, however, from the necessity of devising research techniques in terms of new and broader values.

A. S.

NURTURING SINCERITY IN DRAMATICS

Helen Ericson

IN THE spontaneous, imaginative play of an unspoiled child one may witness a perfect example of creative drama. And in the witnessing, one becomes convinced that dramatization is inherent in the child's nature, and impersonation an instinctive art.

In designating an *unspoiled* child in the rôle of actor, the writer has in mind one who is unconsciously dramatizing, with single eye, unaware of a gallery. Such drama is artless and springs entirely from inner vision. Most children are Christopher Robins who find in the nursery chairs the whole world as their stage.

But upon entering the schoolroom, the dramatic impulse must often, perforce, surrender itself to other ways and purposes. For the accepted adult conception of acting and drama is a performance to be observed. Everywhere in schools, little children are being induced to "act out," for each other and the teacher, their experiences and the stories told to them. This régime ends the spontaneous drama, and, except to certain children, it is an ordeal. To the sensitive child comes a terrifying self-consciousness or a giggly embarrassment; to the aggressive one, a glorious satisfaction of his exhibitionary desires.

This subversion of the dramatic impulse is not intentional on the part of teachers, but is due to a misconception of how it may function naturally in the school life. With little children, drama is a game, played alone or with others, and not a performance. The idea of presenting a drama to entertain or give pleasure to spectators or an audience comes with the maturing years. To draw a line between *playing* and *acting* may seem an overfine distinction, but in that demarcation, in regard to little children certainly, one may make the choice between sincerity and artificiality in their drama.

The most beautiful plays and delightfully spontaneous creative dramas in the lower grades at Sunset Hill School have been those which came about in the free-play periods, in settings made by the screen playhouse behind the piano, the enclosures and structures made of the building blocks, or by the rearrangement of the schoolroom furniture itself. The plays, self-initiated games to the children, were a naïve medley of reality and imagination, the impersonation of their acquaintances and of the folk and animals in tales they loved—the plot unfolding as chance determined. The mousiest little one became an eager participant, the bright flush of cheek and a transported radiance of eye giving evidence of how completely body and mind were fused.

Such plays could never be "put on," not even before a mother, without losing something of their vital essence. They *happen* only when the teacher is an apparently unseeing and unseen, yet ever-vigilant presence. Such plays should form a natural part of the daily school program rather than the "cute" little dramatizations of stories and episodes, which more often constitute the dramatic experience in school. To us, it seems that the dramatic urge will be free, and true creative forces nourished by this spontaneous type of dramatization found in nursery play. In addition, the "dressing up" may be kept to the rudimentary accessories which childhood accepts—"Stuck a feather in his cap, and called it Macaroni!"

Only from such natural drama will satisfactory development result; and it remains for us, the adults, to see that the influences in the child's environment and the experiences which come to him for his imagination to feed upon are such stuff as the finest "dreams are made on." By the light of his creative insight, as he dramatizes the world about him, he can revitalize for himself the worthy aspects of life.

What a tragic loss to childhood, with all the beauties of civilization ready at hand, that often its games consist only of gunplay, robbery, sophisticated frivolities, and underworld jargon!

Almost all of the dramatics in the lower grades of our school are of the spontaneous type, but nevertheless, and without qualm, there are occasions when we impose upon even the youngest children participation in a dramatic performance they have not originated. These performances are usually in the celebration of the yearly festivals, Thanksgiving, Christmas, and patriotic anniversaries. As a preparation for their special rôles, through stories and discussion, the children are initiated into an understanding of the significance and ideals of the celebration.

Many incidents reveal how completely the child may come to identify himself as an important factor in the presentation of the central idea. Self is forgotten and he is borne along and merged in something bigger than himself. And it is this unifying undercurrent in these group dramatic events that we believe valuable for a child.

A change of attitude comes to older children, due to their experiences in witnessing drama in the theater and in reading plays. They want to "give plays." Our experience has been that the transition is best made by the use of puppets. Little girls often discover and find vent for this new feeling about dramatics in their play with paper dolls, and little boys with their tin soldiers. The puppet theater of the third and fourth grades has been a joyous enterprise and comes into constant use. These groups enjoy repeating over and over the traditional dialogues of the old fairy tales and legends. With these children, the drama is more in the speech than in the action. At present, this phase of dramatics is being studied and is still in the experimental stage.

In classes above the primary, a challenging array of original and interesting written drama has accumulated through the years. An esspecial glamour seems to have gathered about a play which grew out of the reading by a sixth-grade group of Kenneth Grahame's *Wind in the Willows*. The children had taken boundless delight in the story, particularly in the author's endowment of the creatures of his tale with the whimsicalities of the Oxford dons of his acquaintance. The subtle combination of human beings and animals intrigued the children, and in the speeches of the creatures they found delectable literary morsels which they seized upon, savoring their deliciousness on the tongue, bandying them about in their conversations with each other. In fact, little dramas were constantly in progress at recess time and on the playground.

With one accord it was decided to write a play. The episode of Mr. Mole's finding his home became the drama under the title of "Home Again!" Many of the lines of the play were incorporated directly from the dialogue of the book, but the plot was carried forward by lines written by the children. The setting was of the simplest, crude benches and tables, and the costuming only such ordinary garments as were easily gathered from the home wardrobe. Animal masks were not to be thought of! Even after twelve years, with any number of other dramatic experiences intervening, this particular play seems to epitomize for these children *the perfect drama*.

At some other time we should like to drag from the closet the skeleton of high-school dramatics, the rattle of whose bones—the annual senior play, the dramatic club play, try-out systems, paid admission, elaborate costuming, and the like—brings haunting and disturbing thoughts. Solving for the high school the problem of more playing and less acting is another story, and one sadly in need of attention.

GROWING UP AND DRAMATICS

Caroline Pratt

WE SHOULD think of dramatics in an elementary school as an important process through which children grow up rather than as a school "subject." I doubt if the productions of children are ever "art" in the adult sense, in spite of the fact that children often produce what adult artists pronounce organized pictures, or sculpture, or bits of versification, or a play. One must not forget that the very fact of being an organism tends toward productions which have more or less formulation. While many animals live in places which they discover, many also produce homes, and these homes have form, as bird nests, ant hills, beaver houses. It is because this tendency toward production is broken up or interfered with that we do not obtain more of what may be called embryonic art from children. The value of preserving this tendency is very great, because when the individual becomes conscious of it, he has something already developed with which to attack his medium. The medium is mere chance; the great thing is the ability to organize.

All play is dramatization in one form or another. Even "organized" play must have originated as dramatic play and branched off into what we call games with set rules and regulations.

Dramatics as a growing-up process begins with very young children. They play, and play, and grow muscularly because they have to. But many things besides muscular growth take place. By handling, by seeing, by smelling, and by experiencing the relationships in these, children discover what can be done with things about them, and a more recognizable "dramatic" play begins. A knowing teacher, supplying the right materials during long play periods, supplying new opportunities to see, to hear, to smell, helps to enrich the simple beginnings, and new productions are made. It is a very familiar sight—children pushing about a train of cars, playing horse, pouring tea. We have always accepted it as "natural" for a child to play in this way, but it is a fairly rare thing for adults to help children enrich and extend this play. And it is quite a new thing to do this in schools.

What the children acquire from this early dramatic play period which will help them in the future, are habits of searching for and using what lies about them. I refer not only to play materials but to facts as well.

They learn to select what is pertinent to their schemes. Playing horse may mean a great deal of horse background or a very little. But to carry on in playing horse, facts must be discovered and materials have to be added, or the play comes to a full stop.

Facts in use are facts related. If a child dramatizes with a doll as a center, she relates her facts until a whole domestic situation is set up. If a boy or girl uses an engine as a center, both add tracks, all sorts of cars, and so on, though the girl may be more interested in dining and sleeping cars, while the boy may explore and play with the details of the engine.

This natural or spontaneous play, if unaided, begins to slough off when organized games begin unless the same or another knowing teacher stands by to help promote it. About this time (seven or eight years of age), play begins to take on a somewhat different form. Different materials are used. Children like to dress and to pretend consciously that they are someone else. Pretend is the essence of drama. It marks quite a change in the growing-up process. Although before this time, children had *been* the horse, the pig, the engineer, now they *pretend* to be. Some people never get to this stage of development. They remain the center of the universe, and believe everything revolves about them. It is indeed a modern thing which is getting into our thinking: that perhaps the universe was not made for man. This may be one of the signs that the race is growing up.

Another thing which interests children at this period is what has gone before. They are beginning to read, and they have been read to. Books are necessarily of the past, and the immediate past is very pertinent to their own lives. Furthermore, if they are going to use this past dramatically, the very fact that it has to be imagined rather than copied conduces to pretense. When a child is pretending, he is saved from self-consciousness by the fact that all the others know he is pretending, and he is not so open to criticism. One child's interpretation is as good as another's.

This playing with costumes and making of properties does not always eventuate in what might be called a drama. Sometimes the children are not interested in presenting it to an audience. They have had their fun, and that's the end of it. I often wonder whether this playing would ever come through in form if the teacher had not a feeling that it should, that time has been wasted if it does not, and therefore helps to bring it through. Bringing it through usually means having a performance in an auditorium and inviting an audience.

One of the most interesting things about these plays of the younger children is the infinite properties they construct—prairie wagons needing a field to operate in, horses, oxen, pasteboard stores large enough for a child to enter; anything they lack is cheerfully made. They use these things in their daily play until after the production, when they are stowed away until forgotten. They bother little with scenery. During this period, one can enter the schoolroom and find children dressed in costumes they have made. They bring the lives of the people into their own daily lives. *The value of drama seems to lie in getting ready for it. Through this getting ready, children broaden their knowledge, their sympathies; they are growing up.*

The next change in the dramatic movement seems to be one of eliminating nonessentials. The children's critical faculty, developed through the dramatic experience as well as in other ways, comes into use. They choose more carefully their situations to be dramatized. They effect closer relationships between dialogue, action, properties, costumes, and stage sets. Not that this has not happened in the former dramatic play, but now it begins to be a conscious effort toward form.

The children search the history and literature with which they are making their contacts and choose a dramatic situation. They try out their parts, suiting their actions to words, or as likely as not, their words to action. They learn to use dialogue, not merely as a passage at arms with another, and for the passing moment, but to indicate the development of the play as a whole. They learn the value of costumes, stage sets, properties, in getting over an idea. They investigate the dance, the music of the period, as well as the decorative art, and they bring these also into relation with their play. All this has been shown in detail in one of the City and Country School publications.*

Some will say that children should not be kept in the play world, that this is not facing reality, that the real world is very different. But this is not a valid criticism of what I am describing, for, though I may have dwelt on the play aspects, the drudgery part is there too. One is too apt to think of a creative artist as one who escapes from real work, that he lives a life of ease and pleasure, that being gifted, he is, therefore, exempt from the drudgery of life. But this is not true. An artist who "comes through" has done it through the hardest kind of work.

The children, too, put through a great deal of drudgery in the making of a play. They learn to face this necessity, that drudgery is a part of any accomplishment. If a shirk appears, his nose is held to the grindstone by his peers.

Far from agreeing that children's play time should not be extended, I hope that dramatic play will be part of their adult lives. I could wish them nothing better than that their future leisure shall go into the making and producing of plays. It would be healthier and more profitable

* *Adventuring with Twelve Year Olds*, by Leila Stott. Greenberg. 1927.

than the passive entertainment which adults demand of professionals, the extreme example of which is watching professional baseball instead of playing it!

In every group of these older children, there are indicated definite talents in dialogue and dramatic technique, in stage sets, in costumes, in acting, in general management, so that the individual child has his opportunity. But the great value of dramatics to children of eleven, twelve, and thirteen, lies in the positive working towards a common end. Individuals constantly stand aside for the benefit of the whole. This is illustrated when the time comes to try out scenes. Small groups get together and present scenes before a class audience, and the parts are assigned in accordance with the judgment of the group. Differences of opinion are met by doing the parts over until the group is convinced. Each child is given a chance, if he wants it. There is a minimum of bad feeling about this. Everyone gets a part, for this method of making a play permits a latitude which makes it possible to create a part if need be.

Perhaps the greatest value of dramatics in elementary schools lies in the opportunity it offers to children to produce an organized picture of which they themselves are the media. Though the children are pretending, they are learning to live together harmoniously, and this alone is an invaluable experience for them.

A PLAY IN THE WALDEN SCHOOL

Berta Rantz

A FIRST-YEAR high-school group in the Walden School made and produced a three-act play called *Fanatic Fancies*. Out of the children's interests and questionings grew a concept; and this concept was developed into a play which expressed their observations, their thoughts, and their humor. Although our high-school groups sometimes produce plays which they have read, they more often make them up themselves. The children realize that to write a play takes a great deal of time and of creative energy. Moreover, at this age, standards are high, and frequently the children are unwilling to sacrifice production to writing. However, it is difficult to find a play that is not too long, that gives everyone in the group an opportunity to act, that is sufficiently mature in subject matter without being beyond the emotional power of the children, and that is expressed in language beautiful enough to withstand the constant repetition of rehearsals. Finally, the satisfaction of subjective expression counterbalances the technical deficiencies of an original play.

What did this group want to write about? People interested them, the effect of people upon one another. Someone in the class suggested writing about a family because, sometimes, a person who seemed to get along well with his family was really in conflict. Someone else wanted to show a person taken out of his own class in society and placed in another in which he had had no experience. Another suggested that it would be interesting to take a person out of one century and place him in another. One girl was especially interested in what it would be like to come out of a past century into a future one—any past into any future.

In naming these conflicts of group with group, or of individuals in relation to groups, the children were unconsciously giving expression to their own problems of adjustment to their families and to the world. For the teacher, this was excellent educational material, being both the substance of drama and the means through the expression of which the children could find growth.

All of the children were interested in the first suggestion; but they soon put aside the idea of family conflict. They said it was too personal, too limited, too serious. It contained, of course, an emotional problem too difficult for them to handle. The more intellectual and fantastic problem of the juxtaposition of the past, present, and future really appealed to them.

To help make actual the ideas which they were expressing in speech, the teacher gave the class exercises in pantomime fitted to the problem. They had been accustomed to such training in pantomime since they were about nine years old and first began to give plays for other children. These pantomimic exercises were for the purpose of making real the contrasts and conflicts contained in the suggestions for a play. The children were given bits to act out: a child appearing for the first time in his class in a new school; a poor man, who knows only cheap movie houses, going to a first-night on Broadway; a country person's first walk on a crowded New York street. Later exercises, first for pantomime, then for action and speech, were: two people of distinctly opposite character —one strong, one weak; one proud, one abject; one excited, one calm; one wise, one foolish. These character contrasts were valuable for creating mood. Then, there were introduced into the exercises contrasts in idea as well as in mood. It was suggested that they act out a meeting between two scholars, one interested in the past, the other in the future. Someone in the class said that they could be two men who, though devoted to opposite ideas, had lived and quarreled amicably for many years.

Immediately after this dramatization, some members of the group wanted to write down what they could remember of the dialogue. The children saw in the exercise exactly what they needed for their play.

When the dialogue was read, everyone, including the writers, agreed that it was weak. They must dramatize again. Thus by action rather than by rote-learning of lines, the characters of the play came to life.

At the next dramatization, the actors established the place, the library of the men's home. They introduced a wife for each man, two secretaries, servants, and a friend. The *dramatis personæ* changed from day to day, being fixed finally only when the characters of the two men were so defined that the support each merited could be well ascertained. As the play grew and clarified, the scholars became: one, a scientist who, abhorring the fumbling waste of this age, searches for a future that will be mechanically perfect; the other, an historian who, hating the restlessness of the present day, longs to find a past in which man lived in peaceful harmony with nature.

In the first scene, the two men are seen preparing for their journeys. The historian is burdened with books, charts, suitcases, shoes, shovels, and other baggage; the scientist is neatly ready with a small, black, electrically equipped case, compact with all requirements, personal and scientific.

Many grave discussions took place in class about time and the eternity of time; the possibility of the coexistence of past, present, and future civilizations; the value of mechanical progress; man's investigations of the past; the question as to whether life moves in great cycles so that man is merely repeating now what he has already done in past ages. Obviously, everything that was possible in classroom discussion was not feasible for use in a play. There were intense arguments, for example, as to whether it was going to be possible on the stage to deal with the simultaneity of time; and the whole shaping of the plot depended upon the outcome of this battle. There was difficulty, too, over this question: how was the historian, by digging into archæological remains, to come upon a living people? The way in which these problems were finally settled may be seen in the following excerpts from the play. Brackett is the historian, Crane is the scientist, Rockland is the friend.

BRACKETT: It is my belief that somewhere a civilization exists in all its primitive perfection. I think that there exists a race of people unaffected by the banishment from Paradise. Their souls remained pure; therefore they remained immortal on earth.

CRANE: Yes—yes—now, Rockland, listen to me.

ROCKLAND: Proceed.

CRANE: I want to find the future. I want to graduate from this confused and undeveloped world to the higher organization of a mechanical state. This would require centuries to develop, but I cannot live so long. This is my belief: as we pass into the present and as the light of time moves on from the past, the future is revealed. If I can leave the light of time which shines only on the present, I will find the future.

ROCKLAND: The world is very nice as it is. God has given us the power to advance this far and in due time will, I hope, give us the power to advance further. Why hurry or put back what will take its own course? . . .

Somewhere, sometime, the class was struck by the futility of what their two leading characters were trying to do. They were not able to handle dramatically a situation in which these men should succeed in their quests. Then one day a member of the class said, "Suppose they each found the wrong place!" Never was a suggestion greeted with happier enthusiasm. The historian would dig his way into Mekanikos, a long-forgotten mechanical civilization; the scientist would contrive his way to a blissful future of song and rustic peace, in a place named Illusia. And both men, baffled, would return to accept the present. This return became the material for a brief epilogue, which was performed in pantomime with laughter for speech.

Naturally enough, it was the scene in a mechanical world which most attracted the group. So many things happened that, when writing time came, idea after idea had to be thrown out. How to limit themselves? They finally decided on a factory in which the creatures of Mekanikos were made. The scene, as finally written, contains a remarkable assortment of beings: mechanical babies that won't cry and that are exchangeable if unsatisfactory; a walking dictionary; laborers; statesmen; a dancer made of a newly invented metal of unusual flexibility; a flirt who will be sold cheap because she is disturbing the factory; a scientist who hits upon the bold idea of injecting a bit of protoplasm into the beings of Mekanikos.

In order to study movement for these characters, work was done in dancing class. The mechanical scene needed mechanical movement; these people had a different rhythm from that developed in Illusia where man lives close to Nature in unburdened simplicity. The mechanical scene, as finally worked out, moved to back-stage music beaten out on tom-tom, triangle, African rattle, and sheet tin. There was additional rhythmic movement and sound from a huge wheel and a balance arm, both worked from back stage throughout the scene.

When the mechanical dancer is being tried out for the first time, Brackett, the poor twentieth-century creature, is much disturbed.

BRACKETT: That isn't dancing! You call that dancing? There's no grace, no freedom of motion, no feeling! Bah! And is that music? If your dancer must dance to that rhythm, for heaven's sake, *stop her, stop her!*

MECHANICAL SCIENTIST: There must be something wrong with him. Our lives are based on that rhythm.

The third scene, that is, the scene in Illusia, was the hardest to write. It was helped the least by preliminary dramatizations. Where they were being satirical about the twentieth century, the dialogue went well.

CRANE: Where are your highly developed mechanisms? Where are the power units of your existence? How do you live? (*Discovers a telephone which the Illusians have just taken out of their museum.*) Is this as far as you've gotten—a telephone?
SPRIG: Oh, is that what you call it? What is it for?
CRANE: You talk into it.
JOY: What do you say?
FEATHER: Whom do you speak to?
ROBIN: Why do you?
CRANE: You can talk to anyone at any distance. You can talk to someone five thousand miles away. Oh, yes, you see I've lived in quite an age. You couldn't do what I've done, discover another world. Dear, dear, it does seem peculiar. You seem to have gone backward instead of forward. . . .
DAWN: Why should you want to talk to people five thousand miles away when there are so many around you?

However, something more than this was needed. The children felt that the scene had to be poetic; but it was difficult to sustain the mood in words. They agreed that a better result could be achieved if they could get their imaginations to working more sympathetically; but they were blocked. This difficulty was holding up rehearsals; for by this time definite parts had been assigned, lines were being learned and costumes were being made. The general feeling of the scene had already been worked out, a background of pleasant hills with no other scenery. The costumes were to be in straight, simple lines and of delicate, harmonious colors. The scene was to open with sweet music and gentle dancing; these had already been composed by members of the group. The actors had worked also on the manner of their speech; it must be beautifully modulated in contrast to the staccato discords of the scene in Mekanikos. All this was good; it was too bad to have to accept poor dialogue. The following quotation is the close of the scene as it was put down in writing at this time:

CRANE: But your life is not for me.
JOY: Won't you stay and live with us a while and maybe you will like our life after all?
CRANE: No, I have my work to do.
DAWN: Oh, do stay.
CRANE: No, I must be going. Good-by, good-by. (*He goes off, repeating his formula.*)

One girl insisted that something could be done and begged for time. She wanted to write alone. She is a girl with a strong poetic gift. The group appreciated the fact that it was a quality like hers which could give something to the scene. Since very little of this had been forthcoming when the group was working together, they were glad to allow her to write alone. By working alone, she was free in the same way as when writing her own stories and poems. She altered some speeches; she added some; she particularly built up the atmosphere of Illusia. The whole class was stimulated by what she had done. In a final dramatization, everyone contributed. This is the close of the scene in its developed form.

CRANE: But your life is not for me.

JOY: You really do not know our life. We do not have pageants all the time. Won't you stay and live with us a while and maybe you will like our life after all?

DAWN: Oh, do stay.

GAY: Yes, do.

FEATHER: } Come, come, don't hurry away.
SPRIG: }

JOY: We will show you our country, Illusia, the big blue river, the high purple mountains and the rolling green fields.

ROBIN: The time is drawing near for our autumn harvest. If you stay you can celebrate with us on top of the purple mountains, dance and sing and frolic in the light of our harvest fire.

DAWN: You can help till the fields after harvest for the products that must be planted early. It's lovely to work in newly turned earth, to smell the fresh dampness.

FEATHER: And then there is the blue river to bathe in after the field work. I'll race you down to the spruce-trimmed shore if—

ROBIN: And you can run in the race against me, when you are strong and cool from the water, and you can be in our leaping contest, do all the things we do.

CRANE: I can't leap. (*To himself.*) Imagine leaping in a contest against this Robin.

FEATHER: We'll teach you. It's easy and it's nice to sail through the air, once you get it.

CRANE: Using my legs to sail on when I have an aeroplane!

DAWN: Come, you'll stay.

CRANE: No, I could not stand living as you do; my world is glorious compared to yours. Oh, no; this is not what I was looking for. Machines— rivers; buildings—mountains and trees. (*Laughs.*) Oh, no, no. Just imagine, I worked eight years to find my Utopia and it's brought me to this.

FEATHER: What a great deal of work you seem to do to enable yourself to avoid it.

CRANE: Well, I have my work, I have my work. Good-by, good-by. (*He goes off repeating his formula.*)

Fanatic Fancies was written by children thirteen and fourteen years old; in its growth, the play reveals much about children of this age. Intellectually, they begin to share an adult world; emotionally, they are much less mature. It is the adjustment between the two kinds of development which makes for the peculiarly varied moods in work. Self-criticism blocks expression; eagerness toward life stimulates it. Play making demands that vision be supplemented by pertinacity and concentration and provides for expression through effort as well as through inspiration.

DRAMATIC PLAY IN THE NURSERY SCHOOL

Harriet M. Johnson

THE small child lives in a self-centered world, the circumference of which is small even if in it is included all of the environment that affects him directly or indirectly. The child himself, however, sets narrower boundaries in terms of his own intimate share in that world's current events. The things that have happened to him and have happened repeatedly are his deepest concern, and as we watch we can trace the lines which have engaged his interest and his emotion. He will usually dramatize the experiences which lie nearest to him, sometimes with startling fidelity, sometimes with an elaboration suggesting that they are inspired either by fantasy or by unconscious desire.

Going to bed and getting up with all the attendant ceremonies—demand for a drink, for an open door, or for a visit to the bathroom—are familiar dramatic stuff.

At seventeen months, Walter laid his doll on its stomach over his knee, patted it and said, "Night, night." He repeated this brief pattern at intervals with no further details. No direct stimulation was given him, but other and older children were about and there were available various materials which might have added realism to his play. These were not conventional toys, clothing or beds and bedding, but things which called for a certain degree of imagination or inventiveness, and which could be used to serve a variety of ends. Apparently a gesture was all that this particular seventeen-months-old child could reproduce from the mass of details that meant being put to bed. At about twenty months, he had adopted some of the properties available and was putting his doll to bed in a small box and spreading pieces of cloth over it. No more realistic details were noted at that time.

At twenty-two months, another child carried out much more complicated doll-bedding play though the stage set was similar. The content and the emotional implications here are very illuminating:

Tom laid his doll on a shelf and spread covers over it. Said very gently, "G'night. Wan' dat shair?" apparently anticipating a familiar demand. Ran off to push up a chair which he placed against doll's "bed." Peeped in at the doll and said, "Have a nice nap," and went across the room. There he picked up an imaginary something which he brought back to the doll saying, "I bring some canny!" The adult near him moved at this point and he called over his shoulder, "Don't wake dolly up. Don't wake her up now." Was reassured and left the doll for a few seconds. On approaching the shelf again he said in a very even tone of voice as if stating an indifferent fact, "See, dollie is wet." Was then heard murmuring, "Any, any more."

Further details are often added, sometimes practical recalls like, "Oh, poor little dolly has a tummy-ache! Poor little dolly!" Or the play grows into a rehearsal of a home episode with details which tempt one to psychoanalytic speculation.

Margaret's mother came to school almost at the end of her patience because of a sudden rebellion at bedtime after two years of serene acceptance of routine. Every ingenious excuse and delay known to children were called upon to defer the hour, and when the room was finally closed Margaret would climb out of her bed, whether she had been pinned in or not, and beat upon the door, howling dolefully, till her parents were almost as hysterical as the baby.

Time and various experimental methods gradually overcame this manifestation, but day after day at school, the drama was reënacted. Margaret and another child alternated in taking the parts of mother and baby, each responding to the proper cue with no coaching, at thirty-two months. The mother would put her baby to bed, cover her carefully and say, "Comfy, dear?" and then "Good night." She had hardly left the bedside before the baby's cries were heard. If they did not come at once the baby was prompted, "Squeal, baby." At the first cry the mother would bustle back, saying, "What's the matter? Want a drink?" or "You wet? Here's a dry pad." It seemed obviously a perfectly understood dramatization of a baby bedeviling its mother at bedtime, except that in this instance every request on the part of the baby was anticipated and met with instant response from the mother.

A rapid survey of a year's notes of children under three years of age shows, besides nap and bedtime skits, records of telephone conversations—to mother or to the grocer ordering various articles of food; the operation of a gramophone when imaginary records of nursery songs were put on the revolving piano stool; and cooking, stirring, baking, and eating with various ingredients mentioned.

Two children under three had a misunderstanding about macaroni, one preparing to serve it for dinner while the other, whose experience was evidently literary rather than gastronomic, said that she was going to put hers on a pony!

Shoe-shining with a small pan for dressing and a pebble or a block for a brush; barbering and shaving, with a doll's cover tucked or pinned about the neck and two blocks for scissors; shampooing with elaborate and vigorous business of rinsing and drying are found repeatedly in the records of our children. Train and boat play, at first hardly more than an announcement as blocks are moved about, grow more and more detailed with experience.

Larry, pushing a box about, announced that he was the moving man. With swinging arms and stamping feet, he proceeded to load large blocks into his cart and was heard to mutter, "Jeeze!" over an especially heavy armful.

A sandwich made of two pebbles with "a flavor" for filling was mentioned; the "scream door" as well as windows went into a building; clothes were washed and wrung out with a very expert twist of hands and wrists and a corresponding screwing-up of facial muscles.

In the nursery school with which I am most familiar, proportional measurements of various parts of the body are regularly taken from time to time by the anthropologist and her assistants. This procedure is not at first popular and constitutes quite an emotional experience until it is understood and accepted as part of the routine. There is usually no dramatic rehearsal of it given by children under twenty-four months but, after that, the records are sure to contain accounts like the following in which the leading actors were recruited from the seniors in the group:

Jane, thirty-four months, led a younger child across the roof and placed him between two sawhorses which she had set up and, saying gently, "Wanna see how *big* Howell's head is," laid a small shovel against his forehead. Turned a wheelbarrow over and urged Margery to sit down to be measured, and continued giving directions in dulcet tones which were an exact imitation of those of an ingratiating adult, and approximated do-mi-sol-do in rhythm.

"*Now* we gotta do a back. Sit down, Margy." Laid a shovel against her back. "*Now*, a s'oulder," with appropriate gestures. "Now a face and a nosses," pressing her shovel against her victim's nose. Occasionally she held the small shovel close to her eyes as if reading, and when another child took her place, she called out over her shoulder after each measurement, "Siss, eight," as if to a recorder. The play went on with further variations for about thirty minutes.

Granted then that dramatic reproduction of familiar and intimate and personal events, with a progressive elaboration of details and widening of setting is a characteristic of early childhood, what of it? Has it significance in the development or in the education of children?

No one who has watched this type of play can doubt that it represents an authentic interest of children. I say authentic because, while adults tend to base their judgments of children's interests upon memories of their own and almost invariably date their appearance too early in the play life, this particular interest, its first appearance, and its early growth history has been discovered by watching children at play. Furthermore, it is indubitably one of the methods of learning practiced by children; first to experience fully, then to recall and relive, and finally to embroider.

These illustrations are echoes of experiences picked up by the way. If education is to use, as a positive asset, this impulse to rehearse past events, it must be prepared gradually to extend the range of children's experiences along intentional and related lines. It is a pedagogical truism that learning proceeds from the known to the unknown. In the education of young children the adventure into new fields must be not only *from* the familiar but *with* it as an accompaniment and a steering wheel. The jogging shuttle is a more appropriate symbol to illustrate excursions of youthful adventurers than even as slow-moving a vehicle as the ox team. Forward and back again it goes till the new and old are closely knit.

An event does not take dramatic form so long as it remains detached from the intimate and the personal; but sometimes in the process of making it his own, a child calls upon fantasy rather than fact. Children seek for relationships between the events which are happening about them, but their conclusions are of necessity limited by the background upon which they draw, and adults often fail them by being so diverted by childish reasoning that they do not see its promise.

A fire extinguisher on a wall is called a statue because of the child's acquaintance with a figure in a niche in a familiar apartment house. A daddy longlegs gets its name because it is "the mother of a baby." If rubbers are put on, it must be raining though there are no clouds in the sky. The moon, visible in the daytime, is asserted to be the sun, and this opinion is upheld with vehemence among the very young. The city child's horse is put to bed with a pillow under its head, and the farmer in the toy village goes to the chain store for milk and takes it back to the cows.

It is the part of education to make a selection from the mass of natural interests of children in the world about them and to give them the opportunity for an introduction to these various phenomena, for investigating them, for raising questions about them, and for coming into actual contact with them through play. The lines of investigation, the total mass of impressions gained by the children, the relationships which are stressed, and appropriate media for dramatic expression remain largely in the hands of the teacher; her task is the delicate one of stimulating interest during the direct experience and of helping in the recall by shared discussion of it afterward.

The dramatic play which follows such an excursion afield gives one the feeling of watching a creative process in which there is a high degree of mental stimulation and an enormous release of emotional power.

A group of six-year-olds discovers by exploration that Manhattan is an island. On the floor with blocks, they map the city as they have seen it, with its lines of traffic and its towering buildings. Discussion leads them to the question of how life can be maintained on an island. Practically, many of them know of tubes, ferries and bridges, but the Holland Tunnel and the Brooklyn Bridge take on new significance when they are approached as man's means of communication with his neighbors. What is it that lies at the other end of these roads, or to what do they give access? What comes into the city by them? What goes out? After each excursion the block community extends its boundaries till it includes farms, factories, and railway systems. A bridge is a real structural problem, but eventually it spans the river, a joy to the eye and a fact in practical human geography. One of the children who had built Manhattan with water all about it decided to make one of the bridges she had seen on a trip to the harbor. She erected some supports on the land, then suddenly stopped with a startled expression. The questions in her mind were almost audible before she finally announced, "There must be some land over there!"

Along with the construction with blocks and in wood and the play with them, power in language grows. Stories have form and concreteness, a vivid phrase describes some detail of experience, and language becomes a familiar tool for experimentation.

Paint and crayons also become vehicles for expression—whether factual, humorous or fanciful.

Dramatic play does not mean learning a part and carrying out on a stage a ready-made and prescribed program. It means first and last, with young and old, *reproducing a personal experience*. The baby is limited to experiences which have come to him through his own muscles and senses; his dramatic form will be expressed largely through muscle and sense recalls. The older child can use events and processes which he has shared only by observing them intimately. If this method of first-hand investigation is consistently carried on, it will mean that ultimately the distant in time and space, that is, the past and the far away, becomes vivid and real and relevant even to children and so an actual and living feature of their environment. To most of us history is largely fiction. To some of the children of today it is as truly a part of the present civilization as it is to the historian, the economist, or the geographer.

A healthy, normally living individual is one whose emotional intake is assured some sort of satisfactory outlet. If and when an intellectual experience is also an emotional one, the need for expression of it is imperative. When children begin to deal with symbols, other avenues are open to them besides that of mimetic representation. Form, color, line can express feelings as surely and as dramatically as a stage presentation. If we regard dramatic play as one of the methods of establishing one's relation with the world in which one lives, and of expressing the feeling, the emotion which is aroused by contacts and experience, we shall find two things happening to us: first, we shall see children in a new perspective, and second, we shall realize the possibilities of modern education as one of the arts.

THE GROWTH OF DRAMATIC FORMS IN THE SCHOOL LIFE

Ellen W. Steele

Two children were playing horse. One, who had never ridden a horse nor had any experience except that of seeing other people ride, gave her horse a bowl of cereal and put him to bed with a sheet and a blanket over him. Another child, who had been to Arizona, had her horse buck and kick out all the stalls in his block stable, while she said, "He is so wild I have to keep him hog-tied all the time." In children's free play, we see the effect that some of the simple facts and habits of the child's life have upon his fantasy. The child's own experience, in which he absorbs his information, completely conditions the kind and quality of his expression.

The younger child's "pretend" world is made of the stuff he takes in from his real world. His play is based essentially on images and recalls from a world about him. These images are reconstructed inside the child and come forth into expression with the particular stamp of his own emotions and free associations. In this sense, fantasy is not the exotic, the unreal, and fairy-tale material, but is close to the world of first-hand experiencing and, at the same time, may take on a purely imaginative character.

It, therefore, behooves us to provide experiences that are of value in the type of information that they give the child, widening his world and at the same time giving him an interesting play background. We need, also, to provide the growing child with such surroundings and materials that he may readily translate his information into his play, thus clarifying and organizing his knowledge.

A five-year-old group at the Rosemary Junior School visited a railroad station. They met the engineer and the fireman who talked to them and let them climb into the engine. They saw the fire, they blew the whistle, and rang the bell. About a week later, they built a train in the court with out-of-door materials. They used a pail turned upside down for a bell, with a rope attached to it leading into the cab of the engine.

DAVID (*climbing onto the coal car*): All aboard! All aboard!

JULIA: You be the fireman and I'll be the engineer. Your name's Mr. Smith, but I must call you Jim.

DAVID: All aboard! All aboard! We're going to New York!

JULIA (*ringing the bell*): Ding dong! Ding dong! Toot! Hoo-oo-oo-oo-oo-oo! You must shovel in the coal, Jim.

DAVID (*chanting*): Port Chester, New York. Now we're at New York! Now we're at New York!

In this case, the dialogue of the engineer and the fireman was more truly a characterization of the real workers they had met, and because of the vividness of experience, the engine itself was a more complete construction, showing a new understanding of parts and how they worked.

But perhaps a still greater value in dramatic play of this type lies in the emotional release that comes to the child when he expresses his feelings through muscular movements and material objects that are natural to his age. Sometimes he completely identifies himself with the object. He becomes an engine, feels a sense of power as he puffs and shuffles across the floor. Or, in playing house, a doll will receive attentions and be put through home situations that the child wishes continued in her own life. A nine-year-old boy, who was always afraid in children's out-of-door games, gained his compensation in the group by playing the rôle of a powerful pirate captain or a thunder god. It seems desirable that some of these urges be compensated in dramatic play instead of in the real world.

In dramatic play the child also comes into gradual social connection with other children. His social connection and adjustments are not forced, but grow out of sharing in play, when sharing is a real need, and making adjustments when the reason for adjusting is concrete and understandable to his own mind.

This play of younger children resembles the dramatic expression of primitive peoples. Its literal quality and its fantasy are both close to the environmental facts, and almost always include satisfying the wish to power of those who are dramatizing. In form there is a likeness too.

Sometimes it is nothing more than putting on a costume and wearing it about. Sometimes there is pantomimic action, rhythmic dance, or whatever chance form may best express the child's feeling. In the presence of this kind of play, the teacher has an opportunity to study the child in action and to discover his qualities.

However, my chief concern is to follow the development of the dramatic impulse and to show its educational meanings for older children. As the children grow older, this dramatic play changes in its combinations and relationships and moves more and more towards conscious forms. If we are wise enough to see what dramatic material, however crude, is most natural for each age, we can continue to build upon it educationally. Information must always remain vivid, even if it moves away from the immediate environment where the child can see and hear and feel to get his facts. The leap to other times and situations and peoples may be safely made if the new facts relate to the old experiences. Then the dramatizing continues to have reality.

An unexpected dramatic situation has developed with the eight- and nine-year-old groups in our school. The eights have a great interest in the life of the Indians of this locality. In the small woods near the school, they dramatize many experiences which they found the Indians had. They are building a bark house, such as the Connecticut Indians used. With their hands, they are making pottery, tools, costumes, and weapons. They selected a place in the woods to erect their house. After it was started, the nine-year-old group came out to build a log cabin. They looked around the grounds and chose a spot that overlapped the Indians' land. When I pointed out to them that the land belonged to the Indians, they said, "But this is the only place with a good view and with space for a garden, and that is big enough for the white people. The Indians must move back to the edge of the woods."

Jane raised the question, "What do you think we ought to pay them for the land?" The teacher asked, "How can we find out?" The answer was, "We could have a meeting with the Indians."

The Indian tribe came into the meeting house of the nine-year-old pioneers. They sat in a semicircle on the floor, and the colonists in a row behind the governor, who was seated at a table. The governor rose and greeted them with, "Welcome, Indians. We took your land. What do you want us to pay for it?"

The chief answered with one word, "Beads."

The governor looked at the others and they nodded, "We will pay beads for it." The governor said, "We want you to trade furs with us, and to let us have peace for fifty years." They passed the peace pipe, and the Indians filed out.

The white settlers then informed me, "We can have the land now.

THE SCENE IN MEKANIKOS FROM "FANATIC FANCIES," A PLAY WRITTEN AND PRO-
DUCED BY CHILDREN OF THIRTEEN AND FOURTEEN

BACKGROUND SCENE FOR A PLAY PAINTED BY CHILDREN TWELVE YEARS OLD

THE LOWER GRADES GAVE AN OUTDOOR STREET FESTIVAL WITH APPLE WOMEN, A BALLAD SINGER, AND TOY VENDERS, USING

We have made a treaty with the Indians and they are going to give it up." When the Indians went back to their classroom, they asked their teacher, "Were the white people always like that?" It seemed an almost too literal living out of American history to me; but they busily began to make the colored beads, and the little Indians pushed back to the edge of the woods.

MEDIEVAL PAPER MAKERS

An eleven-year-old group, studying paper making and printing, decided to make paper themselves as the medieval workers did. They found there were three distinct divisions of the labor, and they organized themselves to cover these fields of work. One group, the vatmen, dipped up the pulp in the molds. They worked with a large tub of pulp, dipping the mold and deckle until the screening was covered with pulp. A coucher removed the pulp from the mold, and the layman attended to the pressing of the paper and the final preparation for use. As nearly as they could, they reënacted the scene of medieval paper making from descriptions and old woodcuts of the period. There was no dialogue, but there was an intensity in the activity that gave it a play feeling.

As the children grow older, the acquisition of information must be more inclusive and proceed along many different lines before they are ready to dramatize in a fine idiom of the people whom they are representing. With a medieval program, after the *Song of Roland* has been read and old legendary material studied—with perhaps a special study of some of the language phrases and words of the time—the children usually create verbally or write a play in which the language in itself gives an atmosphere of the period.

CHILDREN'S PLAYS AS ART FORMS

The main point is that a body of information must be present in the group life. This factual content concerning other times, places, people, and activities grows through the children's play and appears as scenes, pantomimes, stories, dances, and all sorts of incidental dramatic forms. These forms have the kernel of the reality and create the actual dramatic atmosphere, but they are artistic as well. With children, any art expression is a matter of growth.

The play is an art form and, in the adult world, it usually conforms to conventions. Sometimes playwrights experiment with forms, but more often the same old mechanics are used over and over again in the drama of today. With children it is different. They can be as experimental about form in dramatic expression as they can about composition and color in painting. With children, we should not start with a preconceived pattern in mind, but should let the form evolve from the ideas and feelings that are to be expressed.

This was illustrated quite simply to me two years ago when some eight-year-old children, who were living out experiences in primitive life, thus described how the primitive people felt about the sun in winter:

> We worship the sun because it gives us warmth and food.
> When the days are shorter and the nights are longer, he is going away from us.
> But after the winter's cold and ice we will see him coming back, little by little.

Then they described their sun dance.

> First we sat in a circle and made a fire.
> We each made a dance of our own to show how glad we were to get the fire.
> Then we shook our rattles and all danced together.
> We cut trees down and rolled the logs into the fire.
> When they were burning we rolled them round and round, like the sun, to welcome him.
> We stuck our spears into the fire.
> We threw burning disks into the air.
> We danced and waved torches.
> We wore costumes painted like skins.

Their impressions were first enacted in simple pantomime. Then the pantomime became a rhythmic pattern as the rhythms teacher gave it a music background. They repeated the pattern until they were free to lose themselves in the scene. They lived the emotion that the primitives felt about the fire and the sun; their understanding and intensity shaped a truly primitive dance form.

What must the teacher do to help the children live out dramatically the information they take in? First, the children's interests and stage of development must guide her in the selection of what they will study. Facts must be gathered from all sources that produce vivid and real impressions. A wealth of detail is needed with a great deal of making and doing and experiencing until the teacher and the children are saturated with the living content. Then, she must be sensitive to the dramatic situations as they occur, realizing that the evolving and producing of a play is one of the greatest integrating forces in group life. Co-operation and natural social adjustment become realities. Not only does the content organize to this shared end but, in a larger sense, the art and music and rhythms of the school may be drawn in, so that the creative activity extends into all the arts, and the coöperation in producing the play becomes a matter of school life.

In the dramatic art, of all arts, the guidance falls upon the group teacher. In other lines, specialists and artists may be called in, but to me, in dramatics, a director would be superfluous. Only with the teacher can the children live through these first crude stages that give the rich background from which forms grow. And only from such a background, and from the same kind of impulse that produced dramatic expression in primitive tribes and among village folk, can the play arise with such quality that it may be called art expression.

RISE! LADY HILDA FLORADALE!

Rachel Erwin

AT WINBROOK the nine-year-olds when studying the Middle Ages in England and France, produced an original play, "A Christmas in Medieval England." The play was planned by the class as a whole, each scene being written by the children who acted in it. The group had been singing Christmas carols in music class and were interested in finding out the exact meaning of such expressions as "wassail bowl," "boar's head," and "yule log." This led to a good deal of research, as well as to the modeling of a plaster boar's head in the studio.

The problem before the group at the start was how to combine Christmas with the medieval material with which they had become familiar. Very naturally, it resolved into a play dealing with Christmas in a castle, the action centering around a Lady and her two children who wanted her to explain everything that happened. A monk, a crusader, a pilgrim, and a band of minstrels were brought in. Each character, as he entered the hall for refuge from the bitter night, told his story to the children, the mother explaining the unfamiliar terms. The loom was brought down from the crafts room to serve as the Lady's embroidery frame, and ordinary bridge lamps were dismantled to become, with the addition of wax candles, effective candelabra. The minstrels, dragging a real yule log to the fireplace, sang carols and played their psalteries; and the servants brought in the wassail bowl and boar's head which were greeted with songs in which all the characters joined. In the dialogue, the actor vacillated between the use of the medieval "thee" and "thy," and the usual "you" and "your," depending upon the degree to which his imagination had been able to assimilate the material studied.

Later on in the year, this same group staged a miracle play, based upon the story of Abraham and Isaac. This play was freely adapted from one of the old miracle plays often given on Corpus Christi Day. The children's introduction explains how they went about it and shows how the play was an integral part of their study of the Middle Ages.

Every year the Butchers' Guild of Winbrook School gives a pageant play. This year we are giving "Abraham and Isaac." Sometimes we give "Cain and Abel" or "David and Goliath." We always try to give a play that has something to do with our trade of butchering.

We have taken the Brome play of "Abraham and Isaac" and changed it in places. We have made it lots shorter. We have put in two devils and two bad men to make it more exciting.

Our pageant wagon, which we usually pull through the streets and stop at the main corners, has broken down, so we have made this stage to represent a pageant wagon. The top stage is supposed to be Heaven. There you see God and His Angels. The middle stage is Earth. That dragon's head on the right side is Hell Mouth. The devils come through there when they come to Earth to get the bad people.

On the lowest stage behind the red curtain is Hell itself. "Abraham and Isaac" is a miracle play because God interfered just in time and Isaac is saved by a miracle.

At first, they set their hearts on having a real wagon, but on finding no way of hauling one in from the nearest willing farmer, they agreed to see what they could do with material nearer home. The central action took place on a platform raised from the ground on wooden horses. The space below was curtained off in red to represent the dwelling of the two red devils, and brightly painted cardboard wheels were nailed on at the corners. Heaven was accomplished by moving the school junglegym to a position immediately behind the platform. Paper scenery, representing a hill and a great deal of blue sky, was tacked on to cover the scaffolding, while God and His two angels sat on top. Holes were cut in the scenery to allow the angels to climb down the junglegym from heaven and participate at crucial moments in the action on earth while, under cover of the fine red and gold dragon's head, the devils could scramble up from beneath the stage. A beaver board lamb was made in the studio for the sacrifice and placed in a corner of the stage, naïvely visible during the whole action, to be suddenly discovered by Abraham and sacrificed to an accompaniment of loud "baas" sympathetically rendered by the devils below stage.

Thus children find in dramatic presentation one of the best mediums of expressing their feeling for an historical period. Sometimes, however, a play may grow out of a class controversy. An instance of this was a one-act play given by a group of ten-year-olds after studying

"THE WITCH OF THE WELL," A PLAY BASED ON AN ORIGINAL FAIRY STORY WRITTEN
BY A NINE-YEAR-OLD GIRL

IMPROMPTU PLAY WITH NO SCENERY OR COSTUMES SUCH AS THE YOUNGER CHIL-
DREN GIVE VERY FREQUENTLY WITH THEIR OWN CLASSMATES AND TEACHER FOR
AUDIENCE

Euthenics Demonstration School, Vassar

PUTTING OUT A FIRE IN A NEW YORK APARTMENT
HOUSE

Winbrook School, White Plains

FOUR-YEAR-OLDS PLAYING ELVES

Roman history for two months. A point which had interested them all keenly, and which had been the basis of many of their discussions, was the fact that Christ's life could be placed definitely in the history of the world, that it had a chronological setting. This play was planned by the group, and the dialogue written by a ten-year-old girl.

THE RETURN OF A ROMAN WARRIOR

A Christmas Tableau

The background was painted in three panels. On one side was a Roman camp in Egypt; on the other, a galley plowing through the Ægean Sea; and in the center, the skyline of Bethlehem at night. Appropriate tableaux were posed in the foreground of each scene; a soldier and a pirate in front of the two side panels, Mary, Joseph, a shepherd, and an angel in the center. The front stage was arranged to represent a room in a Roman house. A senator and his son were waited on by a slave and held the following conversation:

SENATOR: Did you have a hard fight with the Egyptians?

SON: I admit that the Egyptians are good warriors, but they are traitors. Recently they plotted to kill their captain. He would have been killed, if a woman had not saved him. She was a slave and had to bring him his dinner. She heard them plotting about some poison and so gave him fresh meat.

SENATOR: Let us hear of the battle.

SON: They gave us a hard fight on the Egyptian sands. Our losses were great, but theirs were greater. The Roman soldiers are excellent fighters.

SENATOR: But not all of them. Weren't some of you beaten just the other day by a few miserable pirates?

SON: A few miserable pirates—nothing! There were over three hundred of them in a fleet of six ships. They fought with poisonous snakes as well as stone slingers and swords. They had stones of enormous size on board. Their ships were rowed by Roman slaves which they had captured. I thank the gods I am a free man.

SENATOR: These were cowards. The old Roman legions would have stood firm.

SON: It is true. The Roman Empire is not as good as it used to be. New kings are springing up everywhere. When I went to Syria to collect the taxes, I was putting my horse up at an inn in Bethlehem and I saw three Wise Men. They said there was a little Hebrew baby born there in the inn stable who was to be King of Kings.

SENATOR: Do you believe that? It's a lie!

SON: Why shouldn't I? I saw it with my own eyes. There was a great light around the mother and child. Even King Herod knew about it and sent the three Wise Men who came to his court to find out the meaning of the star. He told the Wise Men that he was going to worship the babe, but he had really plotted secretly to kill him. The Wise Men had a dream in which God told them they were to go back home another way. I, myself, saw the star shining and heard the angels.

With the last words, the children in the tableaux began to sing *Adeste Fideles,* of which they had learned the Latin words.

Plays given in connection with the development of a unit of work are not always written by the children themselves. Occasionally a ready-made play suits their purposes better than an original one. An eleven-year-old group, for example, while studying Elizabethan England, became enthusiastic about Shakespeare and presented scenes from *Twelfth Night* with a real feeling for the atmosphere of the play and a keen appreciation of the humor of the situations. However, the plays which are originated by the group itself usually bring out the best acting, because it is easier for children to identify themselves with characters and situations which they have created than it is for them to interpret the thoughts of others.

During the progress of almost every unit of work, there comes a place where dramatization is a definite help; it may be a way of gaining a deeper understanding of an historical period, or as the culmination of the work on the project, or, as in the Roman play quoted, as a means of establishing a new point of view.

The Witch of the Well, based on an original fairy story written by a nine-year-old girl, is an excellent example of a play given for its own sake. The scene is laid in the Queen's garden, with a fountain in the center and a curved stone seat in the rear, which is just the setting the young dramatist had before her. The characters are the Princess, King, Queen, witch, good fairy, lords, and ladies—the usual fairy-tale people. Naïve touches are revealed in the heroine as a maid instead of a neglected younger sister or a peasant girl, and a butler hovering in the background. The Queen tries to dispose of the Princess, her stepdaughter, with the help of the witch, but is prevented by the good fairy who is evoked by the magic words, "Astasia Magasia, Forum!" pronounced by the heroic maid. The play terminates with the Princess placing a gold chain around the neck of the maid and a ring on the finger of the page, saying, "Rise! Lady Hilda Floradale and Lord Leroy, you shall be my special attendants!"

This play is also a good example of the way in which almost every part of the curriculum can contribute to one undertaking. The writing of the story was the very best kind of creative work in English. The dramatization, as the result of the suggestions and discussions by the group, included the writing of an original song and the use of rhythm and music. The simple properties were constructed and painted in the studio, and the costumes were designed and made by the children.

Perhaps the most technically finished piece of work that has been done at Winbrook was the *Treasure Island* of a twelve-year-old group. They were old enough to be very ambitious in their plans, and they designed and painted elaborate sets for three scenes, which were attached to a wooden framework built for outdoor plays. There was a costume committee, properties committee, and several critics. The need for organization became crucial when the company was invited to repeat its performance at Grasslands Hospital before an audience of doctors, nurses, and patients. This invitation necessitated working out a thoroughly efficient handling of properties and scenery to be used in an unfamiliar environment. After that performance, the class realized as never before how necessary were thoughtful coöperation and careful attention to detail.

In this play, as in practically every one given at the school, every child was an actor. Ability to do good committee work does not excuse anyone from actually taking part in the play, and not infrequently one person must take two or three parts. Our groups are small and the timid, self-conscious child is pushed by social necessity into doing something he might not otherwise be willing to attempt. Indeed, it is the self-conscious child who needs this experience most. At least one of our children, whose lack of self-confidence made her enough of a problem to cause her parents to consult a psychiatrist, improved radically after taking part in a play. She found that her ability to use color with effect was a real help in the construction of the scenery, that others were willing to coöperate with her and looked to her for advice, and this seemed to give her the stimulus to carry through a piece of work in a way that she had never been able to do before.

If dramatics are used, not to train "stars" and to impress parents, but to help each child to develop his powers to the utmost, the result will be improved social adjustment, a sense of responsibility, and above all, happiness.

PUPPETS AND PANTOMIMES

Mabel R. Goodlander

CHILDREN's dramatic adventurings run in no set mold, ranging from improvisations without beginning or end through many variations to the fairly well-constructed play with scenes or acts and well-planned dialogue. I have chosen to illustrate here some of the more elementary forms of dramatic action rather than the well-rounded play.

The puppet or marionette theater offers a wide range of possibilities, with actors and settings crude or elaborate, according to the ability of the makers. The making of the figures may be considered craftwork, but their conception, the composition of the play, the speaking of the parts, and the gestures of the actors fall in the realm of dramatic creation.

The dramatization of seven scenes from the old tale of *Pinocchio* was the work of a class of eight-year-old boys and girls. The initial stimulus came when a child made a small theater in school for some puppets which had been given him. Everyone in the class was finally drawn into the interest, and all shared in making marionettes—which they preferred to puppets—in painting scenery or theater, and in planning the play. The dialogue, composed by the children, was written down by the teacher, and each child made a copy of his own part. The marionettes were very rough in construction, but as the children were satisfied with the square wooden limbs, body and head put together with screw eyes, the teacher did not force suggestions for improvement. Features were gouged out of the flat faces, worsted wool was glued on for hair, and the clothes, cut and sewed with teacher help, were nailed to the bodies. Yet, when in action, these odd little figures had a humorous vitality, as the hidden children manipulated their strings and spoke their thoughts.

Less ambitious than *Pinocchio* was a third-grade puppet show, *Peary and the Meteorite,* inspired by interest in the meteorite in the museum, and the subsequent reading of *The Snow Baby.* The play described the fatal attempt of Eskimos to obtain the meteorite for arrowheads, and Peary's later success. As he says in an epilogue, "Well, I succeeded in taking away the meteorite and if you don't believe me, just go to the Museum of Natural History and see it." At first, everyone responded to the idea of a puppet play. Several contributed to the making of the theater—a gayly painted muslin-covered screen; others concocted puppets of odds and ends of cloth and fur; a small group wrote the short playlet. But finally, the scheme was dropped by everyone except two faithful puppeteers who gave the play on the slightest encouragement for the rest of the year. One boy, who contributed a wonderful dog, evinced no further interest; the one expression satisfied his need in this relation. The enterprise was an excellent example of children's unaided attempts at puppet making, for the teacher kept out of the picture except as an appreciative onlooker.

A circus which was the combined effort of a second and third grade proved a valuable coöperative undertaking and provided plenty of action and occasion for impersonation. The tight-rope walker veiled with her conventionally assured smile a certain tense anxiety as she balanced on the wire. The trained seals and elephants, the clowns and acrobats were more than usually humorous and subtle in their interpretation,

A MARIONETTE SHOW OF PINOCCHIO: FIRE EATER AND THE BLUE FAIRY

WOODEN PUPPETS MADE BY CHILDREN: READING FROM THE LEFT, THEY ARE ARA-BELLA, GOLDILOCKS, JOHN THE BAPTIST, SALOME, AND GEORGE BERNARD SHAW

Winnetka Public Schools

PUPPET SHOWS GIVE WORTH-WHILE DRAMATIC EXPERIENCES

King-Coit School, New York

ART INTERESTS CONTRIBUTE TO THE DEVELOPMENT OF A PLAY

because an understanding teacher had encouraged them to improve their acts through imaginative thought. A circus band, playing on violin, harmonicas, flageolets and drums, added to the spirit of the event.

The painting of posters, the making of costumes, as well as lemonade to sell to the spectators, were related activities. For by this age children want an audience.

An interesting piece of dramatic work was a fifth-grade pantomime, *The Knight and the Princess,* accompanied by music. In this outgrowth of a study of medieval life in the castle, the children indulged in many impromptu jousts or played the jester, especially during the free interpretation of music in the period for rhythmic work. The class teacher, observing this spontaneous interest, told the group of the pantomime she had recently seen at the opera. The response was immediate; the idea of acting to music without words made a strong appeal, and they went to work at once to write the pantomime. Two versions of the theme were finally combined, and the action was worked out by the boys and girls during their rhythmics period. As it developed, the pianist tried various musical accompaniments from which the children helped select the most appropriate. By request, the music teacher taught the minstrels an old Minnelied to sing and play on their psalteries. The joust was a most exciting event, and the jester was amusing in his parody of the fight. After the marriage of the Princess and the winner, who was, of course, the knight wearing her token, the play ended with a stately old dance, a pavon, by the members of the court. No scenery was used, but costumes were insisted upon by the children, who worked on them industriously, each making his own. A gayly covered bench at one end of the long room formed the center of the court group; the play began and ended with a courtly procession.

PLAYS IN A KENTUCKY COUNTY SCHOOL

Elsie Ripley Clapp, Elisabeth Sheffield, and George Beecher

THE BALLARD MEMORIAL SCHOOL is a public rural school in Kentucky, eight miles outside of Louisville, beside the Ohio River. A year ago in September, the school became "progressive." The work changed from that typical of a county school in Kentucky to active learning and living together. Through acquaintance with the living conditions and homes of the children, their parents and the neighbors, and through the use of the environment and of Kentucky history, the attempt was made to establish a kind of education that should meet the needs of the community, interpret the lives of the people, and reveal to them the meanings of their past.

The following accounts by members of the staff tell how plays grew last year in the fourth grade and in the eighth and ninth grades of the school.

THE BOONES IN KENTUCKY

The fourth grade studied the period of Kentucky pioneer life from about 1775 to 1790. They studied the conditions and processes of living of that period. Fortunately, there is an old overgrown quarry just back of our building. After they had read and started finding out about these pioneers, they went out to the quarry and pretended to be pioneers in the wilderness themselves. They blazed a trail, and with the help of the shop, put up a lean-to and a forked-stick fireplace for a night's stop on the way to Boonesboro. In class, they thought out just what necessities pioneers would have to carry with them over the toilsome trail, and looked up in old journals to see if they were right. They brought from home necessities, such as a kettle, salt, cornmeal, guns, gourds, lead, and hunting knives.

With this setting and these properties, they dramatically played time after time, with many variations, the Boone family spending a night on the Wilderness Trail. The men hunted and guarded camp; Mrs. Boone cooked a journey cake for supper; children gathered firewood or berries, went to the spring, watched the cattle and made leaf beds. Although at first there were a tiresome number of Indian attacks, as they read more old journals of real pioneers, they found more sorts of things to have happen, and about which to converse, such as procuring salt and trading skins.

As there were thirty in the class, only half could play at a time, so there was always an audience. It was the demand of this audience that brought the free, unorganized, dramatic play to an ordered act with a plot and climax. Finally, after several repetitions of the play by each group, the better performance was chosen and the teacher took down the words as they acted. When she read them back to the children, they made several logical changes. Afterwards, they often changed slightly as they went along, although they decided to keep near enough to the written words so that the order of speaking would not become mixed.

We had now our very realistic first act, which ended with an Indian attacking Squire Boone, Daniel's brother, who was on guard that night, and carrying him off surreptitiously. There was still the other half of the class that must have parts, so we decided that another act (which became the third act) should be at the Indian Camp to which Squire was carried.

This act was done in pantomime with a dance of exultation when the prisoner was brought in and a most tense scene when Daniel Boone crept stealthily in, after all the Indians had fallen asleep, cut the ropes binding Squire and set him free.

By the time they had worked out these two acts, winter had come and we were studying about life in the forts. In shop they were making log furniture, gun racks, trenchers; they were whittling spoons, splitting hickory brooms, hollowing gourds, dipping candles; washing, carding and spinning wool; rippling, braking, scutching, hackling and spinning flax, and dyeing with vegetable dyes. In the homes of some of these children similar processes are still carried on, so that they had a good deal with which to understand. And many families, rich and poor alike, had relics from these very days that they were willing to lend for a collection.

At this time, we took a trip to Harrodsburg, where there is a complete and accurate reproduction of an old log fort. This trip filled the children's minds with concrete images of the home life of these people, and the touchingly simple little cabins fired their imaginations. When they got home, they decided to have some acts of their play take place in a log cabin. They decided to have the family snowbound and out of food after they had arrived at Boonesboro. In this act, Daniel had to brave the storm in order to keep the fort from starving. One of the children wrote down the words as they were decided upon. It seemed best to have this the second act, and the Indian scene the third act; so Dan rescued Squire while he was out getting food. The walls of the cabin were represented by white lines on a brown curtain and the one room was completely furnished by the things made in shop.

The fourth act showed Daniel returning triumphant with Squire and food. All the neighbors were called in to rejoice, and one of the older children fiddled while family and neighbors had a jubilee dance. There was little conversation and this was taken down as they practiced, as the first act had been.

Where the children really needed help from the grown-ups was on grouping themselves with so many on the small stage, and in being shown how to make their light voices carry in our big gymnasium. Also the costumes were made for them. These were made as accurately as possible (as there are few authentic pictures or descriptions in existence) by copying the present-day mountaineer's dress, which has been barely affected by outside influence since pioneer days.

Thus the play rounded out the study of Kentucky pioneers by bringing into life the facts the children had studied and the implements they had made and used, and by giving each the emotional experience implied in these.

THE OLD MILL FEUD

The eighth grade was studying the period in American history between the settlement of Kentucky and 1840, when Kentucky was an active participant in the development of the Middle West. The emphasis of the study was on the Jacksonian era, which saw the rise of western democracy, the growth of rail and river-boat communication, and the opening of the Mississippi Valley. Since the Ohio River runs in front of the school, only a few hundred yards away, and the old type stern-wheel packets still steam up and down, this phase of history was already well fixed in the minds of the children. The river, and in addition, the still rural character of the life of the people in this community offered a setting out of which dramatic activities could easily spring.

Without having in mind the possibilities of drama, the class studied intensively the period between 1830 and 1840, confining its attention largely to the Ohio Valley, except where necessity made reference to other regions. In studying the building of the first railroad in Kentucky, the members of the class who were writing reports on the mechanical problems had to extend their vision to the East, where the Baltimore & Ohio railroad had preceded the Kentucky builders by several years. In reporting on river boats, likewise, attention had to be given to eastern shipbuilders.

Various phases of the period were worked out by other members of the class to make the picture of 1840 life as real as possible. One or two children, who were totally unsuited to making useful research, found themselves gradually involved in the history program through painting scenes which would contribute to the class project as a whole. One boy, in particular, was fond of an old mill, several miles up in the country, where grain has been ground for an unknown number of years. He himself had played on the giant water-wheel. He was not sure at first what value a painting of the scene would have. For a long while, he was disgruntled at his work. But when a drama began to take shape out of the diverse ideas of the class, he felt a growing pride in his scene of the mill. It was developed into the setting for the first act of the play.

Stories by other members of the class, who exercised some choice of subjects on river life, costumes of the period, conversation, the political campaigns and stories of feuds, all reached the state of vividness and relish which would be unified at one stroke for the whole class by the writing and production of a play. The character of the life of the period,

NIGHT ON THE WILDERNESS TRAIL: "THE MEN HUNTED AND GUARDED CAMP; IRS. BOONE COOKED JOURNEY CAKE FOR SUPPER; THE CHILDREN GATHERED FIRE-WOOD OR BERRIES"

Rogers Clark Ballard Memorial School, Kentucky

HE BOONE FAMILY SNOWBOUND IN THEIR CABIN WHILE DANIEL BRAVES THE STORM O KEEP THE FORT FROM STARVING. THE WALLS OF THE BOONE CABIN WERE REP-ESENTED BY WHITE LINES ON A BROWN CURTAIN AND THE ONE ROOM IS COM-PLETELY FURNISHED BY THINGS MADE IN THE SHOP

THE ARRIVAL OF THE GOVERNOR BY TRAIN (1840) TO MAKE A CAMPAIGN SPEEC (FROM THE PLAY "THE OLD MILL FEUD," WRITTEN AND PRODUCED BY TI EIGHTH GRADE)

Rogers Clark Ballard Memorial School, Kentucky

A CHILD'S SKETCH OF WOLF PEN MILL FOR THE BACKDROP OF A SCENE IN "THE OLD MILL FEUD"

scarcely less rough than the pioneer, though intermixed with cultivation, appealed to the eighth grade nearly as strongly as pioneer and Indian life to the fourth grade; and a cast of plantation owners, river men, blustering adventurers, independent farmers, and cultured ladies was eagerly supplied.

When the slow process of composing the four-act drama under the title of "The Old Mill Feud" was completed, immediate steps were taken to produce the play. The setting for the first act was almost entirely managed by the painter of the mill scene, who had so long hesitated to share in the activities. The second set and the third required a scene along the Ohio River, which was painted by the girls in the class. The second act required the fore part of an actual river boat, because the action revolved around the landing of a packet at the Louisville stage. The third act required a representation of an 1840 train, which was to bring the campaigners for Harrison and Tyler. The difficulties of providing these two vehicles of transportation were already partially solved by a previous study of the evolution of American transportation which the boys had made in the shop. Several models, a flat boat, a Conestoga wagon, and early trains had been drawn or worked in wood. Transferring the ideas onto beaver board was a difficult but only slightly more advanced project for the boys. The setting for the fourth act was provided by a girl who was interested in domestic architectural styles of 1840 and in the new antique furnishings of the interiors. Costumes for the girls proceeded from a combination of history research and practical sewing work, which was part of the girls' home economics course. The costumes for the boys demanded outside help.

HORACE'S SABINE FARM

The Latin class had a somewhat similar experience in producing a dramatization of several scenes connected with its study of first-year Latin and ancient Roman history. The slow progress, which is inevitable in acquiring facility with Latin, of necessity postponed any dramatic possibilities until the spring term. The emphasis in history was turned upon Roman life, and the subject matter in Latin class was centered upon Horace and his Sabine villa. The connection between the two needed only to be cemented by a dramatization in order to verify the history and give opportunity to exercise the Latin. Light in volume as the latter still was, several scenes seemed to offer themselves without requiring a plot, appropriately leading from a rural setting at the villa to a scene near the Forum at Rome where an imperial procession could pass, and finally to a spring festival at the Sabine villa.

The history class supplied much information about historic details. A toga and tunic, which had earlier been made, furnished models for the costumes; painted studies of armor and chariots were patterns for our martial equipment. Materials, which communities more favored with large museums have at first hand, were assembled through research with books, pictures, and slides.

The task of the Latin class was to plan out or rather to permit ideas to grow in Latin dialogue which the scenes seemed to demand. The composition was difficult for pupils with "beginning" vocabularies but was kept as simple as possible. The acting out of the play was really to be a drilling ground for difficulties which the Latin imposed.

Late in the spring, the play was rehearsed outdoors with the assembled properties. Several beaver boards had been painted with architectural wall designs familiar to the history class from Roman pictures. A loom was made in shop for the rural scene, armor and chariot were produced for the procession, and ponies supplied by two boys who lived on farms. The rural side of Kentucky life offered in some ways a relation to the studies of Roman life. The final scene, the rural spring festival on the Sabine farm, was not a great leap for minds familiar with the rural setting in Kentucky.

It is in ways such as these that plays grow and develop with us here in a rural county school in Kentucky. It has seemed to us that these ways are natural with the children and that they are essentially the ways drama has always grown in people's lives. The art involved in these dramatizations was as spontaneous and direct as the other interests.

Other plays of various kinds have also been given by other classes. However, the backgrounds out of which these plays arose were developed within only a few months.

Never before had these children presented the plays they made, nor had they written or painted in ways like these. Two-thirds of the children come from the rural countryside and farms; only one-third are children from homes of opportunity. The success of the plays, the intense interest, the enjoyment, the growth, were due to the fact that they filled a need for all the children, satisfied desires, gave meaning to familiar things around them, or in their own past.

DEVELOPING DRAMATICS IN THE PUBLIC SCHOOL

Frances Presler

THERE's nothing so good for children as a good dramatic experience, and nothing so bad as a bad one. For the difference between these extremes is no less than the difference between honesty and sham, between poise and self-consciousness, between self-assumed social control and bedlam.

"I'M CHIWEE," AND "I'M LOKI," AND
THE PLAY BEGINS

Winnetka Public Schools

THE RICH BACKGROUND OF STORIES IS EXPRESSED
THROUGH CHILDREN'S WEAVING

Out-of-Door School, Sarasota

A STUDY OF THE SEMINOLE INDIANS GREW INTO AN INDIAN FESTIVAL BY THE
WHOLE SCHOOL

THE SECOND GRADE GAVE A PUPPET SHOW OF "MRS. TUBBS"

Perhaps these extremes of possibilities are partly responsible for the feeling of insecurity which many teachers have toward dramatic work. Certainly, in no phase of an activity program is the average grade teacher's need for help greater than in the development of creative dramatics. To understand this, one has only to remember that most of the teachers of the average public school have had no activity training or experience.

Some schools meet this problem by putting dramatics in the hands of a special teacher. Others are unable to do so, or believe, as we do in Winnetka, that much of the value of dramatic experience comes from the daily living together of the group-teacher and children in the atmosphere of the thing they are creating. Where there is an activity adviser, help may be given weekly, either in general development, or with the more acute problems. But still most of the responsibility for this important activity rests with the teacher of the group.

Consequently, schools must find the situations and methods which will help these teachers bring about rich dramatic experiences. The problem is not one of training in artistic play coaching, but of developing ability to use the most educational means of expression we have. It is with this point of view that we have developed the method in use in Winnetka.

THE WINNETKA ACTIVITY PROGRAM

There are advantages as well as problems in public school conditions. Even in small cities, groups are duplicated; there are several rooms of the same grade, and a wide variety of training, experience, and ability on the part of the teachers. The duplication of groups is valuable in that it necessitates a number of parallel activities occurring simultaneously, and permits a comparison of children's interests and responses in a single term that would otherwise take years to make. It also permits the exploration of a wider range of possibilities within each unit, for the observation of a number of simultaneous activities permits comparison and analysis.

The variety of teachers' training and ability necessitates an organization of the activities curriculum equal to the need of the school's weakest teacher, and flexible to the talent of the ablest teacher. Therefore, some organization must be evolved for each school, an organization which will stimulate activity, enrich background, and multiply opportunity, but which will in no measure inhibit ideas, crystallize procedure, or narrow choice.

In the effort to meet this need, we have evolved our social-science activity plan. This activity organization consists of a grade sequence with units of increasing social complexity. We believe that a sequence is more valuable than a combination of isolated units. The particular sequence we have chosen consists of the following types of social groups: Local environment for the first grade; primitive life for second grade; a peasant type of culture for third grade; stars, earth development, ancient man and early civilization for fourth grade; Greek and Roman civilization for fifth grade; and medieval life and the Renaissance for sixth grade. Within these grade levels of social types, there are many units. (For example, peasant cultures of Switzerland, Holland, Russia, France, Norway, and Japan for third grade.)

Thus the teacher and group have a choice of the particular culture they wish to use. One or two of these units to a grade level are used during the year. An organized bibliography for each unit, together with numerous activity suggestions and teacher references, children's story and picture books, mounted pictures, slides, films, museum material, some costumes, facilities for field and museum trips, and miscellaneous work materials for various forms of expression are made available for each teacher. From such organized materials, and through weekly conference, and the assistance of the activity adviser, even an inexperienced teacher can build up for herself and the children a rich background of information, folklore, and imagery. It is from this background that the greater part of our dramatization grows.

DRAMATICS IN THE THIRD GRADE AND ABOVE

In the third grade, the elements of dramatic play are still dominant but are a bit less obvious. A setting which we have found particularly suited to this level is the making of the schoolroom into a social environment, such as a Dutch or a French home, a Viking feast hall or boat, a Swiss kitchen.

New problems of construction again make new demands on the children. When they are full of a background of peasant life, and choose to represent a Dutch room, a visit to such a room at the Art Institute shows the need for a cupboard bed, a large fireplace, a window-seat, foot-warmer and treasure chest. These are made, and the atmosphere of the room-wide environment calls for harmony of dress. Mothers are often enlisted by the children and substantial school clothes of Dutch peasant type soon appear. Some child's dog is pressed into the harness of an improvised milk cart. Cottage cheese is made and served with the morning lunch. Winter brings Dutch skating carnivals. Thus third graders live in the atmosphere of a type of culture within their grasp and enjoyment.

Some favorite story may be developed as a definite dramatization in this natural setting, but more likely an original play will express the children's understanding of the life of the people. Such a play is crude,

"THE GIFT OF THE NILE," AN ORIGINAL EGYPTIAN PLAY BY A FOURTH GRADE

PROPERTIES DESIGNED AND MADE BY THE CHILDREN FOR THE
EGYPTIAN PLAY

DOOR PANELS AND STAINED-GLASS WINDOW OF MEDIEVAL ROOM (ORIGINALS 2 BY 6 FEET) PAINTED BY SIXTH GRADE CHILDREN

Winnetka Public Schools

SIXTH GRADES THROUGH A DEEP INTEREST IN MEDIEVAL MANUSCRIPTS AND BOOKS OF HOURS HAVE FOUND GREAT SATISFACTION IN A MONASTERY SETTING

childlike, and free. It is less finished than dramatization of a story by the same group, but has greater creative value.

Beyond the third grade, we do not know so much about *original* plays in the sense just described. Before going on to the organization of creative dramatics based on stories in the grades above third, let us digress for a moment to describe an organization in the Winnetka schools that seems to us promising from many angles, among them that of shedding light on the possibilities of original plays for children above the third-grade level.

This organization we call "common interest groups" or "vertical groups." It enables a few children from each of a number of grades to come together under an adult adviser for an hour twice a week (in school time, of course) to pursue some common interest. One of these groups in each school is devoted to dramatics. In such groups, we hope to have sufficient freedom and seriousness of purpose to discover some things that older children will do spontaneously.

We believe that dramatic play is the foundation of the necessary honesty of dramatization, and we want to know ways of obtaining this sincerity with older children. Occasionally, a fourth-grade group has played cavemen on the beach with abandon. Fifth grades have lost themselves for a time in a Greek experience. Sixth grades, through a deep interest in medieval manuscripts and Hour Books, have found great satisfaction in a monastery setting. A few times, sixth-grade groups have played at being knights, really forgetting themselves for an hour. Such observations assure us that there are yet unexplored possibilities in this phase of dramatic experience.

The story is, of course, the usual basis for dramatization in the fourth grade and up. But here again, there must be a rich background to supply feeling. Such play is more teacher-directed, and unless it be wisely developed from great familiarity with the story, real feeling and clear concept, it will be artificial and superficial.

After the children are familiar with the entire story they have chosen, the teacher helps them select the parts of the story to play, the parts vital to the story as a unit. The teacher and pupils then plan the organization necessary for these parts. Such discussions are valuable parts of play development, and lead to clear thinking, the exercise of analysis, choice, and judgment.

The process must be a social one. Every child must contribute in some way, and preferably by adding his interpretation to the composite building of the characters of the play. The alert, analytical observation of that part of the group not dramatizing at the moment is as essential for the building of honest, intelligent action and satisfying language expression as is direct participation. If the period has no organization and involves no group effort (in small groups or the whole), it probably has little value.

Children can express only what they feel. If a child asks, "What must I say?" or if he expresses self-consciousness through his action, such handling is defeating the purpose of dramatization. It is nothing less than criminal to plunge a child unprepared into an awkward attempt to represent a character he does not feel himself to be.

Dramatic development is a growth. It moves slowly because it is a thing of spirit expressed from within. We must "linger with energy"; allow time for saturation. Characters may be built up one at a time, made mentally vivid through the child's own experiences, and made physically real by absolute honesty of action. Should a fire be built, for example, there must be real though imaginary logs. These must be lifted, carried, laid down as logs, not allowed to evaporate out of one's arms into thin air.

We never memorize parts because our purpose in dramatization is creation. We would feel that we had allowed the play merely to repeat itself if, in the final performance, nothing was said that had never been said before. The lack of fear about forgetting makes for ease and poise. Children are led to feel that what is said and done does not matter so long as it is what might have been said or done by the people whom the children are pretending to be.

A fourth grade was giving a play of *Dr. Dolittle and His Circus.* Dr. Dolittle was counting his animals. The leopard was missing, a thing which had not happened before. Dr. Dolittle, accepting the situation, sent a "circus hand" in search of the missing one. But the leopard was deep in trouble with a wrecked headdress he could not rearrange. The messenger returned, and the teacher of the group, seated in the audience, was surprised to hear a new turn in the play. A report was given of a sick leopard. Dr. Dolittle replied in tones of real concern, "What! Another sick animal? Really, something must be done about this!"

There are other forms which dramatics may take in school; charades, puppet shows, shadow shows, all of which are apt to use the humor which is the birthright of children. There are pageants with their possibilities for a large number of children to express an idea. There is the creative dance which is dramatic in its action. The form is immaterial; the important thing is to give children this means for living vividly, experiencing richly, expressing beautifully. It does not matter where the teacher teaches, how untrained she may be. If she loves children sincerely, is sensitive to their feeling, is willing to steep herself with the children in a rich background, to work for honesty of expression, and to wait for natural child growth, joy of creative dramatics may be hers.

"LET'S PLAY"

Rebecca J. Coffin

THE five-year-olds had been to visit a lighthouse. Little wonder that blocks were piled, block on block, next day and little wooden men, women, boys, and girls went in and out, up and down the "lighthouse" stairs—stopping here and there to peer out of the windows and comment on the boats that were coming and going in "the harbor." "Let's play" with these children is largely an unconscious individual reliving of vivid experiences which comes about when there is an abundance of materials easily adapted to the needs of the group. In this case, large floor blocks, toy people, and play animals were at hand. The satisfaction at the five-year level is more or less immediate. They build while they plan; and they build for the fun of it! Sometimes someone insists on Miss Stevens's seeing "the people crossing the bridge to the lighthouse" but generally there is no particular need of an audience. Gradually, as the year progresses, there is more request that the play schemes "be saved" from day to day and more related events take place.

The play experiences even at this early age show definite enrichment through content. The children had been playing "boats" for some time, but, following the trip to the lighthouse, there were many additions of more accurate details. Someone brought a flashlight and asked for help in manipulating it; he sought advice as to how to work out a signal system, and bells were rung in accordance with a plan; the harbor boats carried many new kinds of cargoes. The lighthouse approached a new height—more like a real lighthouse, and its location now bore a significant relation to the harbor.

II

In such a play village as was built and "played in" by Miss Wright's six-year-olds, the dramatic play started with the early experiences of the children and was constantly enlarged and enriched by succeeding experiences, either actual or vicarious. Here, too, the form which the play took depended on the materials at hand. The children were ready for more permanent materials than blocks. They were willing to prepare materials with which to play—to make stairways, furniture, dishes, curtains, and to build trucks, wagons, boats, and trains to carry out their scheme. As feature after feature of the village was contributed by first one individual and then another, eager attention was given to discussions led by the teacher and details of information gleaned on trips. Conversations between the doll members of the village community increased daily. As meanings and relationships became more clear to the children, group activities developed. The church with its tall spire and its pipe organ (the music of which was made by a music-box with a sweet tone) often had quite a large audience. The theater soon had to put on plays for the doll audiences and the hospital accepted patients and dismissed them.

III

The coming of the postman is a dramatic event in the eyes of many, but little meaning is attached to his coming except the immediate one—that of delivering a letter. In the unit of work developed by Miss Hughes around the postal service, we have an illustration of how the lives of a group of seven-year-old children were enriched, mainly by opening up possibilities for enriching their dramatic play through content. The following excerpts from a manuscript prepared by Miss Hughes show clearly that the meanings the children were attaching to various aspects of mail service were vital to them and rich in social significance. These children had "lived" mail-truck, boat, and plane experiences in their play. They had questioned, discussed, read, painted, and built! So naturally when they said, "Let's play something for the First Grade," they decided that the play should be "all about mail." It is interesting to notice here that certain new aspects of dramatizations begin to appear with seven-year-olds. They want *to make a play*. They want to make a play *for a certain audience*. They want to make it *all about* something that is wide in implications and has many different aspects.

Finally, after many suggestions and much discussion, the action of the play was limited to "mail today." Each child chose the part he wished to take in the play, the parts including stationery seller, weather man, plane pilot and the "lady who lives in the country." The way of these seven-year-olds in making their play was next to plan what they would do in the play.

Excerpts from Miss Hughes's record of this play are included for the purpose of illustrating to what extent this interest in a dramatic figure—the postman—was enriched.

One morning, Billy, who had chosen to be "a weather man and mechanic at the airport," produced a paper and read the following plan which he had written at home: "I am going out and send up a balloon and look through the field glasses and write down in a little book what the weather is going

SECOND GRADE DRAMATIZATION OF THE ACTIVITIES OF A POST OFFICE

OW MAIL TRAVELS: AT THE AIRPORT THE WEATHER MAN MAKES OBSERVATIONS AND
THE MAIL PLANE LANDS

OW MAIL TRAVELS: THE MAIL BAGS ARE TRANSFERRED FROM THE MAIL BOAT TO
THE TRUCK

OUTSIDE SOKAR'S HOME: "I WISH I COULD LIVE A FAIRY STORY"

INSIDE THE QUEEN'S GARDEN: "SOMEONE HAS BEEN PICKING MY BLUE LOTUS FLOWERS!"

ALONG THE RIVER NILE: "I WILL DO ANYTHING. I WILL BRING YOU THE MAGIC LOTUS BUD IF YOU WILL NOT EAT ME!"

to be and the current of the wind. And then I take the instrument into the hangar and write it on the slate. Then Alex comes and I examine his plane; then Alex comes back and we talk about the plane. Then he gets in it, I spin the propeller, and he flies away."

Ann, "the little girl who writes a letter," told the group that she was "going to make a house and come out of the house, go to the stationery store, buy a pen, ink and paper, go home, write a letter, take it to the Post Office, and send it special delivery to Franklin."

Other children presented individual plans from time to time. Some of these were written at home and read to the group. Other children told the class what they were going to do in their different parts and suggestions and criticisms were freely given and taken.

Costumes were planned and made with the help of Miss Jacobson (home economics), scenery worked out with Miss Joyner (art), and the simple verses which the children made were set to music with the help of Miss Kelly (music).

The play finally resolved itself into a simple rhythmic pantomime, consisting of a series of episodes with original songs in which the children organized and expressed dramatically some of their knowledge and feelings about the transportation of mail and the relationships between the truck driver, engineer, fireman, pilot, postman, and their own lives.

Parts of the play as finally worked out and given in the gymnasium for the parents of the second-grade children and for the children of the first four grades follow:

ANNOUNCER

"We have been studying about mail this year and we thought it would be nice to give a play about mail delivery. Most of the trips we took were to help us learn and understand about mails. One of the trips was to the General Post Office where we saw a number of things besides the Dead Letter Office and the big pneumatic tubes between stations. Another trip was to a dock where a little boat leaves to meet the big steamers lying in quarantine. It gets the mail off and brings it to the city where it sometimes is delivered before all the passengers can land. We have made the songs and the costumes and the scenery, and we hope you will enjoy our play."

HOW MAIL TRAVELS

A little boy and a little girl skip from their houses to the stationery store, buy pens, paper, and ink, and skip home where they can be seen through the windows of their houses writing letters. Another little girl comes out of the stationery store on her scooter and goes to the Post Office, buys an air-mail stamp, and mails a letter as she and the stamp clerk sing the "Stamp Song."

STAMP SONG

Stamps, stamps, stamps, air-mail stamps!
Please may I have some stamps
To take my letter thru the sky?
"Special-deliv'ry stamps?" "Air-mail stamps?"
Yes, you may have some stamps
To take your letter thru the sky.
Stamps, stamps, stamps, good old stamps!
Thank you, Mister Postman,
Good-by, good-by, good-by.

In the airport scene, the weather man is seen sending up two gas balloons, making observations through field glasses, and writing down results on a pad. The airplane comes to the center of the room and the group sings the "Mail Plane Song."

MAIL PLANE SONG

Brr-brr-brr, the mail plane starts on a long, long flight.
Over the countryside it flies thru fog, sleet, snow, and hail.
It goes much faster than the train.
That's why people send mail by plane.

The boat is heard tooting in the distance—it sails up to the dock and the mail bags are transferred to the truck which takes them to the Post Office as the group sings the "Mail Boat Song."

MAIL BOAT SONG

The boat is coming in,
The boat is coming in,
The boat is coming in,
With a toot-toot-toot.

The mail is sliding off,
The mail is sliding off,
The mail is sliding off,
With a bang-boom-bump.

The train appears and travels around the gymnasium, slowing up at the country station to throw off a bag of mail and to catch a bag hung on a crane near the station.

The group sings the "Mail Train Song," and the train disappears.

MAIL TRAIN SONG

Toot, toot, puff, puff,
Ding dong, ding dong.
Away goes the mail train,
Away goes the mail train,

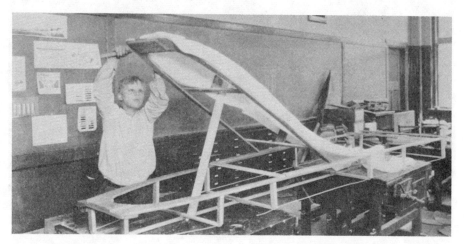

ONE BOY ELECTS TO MAKE THE CROCODILE FOR THE PLAY

CHILDREN SHOW THEIR APPRECIATION OF EGYPT AND HER CONTRIBUTION TO
RECORD-MAKING BY DRAMATIZING "SOKAR AND THE CROCODILE" AND MAKE
THEIR COSTUMES FOR THE PLAY

SIXTH-GRADE PRINTERS MAKING PROGRAMS FOR THE PLAY, "SOKAR AND THE CROCODILE"

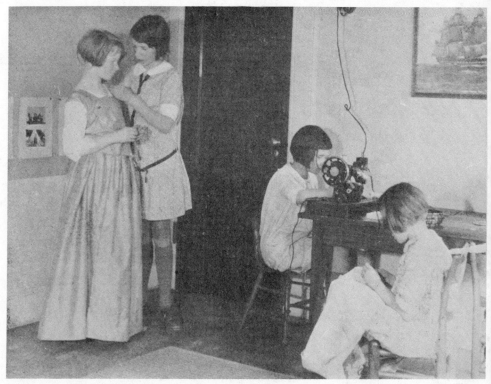

MAKING COSTUMES FOR A PLAY

Singing its song as it speeds along.
Toot, toot, puff, puff,
Bang, bang, bang, bang.
Quickly the mail bag is caught on the fly,
And the train dumps the mail
As it speeds by.

The country postman appears with his horse and wagon, marked "U. S. Mail." A comic touch is introduced here by having the horse run into the center of the room with the postman loudly calling, "Whoa! Whoa!"

The group sings the "Horse Song" while the country postman drives to the station, gets the mail brought in by the train, and delivers some letters and packages to the lady in the country house.

HORSE SONG

Clip, clop, clopperty clop,
Hear the horse's feet.
Jig, jog, joggerty jog,
Coming down the street.
Rumbling, grumbling, rumbling, grumbling,
Down the dusty street.

The play ends with a procession of train, truck, boat, airplane, special-delivery messenger, and so on, following the country postman and his horse out of the gymnasium.

IV

"How can we best share with the fourth and fifth grades the rich store of information and experiences which have come to us in connection with the study of records?" This was the question which the pupils of Miss Barnes's sixth grade asked. Their answer was two assembly programs, the first an information assembly, in which they explained and illustrated the evolution of records. The second assembly, which was given on the following day, expressed their appreciation of Egypt and her contribution to "Records." For this second assembly these children said, "Let's play," and with the help of Miss Barnes chose *Sokar and the Crocodile*. After becoming thoroughly acquainted with the story, they began to make a tentative list of scenes and of characters. They became Sokar, the Princess, Sokar's father, and other characters. They tried out parts. More information was gathered regarding costumes and scenery as the designing, cutting, sewing, and painting for the play progressed.

"Let's play" meant to these children reorganizing all their experiences around the life and times of a boy of ancient Egypt. It meant combining all the elements of drama. It meant unifying all their skill. Because meanings had been made rich through the leadership of the teacher, the parts lived. There was no writing of acts and scenes before the final form had been reached—it was written only for the sake of a permanent record after the play was finished.

Its enrichment through content is not the only aspect of dramatization that interests the writer, though that has been stressed in this article. A school has a large contribution to make toward the whole field of improving "the quality and quantity of seeing, feeling, and hearing on the part of those engaged in this creative activity"—dramatization.

RHYTHM AND DRAMATIC EXPRESSION

Ruth Doing

ONE winter on the Island of Bali, in the Dutch East Indies, I witnessed a performance of a rhythmical drama. In this were combined the chorus, the gamelan or orchestra of pure-toned bells, gongs and drums, and the actors who were dancers. These tillers of the soil are highly developed artists; hence their acting has vitality, a moving quality, and real creative artistry. Although their art gives an effect of great restraint and economy of effort, the whole is infused with a rhythmic vibration that rises to a crescendo so poignantly true and powerful that one is left breathless. When one of the twelve-year-old girl actors seized a dagger, walked with a swift drive of heroic energy toward the Evil One, paused with arm upraised for the length of one moment of tense inaction, then covered the intervening space with a final rush and dexterous thrust, I felt I had not only seen an epic drama consummated but had heard the music of the Avenging Angel himself. Acting comparable to this comes from children in my rhythmic classes. For rhythm is fundamental to movement and expression.

In my work, the organic rhythmic pulsations are regulated by basic movements of the torso and spinal column that exercise the very centers which control the organs and motor responses. Music furnishes the impulsion of these movements; and this organic listening becomes articulate in a gesture of the whole body. The children experience only the best music in these classes; and as the best music is the fruit of the inspiration of artists, the language of spiritual strivings, the substance of poetic ideas, the child is moving in that medium which liberates the artistic forces within himself. Not only does the content of music enrich the child subjectively; it presents the body with many techniques for dramatics. No matter what play material is available, it is immediately converted to the uses of the group urge for rhythmical dramatization. Each child enacts the part which best satisfies his individual rhythm.

RHYTHM IS FUNDAMENTAL TO MOVEMENT AND EXPRESSION

RHYTHMIC EXPRESSION

LITTLE BLACK SAMBO MEETS THE JUNGLE FOLK

IN A PRIMITIVE SUN DANCE EIGHT-YEAR-OLDS EXPRESS THEIR RHYTHMIC CONCEP-
TION OF EARLY MAN'S SUN WORSHIP

Often the dominating leadership of a certain child is intensified because he feels that if he is not the engineer, for instance, the train will not go fast enough. But when the compelling pulse of the play draws him into the line of coaches, he relinquishes his personal rhythm for the time being and is merged into the unity of social participation.

Furthermore, the impulse to speech or vocalization is directly liberated by the forces communicated to the brain from the entire motor organization. This is illustrated in the case of a boy of six who was poorly coördinated. He was very self-conscious, and this took the form of aggressiveness, accompanied by harsh and ugly explosive sounds. One day the group fell into a play of boats; some were tugs towing barges, some steamers, and the like. They lay on the floor and propelled themselves about, using their bodies as dramatic media. They gave off imitative sounds in different pitches, but there was the harmony of orchestration in it all. Ray decided to be the bell buoy; he stood in the middle of the room with arms lightly extended and fell into an easy sway, as if the waves were under him, lifting his body. When this simple coördination was established, he began to sing softly in a lovely tone, without any effort or tension, and kept it up for about eight minutes. He never varied from the pitch and seemed absorbed in listening to it. He was entirely unaware of the other children, although the barges and steamers changed their courses deliberately as they approached the bell buoy and sounded their whistles. Thus, concentration of the entire personality on creative expression such as this brings with it its own technique and through the reality and validity of the experience furnishes an incentive for growth in control. The child returns again and again to a coördination which gives him a feeling of ease and efficiency of movement.

As the child develops, a refinement of rhythmic perception and action makes itself felt in his life. He is more fearless in his attitude toward beauty and in the use of tools for its expression. This is of incalculable value to the adolescent in his efforts to articulate the stirrings of his ego. Now is the time when he connects himself with life and all that has gone before him in human history. We might be as fearless as he in promoting creative undertakings if we had his background of spontaneous initiative.

A cycle of imaginative plays given by children between the ages of twelve and eighteen illustrates the profound nature of the concepts of adolescent children. One play was called *God Through the Ages*, and showed how man in group consciousness had come to worship through fear; how he propitiated the gods; how later science entered and divided man from his instinctive dependence on the unknown; how the institution of the church arose and came under the sway of the state, and the persecutions attending it; how the radicals of a later day suffered much the same treatment at the hands of the conformists; and finally, how man today in individual consciousness carries God in his own heart and is not afraid.

Another play, *Man and the Universe*, opens with a darkened stage. A voice is chanting an original poem, glorifying space and the vibrating ether in which chaos reigns. A mighty wind is heard, first faintly, then with gathering force until the air is vibrant with sound, which diminishes and finally dies away. The wind music was produced by the children, each vocalizing phrases that to him represented the sound of the wind. They had planned to have the total effect represent chaos; hence, each child's wind song was composed by himself and taken down when no other child was present. Each song was in a different key, a different rhythm, and a different melodic progression. Following the mighty wind, nebulæ appeared. These were pure motion and light. Scarfs were attached to sticks and floated from different levels to a central focus of light, first dim white apparitions, then swirling flames in a crescendo of movement. After the earth was formed and cosmic order prevailed, a melody (composed by a boy and played on a pipe of his own making) wooed the first man and woman from the dust and waked to life the little hills. These were mounds of children who soon peopled the earth with gentle-eyed innocents. Responding to the tenderness of the first man and woman, they were gently drawn from the scene.

Their next estate was one of subjection to the mechanical forces of modern times. Groups of people, compelled by machine-driven rhythms, functioned automatically, separately at first, stressing different rhythms and percussion effects, then all together arhythmically, until chaos once more reigned. From this wreckage emerged a host of youths chanting the future and universal order.

In these rhythmic dramas, the *play* is not the thing, no matter how beautiful or stimulating it appears to be. Any attempt to perfect it or to put it in permanent form would defeat its very purpose.

DRAMATICS A MODE OF STUDY

John Merrill

James James
Morrison Morrison
Weatherby George Dupree
Took great
Care of his Mother
Though he was only three.

THIS poem of Milne's is excellent child psychology. James attempts to understand the behavior of grown-ups. In his imagination, his mother does the childish things, and he himself takes on the manners and reactions which he has observed in his parents. Such purposeful imitations as this are made in order to get at the mental experience which gave rise to an act.

Imitation, impersonation, and dramatic play are vital elements in every child's development. They are indispensable factors in his real education. Through the exercise of these elements the young explorer finds significance in things, builds up a consciousness of meaning, lays the foundation of his personality, and begins the framework of his social self. Imitation is the door through which the actor on the stage enters into the lives of others. It is the doorway through which the child enters into life situations. "All the world's a stage" is more than a speech in a play; it is a far-reaching truth.

Dramatic play is one of the child's modes of study. It is not a matter of introducing something new and extraneous into the curriculum of the elementary school; it is merely a problem of using wisely that dramatic tendency which plays so large a part in the child's preschool education and which will, whether we direct it or not, continue to influence the child's whole human experience.

At the time of great impressionability, when patterns of thought and behavior are being rapidly formed, the child should become acquainted with the best that has been written throughout the ages. He should, moreover, have his own personal library. Only that which is ethically sound, essentially true, and beautifully expressed should be introduced to him. There is no place for stories and poems which do not stand the test of essential truthfulness and of real art value. There are nonsense rhymes which are almost perfect bits of writing—real poetry. Many fables are short stories of the finest execution. Numerous folk stories, myths, and hero tales have a technique of incomparable excellence. There is an abundance of world literature from which to choose. Mention is made here of only a few of the possibilities.

"Mother Goose" and other choice nursery rhymes, classic lyrics, fables, and folk tales for the first grade. For the second grade, selected poems from Wordsworth, Keats, Blake, Tennyson, Stevenson, and Walter de la Mare; fairy tales of Grimm, Andersen, and other great writers; and the adventures of Abraham, Isaac, and Jacob from the Old Testament. Among the possible choices for the third grade are the *Uncle Remus* stories, the life of Moses and of David from the Bible, and Defoe's *Robinson Crusoe;* for the fourth grade the Greek myths, and the study of Homer's *Odyssey.*

Continuing through the elementary school, among other good things, are: Howard Pyle's *Robin Hood;* the *Arabian Nights;* the *Viking Tales,* with a portion of William Morris's *Sigurd the Volsung;* Cooper's *Last of the Mohicans;* Irving's *Rip van Winkle;* the Arthurian Cycle; the story of Cuchulain; and selections from Chaucer's *Canterbury Tales.* Accompanying the story material, there should be always a generous allotment of the finest poetry. Moreover, the child should be allowed to linger among his new-born blisses, for out of affectionate lingering grow understanding and self-expression. The child, in the right environment, and unhampered by unwise grown-ups and unchildlike ready-made techniques, brings forth "with newly learned art" his own fruit in his own season.

Literature should be approached in a dramatic spirit. Not every story should be acted, but it should be lingered over until it has become a part of the child's thinking. In the first grade, the return will be largely pantomimic; but before long, characterization, dialogue, and teamwork develop step by step. The teacher should be familiar with the laws of dramatic expression, must try to make conditions right for the child's development, and strive to guide him wisely as he develops in skill and power. The scientific teacher knows that education and not mere entertainment is the actuating purpose.

In the Autumn the first grade made an excursion to the west side of Chicago to see an open market. When they returned to school, they told about their adventure with great joy and eagerness. A. A. Milne's poem, *Market Square,* fitted so well with this experience that the writer, when he visited the class, read them the poem. The next time he met the children, he found them eager to hear the poem again. After this reading, each child was invited to make believe that he had a booth at a fair. The children displayed their wares and talked about them. Then a few children were chosen to pretend that they wanted to purchase a rabbit. In a most free and easy fashion some of the situations in the poem were acted. Everyone played, for the teacher must always be regarded as one of the party and not merely an onlooker. There was very little self-initiated dialogue, but everyone entered zestfully into the play. There was no attempt to play the whole poem. Such an incident as the lad's asking the stall-keeper if he sold rabbits and his disappointment to find that only saucepans or mackerel were on sale was a sufficiently large unit to be stressed, lingered upon, and developed in one day's play.

When, later in the day, the art teacher visited the class and asked what they wished to paint, the children said they wanted to illustrate the story of the rabbits. Their paintings showed an astonishing amount of significant detail and childlike beauty. One child said his picture showed rabbits playing on the "old-gold common." "But," observed the art teacher, "I don't see any rabbits." The young artist replied—and his voice and look indicated his surprise at the art teacher's failure to understand— "The rabbits, you know, are playing in the tall grass."

Only a few poems, either as a whole or in part, can be or should be acted. The ballad, the story-telling poem, occasionally offers possibilities for the playmaker. A lyric poem is complete in itself. Hearing it and saying it gives the child its fulfillment and charm. Once in a great while a lyric, such as Ariel's song, stirs the children to some sort of dramatic expression.

> Come unto these yellow sands,
>   And then take hands:
> Courtsied when you have and kiss'd
>   The wild waves whist:
> Foot it featly here and there;
> And, sweet sprites, the burthen bear.
>   Hark, hark!
>   Bow-wow.
> The watch-dogs bark:
>   Bow-wow.
> Hark, hark! I hear
> The strain of strutting chanticleer
> Cry, Cock-a-diddle-dow.

The third grade knows and loves this Shakespeare lyric. One day recently, some of the children pantomimed the poem while the rest of the class said the verses. A group of fairies in make-believe met in moonlight upon a sandy beach, silently curtsied, and then joined hands. The waves (a group of children who the day before had played surf in the eurythmics class) rolled up on the shore with such force that the fairies threw them a kiss, whereupon the billows were promptly silenced. To the music of imaginary fairy instruments, the dancers executed their dance. Then came the dog's bark, the rooster's warning, and a hasty departure of all the fairies.

The details of the pantomime developed gradually. One child said that the fairies did not hurry away when the dogs barked because they were not certain that the dogs were barking for the sunrise—dogs sometimes bark in the middle of the night; but when the cock crew, the fairies knew they must go, because the rooster always crows at daybreak. Some of the children illustrated the fairy orchestra, the harps, flutes, violins, and drums. They showed how the instruments were played, and how they sounded. The day following, this third grade played Ariel's song at the daily assembly. In a most informal way they pantomimed the story, partly on the stage, and partly on the steps leading to it. They were entirely satisfied with this simple presentation.

In the first and second grades, and even in the third grade, the plays worked out by the children are frequently shared with two or three other grades in a room about forty feet square. The audience is seated in two rows about three sides—sometimes all four sides—of the room. Within the large open square, the children act out their dramatizations. This arrangement gives a large space for acting, does away with arbitrary stage conventions, the necessity of always facing the audience, for example, and fosters a feeling of intimacy. If the occasion is one of importance, a festival day, a party, or some such event, then simple, appropriate costumes and properties are used. When the third grade did a portion of *A Midsummer Night's Dream*, the play was presented on the stage of the main auditorium. The setting and costumes were extremely simple, and the properties confined to those absolutely required by the text. The flowers were designed, made, and painted by the children. For plays done in the lower grades, draperies make an effective background. Screens of various units and sizes take the place of flats and set scenery. Canton flannel or dyed unbleached muslin, hung from barrel hoops, makes effective tree trunks.

For the first six or seven grades there are few, if any, ready-made children's plays worthy of study and presentation. The making of their own dramatization of a great story, such as *Rip van Winkle*, or a portion of a great hero tale, for example, the *Odyssey*, or *Sigurd the Volsung* is, however, a project of the greatest value. It entails affectionate lingering and much intensive work.

As an example of playmaking typical of the methods and procedures carried on in the elementary school, a brief account of a third grade's dramatization of the story of Gideon will perhaps be of value. In their study of some of the Old Testament heroes, the children were read the story of Gideon. They were deeply interested in Gideon's bravery.

When they heard that with only three hundred men he routed the great host of Midian, they declared that Gideon was an even greater leader than Abraham or Moses. There was an immediate acting of as many of the incidents as time permitted. This impromptu playing revealed to the class the fact that their memory of details was rather hazy. They thought it would be an excellent plan for everyone to read the story that evening at home. The next time the class met, they talked over the dramatic possibilities of the story and enumerated the incidents that seemed to have play-making possibilities. There was then and later much reference to the story and many rereadings of the Bible text in order to obtain information or to settle points under discussion. The incidents and characters necessary to the play were selected, and a tentative outline or scenario was placed upon the board. There were several informal playings of the text to test the effectiveness of the material for play use. The children found that there were too many incidents in the Bible account, some of them not practical for stage presentation. More discussion followed, and they finally agreed upon the following outline:

Act I. The Children of Israel, driven by the Midianites, take refuge in the hills. Gideon proclaims his trust in God. The enemy steals his corn. Gideon alone remains fearless. The angel appears and tells Gideon to throw down Baal, and Gideon says he will do so. He places the sheepskin for the test.

Act II. The troubles increase. The worshipers of Baal attempt to kill Gideon. Gideon remains steadfast. He finds the test of the skin satisfactory. Gideon is made leader of the faithful.

Act III. Further test of Gideon. Army is reduced from thirty-two thousand to three hundred, by the test at the stream. The angel again appears to Gideon.

Act IV. Gideon overhears the dream of the Midianite. The attack on the enemy.

Act V. The Israelites attempt to make Gideon king. He refuses, declaring that God alone is their King.

A careful examination of the children's outline will reveal how wise they were in their selection and arrangement of the incidents given in Chapters 6, 7, and 8 of the Book of Judges. They obeyed intuitively the major laws of play-making technique. Wise distribution of exposition, timely introduction of the opposing force, well sustained rising action and suspense, a vivid climax, and a logical and satisfactory resolution, were all skillfully managed. Although the work on the play extended over a considerable length of time, the children did not weary of it. Unfortunately, the play was started late in the school year. The first of June found the play completed but with not sufficient time left in which to present it. However, the teacher of the fourth grade allowed the children ample time in the autumn to stage their play.

The children helped to plan, design, and make the costumes and properties. Some of the members of the senior-class drama course aided in working out an effective lighting scheme and in other ways coöperated with the children in the staging of the play. The stage was hung with gray-green draperies. The entire class was able to participate in the acting because of the large number of characters in the play, and because of the fact that the school considers it advisable and educative to have more than one performance and, as a rule, more than one cast. By limiting the number attending, it was possible to have an audience for more than one performance. During the time devoted to the preliminary playings of their drama, each child had an opportunity to act many rôles. The actual casting of the parts was done as late as possible. Each actor was chosen primarily because of his need for playing a special part. Experience has shown that many a child has found himself as the result of acting the right part in the right play under right leadership.

Not everyone is prepared to direct a play. Playmaking and acting, to be educative, must be carried on in strict obedience to very definite laws. The professional coach, when dealing with amateurs, is very apt to approach the problem from the wrong angle. Appearances and theatrical effects are to him of paramount importance, whereas to the teacher of educative dramatics, richness of ideas, sincerity of expression, rather than the form of expression, are of primary value.

Clearness and vividness of mental images and honesty of expression are often crushed by an untrained teacher's attempts to teach children to act. A negative criticism, for example, may inhibit genuine expression and deter growth. Only a trained teacher, conversant with the laws of the art of dramatic expression, can understand and guide the student as he makes his way through the melodramatic period of development into the realistic realm and finally approaches the desired period of suggestion and real artistry of expression. The trained teacher strives to make conditions right for emotion to function in a worth-while situation; he then labors to direct emotion toward a purposeful, constructive goal. This is an educative act in which intellect, emotion, and will all function purposefully. Where affection is, attention lingers, the intellect acts, will operates, and expansive self-expression follows. All creativeness comes from within.

The dramatic work done in the junior and senior high school is a continuation of that done in the elementary grades, and the principles involved are the same. Therefore, it has seemed wise to stress only the foundation practices.

ILLUSTRATION OF ARIEL'S SONG, THIRD GRADE

Francis W. Parker School, Chicago

AN ORIGINAL SETTING FOR THE SLEEP-WALKING SCENE IN "MACBETH," NINTH GRADE

AN UNDER-SEA SCENE PAINTED BY CHILDREN

A BOAT PAINTED BY CHILDREN AS BACKGROUNDS FOR A PLAY

Francis W. Parker School, Chicago

A SECOND-GRADE GIRL'S PAINTING OF ARIEL'S SONG

Francis W. Parker School, Chicago

A FIRST-GRADE BOY'S PAINTING OF RABBITS ON THE "OLD-GOLD COMMON"

A THIRD GRADE PLAYING "A MIDSUMMER NIGHT'S DREAM"

CUT-OUT SHADOW PLAY OF "THE ARAB
AND HIS CAMEL," BY A SECOND GRADE

SHADOW SHOWS—A GOOD BEGINNING FOR DRAMATIC EXPRESSION FOR THE
TIMID CHILD

When the seventh or eighth grade is reached, the children have grown critical of their own writing and are not fully satisfied with their own plays. Dramatization and original playmaking continue but, gradually, appropriate literary dramas by great writers are used. Here, as in the elementary school, world literature helps to give young people a realization of the meaning of things.

The wise use of the dramatic tendency in the high school is no less imperative educationally than it is in the elementary school. Impersonation and acting are always valuable modes of study. The art of embodying a great dramatic creation and of giving it flesh and blood requires a high degree of sensibility, a keen intelligence, and a trained will. The result of such an art is far-reaching. It is not our desire to make actors or to copy the professional standards of commercial theaters. Our purpose is to use wisely the innate dramatic impulse to further the education of young people.

WORKING AT PLAY AND PLAYING AT WORK

Sarah A. Putnam

WORDSWORTH conceived the child of six as an unconscious actor, constantly fitting together

> Some fragment from his dream of human life . . .
> As if his whole vocation
> Were endless imitation.

At Park School our method is dramatic from the moment a baby enters at four till he graduates at sixteen or seventeen. With slight equipment, we make no circumstance in giving operettas, pageants, tragedies, comedies, original when possible, literary when necessary; but always, whether simple or elaborate, the responsibility is the children's. Within that responsibility lies the continuity of our school doctrine, that the children as much as possible live or experience their learning.

The opportunities for this expression are varied. The primary class, having visited the farm, impersonates the farmer and his pigs, cows, and chickens. A class, studying Japan, interprets the lives of the people and the country by use of very simple plot, music, dancing, and costumes. An intermediate group, absorbed in its work on the British Isles, uses Marshall's *Island Story* and a musical suite for piano students (likewise entitled *An Island Story*) for a series of scenes depicting significant spots in England's story, the children fitting the words to these tunes. The story of lumber was found too prosaic to make into a play.

In a study of the Panama Canal, General Goethals had various discussions with his coworkers, thought through by himself as he worked out the part, and supplemented by the rest of the group as responsible listeners and promoters. The sixth grade, filled with the glamour of India's past, relived the *Ramayana* so exquisitely in costume and in setting, made by their own hands, that even the lofty high-school students were thrilled. Again, a group may wish to convey dramatically the struggle of an epoch, as when the sophomores presented in assembly on succeeding Wednesdays, by means of picture, essay, original playlet, and finally by a rendition of Sheridan's *Critic*, the eighteenth-century battle between artificiality and simplicity, between aristocracy and democracy.

Sometimes there may be an outdoor festival, the cumulative result of the work of all classes with many interests. Such was the Greek Panathenaic celebration that lasted the better part of a day. It began in the morning with a procession to the temple in the grove, where the seniors garbed Athene in her glorious new peplum, helmet, shield, and spear, and a dove let loose from his wicker cage flew above her head and perched on the temple roof, while the children chanted an old hymn to Demeter. Then followed a succession of myths interpreted by each class, ending with a tragedy of Dido and Æneas, treated in blank verse, by the seniors. Then came a Pentathlon, a contest of Greek games, and a rollicking wind-up of the day in an adaptation of *The Frogs* so comic that the gay chorus was loath to cease croaking its inimitable song of "Brekeke-kesh, koash."

Then there are the special days to celebrate in dramatic manner, Halloween, Thanksgiving, Christmas, May Day, and Founders Day (or closing day), in which case the lower and the upper school each executes in its own manner.

The lower-school affairs are always original creations. The junior high-school productions are almost invariably original, as in the semi-Latin, semi-English playlet of a Roman school, or as in adaptations of a story like that of *The Man Without a Country*. The senior high-school productions are occasionally original, as in a Chinese drama given by the senior class in World History, or in the little comedies written for the monthly Drama Club meetings. But more often they are the result of the study of published plays half read, half acted in the Drama Club or carefully prepared as productions at Christmas time and on Founders Day.

By nature, adolescents play-act as much as do younger children, but

GARDEN SCENE FROM "THE FAN" BY GOLDONI, PLANNED AND CONSTRUCTED BY
HIGH SCHOOL STUDENTS EVEN TO THE LIGHTING EFFECTS

THE FOUNTAIN FIGURE OF THE
ABOVE SCENE WAS EXECUTED BY A
GIRL WHO HAD NOT KNOWN SHE
COULD MODEL

Shady Hill School, Cambridge

IDUNA, ODIN, THE DWARF, THE GIANT MIMIR, AND LOKI, HAND PUPPETS MADE BY
CHILDREN FOR A PLAY BASED ON NORSE MYTHS

their stage has now changed. It is no longer the merry puppet stage of the story book; it is instead a confusing shifting stage, sometimes painful in its reality of grown responsibilities thrust close, sometimes bombastically unreal in rebellious flights of imagination. Because of this, an adolescent never is more grateful, more amenable, than when a teacher invites him to let loose this play instinct in a grown-up drama, powerful in expression. He will do many things, otherwise distasteful, in order to qualify for a Drama Club play: wash dishes, clean the costume closet, set up chairs, paint scenery, sew costumes, that he may be included.

Last May we gave an eighteenth-century Italian play, *The Fan*, by Goldoni. Five departments coöperated: English, art, manual training, domestic science, and physics. The seniors took major parts but there were gleanings for underclassmen. And anyone who was allowed to touch paintbrush, hammer, or needle was honored thereby. The committee lists were long indeed.

The scene, wherein the players lived their rôles, was an Italian plaza, with houses converging sharply toward a city gateway. Young artists consulted medieval pictures, studied medieval ornament and costume. The result was a picture, sparkling in color: wall, balcony, awning, and dress, all a gay foil to the actors. The action took place around a fountain, wherein squatted a charming clay baby, executed by a girl who had not known the full scope of her modeling ability. In the building and the lighting, the boys revealed unusual technical skill and maturity.

In the senior year, we go into earnest study of comparative drama for, as city dwellers, the students see many professional plays. This gives an opportunity to direct both their ethical and their artistic senses in the establishment of good taste. Our emphasis lies upon the works of the Greek tragedians, Shakespeare, Masefield, Ibsen, Galsworthy, Shaw, O'Neill, though the range of reading and of study is wide. Much free work is done in extra assignment and in written project. Stauffer's *The Progress of Drama through the Centuries* is a boon to us, though it does not entirely fill our needs. We supplement with many collections, such as those of Dickinson, Clark, Moses, and Shay. Van Doren's *American and British Literature Since 1890*, Lewisohn's *The Modern Drama*, Glenn Hughes's *The Story of the Theatre*, Cheney's *The Theatre*, give us a fine background.

There is life in Æschylus's Agamemnon when you compare the onrush of his fate to that of the fateful end of the lovers in Hugo's *Hernani*, for instance; life in Sophocles' Antigone, when you study the ethical justification of her disobedience with that of the disobedience of Masefield's Nan; or life in Euripides' conception of Alcestis' selfish husband when you compare him with Nora's selfish husband in *A Doll's*

House. There are endless analogies. The fourteenth-century *Everyman* suggests *R. U. R.*, and we search for the meaning behind the symbolism of each era.

EQUIPMENT FOR A PROGRESSIVE-SCHOOL THEATER

Milton Smith

MERELY to have students learn the lines of a play, and say them on any kind of stage, before any sort of setting, with nondescript lighting, is not really educational dramatic art. Students must be given the opportunity to *create* a production. They should design and build their own scenery and costumes; they should experiment with that most wonderful of all dramatic mediums, light; they should try out their ideas of stage and business management. Actors are not more important in the great design than stage hands or ushers. Even the player of the most important character must feel his own subordination to the central idea. Play production of this sort is a synthesis of all the arts and crafts; it involves group activity of a peculiarly socialized sort; it is educational in the truest sense.

For play production, the most important piece of "equipment" is a capable teacher, one who loves the theater, knows its literature, and possesses a working knowledge of the arts and crafts involved in play production. Such a teacher will lead students to rich dramatic experiences whatever the handicaps of the physical equipment of the school. He may resort to boxes, curtains, and lights, such as are described in *The Shady Hill Play Book,* by Katharine Taylor and H. C. Greene. He may be reduced to giving performances with imaginary curtains and properties, as in *The Play Way* by H. Caldwell Cook. Or he may use "central staging," or "dramatic scene shifting," or some of the other devices that I have described in *The Book of Play Production.* But a teacher who can succeed with these handicaps is worthy of a proper place in which to practice real play production with his students. However inspiring a teacher of science may be without a proper laboratory, his work is certain to be more sound and stimulating if he has suitable instruments with which to work.

This is a point which I should like to emphasize. Even in progressive schools (and I almost said, especially in progressive schools!) there seems to be a feeling that good equipment is a handicap. Principals and teachers point with pride to work that is done under unnecessary difficulties. If children are studying printing, there seems to be more virtue in a printed page that is not too bad, considering it has been done with

ROBIN HOOD AND HIS MERRY MEN REHEARSE THEIR PLAY

THE STAR CHILD SINGS TO THE LITTLEST SHEPHERD THE SONG OF THE CHRIST
CHILD'S COMING (ORIGINAL MUSIC BY TEN-YEAR-OLDS)

MINIATURE MODEL (FROM AN ORIGINAL 8 X 12 FEET) OF THE GARDEN SCENE
ADAPTED FROM "THE SLEEPING BEAUTY" AND PLAYED IN SILHOUETTE

CUT-OUT SHADOW PLAY OF "THE MON-
KEY AND THE CROCODILE," CON-
STRUCTED WITH ITS SCREEN BY CHIL-
DREN OF THE SECOND GRADE

MINIATURE MODEL OF THE KITCHEN
SCENE FROM "THE SLEEPING BEAUTY"

A CHURCH WINDOW IN A PLAY BY TEN-YEAR-OLD CHIL-
DREN WHO WERE RELIVING MEDIEVAL TIMES

A SCENE FOR "THE TEMPEST," DESIGNED AND PAINTED BY GUY PÈNE

odds and ends of type on a press that ought to be in a junk heap, than there is in a beautiful page done with fine type on a good press. I have often wondered if this attitude does not arise out of our American worship of ingenuity. But in art—and all the subjects we teach in school are arts—the emphasis should be on the art itself, and not on the ingenious shifts we are put to in order to practice it at all. The real artist is not handicapped by a beautiful instrument. Proper equipment puts the emphasis where it belongs and frees ingenuity to produce a better result.

Most schools are poorly equipped for modern play production. This unfavorable condition is due to the fact that the most important part of the equipment is the building itself, the auditorium and the stage. Almost any large room can be made into a satisfactory laboratory for drawing, painting, crafts, English, or sciences; but play production can be badly and permanently hampered by improper planning for the school stage. A poorly arranged stage, an incorrect proscenium arch, the lack of necessary space here or there, the permanent fixing to the walls of units that should be movable, any of these things can cripple play production. And these "architectural ineptitudes," says Irving Pichel, in *Modern Theaters* (which ought to be studied by all school architects and administrators) "are more likely to be perpetuated, and in time condoned, than those of any other art."

It may be argued (and is!) that school auditoriums are to be used for many things besides play production—for debates and oratory, concerts, assemblies, and graduating exercises. But a stage suitable for all these things may be entirely useless for play production, whereas a stage suitable for play production is just as useful for all of these events. Therefore, every school stage should be built primarily for play production, or if necessary, rebuilt for play production.

A modern theater is a building that has two main parts: an auditorium and a stage. The opening through which the audience hears and sees the performance is called the "proscenium" opening, and it may be closed at will by a curtain. This proscenium wall and opening may, of course, be built in any large room; it may be temporary and movable and may even consist of curtains; but it should be built in the auditorium as a permanent part of the building at the time of construction. All that is in front of this wall is the auditorium, or the "house," in the language of the theater. Many things should be thought of when the auditorium is being planned, the acoustics, the sight lines, the hygienic conditions, and the esthetic appeal. But all these things may be excellent in a school auditorium, and often are, and yet the school may be poorly equipped for play production. It is the stage, or the part of the building that is back of the proscenium wall, that determines its satisfactoriness as a theater.

The first consideration for a stage is the size of the proscenium opening. The minimum practical size is probably 8 feet in height and 15
in width. In an opening smaller than this, the actors, even if they are
children, appear huge and fantastic. The maximum size is probably 15
feet in height and 40 in width. In a bigger opening, actors look dwarfed.
Professional stages rarely have bigger openings than this. Probably the
most useful size is 12 by 24 or 25 feet. Whatever the size of the opening, but especially if it is very large, it should be possible to cut down
its size with a "teaser" and "tormentors." A teaser is a curtain hanging
over the opening; and tormentors are two upright pieces, usually frames
covered with canvas or some other material, one of which stands on
each side of the opening. Both teaser and tormentors should be movable.

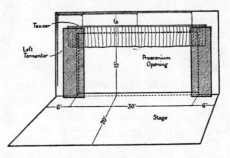

FIGURE I

A stage of correct proportions with minimum off-stage space. Note the movable teaser
and tormentors.

The teaser should never be fastened in a permanent way to the top of
the arch so that it cannot be raised and lowered. The first and most important of all principles in regard to stage equipment is that everything
should be movable and flexible. The teaser should be hung on a pipe, or
wooden batten, suspended from pulleys by two or three ropes, which in
stage parlance are "a set of lines."

After the size of the proscenium opening has been determined, the
next problem is to determine the size and layout of the back-stage space.
There can hardly be too much room back stage, so here the problem is
largely one of determining the minimum limits. The depth, that is, the
distance from the opening to the back wall, should be at least two
thirds of the width of the arch. That is, it should be 18 or 20 feet if the
width of the opening is 25 or 30 feet. On each side of the proscenium
arch, there should be space for actors and the storage of scenery and
properties. The minimum distance on each side of the proscenium arch
should be 5 or 6 feet, as otherwise it is impossible to have doors on the
side of the stage set. The back-stage space need not be symmetrical, and

many professional theaters have more room on one side than the other. The rule is that there should be as much room back stage as may conveniently be allowed. To this end, 'no useless walls should be put in. It is the custom of school architects, even when they build a real proscenium wall and arch, to make a "stage" that is a mere box, usually elaborately plastered and paneled, with dressing rooms on each side of the stage. A real stage should be left bare and open. If the bare stage is unsuitable for assemblies or chapel exercises, an attractive room can easily be created by a set of scenery or a cyclorama of curtains.

The one dimension that remains to be considered is the height of the stage from the floor to the ceiling. Most modern theaters have at least twice as much room above the top of the proscenium arch as below it. At the top, over the stage, is a "gridiron," or network of beams, so that scenery and properties can be handled from above and dragged up out of sight. The school theater should have as much room above the proscenium arch as possible, and never less than six feet. The stage ceiling should never be a mere plaster plane, running out from the top of the proscenium arch. Even the smallest theater can have something that serves as a "grid," even if it is only a beam or two fastened to the ceiling. Two or three I-beams, set over the stage in the ceiling, are a most useful device.

Such an arrangement is invaluable in handling scenery, and also helps to solve the lighting problems. Theater lights should never be permanent fixtures. A few spot lights and one or two strip lights will be quite adequate if they may be moved from place to place, and raised or lowered at will, as they may be in a theater equipped with the rudimentary grid suggested above. It is impossible in such a brief space to discuss lighting (see Figure 2), but the great secret of good lighting is flexibility.

The less finished the back-stage space, the better. It is part of the machinery of play production, and needs no elaborate paneling or painting. Structural beams left exposed provide convenient places for pulleys, lights, and other equipment. The back wall itself should be left plain and unbroken by doors or windows. If roughly plastered, and painted a broken-color blue, it makes a beautiful "sky" when properly lighted. When the auditorium is used for concerts or assemblies, the back wall may be covered with scenery sets or curtains. The floor of the stage, too, is part of the machinery; it should be of soft wood, so that nails and pegs can easily be driven into it.

Nothing has been said about entrances and exits, workshops or storerooms. There should, if possible, be one large door leading off the stage, so that scenery and heavy objects can easily be shifted. Dressing-rooms are desirable, but if the stage is properly arranged as to exits, class-

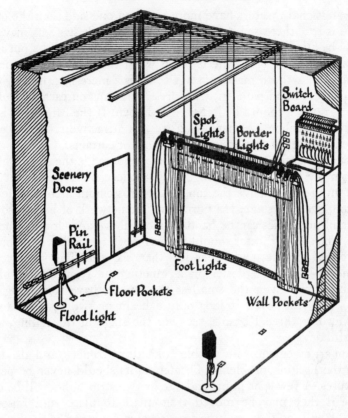

FIGURE 2

Stage suitable for high school plays. Note arrangement of lights, switchboard, large door for scenery, and pin-rail.

rooms (or any other rooms not being used at the time of the performance) will serve, thus saving space. The proper arrangement of space is the main requirement to be kept in mind. Rigging, lights, switchboard, and all the other desirable fixtures can be added later as funds permit; but if the stage is not correctly planned, no amount of equipment can make it adequate.

DRAMA AT SCARBOROUGH SCHOOL

Estelle Hallock

CHILDREN learn in their play with other children far more than they do through the conscious instruction of teachers and parents. When a school recognizes this play value, it is coöperating with the laws of child nature and not working against them. A new school beginning its existence on these principles is fundamentally sound. Scarborough School was founded seventeen years ago with the idea of play as an educational factor at its center.

This country day school is indeed fortunate in having not only a completely equipped theater for indoor plays but much outdoor beauty and space. Each year in the spring, the children of the elementary school give in the tea garden an original play from their study of Greek life. The first play, when the school was young and small, was the story of *Narcissus*. The children created spontaneously a natural, dramatic effect as they ran down the path around the pool while Narcissus studied himself in the water. Another year, the children acted out the story of *Demeter and Persephone* in the Greek style, with a chorus and masks. The children made everything from the play to the masks. They have dramatized *Pandora and Epimetheus*, *The Magic Weathervane* and *Atalanta's Race*. Last year their play was *The Miraculous Pitcher*. When the children turned into trees by slipping behind them, the effect was impressive in its simplicity.

One well-remembered play was a dramatization of the life of *The Big Oak Tree*. The children often play under this oak tree whose great girth taxes the encircling span of six pairs of arms. Wood nymphs told the story of the tree throughout the four seasons; Spring was represented in a beautiful original dance; for Summer, rain drops came as silver balloons attached to the shoulders of the little dancers. Elves carrying branches of oak leaves formed the stage curtain.

Another of the notable plays was a culmination of a reading and library project by the first six grades of the school. Reaching well across the stage was a row of books of dramatic size and color, supported by book-ends consisting of children seated with their backs to the ends of the outside volumes. A group of children in a library atmosphere were mending books and expressing their wish that the book people might come out from between the covers, when in response to their request *Aladdin*, with a cloud of smoke, a child wrapped in mauve shades of cheesecloth from foot to head and beyond, brought the thing to pass. Out from *The Gingerbread Man* stepped a first-grade child, as the original gingerbread man, and second-grade fairies danced out of a volume of *Fairy Tales;* from *Hiawatha* came third-grade children who acted a scene from the poem; fourth-grade children, tiger and all, did *Little Black Sambo* in French; fifth-grade's book was *Treasure Island* and the children presented a swashbuckling pirate episode; sixth grade, who had been studying knighthood, gave a chivalrous incident from *Robin Hood*. From the one volume which bore no title came a little fellow who said that perhaps a child at Scarborough would some day write the book that had no name.

An all-school project which had much educational background was *The River and the Road*. This original pageant in the outdoor theater showed the Indian period, the Dutch Colonial, the English Colonial, and the Revolutionary periods, together with the period of expansion of the historic Hudson on which Scarborough's windows look, and of Revolutionary Road and the Post Road on which her gates open. A student, appropriately costumed and presented as Washington Irving, related the romance of the Hudson Valley.

Since 1927, the school has had a director in charge of the speech and drama in the intermediate school and seventh grade. There the English and history projects are usually the inspiration for her work. The dramatizations are the work of the children, from the choosing of the subject material to the planning, writing, organizing, and costuming of the play. Every pupil in the class has a part, and the children with most difficulties and with greatest need for attention, get leading rôles. Acting of plays in these years of a child's life, as in later years, builds self-confidence and poise, originality and independence. The experience of being somebody also enriches personality. Even more than for recreation and entertainment, does play-acting serve as a teaching device.

Coriolanus, A Roman Feast, Nathan Hale, The First Thanksgiving, Little Women, Dolly Madison, Colonial Lawn Party, Hansel and Gretel, are some of the plays the children in these groups have done. The correlation of this work with other work in the school is shown in the play *Coriolanus* which correlated with Roman history; English (writing the play); shop (making props); art (designing and dyeing costumes); music (original songs); arithmetic (computing costs and amounts of materials for costumes and sets); geography (planning location); speech (play production).

The regular drama classes of the Upper School receive credit toward graduation by offering the dramatic work as a part of the curriculum;

SCENE FROM "THE HOUR GLASS," PRODUCED BY HIGH-SCHOOL STUDENTS

"LA BALLADE DES PENDUS," DRAMATIZED FROM THE FRENCH AND PRODUCED
BY PUPILS

SCENE FROM "MASSE MENSCH," BY ERNST TOLLER, AT THE VASSAR EXPERIMENTAL
THEATER, OF WHICH HALLIE FLANAGAN IS THE DIRECTOR

A JAPANESE NO PLAY OF THE FIFTEENTH CENTURY AT THE VASSAR EXPERIMENTAL
THEATER

time is afforded for serious and systematic study of plays as literature, of the theater as a workshop, and of the art of acting as a means to the cultivation of desirable personality traits in the students. These give not only the cultivation of good speech and posture through practice in acting technique but also enhance appreciation of the motives of human action and emotional response to human problems.

The plays of the Junior School are original dramatizations of their reading, as "The Trial of Rebecca" from *Ivanhoe*, or *The Jester's Purse* from their literature collection, or *The Princess* of Tennyson, or Scott's *Lady of the Lake*. At times, plays like Dunsany's *Gods of the Mountain* and *The Golden Doom*, or scenes from Shakespeare are used. When the tenth-grade English class was studying the development of the drama, they staged the old morality play *Everyman*, employing their own interpretation of symbolism in costume and stage background.

Among the plays given by the Senior School have been Noyes's *Sherwood*, *Antigone*, Miss Peabody's *The Piper*, Rostand's *The Romancers*, *The Wolf of Gubbio*, and plays by Barrie, Yeats, Pinero, Stuart Walker, and many others. In all the dramatic activities, the students choose their special interests and make themselves responsible for the management and production of all the plays given. The school has stimulated drama in other schools in Westchester County by conducting yearly a one-act-play tournament.

VITALITY AT VASSAR

Margaret Ellen Clifford

THE Vassar Experimental Theater is an organization dedicated to vitality in the theater. Some years ago its students, under Hallie Flanagan, refurnished the cellar of the ancient stable in which they were accustomed to take their music and speech lessons, and groan over their Latin prose, and set up theatrical housekeeping. Though the equipment is still inadequate, and the funds insufficient, this has not succeeded in dimming their enthusiasm, or limiting their creative ability. The theater is not, however, another of these "arty" little groups that excuses itself by enthusiasm for shoddy production—the mention of the cellar was perhaps unfortunate in this connection, producing an erroneous impression of egotistic young women in a grubby atmosphere, yearning after "self-expression." It has, on the contrary, a high standard of production, intelligent and imaginative direction, students who do not suffer from the idea that mouthing lines constitutes working in a theater. It is another group to swell the ranks, so confidently spat upon by professionals, of those who are under the impression that the theater is an art and not a pawnshop.

Academically speaking, the theater is composed of three groups: a first-year production group of thirty-five members, an advanced production group of fifteen members, and a play-writing group which is, as is only proper, the core and *raison d'être* of the most characteristic part of the theater's work. These courses are limited to juniors and seniors, and a certain number of hours of work in Dramatic Literature and Creative Writing are prerequisite. Courses in Applied Art, Mechanical Drawing, Rhythmics, Fencing, and the Technique of Speech are suggested as corequisite. The ratio of credit for these courses is the same as that extended to any applied art at Vassar: for four lecture hours and four laboratory hours, students receive four hours of credit.

Work in scene design, lighting, and stage management is scheduled for Friday and Saturday, and, in spite of the extra fee charged for the course, the annual enrollment is twice as large as the theatre can accommodate. The entire expenses of the three courses, with the exception of the salary of the director, are paid from these student fees.

As is proper in an experimental theater, the paramount interest is in premières. The play-writing group is the laboratory for this factory. In the Greenroom, stories are dramatized, scenarios discussed with some violence, plays read to a barrage of uninhibited criticism. Then the chosen plays go into rehearsal; and the authoress who thinks well of her brainchild has a great deal to learn. There is no more valuable or revealing moment in a playwright's life than when she (or he) realizes that the scene that brought tears or laughter to the eye of the reader brings only boredom to an audience because it permits the leading actress to do nothing but sit still in one chair.

There is no danger of a playwright being released from this theater tainted even slightly with the conception that plays are to be read. Plays are to be acted, and acted they will be, though author and director go down to a violent death in the doing. The scene designer proceeds to translate the playwright's idea into terms of paint; the crews into wood and canvas, metal and light; the actors into flesh and blood; the director into scenes and patterns, rhythms and climaxes; and the author realizes that this coördination is what is meant by theater.

For several years now, these students have been doing some thinking in an unorthodox way, and have an eloquent document to that effect in their program of premières. *Blocks*, by Molly Thacher, is a satire on war that ends with the erection of the lifeless bodies of the combatant workers as monuments to their own glory, highly suggestive of a certain well-known statue. *The Prophecy*, by Claudia Hatch, shows the saving of the Ark by the only pagan on board, commenting as coolly on a Christmas myth as Frances Strunsky in *Water and Wine* (concerned wittily with Theseus' desertion of Ariadne on Naxos) does on a Greek one. A wide range of locale inspires these young women; with Florence Clothier, in *She Canna Perish*, it is the Labrador coast; with Charlotte Kohler, in *Down in Egypt's Land*, the American Negro, still enslaved. A wide range of material claims their attention: Eleanor Phelps, in *Troll Hill*, treats of the line between the natural and the supernatural; a play of Molly Thacher's is written expressly for the radio and given through a loud speaker; *Cartoon*, a riotous musical comedy of European politics, is elaborated from a skit in a German newspaper.

Although this theater specializes in premières of student plays, it also stages work of other dramatists, performances in which the emphasis is on experiment in production. The theater made its reputation in the eyes of the world at large by an amusing and brilliant definition of three modern methods of acting and stagecraft, Chekhov's *A Marriage Proposal*, produced three times on one bill, realistically, expressionistically, constructivistically. In *Masse-Mensch*, Toller's play of the individual versus the group, produced in the spring of 1930, a snarling mob swarmed through a terrified audience up the steps onto a stage where a single figure was silhouetted in a pool of light against a great skeleton construction of wood. Last year also saw a highly stylized production of Pirandello's *Each in His Own Way* against black and white hangings, the background of three huge white question marks that changed, as the play grew in intensity, to exclamation points in the second act. Color in costumes and wigs was used with a definite meaning, deepening from pale pink and lavender for the chattering young ladies at the ball, to deep red for the hero and heliotrope for the heroine, characters close to the vortex of emotion in the play. Characters moved as puppets, each in a rhythm of his own. High on a throne, dressed in black velvet, the *raisonneur* of Pirandello's theme seemed part of the scene till he flung back his black hood and revealed his white face, the dot under the question mark.

One important function of the Experimental Theater is its educational relation to the rest of the college. For instance, in connection with a course in the history of drama, it gave a production entitled *Backgrounds of the Modern Theater*. The bill contained a liturgical play of the tenth century, a Japanese No play of the fifteenth century, an incident in the manner of the Commedia dell'Arte, a scene from Shakespeare's *Antony and Cleopatra* (with Cleopatra in a red wig, suggesting the Virgin Queen, and bejeweled dress with Elizabethan ruff), and one act of Beaumarchais's "Barber of Seville." The production showed, far more clearly than any rhetoric, that one possible cause of the blight that has settled on our modern theater is, as Gordon Craig expresses it, that the actor has been "imprisoned in a rectangular box separated from us by a curtain."

After a production, the first meetings of the classes are devoted to discussion. There is self-criticism by the director, by the actors, by the crews, and a harvest of outside criticism avidly gathered by all members of the theater in the highways and byways of the intervening week-end. These students do not want undiscerning approval; they court adverse criticism and hold it up to the light in its turn to determine its value.

The day has passed when our little girl wanted mamma and papa to come to the play to hear her speak her piece; these students are working in a theater. The productions do not meet with unqualified approval —what individual or organization that devotes itself to untrammeled thought does? The director has been accused of being everything from a devotee of Catholic ritual to a Bolshevist spy. Contrary to the popular superstition which holds that every college newspaper proclaims every college play a professional production and every undergraduate actress poised triumphant on the sill of Broadway, the *Vassar Miscellany News* has always been distinctly cool in its critical attitude.

In fact, it habitually expresses a reserved disappointment that the theater is not living up to its own high standard—a somewhat baffling criticism, as research reveals it has been saying so since the theater's first production.

But the most valuable criticism the theater receives is that which comes through its own medium, the theater. Contrary to the system erroneously followed in so many of our college courses, the instructor does not give an examination to the students; the students give it to the instructor. The difference lies not in less mental training required, but in more amusement gained, as the examination is in the form of a revue satirically concerned with the deeds and misdeeds for the past year of the director, technician, students, audiences, and the college in general. This use of their own tools to write their epitaphs is the most discerning criticism they receive.

While the main purpose of these courses is general, not vocational, to create not so much actresses and playwrights as an intelligently critical and theatrically minded audience, an increasing number of its students is going out into every phase of active theatrical work. Some are teaching, starting secondary-school theaters of their own; some are acting on Broadway or in stock companies; some are designing sets and costumes for Broadway and little-theatre producers; and there is an increasingly great demand for girls trained in this valuable branch of the applied arts.

Periodically, in our current literature, a great deal of agonizing is done about the state of our theater, blaming everything from the ticket speculators to the farm problem; the most fatal illness is infrequently stated—lack of ideas. Here is the prescription on Broadway's doorstep.

THE CAROLINA PLAYMAKERS

Ralph Westerman

In an age devoted to domination, it is not often that one finds an individual who never permits his enthusiasm to overshadow the convictions of his followers. No doubt, this is the secret of the stimulation that embryonic playwrights find in Professor Frederick Koch's playwriting course at the University of North Carolina.

Professor Koch's class procedure is very simple. In fact, one can scarcely detect any definite plan of action—which is, in itself, a powerful agent of inspiration. A routine method of instruction would be fatal to creative possibilities. Drama does not readily lend itself to foregone conclusions.

Any student in the Playwriting course asked to define the most vital phase of the instruction will invariably refer to the informality and frankness of the discussions having to do with creative writing. Each student is an individual, with his unique likes and dislikes, his own peculiar flair and, as one student expressed it, his "spiritual limitations." This is always taken into consideration when dealing with the projected creation of the playwright. All types of plays are encouraged; all kinds of criticisms are invited; and no one ever feels hurt or neglected because his play receives less attention than the play of a fellow dramatist.

Each student is required to write two one-act plays a quarter. Each play is read by the author before the entire group. Then open discussion follows, and the play is evaluated from various angles of plot, characterization, motivation, and other units of play construction. These criticisms are carefully noted by the author. Needless to say, he usually profits by them.

The folk drama is encouraged because of its intrinsic possibilities. Professor Koch is convinced that a purely localized drama, from the angle of plot and characterization, may also symbolize the wider horizons of the human emotions. Thus, the intimate and the provincial transcend their artificial boundaries and reach out to touch the fundamental truth of life in all places.

However, there are many students in the group from outside the state, and they cannot be expected to produce authentic "Carolina Folk Plays." These students are encouraged to write about life as they know it. Consequently, a wide variety of plays is turned out in each quarter. Every drama has a chance to find its way to a critical audience, for students are urged to try out their plays in a studio production. Friends are invited, cards are passed around, and criticisms are noted. The play is revised, always with an eye to a public production in The Playmakers Theater. Of course, this possibility is no small factor in the effort put forth by the young playwright. If the play is especially well done, it may find a place in the Playmakers repertory and be taken on tour.

Since 1930, when Professor Koch asked me to assist him in his playwriting course, I have read more than thirty one-act plays and listened to half as many plans for future creations. Let us consider a few representative examples. The first I have in mind deals with Carolina fisherfolk of Nag's Head. The setting is the sitting room of an average family of the type referred to. The scene opens with a charming duologue between a man and a small boy. The former is mending his net, an activity that never fails to suggest the eternal symbol of struggle, romance, and the more definite association with spiritual values. This play is a comedy concerning a man's love for children, and his shrewish wife's final realization that in order to compete with the situation she must change her tactics.

In the field of the sophisticated drama, we have a play dealing with a fear complex. The setting is the porch of a bungalow in Death Valley, California. The young and sensitive wife has a terrific fear of the desert, but in order that her husband may find inspiration, she attempts to stifle her obsession. A friend, a young doctor, through the medium of psychoanalysis, finally cures her.

One student has written a travesty upon our compact civilization. The main humor of the play centers about a scientist who has succeeded in concentrating foods. The "Chamber of Commerce" idea is used in order to defeat a deadlier ambition. Youth wins, and nature returns to her element.

In the field of propaganda, we have a mechanistic drama dealing with the timely problem of Machine versus Man. The Machine wins. In this type of play, we enter the Russian-German school of the theater. We are convinced that it is a healthy sign when students write dramas of this type.

Then, too, there is the philosophical drama, dealing with supersensitive persons who are "sick with consciousness but cannot create." This play approaches a type of poetical drama. Another play, dealing with race prejudice, caused quite a bit of discussion when it was read.

It will be seen, from considering these types of plays, that Professor Koch's course in playwriting is not limited to the folk drama. Every idea is seriously considered, regardless of its sophistication or conventionality. The only rule laid down concerns the sincerity of the creator, which is, after all, the basis of any art.

Professor Koch thus states the purpose of the Carolina Playmakers, the producing organization of the University playwrights: "The Carolina Playmakers is an organization in which the school—whether it be a university, college, normal school, high school, or rural school—is conceived as a radial center of communal expression through the production of original plays. The aim of The Carolina Playmakers is to translate the spirit of Carolina into plays truly representative of the life of the people, of the folk of North Carolina. The idea is communal—an institution of neighborliness, of the common good, and the common happiness. It is a society of amateurs, of *amatores*, in the original sense of the word. For the spirit of communal play cannot be formed by the machinery of modern organization merely; it must come spontaneously from the heart of man. It must be an expression of the joy of the worker in striving to create, to form something into beauty—into poetry."

"There remains to be written," says he, "the many-sided drama of the thrilling new life of Carolina today—of her contribution to America." The folk drama will always remain a paramount feature of playwriting, but the energies of the dramatists will not stop there. We who work with embryo writers are fully assured of the coming of a drama more devoted to significant ideas than to the usual emotional triangles.

Three volumes of plays written by these young Carolina playmakers have been published. *The Carolina Play-Book* is issued four times a year. Each copy contains one of the new plays we have referred to.

It is paradoxical to note that playmaking and play producing at the University of North Carolina are highly organized, and yet unhampered in their natural development. No one has ever thought of compromising in regard to the discussion or the projection of an idea. This has been the inspiration behind the productivity at Chapel Hill. Professor Koch holds the conviction that the mind must be free from fear of commercial conventionality.

All things considered, it is the student who profits most by this dramatic construction. The "machinery" of the organization is secondary; the creative possibilities of the human mind are always the vital issue. This theory seems to be reasonably sound; it is the power that stimulated such significant personalities as Paul Green, Thomas Wolfe, and Jonathan Daniels. Countless other students of English 31 have been given a mental and spiritual balance by their participation in creative dramatics. So playwriting at the University of North Carolina is taken seriously, but the main objective is never lost sight of—to encourage a drama vibrant with the sincere wonder of life, regardless of vain prejudices.

THE VERSE-SPEAKING CHOIR

Virginia Somes Sanderson

LET us bring poetry back again into group life. Let us share it with one another instead of reading silently to ourselves the bits we like, or, half-ashamed, reciting favorite lines aloud in the sanctuary of some private room. Why should people not meet in groups and enjoy poetry together, speaking it aloud in unison? Let each member of such a gathering do his part in re-creating the author's thought and mood, and he will come to gain new appreciation of poetic expression, new power of vocal interpretation, together with a fine coördination of voice and body. Let there be more Verse-Speaking Choirs!

I am not referring here to choirs that chant verse, all members maintaining a fixed pitch and changing it only at the direction of a leader. Nor am I speaking of something possible only for those whose voices are beautiful, controlled instruments of expression. Nor do I mean by a Verse-Speaking Choir a costumed group that combines dancing and chanting in an effort to interpret poetry.

The Verse-Speaking Choir of which I write is for any group of people who wish to gather under a leader who understands that true leadership requires a drawing out of the ideas of those who form the group, not an imposing of his own theories, nor an attempt to arrive at a uniform interpretation.

Fifteen or twenty people are best for a beginning. Eight or twelve will do. Broadly speaking, all voices can be roughly classified as high, middle, or low in median pitch; and this forms the first and only arbitrary division of the group. It must be remembered, however, that an important aim is the development of the individual's range so that one who belongs to the high-voiced group may be able also to speak with the middle, or even the low group. Of course, those with high voices will never reach the low tones of the low-voiced group, but they may develop such range that their lowest tones will serve as overtones of the low-voiced group, when all speak together on a low register.

A poem is chosen and each member is given a copy. Dramatic poetry, verse with compelling rhythm and vivid words suggestive in sound of their meaning, poems with strong expression of emotion or situation, and poems which present contrasted moods are best for a start. Delicate lyrics, selections from the Bible, and humorous poetry are the most difficult to give, perhaps because they require a flexibility of voice and a depth and control of emotion that comes with experience in interpretation. So we start with *Jazz Fantasia*, by Carl Sandburg, or *The Congo*, by Vachel Lindsay. We read it together, aloud. The result is not inspiring.

It becomes evident at this first reading that, in certain ways, we are limited in our individual interpretation. We must all hold to the same rate of speed in speaking together, and pause in the same places for the same length of time. We will have to be especially careful of our enunciation and take heed as individuals not to dominate the group voice. We decide it will be well to vary the reading by having the high voices take certain lines or parts of lines. The middle and low voices must also have their chance to speak. Some lines will be given by individuals. The entire group voice will be needed for others which require unusual emphasis or volume. How the division will be made and which voices will take certain lines must be determined by the group concerned after a careful study of the poem.

> Drum on your drums,
> Batter on your banjos,
> Sob on your long, cool, winding saxophones.
> Go to it, O jazzmen!

In the first reading this suggests that the low voices may well carry the drum sounds; the high and middle voices may choose between banjos and saxophones; while the group voice will be needed for the command, "Go to it, O jazzmen!" In many poems, however, which are less indicative than this one, the group will enjoy experimenting a little, trying out various ways before deciding on which is most satisfactory. Every member will have suggestions. The wise leader will try as many of these as possible; but, in arriving at a decision, both leader and group should choose the interpretation which seems to them best able to bring out the thought and mood of the poem.

One important thing to remember is that imitation of the leader or of individual members of the group is not to be permitted. The aim is not to select a "best" interpretation and model our group presentation after it, but to create a group interpretation which is not based on any one individual's idea nor even on the ideas of several individuals. We do not want a model, or one uniform interpretation. The group product may be slower of realization, but after all, the creative effort of the group is what counts, and not mere acceptance or revision of a suggested interpretation. Incidentally, in an average group, there will be self-conscious members to whom the idea of giving individual interpretations would be sufficient to cause withdrawal from the group. Experience has shown that self-consciousness is lost when one can offer suggestions without being called on to demonstrate them by himself, and when one feels himself to be a working unit rather than an individual performer. It is interesting to note the free expression of voice and body when a timid member of a group expresses himself in company with ten or twelve others. They are his protection, and so he "lets himself go."

An interesting aspect of the Verse-Speaking Choir is that it allows individual interpretation within the group, so far as tone color, inflection, and emphasis go. Audiences always comment on the fact that, although they hear one general interpretation, they can also distinguish individual variations by concentrating attention upon a chosen member. In a choir of twelve, which maintained the same rate of speed and length of pause, there were five different interpretations of the line in the Twenty-third Psalm, "I will fear no evil, for Thou art with me." Some members of the choir felt that "with" was the most important word to stress; others insisted that "Thou" required most emphasis; and still others felt the two words were equally important. One individual gave all four last words equal stress, speaking them with deep emotion, while another brought out the "Thou" and "me" relationship. Inflection and tone color varied with each member, and ranged from tones of joy and exultation to deep, serious expressions of conviction and abiding faith. All were agreed that, with this type of poetic expression, the conversational tone was inappropriate, and so used an elevated but sincere quality.

It is interesting to record that, in interpretation of the Psalms, bodily expression was of great assistance in attaining the proper frame of mind. Only when all members of the group stood as tall as possible without rising on their toes, heads flung back and with eyes that looked beyond the limits of the room, were they able to feel within them the spirit of communion with God, such as was common in the days of the Old Testament when men were not afraid to talk with Him. The interpretation of this Psalm never failed to stir audiences; in spite of individual variations, it left a single impression, and was far more moving than any chanting or antiphonal speaking could be.

In working with poetry of the commonplace and everyday, bodily expression plays an equally important part with vocal interpretation. After the lines have been assigned, and when the group interpretation is definitely swinging into shape, suggestions for accompanying bodily movements are called for. Will pantomime and body expression help our interpretation? If so, what shall we do? Always there will be variation between different groups, even though they are working on the same poem. Two choirs, each of which worked with Vachel Lindsay's *Congo*, illustrate this point. The first group decided to plan a patterned movement with all members of the group moving together elbow to elbow and foot to foot. During the interpretation, any change in position was synchronized; arm and body movements, while not identical, were very similar, and the result of much experimentation and discussion. The second group decided to leave the definite movement to each individual and only determine for the group the motion to be delineated. Thus, on the line, "Then I had religion, then I had a vision," some of the group raised their hands to heaven; others fell on their knees; still others staggered back, hands before their faces as if to mask them from some dazzling light. The first group had interpreted the line by having one individual step forth from the line, eyes fixed on some distant horizon, and say the line while the rest strained their eyes to see what he was seeing. Both groups were impressive.

And the joy of it! The satisfaction of making a poem come to life! The happiness of knowing that the way the group says a certain line is the result of your suggestion! The sense of release when you raise your voice in company with others and feel appreciation of the thought and mood sweep through your tones.

Groups become increasingly enthusiastic as they work together. Poems are memorized, but no one is aware of the process. Voices gradually improve in range, flexibility, control, and tone quality. Enunciation picks up marvelously. Bodies become more capable of expression. Self-consciousness falls away. There is a quickening of aural perception.

Books and magazines are searched for Verse-Speaking Choir material. Poems are exchanged. Three or four members of the group interpret some favorite poem for the others. A fine friendly feeling is aroused. We are drawn together in appreciation and understanding. We learn to give and take constructive criticism. We learn to agree to disagree. We are able to see the value of other interpretations even though we continue to prefer our own.

It is obvious that in working in and for such a Choir there are certain dangers and difficulties which must be guarded against. Imitation has already been mentioned. The individual members must be careful lest they strain their voices in an attempt to secure variety and volume of tone too quickly. Too confident members should not be allowed to rule the group; individuality must be maintained but subordinated. Interpretation must not be allowed to become "sing-song" nor mechanical. Rhythm and melody must be secondary to the thought and feeling of the poem. In spite of all these warnings, the undertaking is worth the effort. Let us bring poetry back into group life!

DRAMA AND THE UNSEEN CURRENTS

Irene Lewisohn

IN SCANNING the history of mankind, both in its primitive cultures and in its more developed civilizations, one cannot overlook a common impulse that has taken form in some sort of dramatic expression. If we are studying a tribal state of society, we must realize the importance of rituals that show the tribe's relation to its social state. If we are touching even superficially the life of any great epoch or race, we must recognize the scope of its development, in part at least, through what remains to us of its drama. It is just as unthinkable to have a knowledge of the life of the Pacific Islanders, for example, without observing their tribal, seasonal, or initiation ceremonies, as it is to gain a concept of Greek thought and manner of living without some knowledge of Æschylus, Sophocles, Euripides, and the other great dramatists. Progressive education, as I understand it, is a release of the individual's capacities to meet the problems of life, and the life of today and tomorrow is inevitably bound up with the life of yesterday; in fact, we are beginning to realize that yesterday, today, and tomorrow are one.

If it is true that a common impulse toward dramatic expression can be found wherever life in any social state has prevailed, it must be no less true that it is here in our complex, highly mechanized civilization. Nor is it unnatural that here where the emphasis is on the materialistic, on the physical side of life, the impulse toward dramatic expression should be contrastingly intense and deep. It is significant that educators who, in the literal sense of the word, are leading the youth of our land out to a wider understanding of life are sensitive to this deep impulse. They are trying to meet its needs by establishing dramatic departments in universities, in schools, and in stimulating theater movements in many communities.

Objectively, we are surrounded by many unfortunate results of this impulse. No generation has burst forth with such a flood of expression as the mechanism of this age has made possible. Motion pictures on every street corner, radios in every home, indicate an intoxication no less insidious than their forerunner, the saloon. The glamour of Hollywood, the lure of the "mike," is a constant call to the youth with an ounce of personality to sell, and the ruin of many a talent that might unfold if nurtured in less blatant light. In the theater, too, with the exception of special independent or art groups, the appeal is to the sensational and tawdry; and it is rare, indeed, that drama as an art is made visible. Speed, in every variety of syncopation, lurid transcriptions of front-page journalism, are the sum of the countless "shows that get over." These are the almost invariable offerings made to satisfy the instinctive craving for adventure and romance that seem likely to be tricked into hard-boiled sentimentality. It is not my intention to sketch the manifold ways in which the impulse for dramatic expression is revealed in this or any other age. I merely restate the obvious fact that this fundamental instinct discloses itself now, as it always has, through the forms of the day; and the result is as important a comment on the life of our time as have been, and are, the drama and rituals of any state of society.

But the life of our day is not all mechanism. There is as deep a searching after truth in art and in science as the world has ever witnessed; and we are surely looking toward a more mature existence that will place the physical and material aspects in their proper proportion. Professor Albert Einstein has called this searching a cosmic religious sense. In his article, *Religion and Science,* he says:

How can this cosmic religious experience be communicated from man to man, if it cannot lead to a definite conception of God or to a theology? It seems to me that the most important function of art and science is to arouse and keep alive this feeling in those who are receptive.

The art of drama is one of the most vital means of communication between man and man. The cosmic religious sense that flows through this generation must find its corresponding dramatic expression. It does in such plays as *Green Pastures,* where it touches an unconscious depth that sweeps away even race differences. Perhaps it has been this same searching that has been the keynote of the Neighborhood Playhouse. As I glance over our repertoire of more than fifteen years, I find a series of productions that consistently emphasizes this spiritual pilgrimage. The mystical Chasidic legend, *The Dybbuk,* the classic of Sanscrit and Buddhist culture, the *Little Clay Cart,* the fourteenth-century French miracle play, *Guibour,* the episodes of a jazzed and sordid New York, *Pinwheel,* are just a few high spots that indicate our trend in the field of spoken drama; and the dramatic version of Whitman's poem, *Salut au Monde,* and, more recently, the performances of symphonic music with stage and orchestra, carry the same motive. It has not been a haphazard accident that placed themes such as these in our repertoire. It has been a recognition of a fundamental need to touch universal forces, to feel in tune with racial currents that have swept through the ages, to reach beyond the problems of individual effort and achievement into the plane of world consciousness. Our effort has been to build a bridge between the reality of today and the ceaseless flow of eternal life.

Not in theme only, but dedicated to beauty of form in line, in word, in color, in light, in sound, in movement—in short, an art product of that instinct toward dramatic expression—this has been our goal, an act of creation that might contain in its essence the sum of human searching, just as white contains the colors of the spectrum and in its purity is akin to black. This is drama, the juxtaposition of Yes and No, of light and darkness, of weakness and strength, and of all the opposites that give life its drive.

The latest of these excursions into new modes has been the production of symphonic music with stage and orchestra above referred to: Ernest Bloch's *Israel*, Richard Strauss's *Ein Heldenleben* (The Life of a Hero), and Charles Martin Loeffler's *A Pagan Poem*, as examples of the major works of three programs, demanded a new interpretation of the scores from a dramatic standpoint instead of a literal rendering of program notes or rhythmic patterns. An understanding of the inner drama behind the music revealed the first as the aspiration of a race through atonement rituals shown symbolically at the Wailing Wall; the second, as man in a dual rôle, his objective self observing the struggle of his psyche and his ultimate integration; the third, as the ascent of the soul through the three classic planes of existence. Architectural settings that allowed movement in varied planes and grouping of the human form in plastic patterns were required. No traditional dance could break the structure of the musical scores. Gesture built on modern lines, vital, simple, direct, and broad in phrasing; lighting blended to synchronize with the dynamics of the music; costumes planned to give free play to the body and yet suggest in outline the atmosphere of Wailing Wall, psychic fantasy, or ancient grove—all of these mediums had to be scaled to the breadth of full symphony orchestra so completely that sound and sight might blend into one emotional mood. That was the task we set ourselves, the challenge to all the artists working with us and, according to the response of the audience, achieved to no small degree.

The building up of new techniques has also called into being a school, the Neighborhood Playhouse Studios. This school has no academic earmarks. It is rather an association of artists eager to pass on to youth the results of their experience in their own particular craft and to help the students find within themselves the ways and means to make these tools their own. The students come with a desire for an experience that will help them understand theater as a unified expression of the arts, for a release of their capacities not only along the paths of their previous training, but in all the elements that theater, in terms that are new and yet old, demands. To convey to an audience the true character of a rôle, the mood of a song or dance pattern, the atmosphere of a background or costume, it is necessary to probe inside and evoke the life of that rôle, or song, or dance, or setting. In any production, just as in human intercourse, it is vital to find the proper relation of the parts to the whole, to balance the tone color with the movement and the line in whatever problem is presented. To create under direction of the staff is not only encouraged but demanded, and it is interesting to observe how quickly students respond in fields hitherto completely closed to them. Study and expression of this intensive kind can only be carried on in small groups, by personal contact and inspiration from both student and teacher. Added to this is the spur of immediate practice. Instead of abstract theory, all of the work of the students is focused on production, either for the Junior Holiday performance in some theater, or for a private spring demonstration.

This method is also carried on with our Junior students, a group of children of school and high-school age who come for special training in movement and voice in folk song and speech. Although one or two rehearsals a week is all their school program will allow, over the years these young people acquire a skill and style that flower amazingly in performance.

What is it preserves this unconscious beauty? I incline to lay it to many influences—play of the imagination in ordered rhythmic patterns, touch with basic cultures in the folk life of many peoples, contact through the mediums of theater with the essence of art, understanding and discipline of art forms of today and of all times, release of the impulse toward creative expression, relation of the individual to the ceaseless flow of universal life.

In nourishing and stimulating this germ of theater expression under the name the Neighborhood Playhouse, it is our hope that we may tune in on the unseen currents that are slowly but surely effecting a more sensitive vision of life and, therefore, of art. It is folly to prophesy; but the time may soon be ripe when more of our world may yearn for that cosmic experience to which Professor Einstein alludes. Those of us working in any of the arts, including the art of education and the art of drama, may join hands with the scientists in not only "keeping alive the feeling" already existing but in preparing for a new epoch of spiritual, psychic, and individual growth.

SHANKEUM, PRINCESS OF
HAN

EMPEROR

BUDDHA

A MASK

HANCHENYU, KHAN OF THE
TARTARS

Beaver Country Day School

COSTUME PLATES FOR "SORROW OF HAN" MADE BY STUDENTS

A DRESS REHEARSAL OF "IPHIGENIA IN TAURIS" GIVEN IN AN AMPHITHEATER

SHADOW SHOWS OFFER OPPORTUNITIES
FOR DRAMATIC HUMOR

CURTAIN DESIGNED AND PAINTED BY A FIFTH GRADE

MAKING STAGE SCENERY

Marion P. Leggette

STAGE scenery is expensive. Few elementary schools can afford more than one outdoor and one indoor set. Many schools have none. West Raleigh was in the latter class, when one spring the fifth grade burst forth with an unusual bit of creative drama, an operetta. The leaders of the group demanded a Colonial garden set similar to one they had seen in a local theater. The children declared their intention to paint the scenery themselves if the teacher would help.

A knowledge of industrial arts, a short course in oil painting, and a soul to dare, were the teacher's only preparation for this task which her pupils had set for her. The class consulted geographies, encyclopedias, and travel pamphlets to determine how the required garden in Trenton, New Jersey, would appear in the month of May.

It was decided that a beautiful landscape painted on a backdrop would serve for this operetta and that it could also be used for other performances, if the close-ups were worked out in reality upon the stage itself.

The class visited a local theater. The manager allowed them to examine the scenery closely. He showed them how lighting effects are obtained. He called their attention to the fact that the scenery painter had put all the paint on flat, that there were no fine details; shadows were purple; the lights were yellow; plants were mere splashes of color.

Mindful of all they had seen, each of the children designed a miniature backdrop. Showcard colors and wash brushes were used with heavy watercolor paper. The class voted for the best design; when one was finally selected, the work began in earnest.

Careful measuring of the stage showed that the backdrop must be 24 feet high and 30 feet long. Four widths of 90-inch sheeting, eight yards long, were purchased. These the children sewed together so that the seams would be perpendicular to the floor. A two and one-half inch hem was made at both top and bottom. Iron piping was inserted in the top hem so that ropes could be attached to hold the curtain up. Pipe of the same size was used in the bottom to stretch the sheeting.

The paints used were alabastine dry positive colors, mixed dry until the desired colors were obtained. Water was added until a thin smooth paste resulted. Three pounds of white fish glue, dissolved in boiling water, was added to the prime coat. This sizing, applied with five-inch paint brushes, gave body to the sheeting, and made the paint stick like oils.

When the curtain was ready, the question arose as to how the small design could be sketched upon so large a canvas. Having drawn to scale in arithmetic, the class readily took to the suggestion to mark the curtain and small design off in an equal number of squares. The squares were numbered. It was then an easy matter to sketch in square number one of the backdrop what appeared in square number one of the small design. Large soft lead pencils were used for sketching.

Since all of the children could not paint at one time, they decided to paint in relays. (There were fifty-eight children in the class!) Ten was found to be the best number for good work. Each group had a captain who was responsible for the work done during his hour. The tops of the extension ladders were the most popular positions. No one ever tired of coming down to view the scene as a whole and climbing the ladder again to put on a finishing touch. When the backdrop was completed, the boys built a garden wall of white slats. They made a very effective garden scene with ivy, moss, flowers, and potted plants.

The scenery made the operetta a success. After the performance, many youngsters were seen pointing out to their parents the specific spots which they themselves had painted. Although these youthful artists are now in junior high school, the stage scenery remains where it was hung. As a school project, it is the pride of the community.

A SELECTED LIST FOR THE SCHOOL THEATER

Prepared by Marjorie Seligman

I. REFERENCE BOOKS

ACKLEY, EDITH FLACK—Marionettes. Illustrated. Stokes, 1929.
A book for children telling how to make and use marionettes. Five plays.

BROWN, CORINNE—Creative Drama in the Lower School. Illustrated. Appleton, 1929.
This covers the field of dramatics for the younger children; in addition to material on the presentation of plays, there are chapters on dances, puppets, and pageantry.

COLLINS, LILLIAN FOSTER—The Little Theater in School. Illustrated. Dodd, Mead, 1930.
Dramatics in the school interestingly discussed and four very delightful plays written for children are included.

COOK, H. CALDWELL—The Play Way. Stokes, 1919.
Although written in 1915, this book should be read by teachers. It tells of the play way at Perse School, England.

DABNEY, EDITH, and WISE, C. M.—A Book of Dramatic Costume. Illustrated. Crofts, 1930.
This book is especially adapted to meet school requirements; it presents in line drawings a selection of the costumes of most of the peoples and periods. This is followed by an illustration of a set from some play in which the particular costumes may be used.

D'AMICO, VICTOR E.—Theater Arts. Manual Arts Press, 1931.
A volume of practical helpfulness on the arts contributing to a school theater.

EVANS, MARY—Costume Throughout the Ages. Illustrated. Lippincott, 1930.
An unusually interesting recent book. The first section gives the development of dress from the Egyptian, Greek, and Roman to the present day. The second part deals with national costume in Europe, Northern Africa, Asia, and America. There are over two hundred photographs.

GRIMBALL, ELIZABETH B., and WELLS, RHEA—Costuming a Play. Illustrated. Century, 1925.
A helpful handbook on the development of costume. The illustrations are particularly good, and the text simple and concise.

FISH, HELEN RANDLE—Drama and Dramatics. Illustrated. Macmillan, 1930.

A volume whose purpose is to give the student an idea of some of the principles on which plays are made and by which they may be judged. Six one-act plays are included with directions for acting and producing.

LINCOLN SCHOOL STAFF—Curriculum Making in an Elementary School. Illustrated. Ginn, 1927.

Pages 74-130 contain a discussion of dramatic play; also how units of work are unified through play making.

MACKAY, CONSTANCE D'ARCY—Children's Theaters and Plays. Illustrated. Appleton, 1927.

An interesting account of the activities of American, English, French, Italian, and other European children's theaters. The latter half of the volume devotes itself to the more practical problems of production.

MERRILL, JOHN, and FLEMING, MARTHA—Play Making and Plays. Illustrated. Macmillan, 1930.

Divided into four parts, this recent volume presents the Dramatic Impulse, the Educative Use of the Dramatic Impulse, notes on and illustrations of original play making, and finally an excellent bibliography containing a list of plays for production and study.

MILLS, WINIFRED H., and DUNN, LOUISE M.—Marionettes, Masks and Shadows. Illustrated. Doubleday, 1927.

Beautiful and complete, giving the history of marionettes, masks, and shadow shows, how to make them, and several plays for each. Good bibliographies.

MITCHELL, ROY—The School Theater. Illustrated. Brentano's, 1925.

A practical little handbook on production in the school; of particular interest is the chapter on "Adaptation to Conditions," in which Jacques Copeau's method of staging is described.

NAUMBURG, MARGARET—The Child and the World. Harcourt, Brace, 1928.

The fourteenth dialogue tells of play making in the Walden School, and how the school of the future may center around a theater of arts and crafts.

SELDEN, SAMUEL, and SELLMAN, HUNTON D.—Stage Scenery and Lighting. Illustrated. Crofts, 1930.

The first half of this volume is devoted to the design, planning, construction, painting, assembling, and shifting of scenery. The latter half includes all the necessary information for lighting control and effect. A really invaluable book.

SMITH, MILTON—The Book of Play Production. Illustrated. Appleton, 1926.

An excellent handbook on production in general. Of particular help are the chapters on scenery and lighting.

STODDARD, ANNE, and SARG, TONY—A Book of Marionette Plays. Greenberg, 1927.

Five plays and directions for constructing marionettes and stage.

WARD, WINIFRED—Creative Dramatics for Upper Grades and Junior High School. Illustrated. Appleton, 1930.

During the past six years the public schools of Evanston, Illinois, have made use of this text. The author is outstanding in the field of educational dramatics.

II. VOLUMES OF PLAYS

BELL, LADY—Fairy Tale Plays. Illustrated. Longmans, Green, 1896.

A favorite collection of popular fairy tales, dramatized with music.

BUTLER, MILDRED ALLEN—Literature Dramatized. Illustrated. Harcourt, Brace, 1926.

Very short scenes dramatized from young people's classics, such as *Alice in Wonderland, Little Women, The Prince and the Pauper, Treasure Island, Odyssey, Ivanhoe, Rip van Winkle,* etc.

FIELD, RACHEL—Patchwork Plays. Illustrated. Doubleday, Doran, 1930.

A new volume of plays of real imagination and charm.

FYLEMAN, ROSE—Eight Little Plays for Children. Illustrated. Doubleday, Doran, 1925.

Some very short and charming plays for the younger children. Six of these have only three in the cast.

Seven Little Plays for Children. Illustrated. Methuen, London, 1923.

Another volume of delightfully imaginative plays by the popular English poetess.

GOLDSMITH, SOPHIE L.—Wonder Clock Plays. Illustrated. Harper's, 1925.

Five dramatizations from Howard Pyle's *The Wonder Clock.* These play about one and one-half hours, and are especially suited for out-of-door presentation.

GOODLANDER, MABEL R.—Fairy Plays for Children. Illustrated. Rand, McNally, 1915.

Very simple dramatizations which were given by the primary children of the Ethical Culture School, New York City.

JAGENDORF, M. A. (Editor)—One-Act Plays for Young Folks. Illustrated. Brentano's, 1924.

Thirteen plays for children from six to fifteen, all of which have been successfully produced by a children's theater. The majority of these plays, which are imaginative, lend themselves to out-of-door production.

JASSPON, ETHEL REED, and BECKER, BEATRICE—Ritual and Dramatized Folkways. Illustrated. Century, 1925.

An excellent collection of short ceremonies, pantomimes, plays, and dramatized ballads. Highly recommended for camp use.

MACKAY, CONSTANCE D'ARCY—The House of the Heart. Illustrated. Holt, 1909.

Plays of fantasy, including two Christmas favorites, On Christmas Eve and The Christmas Guest.

The Silver Thread. Illustrated. Holt, 1910.

A collection of interesting folk plays, which have long been popular.

MOSES, MONTROSE J. (Editor)—A Treasury of Plays for Children. Illustrated. Little, Brown, 1921. Another Treasury of Plays for Children. Illustrated. Little, Brown, 1926.

Two unusually fine anthologies of plays both long and short, for children to read and to produce. They include such favorites as Racketty Packetty House, Treasure Island, The Little Princess, The Toy Maker of Nuremberg, Alice in Wonderland, and Make Believe.

MAJOR, CLARE TREE—Playing Theater, Six Plays for Children. Illustrated. Oxford University Press, 1930.

Mrs. Major has long been known as a pioneer in the Children's Theater movement. This is her first volume of published plays. Since these have all been successfully produced by her this collection should prove to be a valuable one.

OLLER, MARIE, and DAWLEY, ELOISE K.—Little Plays from Greek Myths. Illustrated. Century, 1928.

Short dramatizations from Greek mythology, which have been tried with success by the students of the Washington Irving High School, New York City.

OULD, HERMAN—New Plays from Old Stories. Illustrated. Oxford University Press, 1924.

Peter the Pied Piper, The Princess in the Sleeping Wood, Rip van Winkle are dramatized by a well-known English playwright.

PRICE, OLIVE M.—Short Plays from American History and Literature. Vol. I, 1925. Vol. II, 1928.

Dramatizations of varying lengths which have been successfully tried in Pittsburgh schools.

SANFORD, A. P., and SCHAUFFLER, ROBERT HAVEN (Editors)—Little Plays for Little People. Dodd, Mead, 1929.

An excellent anthology of simple plays for important occasions in the school year.

SANFORD, A. P. (Editor)—Outdoor Plays for Boys and Girls. Dodd, Mead, 1930.

A varied selection of plays which is already greatly in demand for junior members of summer camps.

SCHAUFFLER, ROBERT HAVEN, and SANFORD, A. P. (Editors)—Plays for Our American Holidays. Dodd, Mead, 1928. 4 vols.

An extremely helpful collection of plays. This includes: Vol. 1, Plays for Christmas and Other High Days; Vol. 2, Plays for Festivals; Vol. 3, Plays for Patriotic Days; Vol. 4, Plays for Special Celebrations.

SMITH, EVELYN—Little Plays from Shakespeare. Thomas Nelson, Series 1 —1926; Series 2—1927.

Short scenes taken from Shakespeare, each in itself making a complete play.

TAYLOR, KATHARINE, and GREENE, HENRY COPLEY—The Shady Hill Play Book. Macmillan, 1928.

A volume of really unusual plays in English and French, the result of experimental work at the Shady Hill School, Cambridge, Mass.

THOMAS, CHARLES SWAN (Editor)—The Atlantic Book of Junior Plays. Little, Brown, 1924.

A well-balanced anthology of one-act plays for reading and production in the Junior High School.

WEBBER, JAMES PLAISTED, and WEBSTER, HANSON HART—Short Plays. Houghton Mifflin, 1925.

This interesting collection of one-act plays is divided into several sections. Plays of Fancy, Plays with a Literary Background, and Plays based on History and Tradition; the latter part of the volume consists of practical suggestions to students and teachers.

WRIGHT, HARRIET S.—New Plays from Old Tales. Macmillan, 1921.

Plays of real charm on such tales as Aucassin and Nicolette, The Birthday of the Infanta, Pilgrim's Progress, and Feathertop.

III. LIST OF PRACTICAL HELP

OGLEBAY, KATE, and SELIGMAN, MARJORIE (Compilers)—Plays for Children. H. W. Wilson, 1928.

A selected list of plays for children, ages 6 to 14.

FRANKENSTEIN, LOUISE, and SELIGMAN, MARJORIE (Compilers)—Plays for junior and senior high school. H. W. Wilson.

KOCH, FREDERICK, and STROBACH, NETTINA—Plays for Schools and Little Theaters. University of North Carolina Press, 1930. Bulletin No. 8.

Annotated lists of full-length plays, short plays, plays for children, books about the theater, and books of plays.

INDEX OF CONTRIBUTORS

KATHARINE A. BARBER

was a teacher of English in East High School, in Rochester.

page 200

GEORGE BEECHER

teaches in the junior high school of the Rogers Clark Ballard Memorial School, Louisville, Kentucky. He is a graduate of Yale University.

page 287

MATTHEW WILSON BLACK

is Assistant Professor of English in the University of Pennsylvania.

page 245

FREDERICK GORDON BONSER

whose life was a rich and lasting contribution to education, died June, 1931. For many years he was a member of the faculty of Teachers College and director of Speyer School. "Always an ardent advocate of the educational philosophy of John Dewey, his chief concern was for the betterment of schools through richer curricula and the better training of teachers. His work gave industrial arts, history, and science in the schools a richer content and a greater social significance. He was keenly sensitive to the value of art in life."

pages 22 *and* 245

CALVIN B. CADY

after teaching a number of years at Oberlin College and the University of Michigan, became convinced of the need for a new type of work in the field of music. Since then, he has been active in writing books and articles on teaching, and in training teachers in the new approach to music. Since 1915

he has been educational director of the work in the Music Education School in Portland, Oregon.

page 132

FLORENCE CANE

is the director of art and teacher of painting in the Walden School. She has also been conducting classes in creative art for children and teachers at the Westchester Work Shop of the Westchester County Recreation Commission.

page 42

NORVAL CHURCH

is Assistant Professor of music education at Teachers College, Columbia University.

page 103

ELSIE RIPLEY CLAPP

formerly of the Rosemary Junior School, is head of the Rogers Clark Ballard Memorial School, a rural county school in Jefferson County, Kentucky.

page 287

SARAH N. CLEGHORN

is well known as a writer. For several years she has taught English at Manumit School, Pawling, New York.

page 193

MARGARET ELLEN CLIFFORD

is a former student of Miss Hallie Flanagan, the director of the Experimental Theater at Vassar, and is now conducting a children's theater at Briarcliff, New York.

page 322

REBECCA COFFIN

is the principal of the lower school of Lincoln School, New York.

page 297

SATIS N. COLEMAN

has charge of the creative music in the Lincoln School of Teachers College, New York, where she has been conducting experiments since 1919. During the summer she gives courses to teachers in Columbia University. She is the author of *Creative Music for Children, Bells, The Drum Book, Children's Symphonies*, and other books on creative music.

page 91

RACHEL A. COOGLE

teaches in the Morgantown, West Virginia, High School.

page 184

L. YOUNG CORRETHERS

has made a special study of the modern art tendencies in this country and abroad. He is instructor at the Keith Country Day School at Rockford, Illinois, and he has written and produced many plays on art subjects for children.

pages 23 *and* 152

KATHERINE K. DAVIS

is a graduate of Wellesley College, where she also taught in the Music Department. She has also studied with Mr. Surette and taught in the Concord, Massachusetts, Academy, and at the Shady Hill School in Philadelphia.

page 75

RUTH DOING

teaches rhythmics in several progressive schools in New York City. She is head of the Ruth Doing School of Rhythmics and of the Gardner-Doing Camp in the Adirondacks.

pages 98 *and* 302

FRANCES DORWIN DUGAN

is associate director of the Seymour School, Boston, a private school for girls.

page 198

PETER W. DYKEMA

is a pioneer in a community music movement, and has served its cause in a variety of ways. For several years he was in charge of the music at the Ethical Culture School in New York. Later he was Professor of music at the University of Wisconsin, and at present is acting in a similar capacity at Teachers College, Columbia University.

page 108

ETHEL M. ERICSON

teaches English at Wadleigh High School, New York, and has for years contributed to magazines and newspapers.

page 205

HELEN ERICSON

formerly head of the Riverside School, is now director of the Sunset Hill School in Kansas City, Missouri. This year she is on leave of absence at the Spence School, New York, where she is helping to reorganize the secondary department.

pages 59 *and* 259

RACHEL ERWIN

is the director of the Winbrook School, White Plains, New York, and has been an active worker in the Progressive Education Association.

page 281

ELIZABETH BYRNE FERM

was for many years connected with the Modern School at Stelton. Her interest in education of the new type extends back over a number of years, during which she and Mr. Ferm organized and conducted the Children's Neighborhood Playhouse in New Rochelle, and a similar undertaking later in New York City.

page 36

JOHN L. FOLEY

is a member of the English faculty of the George Washington High

School, New York City. He is also a writer of special articles and a lecturer on English.

page 236

MABEL R. GOODLANDER

is the director of the Ethical Culture Branch School in New York City.

page 285

HELEN GOODRICH

has been head of the music department of the Francis W. Parker School in Chicago for almost three decades.

page 111

ESTELLE HALLOCK

is the director of dramatics at Scarborough School, Scarborough, New York.

page 319

LULU M. HOOD

is head of the English Department of the Girls' Latin School of Chicago, a private college preparatory school.

page 182

FLORENCE E. HOUSE

is in the Department of Industrial Arts in Teachers College. She has had a broad experience in teaching in progressive schools, and is at present at Rosemary Junior School, Greenwich, Connecticut.

page 34

FLORENCE S. HOYT

teaches English in Bryn Mawr School, Baltimore, a private college preparatory school for girls.

page 191

HARRIET M. JOHNSON

is the director of the Nursery School and co-director of the Cooperative School for Student Teachers, New York City. She is author of *Children in the Nursery School*, and a member of the National Committee on Nursery Schools. She is well known for her experimental work with pre-school children.

page 271

ROSE KHOURIE

is Director of Art and the Industrial Arts Department in the Elementary School of the Jewish Center, New York City.

page 159

HELEN W. LEET

is a graduate of Barnard College and teaches English and History at Greenwich Academy, Greenwich, Connecticut.

page 188

EVA LE GALLIENNE

is the founder and director of the Civic Repertory Theater in New York City. She believes that "the true theater of America must be created by the people themselves. Their demand will create the supply. The theater must be an integral part of the life of the community." Her theater on Fourteenth Street is noted for the sincerity and vigor of its productions; it has educated the public as well as actors to the advantages of repertory.

page 254

MARION P. LEGGETTE

is a teacher in the public schools of Raleigh, North Carolina.

page 337

JOHN A. LESTER

is head of the department of English at Hill School, a private school for boys, at Pottstown, Pennsylvania. He is a frequent contributor to educational magazines.

page 197

WILLY LEVIN

brings to her teaching a rich and varied experience. She was born in Russia, studied art in Paris and Munich, and in America at Alfred University. She has also worked in sculpture at Mr. Archipenko's studio. She has organized classes at the Educational Alliance, Hamilton Grange School, and the Hoffmann School. She is now connected with the Brooklyn Ethical Culture School.

page 27

IRENE LEWISOHN

and her sister, ALICE LEWISOHN, have been training young people of the Henry Street Settlement of New York in festival plays, ritual dances, and spoken drama since 1907. In 1915, this became the Neighborhood Playhouse of Grand Street and until 1927, when it was reorganized, it had a marked influence not only on community drama but, through the actors trained there, on the commercial theater as well. Since 1927, programs have been carried out, and after-school classes in dancing, pantomime, the sung and spoken word, and an intensive course in arts relating to the theater have been conducted.

page 333

ROSEMARY LILLARD

is director of music at Greenwich, Connecticut.

page 125

P. H. B. LYON

is Rector of Edinburgh Academy, of Edinburgh, Scotland.

page 185

PEPPINO MANGRAVITE

is an artist of the modern school and his paintings are represented in various museums and private collections. During the last ten years he has dedicated considerable time to art teaching and has made an extensive study of the various methods in art education. He now heads the Art Departments of the Ethical Culture Schools and conducts classes in painting and drawing at Sarah Lawrence College.

page 29

HUGHES MEARNS

Interested readers will welcome another contribution from the author of *Creative Youth* and *Creative Power*. Mr. Mearns is at present conducting courses in creative education at New York University. He is the author of several novels and is a frequent contributor to magazines.

pages 13 *and* 143

JOHN MERRILL

is the author of *Playmaking and Plays* and the director of dramatics of the Francis W. Parker School, Chicago.

page 305

LUCY SPRAGUE MITCHELL

has been actively engaged in experimental work with children for many years at the Bureau of Educational Experiments in New York. Her interest in children's language development led to the publishing of the *Here and Now Story Book* and the *Here and Now Primer*. Her work with older children led to the publishing of *Horses Now and Long Ago* and *North America*, a fascinating beginning geography. She is at present co-director with Harriet Johnson of the Co-operative School for Student Teachers in New York City.

pages 40 *and* 167

LUCIA BURTON MORSE

Director of Avery Coonley School, Downers Grove, Illinois. Miss Morse was one of the founders and a most active supporter of the Progressive Education Association.

page 206

MABEL MOUNTSIER

teacher of English and Editor of *Singing Youth*, an anthology of poems by children, has made a wide personal investigation of published writings of children, both prose and poetry.

page 232

MARGARET NAUMBURG

founded the Walden School eighteen years ago under the name of The Children's School. She is now an adviser-director of the school. She has written educational articles for various journals and recently published her book, *The Child and the World*.

page 50

ELIZABETH NEWMAN

is on the faculty of the Seymour School of Musical Re-Education, New York City. She has compiled a collection of folk songs entitled *The Children's Own Book* (published by Carl Fischer) so arranged as to make playing simple and possible for even small children.

page 86

IDA RHEA PEARSON

studied with Professor Merriam at the University of Missouri. She has also done post-graduate work in dancing and physical education at the University of Wisconsin. Recently she has been doing special work in the Ethical Culture Branch School in New York.

page 162

EDITH POTTER

has for several years directed the music education of the Avery Coonley School at Downers Grove, Illinois, and her development of work with very young children has been of an original and interesting nature.

page 116

CAROLINE PRATT

is the founder and director of the City and Country School in New York City.

page 262

FRANCES PRESLER

is the supervisor of creative activities in the Winnetka Public Schools, Winnetka, Illinois.

page 292

SARAH A. PUTNAM

is a teacher of English in the Park School of Baltimore.

page 311

BERTA RANTZ

has charge of dramatics in the Walden School, New York City.

page 265

VIRGINIA SOMES SANDERSON

has been conducting Verse-Speaking Choirs at the summer sessions of Mills College, California, in Dr. Harry Allen Overstreet's summer school for adults.

page 329

MARJORIE SELIGMAN

has charge of the Drama Book Shop in New York City.

page 339

NELLIE B. SERGENT

teacher of English at Evander Childs High School, New York, is a graduate of Smith College, and a former student in the poetry classes of Professor John Erskine at Columbia. She is the author of a new book called *Younger Poets*.

page 202

HARRIET AYER SEYMOUR

was educated musically in the best conservatories in this country and abroad. She taught for a number of years in the Institute of Musical Art, New York, and in one of the largest music school settlements in the country. She is now the director of the Seymour School of Musical Re-Education in New York City, which prepares teachers of music.

page 81

ELISABETH SHEFFIELD

has charge of the fourth grade in the Rogers Clark Ballard Memorial

School, Louisville, Kentucky. She was formerly teacher of the ten-year-old group of the Rosemary Junior School.

page 287

MILTON SMITH

author of *The Book of Play Production*, has charge of dramatics in Sarah Lawrence College, Bronxville. He was formerly at the Horace Mann School, New York City.

page 314

ELLEN W. STEELE

is head of the Junior School, Rosemary Hall, Greenwich, Connecticut. She was formerly connected with the City and Country School, also the Beaver School of Boston.

pages 51, 125 *and* 276

THOMAS WHITNEY SURETTE

Mr. Surette has for many years been a leader working for better music in home, school, and college. He has been a potent force in changing the attitude toward music in the liberal college and also acts as consultant to a number of schools. In the Concord Music Series he is supplying a better type of music for school use. From his summer school at Concord, teachers go forth each year to develop the new methods in schools all over the country.

page 69

RALPH WESTERMAN

is assisting Dr. Frederick Koch in his playmaking course at the University of North Carolina. He is also business manager of the Carolina Playmakers.

page 326

EVA LOUISE WILDE

formerly critic teacher in the Normal School at Johnson, Vermont, and more recently head of the Lower School at the Park School of Cleveland, Ohio, now occupies the same position at the Castilleja School in Palo Alto, California.

page 154

AMERICAN EDUCATION:
ITS MEN, IDEAS, AND INSTITUTIONS
An Arno Press/New York Times Collection

Series I

Culver, Raymond B. **Horace Mann and Religion in the Massachusetts Public Schools.** 1929.

Curoe, Philip R. V. **Educational Attitudes and Policies of Organized Labor in the United States.** 1926.

Dabney, Charles William. **Universal Education in the South.** 1936.

Dearborn, Ned Harland. **The Oswego Movement in American Education.** 1925.

De Lima, Agnes. **Our Enemy the Child.** 1926.

Dewey, John. **The Educational Situation.** 1902.

Dexter, Franklin B., editor. **Documentary History of Yale University.** 1916.

Eliot, Charles William. **Educational Reform: Essays and Addresses.** 1898.

Ensign, Forest Chester. **Compulsory School Attendance and Child Labor.** 1921.

Fitzpatrick, Edward Augustus. **The Educational Views and Influence of De Witt Clinton.** 1911.

Fleming, Sanford. **Children & Puritanism.** 1933.

Flexner, Abraham. **The American College: A Criticism.** 1908.

Foerster, Norman. **The Future of the Liberal College.** 1938.

Gilman, Daniel Coit. **University Problems in the United States.** 1898.

Hall, Samuel R. **Lectures on School-Keeping.** 1829.

Hall, Stanley G. **Adolescence: Its Psychology and Its Relations to Physiology, Anthropology, Sociology, Sex, Crime, Religion, and Education.** 1905. 2 vols.

Hansen, Allen Oscar. **Early Educational Leadership in the Ohio Valley.** 1923.

Harris, William T. **Psychologic Foundations of Education.** 1899.

Harris, William T. **Report of the Committee of Fifteen on the Elementary School.** 1895.

Harveson, Mae Elizabeth. **Catharine Esther Beecher: Pioneer Educator.** 1932.

Jackson, George Leroy. **The Development of School Support in Colonial Massachusetts.** 1909.

Kandel, I. L., editor. **Twenty-five Years of American Education.** 1924.

Kemp, William Webb. **The Support of Schools in Colonial New York by the Society for the Propagation of the Gospel in Foreign Parts.** 1913.

Kilpatrick, William Heard. **The Dutch Schools of New Netherland and Colonial New York.** 1912.

Kilpatrick, William Heard. **The Educational Frontier.** 1933.

Knight, Edgar Wallace. **The Influence of Reconstruction on Education in the South.** 1913.

Le Duc, Thomas. **Piety and Intellect at Amherst College, 1865-1912.** 1946.

Maclean, John. **History of the College of New Jersey from Its Origin in 1746 to the Commencement of 1854.** 1877.

Maddox, William Arthur. **The Free School Idea in Virginia before the Civil War.** 1918.

Mann, Horace. **Lectures on Education.** 1855.

McCadden, Joseph J. **Education in Pennsylvania, 1801-1835, and Its Debt to Roberts Vaux.** 1855.

McCallum, James Dow. **Eleazar Wheelock.** 1939.

McCuskey, Dorothy. **Bronson Alcott, Teacher.** 1940.

Meiklejohn, Alexander. **The Liberal College.** 1920.

Miller, Edward Alanson. **The History of Educational Legislation in Ohio from 1803 to 1850.** 1918.

Miller, George Frederick. **The Academy System of the State of New York.** 1922.

Monroe, Will S. **History of the Pestalozzian Movement in the United States.** 1907.

Mosely Education Commission. **Reports of the Mosely Education Commission to the United States of America October-December, 1903.** 1904.

Mowry, William A. **Recollections of a New England Educator.** 1908.

Mulhern, James. **A History of Secondary Education in Pennsylvania.** 1933.

National Herbart Society. **National Herbart Society Yearbooks 1-5, 1895-1899.** 1895-1899.

Nearing, Scott. **The New Education: A Review of Progressive Educational Movements of the Day.** 1915.

Neef, Joseph. **Sketches of a Plan and Method of Education.** 1808.

Nock, Albert Jay. **The Theory of Education in the United States.** 1932.

Norton, A. O., editor. **The First State Normal School in America: The Journals of Cyrus Pierce and Mary Swift.** 1926.

Oviatt, Edwin. **The Beginnings of Yale, 1701-1726.** 1916.

Packard, Frederic Adolphus. **The Daily Public School in the United States.** 1866.

Page, David P. **Theory and Practice of Teaching.** 1848.

Parker, Francis W. **Talks on Pedagogics: An Outline of the Theory of Concentration.** 1894.

Peabody, Elizabeth Palmer. **Record of a School.** 1835.

Porter, Noah. **The American Colleges and the American Public.** 1870.

Reigart, John Franklin. **The Lancasterian System of Instruction in the Schools of New York City.** 1916.

Reilly, Daniel F. **The School Controversy (1891-1893).** 1943.

Rice, Dr. J. M. **The Public-School System of the United States.** 1893.

Rice, Dr. J. M. **Scientific Management in Education.** 1912.

Ross, Early D. **Democracy's College: The Land-Grant Movement in the Formative Stage.** 1942.

Rugg, Harold, et al. **Curriculum-Making: Past and Present.** 1926.

Rugg, Harold, et al. **The Foundations of Curriculum-Making.** 1926.

Rugg, Harold and Shumaker, Ann. **The Child-Centered School.** 1928.

Seybolt, Robert Francis. **Apprenticeship and Apprenticeship Education in Colonial New England and New York.** 1917.

Seybolt, Robert Francis. **The Private Schools of Colonial Boston.** 1935.

Seybolt, Robert Francis. **The Public Schools of Colonial Boston.** 1935.

Sheldon, Henry D. **Student Life and Customs.** 1901.

Sherrill, Lewis Joseph. **Presbyterian Parochial Schools, 1846-1870.** 1932 .

Siljestrom, P. A. **Educational Institutions of the United States.** 1853.

Small, Walter Herbert. **Early New England Schools.** 1914.

Soltes, Mordecai. **The Yiddish Press: An Americanizing Agency.** 1925.

Stewart, George, Jr. **A History of Religious Education in Connecticut to the Middle of the Nineteenth Century.** 1924.

Storr, Richard J. **The Beginnings of Graduate Education in America.** 1953.

Stout, John Elbert. **The Development of High-School Curricula in the North Central States from 1860 to 1918. 1921.**

Suzzallo, Henry. **The Rise of Local School Supervision in Massachusetts. 1906.**

Swett, John. **Public Education in California. 1911.**

Tappan, Henry P. **University Education. 1851.**

Taylor, Howard Cromwell. **The Educational Significance of the Early Federal Land Ordinances. 1921.**

Taylor, J. Orville. **The District School. 1834.**

Tewksbury, Donald G. **The Founding of American Colleges and Universities before the Civil War. 1932.**

Thorndike, Edward L. **Educational Psychology. 1913-1914.**

True, Alfred Charles. **A History of Agricultural Education in the United States, 1785-1925. 1929.**

True, Alfred Charles. **A History of Agricultural Extension Work in the United States, 1785-1923. 1928.**

Updegraff, Harlan. **The Origin of the Moving School in Massachusetts. 1908.**

Wayland, Francis. **Thoughts on the Present Collegiate System in the United States. 1842.**

Weber, Samuel Edwin. **The Charity School Movement in Colonial Pennsylvania. 1905.**

Wells, Guy Fred. **Parish Education in Colonial Virginia. 1923.**

Wickersham, J. P. **The History of Education in Pennsylvania. 1885.**

Woodward, Calvin M. **The Manual Training School. 1887.**

Woody, Thomas. **Early Quaker Education in Pennsylvania. 1920.**

Woody, Thomas. **Quaker Education in the Colony and State of New Jersey. 1923.**

Wroth, Lawrence C. **An American Bookshelf, 1755. 1934.**

Series II

Adams, Evelyn C. **American Indian Education. 1946.**

Bailey, Joseph Cannon. **Seaman A. Knapp: Schoolmaster of American Agriculture. 1945.**

Beecher, Catharine and Harriet Beecher Stowe. **The American Woman's Home. 1869.**

Benezet, Louis T. **General Education in the Progressive College. 1943.**

Boas, Louise Schutz. **Woman's Education Begins. 1935.**

Bobbitt, Franklin. **The Curriculum. 1918.**

Bode, Boyd H. **Progressive Education at the Crossroads. 1938.**

Bourne, William Oland. **History of the Public School Society of the City of New York. 1870.**

Bronson, Walter C. **The History of Brown University, 1764-1914. 1914.**

Burstall, Sara A. **The Education of Girls in the United States. 1894.**

Butts, R. Freeman. **The College Charts Its Course. 1939.**

Caldwell, Otis W. and Stuart A. Courtis. **Then & Now in Education, 1845-1923. 1923.**

Calverton, V. F. & Samuel D. Schmalhausen, editors. **The New Generation: The Intimate Problems of Modern Parents and Children. 1930.**

Charters, W. W. **Curriculum Construction. 1923.**

Childs, John L. **Education and Morals. 1950.**

Childs, John L. **Education and the Philosophy of Experimentalism.** 1931.
Clapp, Elsie Ripley. **Community Schools in Action.** 1939.
Counts, George S. **The American Road to Culture: A Social Interpretation of Education in the United States.** 1930.
Counts, George S. **School and Society in Chicago.** 1928.
Finegan, Thomas E. **Free Schools.** 1921.
Fletcher, Robert Samuel. **A History of Oberlin College.** 1943.
Grattan, C. Hartley. **In Quest of Knowledge: A Historical Perspective on Adult Education.** 1955.
Hartman, Gertrude & Ann Shumaker, editors. **Creative Expression.** 1932.
Kandel, I. L. **The Cult of Uncertainty.** 1943.
Kandel, I. L. **Examinations and Their Substitutes in the United States.** 1936.
Kilpatrick, William Heard. **Education for a Changing Civilization.** 1926.
Kilpatrick, William Heard. **Foundations of Method.** 1925.
Kilpatrick, William Heard. **The Montessori System Examined.** 1914.
Lang, Ossian H., editor. **Educational Creeds of the Nineteenth Century.** 1898.
Learned, William S. **The Quality of the Educational Process in the United States and in Europe.** 1927.
Meiklejohn, Alexander. **The Experimental College.** 1932.
Middlekauff, Robert. **Ancients and Axioms: Secondary Education in Eighteenth-Century New England.** 1963.
Norwood, William Frederick. **Medical Education in the United States Before the Civil War.** 1944.
Parsons, Elsie W. Clews. **Educational Legislation and Administration of the Colonial Governments.** 1899.
Perry, Charles M. **Henry Philip Tappan: Philosopher and University President.** 1933.
Pierce, Bessie Louise. **Civic Attitudes in American School Textbooks.** 1930.
Rice, Edwin Wilbur. **The Sunday-School Movement (1780-1917) and the American Sunday-School Union (1817-1917).** 1917.
Robinson, James Harvey. **The Humanizing of Knowledge.** 1924.
Ryan, W. Carson. **Studies in Early Graduate Education.** 1939.
Seybolt, Robert Francis. **The Evening School in Colonial America.** 1925.
Seybolt, Robert Francis. **Source Studies in American Colonial Education.** 1925.
Todd, Lewis Paul. **Wartime Relations of the Federal Government and the Public Schools, 1917-1918.** 1945.
Vandewalker, Nina C. **The Kindergarten in American Education.** 1908.
Ward, Florence Elizabeth. **The Montessori Method and the American School.** 1913.
West, Andrew Fleming. **Short Papers on American Liberal Education.** 1907.
Wright, Marion M. Thompson. **The Education of Negroes in New Jersey.** 1941.

Supplement

The Social Frontier (Frontiers of Democracy). Vols. 1-10, 1934-1943.